T0324271

Reliability Modeling
with Computer and
Maintenance Applications

Reliability Modeling
with Computer and
Maintenance Applications

Editors

Syouji Nakamura
Kinjo Gakuin University, Japan

Cun Hua Qian
Nanjing Tech University, China

Toshio Nakagawa
Aichi Institute of Technology, Japan

World Scientific

NEW JERSEY · LONDON · SINGAPORE · BEIJING · SHANGHAI · HONG KONG · TAIPEI · CHENNAI · TOKYO

Published by

World Scientific Publishing Co. Pte. Ltd.
5 Toh Tuck Link, Singapore 596224
USA office: 27 Warren Street, Suite 401-402, Hackensack, NJ 07601
UK office: 57 Shelton Street, Covent Garden, London WC2H 9HE

British Library Cataloguing-in-Publication Data
A catalogue record for this book is available from the British Library.

ISBN 978-981-3224-49-0

Printed in Singapore

Preface

In this book, I(Prof. Syouji Nakamura) will retire from Kinjo Gakuin University on March 31, 2017. This commemorative publication was made by the World Scientific Publishing, where I have already published two co-edited books from World Scientific Publishing.

I started my research, when I worked at Bank of Nagoya, where I worked for 22 years in the computer department. During that time, I began my doctorate in operations research and economics at Nagoya City University. After submitting my research for review, I was offered a tenured professorship at Kinjo Gakuin University. I was awarded the degree finally in 2003.

Since that time, I have actively published many papers at numerous international workshops of distinguished professors such as Professor Toshio Nakagawa, Professor Shunji Osaki, Dr. Kazug Okumoto, Professor Shigeru Yamada, Professor Tadashi Dohi, and other well-known researchers. I was engaged with researchers who knew me well at international conferences and workshops. Graciously, more than twenty excellent writers from around the world have cooperated with this work.

This book is composed of four parts by their active cooperation: Part1 consists of five papers about computer systems with a maintenance policy. Part 2 has five papers regarding reliability analysis. In Part 3 there are four papers about reliability applications. Finally, Part 4 has four papers about maintenance policy. These four parts address the areas for future research while providing an overview of current developments and useful methods for practical application and reliability. This book will be useful to students, technicians, and serve as a reliability textbook and guidebook for research.

Finally, we, the contributors and I, would like to thank the editor, Chelsea Chin, for her support and the World Scientific Publishing Company for providing this opportunity to publish this book.

Syouji Nakamura, Kinjo Gakuin University, Japan
Cun Hua Qian, Nanjing Tech University, China
Toshio Nakagawa, Aichi Institute of Technology, Japan

Contents

Reliability Analysis   101

PART 1
Computer System

Chapter 1

An Overview of Practical Software Reliability Prediction

Kazuhira Okumoto

Software and Systems Reliability Engineering,
Bell Labs CTO, Nokia

1 Introduction

In recent years many product suppliers have been implementing complex software-controlled systems with a large number of software features on a short development schedule. In the telecommunication industry, a critical customer operational issue is on system performance, especially in terms of system outages impacting the service availability for their end users. As a result, service providers frequently ask their product suppliers for software reliability and availability measurements. For example, service providers ask for a 5 9's system availability requirement which is equivalent to 5.26 downtime minutes/year.

In this paper we focus on software defects found by testers and customers. The following terms are used interchangeably: defects = faults and failures = outages. There is a significant difference between defects and failures. Only a few defects will result in failures in the field. A release contains a set of new software features (or functionalities) which are developed (including requirements specification, software design and coding), tested against the requirements. Once the test phase is completed, it is delivered to customer site for acceptance test (or site test) and finally deployed for commercial operation (or in-service).

A software failure is defined as a system outage caused by a software defect during an operation period. Software reliability represents the probability of the system operating without a software failure during a specified period of time. It is associated with software failure rate. Software availability is the probability of the software system being up and running for a duration of time. It is measured in practice in terms of annual downtime minutes. Both software reliability and availability metrics are defined for an operation period.

This paper provides an overview of practical software reliability prediction, as described in [Okumoto (2016)] . The approach is illustrated in Fig. 1 which involves several steps. An automated tool will be described for generating key quality and reliability metrics and associated charts. Actual defect and outage data taken from large-scale software development projects will be used to illustrate and validate the proposed approach.

1.0.1   *Software Reliability Growth Model*

A key step for software reliability prediction is defect prediction during an operation period based on test defect data using a mathematical model. Software defect prediction models are known as software reliability growth models (SRGMs). Over 200 SRGMs have been developed since early 1970s (e.g. [Jelinski and Moranda (1972); Schick and Wolverton (1973); Schneidewind (1975); Musa (1975); Goel and Okumoto (1979); Yamada et.al. (1983); Musa et.al. (1987); Musa (1993); Wallance and Coleman (2001); Okamura et.al. (2001); Jeske et. al. (2005); Zhang and Pham (2006)]).

Most models assume that there are a finite number of defects in any piece of software and each defect will be found according to a certain statistical distribution. Most of those frequently used models can be systematically sorted in terms of the shape of the distribution function (i.e. an exponential curve or an S-shaped curve). Exponential models assume that each defect will be found at a constant rate through various test phases. Some representatives of exponential models can be found in [Jelinski and Moranda (1972); Schneidewind (1975); Musa (1975); Goel and Okumoto (1979); Musa (1993)]. S-curve models assume various types of S-shaped distributions such as Weibull, Gamma, logistic functions to match with actual data trends (e.g. [Schick and Wolverton (1973); Yamada et.al. (1983)]). Exponential models are simple with only two parameters. S-curve models have flexibility in describing different shapes of the trend since they have more than two parameters.

There have been many comparison studies performed and various tools were developed for evaluating individual models in terms of how well each

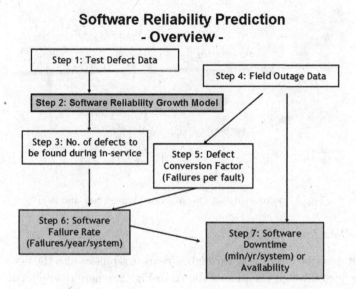

Fig. 1   An overview of software reliability and availability predictions

model fits to the data (e.g. [Lyu (1995); Okamura and Dohi (2013)]). For a successful implementation of software reliability practice we also need to integrate this practice into software design for reliability [Asthana and Okumoto (2012)]. However, there is no single model which can be used in every situation [Wikipedia (Retrieved 2016)]. Predicting software reliability and availability based on internal test defect data can be challenging.

We also incorporate changes in software content during test phases with the multiple-curve approach. The idea of piecewise application of SRGMs is not exactly new. For example, a concept for evolving software content was originally discussed in [Musa et.al. (1987)].

Most SRGMs (e.g. [Musa (1993); Wallance and Coleman (2001); Okamura et.al. (2001)]) assume an extension of the curve to represent defects to be found during an operation period. It will be demonstrated that there are discontinuities in defect trend from internal test phase to customer site test and operation periods due to the changes in test intensity and operational profile as originally described in [Musa (1975)].

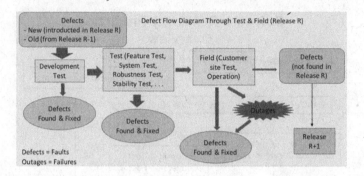

Fig. 2   Software defect flow diagram through test and field

1.0.2 *Data Requirements*

We first describe defect flow through various test phases into the field. Each feature goes through the phases shown in Fig. 2, where requirement specification and design & coding phases are combined in one box representing a development phase. We are focusing on test phases and beyond. Once internal test phase is completed, the release is delivered to customer site for acceptance test and then deployed to commercial sites for operation. There are many activities overlapping at a same point in time. At the start of testing there are a certain number of new defects introduced through software design and coding phases for the release. In addition, there are old or base defects which were not found in the previous release and carried over into the current release. Some defects are found and removed during a development test phase.

We now summarize a set of key data requirements.

- Software defects which were found by testers or customers. In practice, defect data are sorted on a weekly basis.
- Software defects which were found and fixed, excluding duplicates. We are basically looking for unique software defects which actually require fixes by software designers.
- High severity defects. We focus on high severity defects representing severity 1 (emergency) & severity 2 (critical) defects. They are highly correlated to system stability and may trigger a failover or a reboot. Software failure rate is a function of residual high severity defects, known but not yet fixed high severity defects, and operational profile and configuration of deployed systems.

- Software outage data, including outage frequency and annual downtime.
- Key project milestone dates such as delivery dates for customer acceptance test and commercial deployment.

1.0.3 *Software Defect Data*

Telecommunication products include wireless network systems such as base station controller, radio network controller, remote radio heads and core network. We have selected two most complex, large-scale software development projects (Project A and Project B). They represent critical elements of wireless communication network and generate a relatively large number of defects because of the software size and complexity. The data sets help provide statistically meaningful results for the purposes of prediction and validation.

Project A represents a key wireless product which is responsible for the control and management of radio resources in a wireless network. Earlier releases contained new features with over 500 KNCSL (1,000 non-commentary source lines) and then gradually slowed down to less than 100 KNCSL. It uses a traditional delivery scheme of one delivery per release. The data sets used in this paper cover 11 releases over 5 years, including a major hardware platform change, which resulted in redesigning the software architecture.

Project B represents a radio access part of the latest mobile network technology. It performs tasks similar to those performed by a product described in Project A, plus radio frequency transmitters and receivers used to directly communicate with mobile devices. It is based on a highly complex hardware design and sophisticated software architecture to meet high data rate requirements. Many complex new features are required to meet fast growing markets demand. Recent releases contain over 1 MNCSL new features and deploy a new delivery scheme of multiple deliveries per release to satisfy the needs for additional features by multiple customers.

2 Software Defect Prediction Model

2.0.1 *Non-homogeneous Poisson Process (NHPP) Exponential Model*

If software content is relatively stable, it is reasonable to assume that there are a finite number of defects and each defect will be found and removed at a constant rate through various test phases. This is the basic assumption of an exponential model. It is simple, flexible and based on well-understood assumptions, as discussed in details in [Musa et.al. (1987)]. When a major change is made to the software, it generates a new wave of software defects. For each wave of software defects we apply an exponential model.

As defects are found and removed, encountering additional severe defects is less likely. This defect find process can be formulated as a stochastic process in terms of time-varying defect find rate. Since we count defects as they are exposed, it seems logical to statistically formulate the number of high severity defects found during test as a Poisson process with a time-varying mean value function, which is known as a non-homogeneous Poisson process (NHPP), e.g. [Musa (1993)].

For a defect find process, $N(t)$, the probability of finding n high severity defects by time t is expressed in general as a Poisson distribution with the mean value function, $m(t)$, as:

$$P\{N(t) = n\} = \frac{m(t)^n \exp\{-m(t)\}}{n!} \tag{1}$$

Note that $m(t)$ represents the average number of defects found by time t.

An exponential model is described as an NHPP with the mean value function:

$$m(t) = a\{1 - \exp(-bt)\}. \tag{2}$$

The parameters a and b represent total defects in the software and the rate at which each defect is found, respectively. Note that we will be using the model for each period. The parameter a should be interpreted as the number of defects associated with each period.

Each defect of total a defects is assumed to be found according to an exponential distribution with a rate of b. The associated mean value function is time-dependent. Hence it is called an exponential NHPP model. The corresponding defect intensity function or defect rate can be derived as the derivative of the mean value function (2):

$$\lambda(t) = ab \exp(-bt). \tag{3}$$

If $b > 0$, $m(t)$ levels off exponentially, converging to $a > 0$, and $\lambda(t)$ decreases exponentially. If $b- > 0$ and $a- > \infty$, $m(t)$ becomes a straight line and $\lambda(t)$ becomes constant. It is a stationary Poisson process. If $b < 0$ and $a < 0$, both $m(t)$ and $\lambda(t)$ increase exponentially. Although most of the time $b > 0$, there are a few cases with $b- > 0$ during site test and in-service periods and $b < 0$ in early test phases. It should be pointed out that the basic assumption of a finite number of defects is violated for

$b = 0$ or $b < 0$. However, it will be useful in explaining different trends for individual test periods within the same release. We will discuss further with actual data later.

The maximum likelihood method is a commonly used statistical method for estimating the parameters a and b for a given set of defect data. The maximum likelihood estimates for a and b are chosen to maximize the likelihood function and obtained by solving nonlinear equations as described in [Okumoto (2016)]. It also explains how to derive confidence intervals for a and b. Note that the approximate confidence interval is used here for practical purposes. It's not a theoretical interval. The 90% confidence interval is used here for practical purposes due to data variation although 95% or higher is preferred.

2.0.2 *Automated Tool*

We developed an automated tool with a spreadsheet for deriving the maximum likelihood estimates and confidence limits for a and b, incorporating a built-in function, solver. Below is a brief description of input and output with the procedure.

Input data include cumulative defect data by week and project milestone data such as the delivery and service-in dates. In addition, we need the rate reductions from the end of internal test to customer site test and from customer site test to in-service, respectively. The can be derived from previous release data. Other input data related to reliability and availability predictions will be addressed in next section.

Once input data are provided, it will automatically generate key quality and reliability metrics when the "Update" button is clicked, as shown in Fig. 4.

The automated tool generates the prediction of residual defects at the delivery and customer found defects during site test and operation phases as shown in 5. The prediction method for software reliability will be described in Section 3.

In addition, it generates charts of predicted curves for cumulative view and weekly view, along with actual data being used for prediction. The predicted curves include the exponential model and predicted customer found defect curves for site test and operation phases, as shown in Fig. 6.

As discussed in [Okumoto (2016)], the customer found defect curves typically become a straight line. Only critical fixes were delivered to avoid possible system breakages. The defect curves slow down as it moves from

Date	Week (x)	Cumulati ve Defects (y)	Input Data for Predictio n?	Input	
1-Jan-15	1	1		**Project Milestone Data**	
8-Jan-15	2	2		Delivery week =	46
15-Jan-15	3	2		Service-in week =	60
22-Jan-15	4	3			
29-Jan-15	5	3		**Defect Rate Changes**	
5-Feb-15	6	3		Rate Reduction at Site Test =	54%
12-Feb-15	7	3		Rate Reduction at In-service =	65%
19-Feb-15	8	3			
26-Feb-15	9			**Reliability Data Assumptions**	
5-Mar-15	10			%High Sev =	35%
12-Mar-15	11			%HighSev found in operation =	75%
19-Mar-15	12			Defect Conversion Factor =	0.13
26-Mar-15	13		yes		
2-Apr-15	14		yes		
9-Apr-15	15		yes		
16-Apr-15	16		yes		
23-Apr-15	17		yes		
30-Apr-15	18		yes		
7-May-15	19		yes		
14-May-15	20		yes		
21-May-15	21		yes		
28-May-15	22		yes		
4-Jun-15	23		yes		
11-Jun-15	24		yes		
18-Jun-15	25		yes		

Fig. 3   Sample automated tool for NHPP exponential model (Input)

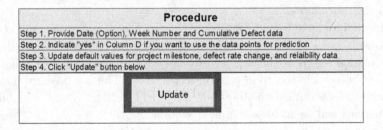

Procedure
Step 1. Provide Date (Option), Week Number and Cumulative Defect data
Step 2. Indicate "yes" in Column D if you want to use the data points for prediction
Step 3. Update default values for project milestone, defect rate change, and relaibility data
Step 4. Click "Update" button below

Update

Fig. 4   Sample automated tool for NHPP exponential model (Procedure)

formal test, site test, and to in-service. This is due to the changes in operational profile, where the intensity of test significantly changes.

If actual data are available for site test and operation phases, it will show actual data along with the predicted curves, as illustrated in Fig 7.

Repeating this procedure for each data period of new trends for the entire data set, we can find a set of best fitted curves to describe the entire data set. In next section we will demonstrate that the multiple curve approach is flexible enough to describe any type of trends.

Output			

Model Parameter Estimation & Confidence Limits			
Parameter	Estimate	Lower Limit	Upper Limit
a_new (a+y0)			
b			

Software Defect Prediction			
Release R	Estimate	Lower Limit	Upper Limit
Total Defects			
Residual Defects at Delivery			
Defects During in-service			

Defect Find Rate		
Defect Rate at Delivery		defects/week
Defect Rate during Site Test		defects/week
Defect Rate during In-service		defects/week

Software Reliability & Availability Prediction				
Release R	Estimate	Lower Limit	Upper Limit	Unit
SW Ffailure Rate				failures/yr
SW Downtime				minutes/yr
SW Availability				

Fig. 5   Sample automated tool for NHPP exponential model (Output #1)

2.0.3   *Defect Data Analysis-Example B*

In this section we will use a defect data set of Release R3 from Project B and illustrate the multiple curve approach for multiple deliveries per release. As described in Section I, Project B is a very complex system with a large number of new features and hence it generates a lot more defects. There were over 1,000 defects found but we are using only high severity defects here, which are roughly $\sim 33\%$ of total defects. The delivery plan was devised to incorporate customersf needs for certain features first and then additional features at a next delivery. There were three deliveries within the release.

After a careful investigation of the defect data, we divided into 6 distinct periods (P1 through P6) where different curves were needed. For each period we applied an NHPP exponential model. Both cumulative and weekly views are shown in Fig. 8.

Each predicted curve shows a very close fit to the actual data for the period. There are many activities overlapping or in parallel for each period. It also shows a typical weekly view of software defect rate, where multiple

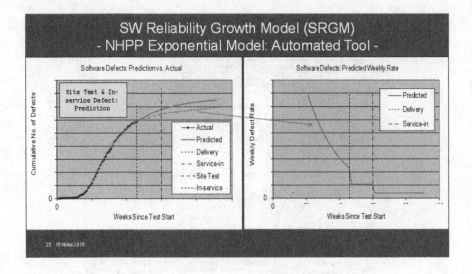

Fig. 6   Sample automated tool for NHPP exponential model (Output #2)

deliveries are deployed. When a new curve starts, the weekly curve jumps up and begins decreasing exponentially, like a saw wave. As discussed in previous section, the customer found defect curves (P5 and P6) become a straight line.

2.0.4   *New Code Arrival Rate vs. Defect Data*

A statistical correlation study of defect data with new code arrival rate is in progress. As illustrated in Fig. 9, both new code arrival rate and defect trend can be well represented by a NHPP exponential model for each segment of time, respectively. A preliminary study shows that new code arrival rate is a good leading indicator for defect trends. Our goal is to predict the test defect trend based on new code arrival rate. This will provide an early indication of test defect trend at a planning phase.

3   Software Reliability and Availability Predictions

In section II we demonstrated that successive NHPP exponential models can precisely capture an entire defect trend from internal test phases to site test and operation periods. We will first present a method for predicting high severity defects during an operation period based on internal

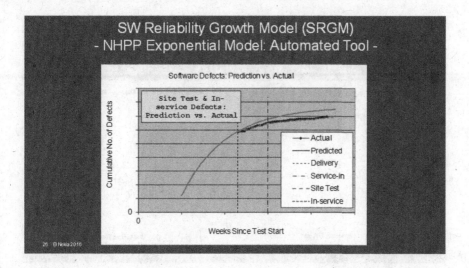

Fig. 7   Sample automated tool for NHPP exponential model (Output #3)

test defect data. We will then address software reliability and availability predictions.

3.0.1   *Software Defect Prediction during Operation Period*

In Section 2 we demonstrated with the multiple curve approach that not all features are ready for test at the startup of test phase. The last curve prior to the delivery represents the final product. Using the last predicted curve prior to the delivery, we can find the total number of defects from parameter a. Subtracting actual defects found at delivery from the total defects, we can find the number of defects not yet found at delivery or the delivered defects. In addition, there are some defects found but not yet fixed at delivery although they are typically small. The sum of the above two metrics will represent the number of defects delivered or remaining at delivery, which is the basis for predicting field outages.

Note that the curve should be always above the actual data after the delivery. The difference between the curve and the last actual data point indicates the defects not found in this release and they will become a part of the next release.

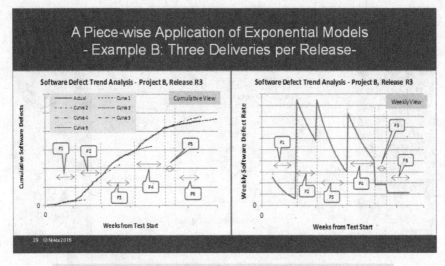

Fig. 8   Cumulative view of defect data and curves

3.0.2   *Software Reliability and Availability Prediction*

We have summarized a general procedure for predicting software reliability and availability in 11. Table 1 summarizes the practical calculation steps of delivered software defects, software reliability and software availability. The formulas and numbers are provided to illustrate the procedure.

First, we need to recognize that not all delivered defects will be found during the operation period, as illustrated in Fig. 7. Previous release data or historical data from other projects will be helpful for determining the percent of delivered defects to be found during the operation period.

Next, we need to convert defects into outages since not all high severity defects will result in outages. A defect conversion factor is introduced to map high severity defects into outages. It is basically a ratio of outages to high severity defects from the field. In our experience from various products the defect conversion factor is reasonably constant from release to release within a same project, but it significantly varies from project to project,

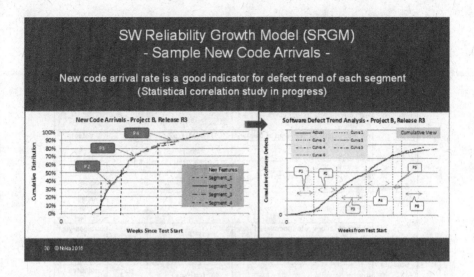

Fig. 9   New code arrival rate vs. defect trend

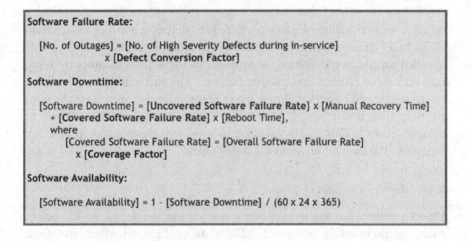

Fig. 10   Procedure for predicting software reliability and availability

depending on how outages are reported.

To achieve a high availability system most systems are designed to detect a failure and recover automatically via a reboot or a switch-over to a standby unit. It brings the system quickly back to normal operation. It is

Table 1   Software Reliability Prediction - Example for illustration purpose

Analysis Phase	Key Metrics	Formula	Release No.	Unit
Software Defect Prediction	Total high sev defects	(a11)	230	defects *
	High sev defects found at delivery	(a12)	200	defects *
	High sev defects not yet found at delivery	(a1)=(a11)-(a12)	30	defects
	High Sev defects found but not yet fixed at delivery	(a2)	2	defects **
	High Sev defects delivered at delivery	**(a)=(a1)+(a2)**	**32**	**defects**
Software Reliability	% high Sev defects to be found during in-service	(b0)	15%	percent **
	In-service duration	(b1)	6	months
	High Sev defects per year to be found during in-service	(b)=(a)x(b0)x12/(b1)	10	defects / year
	Defect conversion factor	(c)	0.04	outages / system / defect **
	Software failure rate (uncovered failures only)	**(d)=(b)x(c)**	**0.38**	**outages/year / system**
Software Availability	Average recovery time for uncovered failure	(e)	45	minutes / outage **
	Annual downtime	**(f)=(d)x(e)**	**17.3**	**minutes / year / system**
	Software Availability	**(g)=1-(f)/(60x24x365)**	**99.9967%**	**percent**

* can be derived from defect trend analysis
** can be derived from previous release data

called a covered failure. If the system fails to detect or auto recover, it will result in a customer perceived outage which requires a manual recovery. It is called an uncovered failure. A coverage factor is used to properly separate uncovered failures and covered failures. The coverage factor is defined as the percent of covered failures and it plays an important role if the auto recovery time is not trivial. It usually requires a separate internal tool to measure covered failures. In practice, only customer perceived outages are reported. We assume uncovered failures only.

3.0.3   *Use of Confidence Limits*

Defect prediction is made based on a certain sample size of weekly defect data, as discussed in Section 2. The data contain statistical variation. Predicted mean is shown as (a11) in Table 1 which corresponds to parameter a of the NHPP exponential model. Note that it does not indicate the prediction accuracy. Statistical confidence limits provide additional insight to the accuracy of reliability prediction [Okumoto (2016)].

As more defect data become available, the confidence interval becomes smaller if actual data follow the model prediction. In practice, the underlying model is considered reasonable if the confidence intervals continue

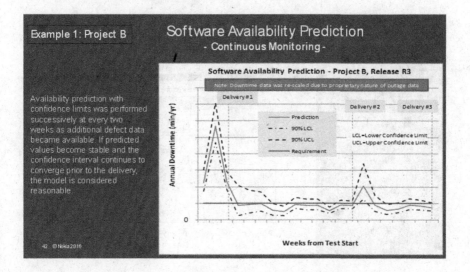

Fig. 11   Changes in availability prediction over time

to get smaller as more data points are added. Combining the stability of predicted values and the convergence of confidence intervals will provide a good indication of model validation.

We will now illustrate the usefulness of confidence limits using defect and outage data from Release R3 of Project B. This project uses three major deliveries per release, as discussed in Section 2. Note that the downtime data was rescaled due to the proprietary nature of outage data. The 10-minute downtime requirement was assumed here for the purpose of discussion.

Availability prediction with confidence limits was performed successively at every two weeks as additional defect data became available. Fig. 11 shows predicted values of availability over time along with confidence intervals. It will provide insight to validate the underlying model in terms of the stability of predicted values and confidence interval.

Fig. 12 indicates that availability predictions quickly converged with reasonably small confidence intervals prior to Delivery #2 and Delivery #3, respectively. It is an indication of the validity of the underlying model. This validation method is especially useful when we do not have sufficient historical data from previous releases or actual outage data are not readily available. Note that Delivery #1 was for site test only to demonstrate the features at customerfs site, not so much to focus on the system stability. In

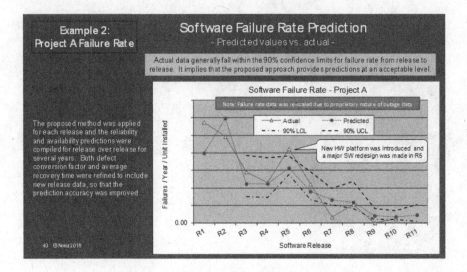

Fig. 12   Release-over release software reliability prediction

next section we will present a case for model validation where actual outage data from many releases are available.

4   Reliability and Availability: Model Validation

In this section we will validate model predictions against actual data in a practical way due to the complex nature of outage data. Project A is used to illustrate the validation of the underlying model. As described in Section 1, Project A represents a large-scale software development for a key telecommunication product with a high availability redundant hardware configuration.

The proposed method summarized in Table 1 was applied for each release and the reliability and availability predictions were compiled for release over release for several years. Both defect conversion factor and average recovery time were refined to include new release data, so that the prediction accuracy was improved.

Fig. 12 and Fig. 13 show predicted software reliability in terms of failure rate and software availability in terms of annual downtime, respectively. Due to the proprietary nature the outage data were re-scaled. Outage data represent unplanned, customer-reported, and uncovered failures, including full and partial outages. They were collected from over 400 systems being

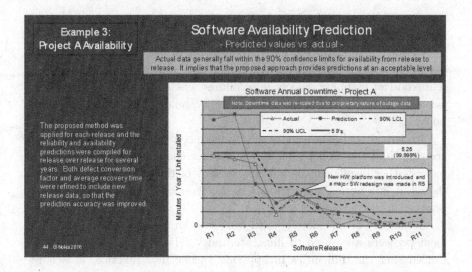

Fig. 13   Release-over-release software availability prediction

deployed in the field. Actual outage data were also overlaid in Fig. 12 and Fig. 13 to compare against predictions so that the accuracy of predictions can be visually observed. In the following we summarize several key findings. Actual data generally fall within the 90% confidence limits for both reliability and availability from release to release. It implies that the proposed approach provides

5   Conclusion

An overview of practical software reliability prediction was provided. The proposed approach consists of three major phases: field defect prediction, reliability and availability predictions. A piecewise application of NHPP exponential models was used to precisely capture an entire defect trend from internal test phases to customer site test and operation phases. The need for multiple curves was explained in terms of software content changes and test resources allocation such as testers, lab time and test cases. The last curve prior to the delivery represents a final product, which should be the basis for defect prediction. That is, defect data generated from an incomplete product is not important for reliability prediction.

An automated tool was developed for generating statistical estimates of the model parameters, the predicted curve, and key quality and reliability metrics. The metrics are useful for determining whether the software release is ready for delivery.

We have demonstrated that both software defect and failure processes during an operation period are considered as a stationary Poisson process. A method of mapping defects into failures was addressed so that we can calculate software reliability and availability, analogous to hardware reliability.

Statistical confidence limits were introduced to address the prediction accuracy and the model validation. A wider confidence interval typically means either insufficient data or inadequacy of the underlying model. Although it is a normal approximation, it is good enough for practical purposes.

Actual defect and outage data from two large-scale software development projects were used to illustrate and validate the proposed method. Considering the difficulties in applying theory into practice, it is a remarkable accomplishment. The proposed approach has been successfully implemented for software reliability assessment of key telecommunication products over several years. It is made flexible to apply to other software development projects.

References

Okumoto, K. (2016). Experience report: Practical Software Availability Prediction in Telecommunication Industry, *International Symposium on Software Reliability Engineering*.

Jelinski, Z., and Moranda, P. B. (1972). Software reliability researchh, (W. Feiberger, Editor), *Statistical Computer Performance Evaluation*, Academic, New York, pp. 465–484.

Schick, G. J., and Wolverton, R. W. (1973). Assessment of software reliability, *Proceedings of Operations Research*, Physica-Verlag, Wurzburg-Wien, pp. 395–422.

Schneidewind, N. F. (1975). Analysis of error processes in computer software, *Proceedings of the International Conference on Reliable Software, IEEE Computer Society*, pp. 337–346.

Musa, J. D. (1975). A theory of software engineering and its application, *IEEE Transactions on Software Engineering*, SE-1:3, pp. 312–327.

Goel A. L., and Okumoto, K. (1979). Time-dependent error-detection rate model for software reliability and other performance measures, *IEEE Transactions on Reliability*, pp. 206–211.

Yamada, S., Ohba, M., and Osaki, S. (1983). S-shaped reliability growth modeling for software error detection, *IEEE Transactions on Reliability*, pp. 475–478.

Musa, J. D., Iannino, A., and Okumoto, K. (1987). *Software Reliability: Measurement, Prediction, Application*, (McGraw-Hill, New York).

Musa, J. D. (1993). Operational profiles in software-reliability engineering, *IEEE Software*, pp. 14–32.

Wallace. D., and Coleman, C. (2001). Application and improvement of software reliability models, *Hardware and Software Reliability (323-08), Software Assurance Technology Center (SATC)*.

Okamura, H., Dohi, T., and Osaki, S. (2001). A reliability assessment method for software products in operational phase proposal of an accelerated life testing model, *Electronics and Communications in Japan*, pp. 25–33.

Jeske, D. R., Zhang, X. and Pham, L. (2005). Adjusting software failure rates that are estimated from test data, *IEEE Transactions on Reliability*, pp. 107–114.

Zhang, X. and Pham, H. (2006). Software field failure rate prediction before software deployment, *Journal of Systems and Software*, pp. 291–300.

Lyu, M. R. (1995). *Handbook of Software Reliability Engineering* (Computer Society Press, Los Alamitos and McGraw-Hill, New York).

Okamura, H., and Dohi, T. (2013). SRATS: Software reliability assessment tool on spreadsheet, *Proceedings of The 24th International Symposium on Software Reliability Engineering (ISSRE 2013)*, IEEE CPS, pp. 100–117.

Asthana, A., and Okumoto, K. (2012). Integrative Software Design For Reliability: Beyond Models and Defect Prediction, *Bell Labs Technical Journal* **17**, 3, pp. 39-62.

Wikipedia. (Retrieved 2016). *List of software reliability models*, `https://en.wikipedia.org/wiki/List_of_software_reliability_models`.

QuEST Forumfs. (2007). *TL 9000 Measurements Handbook Release 4.0.*

Kimura, M., Toyota, T., and Yamada, S. (1999). Economic analysis of software release problems with warranty cost and relaibility requirement, *Reliability Engineering & System Safety*, pp. 49–55.

Yang, B., and Xie, M. (2000). A study of operational and testing reliability in software reliability analysis, *Reliability Engineering & System Safety*, pp. 323–329.

Ukimoto, S., and Dohi, T. (2013). A software cost model with reliability constraint under two operational scenarios, *International Journal of Software Engineering and Its Applications*, **7**, 1.

Chapter 2

NHPP-based Software Reliability Assessment using Wavelets

Xiao Xiao[1] and Tadashi Dohi[2]

[1] *Department of Management Systems Engineering,*
Tokyo Metropolitan University,

[2] *Department of Information Engineering,*
Hiroshima University

1 Introduction

The quantitative assessment of software reliability is one of the main issues in software engineering. Over the last four decades, researchers have investigated a variety of quantitative methods for supporting decision making in real software development processes. A range of software reliability models (SRMs) have been proposed [Lyu (1996); Musa *et al.* (1987); Pham (2000)], taking different approaches to estimate quantitative software reliability, defined as the probability that a software system will not fail during a specified period of operation. Among these, non-homogeneous Poisson process (NHPP)-based SRMs have become widely-used in the software testing phase to assess the software reliability, identify the number of remaining faults in software, and determine the software release schedule.

The mean value function is a unique parameter that supports the probabilistic property of NHPP-based SRMs. The estimation methods can be broadly classified into Bayesian and non-Bayesian. Kuo and Yang (1996) proposed a general Bayesian estimation framework based on the well-known Markov chain Monte Carlo (MCMC) method, for representative NHPP-based SRMs with and without bounded mean value functions. Basu and

23

Ebrahimi (2003) analyzed different Bayesian SRMs with a piecewise constant failure rate and a martingale process prior, and proposed general techniques for estimating the marginal likelihood of the proposed SRMs, as well as of many existing SRMs. Okamura *et al.* (2007) developed a variational Bayesian approach that allowed the computation time of the MCMC-based algorithms of Kuo and Yang (1996) to be shortened.

Outside the Bayesian framework, maximum likelihood estimation (MLE) is a commonly used technique for estimating the model parameters of an NHPP-based SRM when formulated as a parametric model. However, as Ohishi *et al.* (2009) and Okamura *et al.* (2004; 2006) have pointed out, MLE performs poorly when the mean value functions are strongly nonlinear and there are multiple parameters, making it challenging to obtain exact solutions. They proposed the use of iterative Expectation Maximization (EM) algorithms to provide the numerical stability. However, due to the ill-posed nature of the likelihood equations, the variance of the maximum likelihood (ML) estimator can be quite high, particularly in applications involving very low counts. In addition, ML estimators in NHPP-based SRMs are inconsistent, and do not converge to the real (but unknown) parameters even if the number of software faults increases to infinite. Jeske and Pham (2001) and Zhao and Xie (1996) have investigated the inconsistency phenomena of ML estimators of specific NHPP-based SRMs both theoretically and empirically. Nayak *et al.* (2008) proved an inconsistency result for general NHPP-based SRMs with bounded mean value functions.

Although over one hundred parametric NHPP-based SRMs have been reported in software reliability research, it is well known in the software reliability engineering community that no uniquely best parametric NHPP-based SRM exists that can address every type of software-fault data. This is not to suggest that parametric NHPP-based SRMs are not useful for estimating software reliability in practice, but to recognize their inherent limitations. From this point of view, non-parametric methods can be used to describe the software debugging phenomena, which are different in each testing phase.

Frequentist approaches based on non-parametric statistics within a non-Bayesian framework have been proposed to estimate quantitative software reliability. Sofer and Miller (1991) used an elementary piecewise linear estimator of the NHPP intensity function, which is the derivative of the mean value function, from the software-fault detection time data, and proposed a smoothing technique using quadratic programming. Gandy and Jensen (2004) used a kernel-based estimator for the non-parametric estimation of the NHPP intensity function. Though their estimator is statistically consistent, and has good asymptotic properties, it requires multiple time-series samples of the software-fault data. As the authors have acknowledged [Gandy and Jensen (2004)], it is often inapplicable when the software product is tested by a single team. Barghout *et al.* (1998) also proposed a kernel-based non-parametric estimation technique for order statistics-based SRMs, using likelihood cross validation and prequential likelihood approaches to estimate the bandwidth. Wang *et al.* (2007) applied a similar kernel method to NHPP-based SRMs, using a local likelihood method with a locally weighted log-likelihood function. Strictly speaking, this approach is not non-parametric, because the logarithmic intensity function is approximated by a parametric linear function.

Although non-parametric methods have received considerable attention in software reliability assessment, it is widely recognized that kernel-based non-parametric estimation and simulation-based approaches such as MCMC incur high computation costs. This motivated us to seek a high-speed and low-cost solution. We therefore adopted a data-driven approach, and proposed wavelet shrinkage estimation (WSE) [Xiao and Dohi (2009)]. WSE has advantages over other commonly used techniques: (i) it is a non-parametric estimation that does not require the parametric form of the mean value function to be specified, and (ii) it allows time series analysis to be conducted accurately and at high speed. In some cases, the computation cost may be close to or greater than model selection using parametric SRMs. However, the WSE does not require optimization problems to be solved, making the implementation of the estimation algorithms relatively straightforward.

In this chapter, we introduce our proposed wavelet approaches to NHPP-based software reliability assessment. The remainder of this chapter is organized as follows. Section 2 briefly introduces NHPP-based SRMs and provides an overview of the wavelet-based approaches that have been developed for software reliability assessment. Section 3 discusses multiresolution representation, and gives a worked example. The multiresolution representation is used in the wavelet expansion of the software reliability measure in NHPP-based SRM. Readers who are already familiar with wavelet analysis may skip this section. Section 4 presents our data-transform-based wavelet shrinkage estimation (DT-WSE) technique for software reliability assessment. Section 5 presents numerical examples to demonstrate the effectiveness of DT-WSE. Section 6 presents our conclusions and suggests directions for future research.

2 Wavelet Approaches to NHPP-based Software Reliability Modeling

2.1 *NHPP-based SRM and its Parametric Estimation*

Let $N(t)$ denote the number of software faults detected by testing time t, and let this be a stochastic point process in continuous time. The stochastic process $\{N(t),\ t \geq 0\}$ is said to be an NHPP if the probability mass function at time t is given by

$$\Pr\{N(t) = m\} = \frac{\{\Lambda(t)\}^m}{m!}\exp\{-\Lambda(t)\}, \quad m = 0,\ 1,\ 2,\ldots, \qquad (1)$$

$$\Lambda(t) = \int_0^t \lambda(s)ds, \qquad (2)$$

where $\Lambda(t) = E[N(t)]$ is the mean value function of the NHPP, and means the expected cumulative number of software faults taking place within time t. In Eq. (2), $\lambda(t)$ is the *rate function* of the NHPP, and represents the software failure rate at time t. For clarity, we call the NHPP defined in continuous time the C-NHPP.

Suppose that the number of software faults detected through a system test is observed at discrete time $i = 0,\ 1,\ 2,\ldots$. Let Y_i denote the number of software faults detected at testing date i, and $N_i = \sum_{k=0}^{i} Y_k$ its cumulative value. Here $Y_0 = N_0 = 0$ can be assumed without any loss of generality. The stochastic process $\{N_i : i = 0,\ 1,\ 2,\ldots\}$ is said to be a discrete non-homogeneous Poisson process (D-NHPP) if the probability mass function at time i is given by

$$\Pr\{N_i = m\} = \frac{\{\Lambda_i\}^m}{m!}\exp\{-\Lambda_i\}, \quad m = 0,\ 1,\ 2,\ldots, \qquad (3)$$

$$\Lambda_i = \sum_{k=0}^{i} \lambda_k, \qquad (4)$$

where $\Lambda_i = E[N_i]$ is the mean value function of the D-NHPP, and means the expected cumulative number of software faults detected by testing date i. In Eq. (4), the function $\lambda_i = \Lambda_i - \Lambda_{i-1}$ $(i \geq 1)$ is called the *software intensity function* of the D-NHPP, and represents the expected number of faults detected at testing date i, *i.e.*, $\lambda_i = E[Y_i]$. Note that D-NHPP is obtained by projecting the sample pass of the C-NHPP onto discrete-time axis. That is, the software intensity function is essentially identical to the rate function. However, we purposely distinguish D-NHPP from C-NHPP to make the following discussions be consistent.

Because both the C-NHPP and D-NHPP are governed by mean value function, model estimation is reduced to identifying the mean value function from the observed software-fault data. In parametric models, many types of reliability growth patterns in software debugging can be represented by assuming a shape for the mean value functions in testing time. For example, if we assume the software fault-detection time distribution to follow an exponential distribution, we can derive the Goel-Okumoto C-NHPP-based SRM [Goel and Okumoto (1979)] with the mean value function $\Lambda(t) = \omega(1 - \exp(-\beta t))$, where ω and β are real number parameters. A growing body of work has addressed C-NHPP-based SRMs with different software fault-detection time distributions [Xiao *et al.* (2012); Xiao and Dohi (2013,a); Xiao (2015)]. The equilibrium distribution, the extreme value distribution, the Weibull-type distribution, and the Marshal-Olkin distribution have all been considered. Yamada *et al.* (1984), and Yamada and Osaki (1985) have developed a number of D-NHPP-based SRMs that are analogous with C-NHPP-based SRMs. A representative D-NHPP-based SRM uses the discrete Weibull distribution with the mean value function $\Lambda_i = \omega(1 - p^{i^r})$, where ω, p, and r are real number parameters. When the mean value function is assumed in parametric form, the unknown model parameters may be estimated from the realizations of $N(t)$ or N_i. ML estimation is a widely used technique, in which the estimate of the unknown model parameters is the one that maximizes the log likelihood function of the C-NHPP or D-NHPP.

Quantitative software reliability can be estimated once the mean value function has been identified, either using the parametric approach noted above, or a non-parametric approach discussed in Section 2.2 below. Let $\hat{\Lambda}(t)$ and $\hat{\Lambda}_i$ be the estimates of the mean value function of the C-NHPP and D-NHPP, respectively. Suppose that software testing terminates at time t_e, at which point the product is released to the user or the market. The software reliability, expressed as the probability that no fault will arise in the operational period $[t_e, t_e + x)$, is then defined as follows:

$$R(x \mid t_e) = \exp\left\{ -[\hat{\Lambda}(t_e + x) - \hat{\Lambda}(t_e)] \right\}. \tag{5}$$

For the D-NHPP, the software reliability is given by

$$R(x \mid t_e) = \exp\left\{ -[\hat{\Lambda}_{t_e+x} - \hat{\Lambda}_{t_e}] \right\}. \tag{6}$$

2.2 *Non-parametric Estimation using Wavelets*

In the non-parametric formulation of C-NHPP- or D-NHPP-based SRMs, the mean value function is not assumed to be a smooth function, and is identified directly from its realization. Alternative approaches have often focused on the rate function $\lambda(t)$ or the software intensity function λ_i, because the estimate of the mean value function can be derived by integrating $\lambda(t)$ or summing λ_i. In our wavelet-based approach, the rate function $\lambda(t)$ and the software intensity function λ_i are estimated from the observed data.

Recent years have seen significant developments in the use of wavelet-based statistical methods. Representation of an arbitrary function by the series expansion in terms of orthogonal basis functions has become familiar, a clear example being the widely-used Fourier expansion with sines and cosines of different frequencies. The wavelet bases used in wavelet expansion are applicable to a wide class of function spaces, and are useful by virtue of their special structure [Daubechies (1992)]. Wavelet-based techniques have been well established in statistical applications, and particularly in areas such as non-parametric regression, probability density estimation, and time-series analysis, *etc.* Among them, wavelet-shrinkage techniques have emerged as powerful methods for the non-parametric estimation of objectives that may be primarily characterized as spatial variables.

We applied these wavelet-shrinkage techniques to the estimation of the software intensity function λ_i of the D-NHPP. Consider the following non-parametric regression model:

$$S_i = z_i + \epsilon_i, \quad i = 1, 2, \ldots, n, \tag{7}$$

where z_i is the expectation of Gaussian random variable S_i at discrete time i, and noise ϵ_i is Gaussian random variable with mean 0 and variance σ^2. One of the basic approaches used in Gaussian non-parametric regression is to expand the unknown function z_i as a wavelet series, and thereby to transform the problem to the non-parametric estimation of the wavelet coefficients, based on the data. Donoho and Johnstone (1994; 1995; 1998), and Donoho *et al.* (1995) have proposed non-linear wavelet estimators of z_i using a reconstruction from judicious selection of the empirical wavelet coefficients, and suggested the extraction of the significant wavelet coefficients using *thresholding*. They proposed a denoising procedure with three steps: (i) expansion of the observations of z_i (the time-series data) to obtain the empirical wavelet coefficients, (ii) removal of the noise from the empirical wavelet coefficients using thresholding, where the empirical wavelet coefficients are set to 0 if the absolute value is below a certain threshold level, and (iii) application of the inverse wavelet transform to the denoised wavelet coefficients to obtain the estimator of the unknown function z_i.

The success of this wavelet-shrinkage denoising procedure is highly dependent on the properties of the Gaussian noise ϵ_i, assumed in the Gaussian non-parametric regression model Eq. (7). Our approach, however, used the following Poisson non-parametric regression model:

$$Y_i = \lambda_i + \eta_i, \quad i = 1, 2, \ldots, n, \tag{8}$$

where Y_i is Poisson random variable that denotes the number of software faults detected at testing date i, and noise η_i is Poisson white noise. Here, the goal is to recover the underlying software intensity function λ_i from software-fault count (group) data containing Poisson noise η_i. It is clearly inappropriate to apply the above wavelet-shrinkage denoising procedure directly to the Poisson non-parametric regression model (8). Two approaches can be applied to address this. The straightforward approach involves preprocessing the Poisson count data using normalizing and variance-stabilizing data transformation. After preprocessing, the standard wavelet-shrinkage denoising procedure [Donoho and Johnstone (1994, 1995, 1998); Donoho *et al.* (1995)] can be applied as though the noise were truly Gaussian. In previous work [Xiao and Dohi (2013b)], we applied this approach to the estimation of the software intensity function λ_i. A detailed explanation will be presented in Section 4.

A second approach is to apply a suitable level-dependent threshold to the empirical wavelet coefficients of the original Poisson count data. The translation-invariant denoising approach of Coifman and Donoho (1995) can be used in conjunction with these level-dependent thresholds to yield smooth estimates. We discussed this approach in detail in a previous study [Xiao and Dohi (2013c)]. We have also developed a Daubechies wavelet-based estimator that can be used to estimate the rate function $\lambda(t)$ of a C-NHPP [Xiao and Dohi (2012a)].

3 Multiresolution Representation

Multiresolution analysis [Mallat (1989)] is now considered one of the standard tools in image processing. It represents an arbitrary function of time t by an approximation component and a detail component. For an arbitrary function $f(t)$, the multiresolution representation is given by

$$f(t) = f_{j_0}(t) + \sum_{j=j_0}^{+\infty} g_j(t), \quad t \in (-\infty, +\infty), \tag{9}$$

where $f_{j_0}(t)$ is the level-j_0 approximation representing the global average of function $f(t)$ over the entire range of time t, while $g_j(t)$ is the level-j detail representing the difference between the global average and the function $f(t)$ in a certain subinterval of time t. Parameter j is called the resolution level, and the primary resolution level j_0 is generally set to 0. A sufficiently accurate representation of function $f(t)$ can be obtained by summing function $g_j(t)$ as many times as possible. In practice, however, it is unfeasible to sum function $g_j(t)$ infinitely. From the size of the observed data, the highest resolution level J can be determined, and function $g_j(t)$ is summed from 0 to $J-1$. The level-J multiresolution representation of function $f(t)$ is therefore normally obtained as follows:

$$f_J(t) = f_0(t) + \sum_{j=0}^{J-1} g_j(t). \tag{10}$$

Additionally, the level-j approximation and level-j detail are defined as

$$f_j(t) = \sum_{k=-\infty}^{\infty} c_{j,k} \phi_{j,k}(t), \tag{11}$$

and

$$g_j(t) = \sum_{k=-\infty}^{\infty} d_{j,k} \psi_{j,k}(t), \tag{12}$$

respectively. The level-j approximation $f_j(t)$ is expanded by the so-called *scaling coefficients* $c_{j,k}$ and an orthonormal basis $\phi_{j,k}(t)$. The orthonormal basis $\phi_{j,k}(t)$ is constructed by introducing the integer parameters j and k into the *father wavelet* (scaling function). Similarly, the level-j detail $g_j(t)$ is expanded by the so-called *wavelet coefficients* $d_{j,k}$ and an orthonormal basis $\psi_{j,k}(t)$. The orthonormal basis $\psi_{j,k}(t)$ is constructed by introducing the integer parameters j and k into the *mother wavelet* (wavelet function). Many wavelets can be used to construct the basis. The simplest is the Haar wavelet [Haar (1910)]. The Haar father wavelet and Haar mother wavelet are defined as follows:

$$\phi(t) = \begin{cases} 1 \ (0 \leq t \leq 1) \\ 0 \ (\text{otherwise}), \end{cases} \tag{13}$$

$$\psi(t) = \begin{cases} 1 \ (0 \leq t < 1/2) \\ -1 \ (1/2 \leq t < 1) \\ 0 \ (\text{otherwise}). \end{cases} \tag{14}$$

The system of orthogonal functions is normally generated using real number parameters, as

$$\psi_{a,b}(t) = |a|^{-1/2} \psi(a^{-1}t - a^{-1}b), \quad (a, \ b \in R). \tag{15}$$

Discretizing the parameters, and setting $a = 2^{-j}$, $b = 2^{-j}k$, yield

$$\psi_{j,k}(t) = 2^{j/2}\psi(2^j t - k), \quad (j, \; k \in Z). \tag{16}$$

Here, the parameters j and k are called the scaling parameter and shift parameter, respectively. Then, the orthonormal basis generated using the Haar wavelet is obtained as follows:

$$\phi_{j,k}(t) = 2^{j/2}\phi(2^j t - k) = \begin{cases} 2^{j/2}, & 2^{-j}k \leq t \leq 2^{-j}(k+1) \\ 0, & \text{otherwise,} \end{cases} \tag{17}$$

$$\psi_{j,k}(t) = 2^{j/2}\psi(2^j t - k) \begin{cases} 2^{j/2}, & 2^{-j}k \leq t < 2^{-j}(k+1/2) \\ -2^{j/2}, & 2^{-j}(k+1/2) \leq t < 2^{-j}(k+1) \\ 0, & \text{otherwise.} \end{cases}$$
$$\tag{18}$$

The multiresolution representation of function $f(t)$ is then obtained with finite resolution:

$$f_J(t) = f_0(t) + \sum_{j=0}^{J-1} g_j(t) = \sum_{k=0}^{2^0-1} c_{0,k}\phi_{0,k}(t) + \sum_{j=0}^{J-1}\sum_{k=0}^{2^j-1} d_{j,k}\psi_{j,k}(t)$$

$$= c_{0,0}\phi_{0,0}(t) + \sum_{j=0}^{J-1}\sum_{k=0}^{2^j-1} d_{j,k}\psi_{j,k}(t). \tag{19}$$

The properties of the orthonormal basis allow the coefficients to be obtained by taking the inner product of function $f(t)$ and the orthonormal basis. This gives the scaling coefficient and the wavelet coefficient:

$$c_{j,k} = \int_{-\infty}^{\infty} f(t)\phi_{j,k}^*(t)dt, \tag{20}$$

$$d_{j,k} = \int_{-\infty}^{\infty} f(t)\psi_{j,k}^*(t)dt, \tag{21}$$

where "*" denotes a complex conjugation.

We now present an example of this multiresolution representation, for better understanding. Consider the target function $f(t)$, $t \in (-\infty, +\infty)$.

$$f(t) = \begin{cases} 56, & 0 \leq t < 1/8 \\ 40, & 1/8 \leq t < 2/8 \\ 8, & 2/8 \leq t < 3/8 \\ 24, & 3/8 \leq t < 4/8 \\ 48, & 4/8 \leq t < 5/8 \\ 48, & 5/8 \leq t < 6/8 \\ 40, & 6/8 \leq t < 7/8 \\ 16, & 7/8 \leq t < 1 \\ 0, & \text{otherwise.} \end{cases} \tag{22}$$

Since it has eight observation points, the highest resolution level J is $\log_2 8 = 3$. We can calculate the level-1, level-2, and level-3 approximation of $f(t)$ as follows:

(1) level-1 approximation $f_1(t)$

From Eq. (19), $f_1(t) = f_0(t) + g_0(t)$. Since

$$\phi_{0,0}(t) = \phi_{0,0}^*(t) = \begin{cases} 1, & 0 \leq t \leq 1 \\ 0, & \text{otherwise}, \end{cases} \tag{23}$$

$$c_{0,0} = \int_{-\infty}^{\infty} f(t)\phi_{0,0}^*(t)dt = \int_0^1 f(t)\phi_{0,0}^*(t)dt = \int_0^1 f(t)dt$$

$$= \int_0^{1/8} 56dt + \int_{1/8}^{2/8} 40dt + \cdots + \int_{7/8}^1 16dt = 35, \tag{24}$$

we have

$$f_0(t) = c_{0,0}\phi_{0,0}(t) = \begin{cases} 35, & 0 \leq t \leq 1 \\ 0, & \text{otherwise}. \end{cases} \tag{25}$$

Similarly, since

$$\psi_{0,0}(t) = \psi_{0,0}^*(t) = \begin{cases} 1, & 0 \leq t < 1/2 \\ -1, & 1/2 \leq t < 1 \\ 0, & \text{otherwise}, \end{cases} \tag{26}$$

$$d_{0,0} = \int_{-\infty}^{\infty} f(t)\psi_{0,0}^*(t)dt = \int_0^1 f(t)\psi_{0,0}^*(t)dt = \int_0^{1/2} f(t)dt - \int_{1/2}^1 f(t)dt$$

$$= \left\{ \int_0^{1/8} 56dt + \cdots + \int_{3/8}^{4/8} 24dt \right\} - \left\{ \int_{4/8}^{5/8} 48dt + \cdots + \int_{7/8}^1 16dt \right\}$$

$$= -3, \tag{27}$$

we have

$$g_0(t) = \sum_{k=0}^{2^0-1} d_{0,k}\psi_{0,k}(t) = d_{0,0}\psi_{0,0}(t) = \begin{cases} -3, & 0 \leq t < 1/2 \\ 3, & 1/2 \leq t < 1 \\ 0, & \text{otherwise}. \end{cases} \tag{28}$$

The level-1 approximation $f_1(t)$ is therefore calculated as follows:

$$f_1(t) = f_0(t) + g_0(t) = \begin{cases} 32, & 0 \leq t < 1/8 \\ 32, & 1/8 \leq t < 2/8 \\ 32, & 2/8 \leq t < 3/8 \\ 32, & 3/8 \leq t < 4/8 \\ 38, & 4/8 \leq t < 5/8 \\ 38, & 5/8 \leq t < 6/8 \\ 38, & 6/8 \leq t < 7/8 \\ 38, & 7/8 \leq t < 1 \\ 0, & \text{otherwise}. \end{cases} \tag{29}$$

(2) level-2 approximation $f_2(t)$

From Eq. (19), $f_2(t) = f_0(t) + g_0(t) + g_1(t)$. Since

$$\psi_{1,0}(t) = \psi_{1,0}^*(t) = \begin{cases} \sqrt{2} & , \ 0 \le t < 1/4 \\ -\sqrt{2} & , \ 1/4 \le t < 2/4 \\ 0 & , \ \text{otherwise,} \end{cases} \tag{30}$$

$$\psi_{1,1}(t) = \psi_{1,1}^*(t) = \begin{cases} \sqrt{2} & , \ 2/4 \le t < 3/4 \\ -\sqrt{2} & , \ 3/4 \le t < 1 \\ 0 & , \ \text{otherwise,} \end{cases} \tag{31}$$

$$
\begin{aligned}
d_{1,0} &= \int_{-\infty}^{\infty} f(t)\psi_{1,0}^*(t)dt = \int_0^1 f(t)\psi_{1,0}^*(t)dt \\
&= \sqrt{2}\int_0^{1/4} f(t)dt - \sqrt{2}\int_{1/4}^{2/4} f(t)dt \\
&= \sqrt{2}\left\{ \int_0^{1/8} 56dt + \int_{1/8}^{2/8} 40dt \right\} - \sqrt{2}\left\{ \int_{2/8}^{3/8} 8dt + \int_{3/8}^{4/8} 24dt \right\} \\
&= 8\sqrt{2},
\end{aligned}
\tag{32}
$$

$$
\begin{aligned}
d_{1,1} &= \int_{-\infty}^{\infty} f(t)\psi_{1,1}^*(t)dt = \int_0^1 f(t)\psi_{1,1}^*(t)dt \\
&= \sqrt{2}\int_{2/4}^{3/4} f(t)dt - \sqrt{2}\int_{3/4}^{1} f(t)dt \\
&= \sqrt{2}\left\{ \int_{4/8}^{5/8} 48dt + \int_{5/8}^{6/8} 48dt \right\} - \sqrt{2}\left\{ \int_{6/8}^{7/8} 40dt + \int_{7/8}^{1} 16dt \right\} \\
&= 5\sqrt{2},
\end{aligned}
\tag{33}
$$

we have

$$g_1(t) = \sum_{k=0}^{2^1-1} d_{1,k}\psi_{1,k}(t) = d_{1,0}\psi_{1,0}(t) + d_{1,1}\psi_{1,1}(t)$$

$$= \begin{cases} 16 & , \ 0 \le t < 1/4 \\ -16 & , \ 1/4 \le t < 2/4 \\ 10 & , \ 2/4 \le t < 3/4 \\ -10 & , \ 3/4 \le t < 1 \\ 0 & , \ \text{otherwise.} \end{cases} \tag{34}$$

The level-2 approximation $f_2(t)$ is therefore calculated as follows:

$$f_2(t) = f_0(t) + g_0(t) + g_1(t) = \begin{cases} 48, & 0 \le t < 1/8 \\ 48, & 1/8 \le t < 2/8 \\ 16, & 2/8 \le t < 3/8 \\ 16, & 3/8 \le t < 4/8 \\ 48, & 4/8 \le t < 5/8 \\ 48, & 5/8 \le t < 6/8 \\ 28, & 6/8 \le t < 7/8 \\ 28, & 7/8 \le t < 1 \\ 0, & \text{otherwise.} \end{cases} \tag{35}$$

(3) level-3 approximation $f_3(t)$

In a similar fashion, the level-2 detail component $g_2(t)$ can be calculated by

$$g_2(t) = \begin{cases} 8, & 0 \le t < 1/8 \\ -8, & 1/8 \le t < 2/8 \\ -8, & 2/8 \le t < 3/8 \\ 8, & 3/8 \le t < 4/8 \\ 0, & 4/8 \le t < 5/8 \\ 0, & 5/8 \le t < 6/8 \\ 12, & 6/8 \le t < 7/8 \\ -12, & 7/8 \le t < 1 \\ 0, & \text{otherwise.} \end{cases} \tag{36}$$

The level-3 approximation $f_3(t)$ can therefore be calculated as follows:

$$f_3(t) = f_0(t) + g_0(t) + g_1(t) + g_2(t) = \begin{cases} 56, & 0 \le t < 1/8 \\ 40, & 1/8 \le t < 2/8 \\ 8, & 2/8 \le t < 3/8 \\ 24, & 3/8 \le t < 4/8 \\ 48, & 4/8 \le t < 5/8 \\ 48, & 5/8 \le t < 6/8 \\ 40, & 6/8 \le t < 7/8 \\ 16, & 7/8 \le t < 1 \\ 0, & \text{otherwise.} \end{cases} \tag{37}$$

4 Wavelet Shrinkage Estimation for D-NHPP-based Software Reliability Assessment

In this section, we use the data-transform-based wavelet shrinkage estimation (DT-WSE) [Xiao and Dohi (2013b)] to estimate the software intensity function λ_i of the D-NHPP-based SRM. Usually, the realizations of the target function λ_i are observable, and noise may be present in the observations. We consider the problem of estimating the target function λ_i $(i = 1, 2, \ldots, n)$ from such noisy software-fault count data y_i $(i = 1, 2, \ldots, n)$, which is the realization of Poisson random variable Y_i in Eq. (8). The fundamental idea is to remove the noise from the empirical wavelet coefficients to obtain a noise-free estimator of the target function.

As noted in Section 2.2, a problem arises when the standard wavelet-shrinkage denoising procedure [Donoho and Johnstone (1994, 1995, 1998); Donoho *et al.* (1995)] is used to remove the noise η_i in Eq. (8), because this procedure is designed to remove Gaussian white noise, whereas η_i is Poisson white noise. To overcome this problem, we employ normalizing and variance-stabilizing data transformation. The DT-WSE designed for the estimation of software intensity function λ_i of the D-NHPP has three steps: (i) pre-processing the Poisson count data y_i by data transformation, (ii) applying the standard wavelet-shrinkage denoising procedure to remove the noise from the empirical wavelet coefficients, and (iii) using inverse data transformation to obtain the estimator of λ_i.

Three well-known normalizing and variance-stabilizing transforms are the *Bartlett transform* [Bartlett (1936)], the *Anscombe transform* [Anscombe (1948)], and the *Fisz transform* [Fisz (1955)]. Applying any of these, the software-fault count data y_i, which follow the D-NHPP with an unknown mean value function, are transformed to the approximately Gaussian data y_i', which can be regarded as the realizations of the normally distributed random variables Y_i' $(i = 1, 2, \ldots, n)$. Additionally,

$$Y_i' = \lambda_i' + \eta_i', \quad i = 1, 2, \ldots, n, \tag{38}$$

where λ_i' is the transformed software intensity function at testing date i, and η_i' is Gaussian white noise. For example, *Anscombe transform* (AT) [Anscombe (1948)] is a natural extension of the well-known *Bartlett transform* [Bartlett (1936)], and is the most fundamental data-transform tool in statistics. Taking the AT, the random variables $Y_i' = 2\sqrt{Y_i + 3/8}$ $(i = 1, 2, \ldots, n)$ can be approximately expressed as the Gaussian random variables with $N(2\sqrt{\lambda_i + 1/8}, 1)$ so that the realizations

$$y_i' = 2\sqrt{y_i + 3/8}, \quad i = 1, 2, \ldots, n, \tag{39}$$

can be regarded as samples from $N(\lambda_i', 1)$, where $\lambda_i' = 2\sqrt{\lambda_i + 1/8}$. Here, $N(\mu, \sigma^2)$ denotes normal distribution with mean μ and variance σ^2.

Utilizing the multiresolution representation introduced in Section 3, the transformed target function in Eq. (38), λ_i' ($i = 1, 2, \ldots, n$), can be expressed as

$$\lambda_i' = a_{0,0}\phi_{0,0}(i) + \sum_{j=0}^{J-1}\sum_{k=0}^{2^j-1} b_{j,k}\psi_{j,k}(i), \tag{40}$$

where

$$a_{j,k} = \sum_{i=1}^{n} \lambda_i'\phi_{j,k}(i), \tag{41}$$

$$b_{j,k} = \sum_{i=1}^{n} \lambda_i'\psi_{j,k}(i), \tag{42}$$

are called the *discrete scaling coefficients* and the *discrete wavelet coefficients*, respectively. The $a_{j,k}$ and $b_{j,k}$ are related to their continuous counterparts $c_{j,k}$ (Eq. (20)) and $d_{j,k}$ (Eq. (21)) by the relationships $c_{j,k} \approx a_{j,k}/\sqrt{n}$ and $d_{j,k} \approx b_{j,k}/\sqrt{n}$. The factor $\sqrt{n}$ arises from the difference between the continuous and discrete orthonormality conditions [Abramovich *et al.* (2000)]. Let y_i' ($i = 1, 2, \ldots, n$) be the observation of λ_i'. The *empirical discrete scaling coefficients* $\alpha_{j,k}$ and the *empirical discrete wavelet coefficients* $\beta_{j,k}$ of λ_i' can then be calculated using Eq. (41) and Eq. (42), with λ_i' replaced by y_i'.

Many types of wavelet have been presented in the literature, and can be used to generate the orthonormal basis $\phi_{j,k}(i)$ and $\psi_{j,k}(i)$. The Haar wavelet [Haar (1910)], Daubechies wavelet [Daubechies (1992)], and Meyer wavelet [Meyer (1993)] are representative discrete wavelet transforms, and well-known continuous wavelet transforms include the Shannon wavelet [Cattani (2006)] and Morlet wavelet [Grossmann and Morlet (1984)]. We use the Haar wavelet because it is the most basic, and is appropriate to handle discrete time-series data. The Haar father wavelet and the Haar mother wavelet are given in Eq. (13) and Eq. (14), respectively.

The noise in the empirical discrete wavelet coefficients $\beta_{j,k}$ can be removed using the thresholding method [Donoho and Johnstone (1994, 1995, 1998); Donoho *et al.* (1995)]. Although a range of thresholding schemes have been presented, the most common approaches are *hard thresholding*,

$$\delta_\tau(u) = u 1_{|u|>\tau}, \tag{43}$$

and *soft thresholding*,

$$\delta_\tau(u) = \text{sgn}(u)(|u| - \tau)_+, \tag{44}$$

for a fixed threshold level τ (> 0), where 1_A is the indicator function of an event A, $\text{sgn}(u)$ is the sign function of u, and $(u)_+ = \max(0, u)$. Hard thresholding is a 'keep' or 'kill' rule, while soft thresholding is a 'shrink' or 'kill' rule. Both thresholding methods are employed to remove the noise from the empirical discrete wavelet coefficients $\beta_{j,k}$. If too high a threshold is set, this may remove important parts of the original function, whereas too small a threshold will allow noise to persist in the selective reconstruction. Hence, the choice of threshold is significant. Many methods have been proposed for determining the threshold level (see, for example, [Besbeas *et al.* (2004)]). We use the universal threshold [Donoho and Johnstone (1994)] and the 'leave-out-half' cross-validation threshold [Nason (1996)]:

$$\tau = \sqrt{2\log n}, \tag{45}$$

$$\tau = \left(1 - \frac{\log 2}{\log n}\right)^{-1/2} \tau\left(\frac{n}{2}\right). \tag{46}$$

Details of $\tau(n/2)$ are given in [Nason (1996)].

From above, the function

$$\vec{w} = (\vec{\alpha}_0, \ \delta_\tau(\vec{\beta}_0), \ \delta_\tau(\vec{\beta}_1), \ldots, \ \delta_\tau(\vec{\beta}_{J-1}))^T \tag{47}$$

is the denoised coefficient matrix, and is used to construct the estimator of the transformed target function λ_i'. Here, $\vec{\alpha}_0 = (\alpha_{0,0}, \alpha_{0,1}, \cdots, \alpha_{0,2^j-1})^T$, and $\vec{\beta}_j = (\beta_{j,0}, \beta_{j,1}, \cdots, \beta_{j,2^j-1})^T$. Finally, the algebraic inverse of the data transform can then be used in the third step of the DT-WSE. Xiao and Dohi (2012) compared the accuracy of DT-WSE using different data transforms, while Tada *et al.* (2016) investigated the influence of the bias of the algebraic inverse data transform.

5 Performance Evaluation

In this section, we give a numerical example to demonstrate the effectiveness of the DT-WSE. The software-fault count data (group data) used was the J1 data set from [Lyu (1996)]. The final testing date was $n = 62$, and the total number of detected faults was $x_n = 133$. The mean square error (MSE) and log likelihood (LL) were used as the goodness-of-fit measures, where

$$\text{MSE}_1 = \frac{\sqrt{\sum_{i=1}^n (\hat{\Lambda}_i - x_i)^2}}{n}, \tag{48}$$

$$\text{MSE}_2 = \frac{\sqrt{\sum_{i=1}^n (\hat{\lambda}_i - y_i)^2}}{n}, \tag{49}$$

Table 1.1 Goodness-of-fit test Results.

Proposed methods	MSE$_1$	MSE$_2$	LL
AT(h, ut)	2.573	0.316	-145.390
AT(h, lht)	0.114	0.014	-60.324
AT(s, ut)	2.573	0.316	-145.390
AT(s, lht)	0.115	0.010	-60.118
Existing methods	MSE$_1$	MSE$_2$	LL
MLE(GE)	0.666	0.407	-142.071
MLE(NB)	1.077	0.415	-137.648
MLE(DW)	0.666	0.407	-142.071
LLE(K)	0.869	0.257	-115.046

$$LL = \sum_{i=1}^{n}(x_i - x_{i-1})\ln[\hat{\Lambda}_i - \hat{\Lambda}_{i-1}] - \hat{\Lambda}_n - \sum_{i=1}^{n}\ln[(x_i - x_{i-1})!]. \quad (50)$$

Here, $\hat{\Lambda}_i$ and $\hat{\lambda}_i$ denote the estimates of the mean value function and the intensity function of D-NHPP, respectively. And y_i denotes the number of software faults detected at testing date i, while $x_i = \sum_{k=0}^{i} y_k$ is its cumulative value. Four thresholding techniques were compared: hard thresholding (h) with soft thresholding (s), and the universal threshold (ut) with the 'leave-out-half' cross-validation threshold (lht), yielding a total of four DT-WSEs when the Anscombe transform was used. Here, AT($\cdot$, $\cdot$) denotes the DT-WSE with the Anscombe transform. The performance evaluation of the DT-WSEs with Fisz transform, Bartlett transform, and *Freeman and Tukey transform* [Freeman and Tukey (1950)] can be found in [Xiao and Dohi (2012, 2013b)]. We also estimated the software intensity function using three parametric D-NHPP-based SRMs, applying the MLE to estimate the model parameters for comparison. The mean value functions of these three parametric D-NHPP-based SRMs were assumed to be $\Lambda_i^{\text{GE}} = \omega\{1 - (1 - p)^i\}$, $\Lambda_i^{\text{NB}} = \omega\{\sum_{k=1}^{i} \frac{(r+k-1)!}{(r-1)!k!} p^r (1 - p)^{k-1}\}$, and $\Lambda_i^{\text{DW}} = \omega\{1 - p^{i^r}\}$, respectively, denoted as MLE(GE), MLE(NB), and MLE(DW). The parameters ω, p, and r are real number parameters. Additionally, local likelihood estimation [Wang *et al.* (2007)] with the kernel function $K(u) = 3/4(1 - u^2)I_{[-1,1]}$ was selected from the existing non-parametric estimation methods, and denoted as LLE(K). The goodness-of-fit results are shown in Table 1.1. f

It can be seen that the DT-WSEs minimized MSE_1 and MSE_2 in the data set, and maximized LL although no parametric form was assumed for the software intensity function. This result is not surprising, because the output of the DT-WSE without denoising constitutes the input data. In cases where the effects of denoising are significantly smaller, the resulting MSE of the number of faults also tends to be small. It is interesting to note that the DT-WSEs outperformed the MLE in maximizing the log likelihood. These experimental results suggest the potential applicability of wavelet-based estimation methods using different thresholding schemes. The methods employed here incur far less computational costs than the MLE (with estimates generated in under one second). This is a significant advantage, in addition to the fact that practitioners do not request much time and effort to implement the wavelet-based estimation algorithms. The table also demonstrates that, due to the non-parametric nature of the LLE, a better goodness-of-fit was achieved than those of the parametric estimation techniques discussed above. However, the LLE failed to outperform the DT-WSE on any of the goodness-of-fit criteria. This further demonstrates the power of the DT-WSE within the non-parametric framework.

6 Conclusion

In this chapter, we used wavelet-based techniques to estimate the software-fault detection process in software testing. In spite of being non-parametric, numerical experiments using real data demonstrated that our wavelet-based estimation method had a goodness-of-fit performance superior to that of the conventional MLE and LLE, in some cases. We confirmed the potential applicability of wavelet-based estimation methods to software reliability assessment. This approach does not require the use of difficult model selection procedures, and offers greater computational efficiency in the judgment of convergence and selection of initial parameters.

The most serious disadvantage of non-parametric estimation techniques is the difficulty of predicting future debugging behavior from the observation point. In parametric SRMs, it is possible to predict the behavior of the software-fault detection process at an arbitrary future time, if the estimated parameters can be plugged into the mean value function and intensity function. However, non-Bayesian and non-parametric SRMs [Gandy and Jensen (2004); Sofer and Miller (1991); Wang *et al.* (2007)] are defined on the limited information available at the observation point. One available prediction method is the sequential one-stage look-ahead prediction, as Barghout *et al.* (1998) used. We used this to predict the software reliability on the following day. The predictive performance of the proposed method can be found in [Xiao and Dohi (2013b,c)].

Along with the popularization of new testing techniques, measurement units other than calendar time may become more appreciated in test data collections. In recent years, the number of test cases has become to be considered as the measurement unit instead of calendar time [Ishii *et al.* (2008); Shibata *et al.* (2007)]. However, it should be noted that our method is certainly not restricted to the analysis of test data using calendar time. Our method can also analyze such test data using other measurement units as long as the number of detected faults is recorded on equally-spaced intervals. We will give numerical assessment to show the applicability of our method to the other type of test data in the future.

Attention also should be paid to the overestimation of quantitative software reliability that arises from using the testing time as the unit of measurement for the software-fault data. Chen *et al.* (2001) pointed out that this may not be the best way of representing the testing effort, because additional testing time may be considered *ineffective*. This critique can be applied not only to the use of calendar time, but also the number of test cases. They suggested an adjustment to the raw software-fault data, to be applied before estimating software reliability. Their approach was to turn back the testing time if the interval of testing time neither increased the testing coverage nor caused the program to fail on execution. This allowed the overestimation of quantitative software reliability to be corrected. Although their approach was evaluated using software failure time data, we believe it to be applicable to the software-fault count data used in the present study. The calibration of the ineffective testing time is beyond the scope of the present study, but we remain interested in applying this approach to the preprocessing of the observed software-fault count data. We consider their approach to be fundamentally consentient with a wavelet-based approach from the viewpoint of *denoising*.

Moreover, one should be aware that the assumption about statistical independency between different software faults might be a little strong. A more realistic situation is one where the detection of one software fault may directly lead to the detection of a related one, or make it more difficult to find other faults. As Debroy and Wong (2009) indicated, there is a nontrivial interference between multiple software faults in the same program. Therefore, the over-simplified assumption is not very preferable. In practice, the software testers often encounter such a situation that the software debugging effort alternates between high and low states. To illustrate the detection phenomenon relevant to the dependency between different software faults, Ando *et al.* (2006) introduced the so-called *Markov modulated Poisson processes*, and developed Markov modulated software reliability models. As in their work, it is necessary to employ a more complex stochastic process if we do not assume statistical independence between different software faults. However, in the field of wavelet analysis, the techniques for such a complex stochastic process have not been well established mathematically. Therefore, at this point, the wavelet-based estimation method for software reliability assessment is still restricted to NHPP. As future work, we are interested in developing new wavelet-based methods for a more realistic situation, depending upon the progress of mathematical establishment.

References

Abramovich, F., Bailey, T. C. and Sapatinas, T. (2000). Wavelet analysis and its statistical applications, *The Statistician*, vol. 49, no. 1, pp. 1–29.

Ando, T., Okamura, H. and Dohi, T. (2006). Estimating Markov modulated software reliability models via EM algorithm, *Proceedings of the 2nd IEEE International Symposium on Dependable, Autonomic and Secure Computing* (DASC'06), pp. 111–118, IEEE CS Press.

Anscombe, F. J. (1948). The transformation of Poisson, binomial and negative binomial data, *Biometrika*, vol. 35, no. 3-4, pp. 246–254.

Barghout, M., Littlewood, B. and Abdel-Ghaly, A. (1998). A non-parametric order statistics software reliability model, *Software Testing, Verification and Reliability*, vol. 8, no. 3, pp. 113–132.

Bartlett, M. S. (1936). The square root transformation in the analysis of variance, *Supplement to the Journal of the Royal Statistical Society*, vol. 3, no. 1, pp. 68–78.

Basu, S. and Ebrahimi, N. (2003). Bayesian software reliability models based on martingale processes, *Technometrics*, vol. 45, no. 2, pp. 150–158.

Besbeas, P., De Feis, I. and Sapatinas, T. (2004). A comparative simulation study of wavelet shrinkage estimators for Poisson counts, *International Statistical Review*, vol. 72, no. 2, pp. 209–237.

Cattani, C. (2006). Connection coefficients of Shannon wavelets, *Mathematical Modelling and Analysis*, vol. 11, no. 2, pp. 117–132.

Chen, M. H., Lyu, M. R. and Wong, W. E. (2001). Effect of code coverage on software reliability measurement, *IEEE Transactions on Reliability*, vol. 50, no. 2, pp. 165–170.

Coifman, R. R. and Donoho, D. L. (1995). Translation-invariant de-noising, In *Wavelets and Statistics, Eds. A. Antoniadis and G. Oppenheim, Series Lecture Notes in Statistics*, vol. 103, pp. 125-150, New York, USA: Springer-Verlag.

Daubechies, I. (1992). *Ten Lectures on Wavelets*, SIAM, Pennsylvania.

Debroy, V. and Wong, W. E. (2009). Insights on fault interference for programs with multiple bugs, *Proceedings of 20th International Symposium on Software Reliability Engineering* (ISSRE'09), pp. 165–174, IEEE CS Press.

Donoho, D. L. and Johnstone, I. M. (1994). Ideal spatial adaptation by wavelet shrinkage, *Biometrika*, vol. 81, no. 3, pp. 425–455.

Donoho, D. L. and Johnstone, I. M. (1995). Adapting to unknown smoothness via wavelet shrinkage, *Journal of the American Statistical Association*, vol. 90, no. 432, pp. 1200–1224.

Donoho, D. L. and Johnstone, I. M. (1998). Minimax estimation via wavelet shrinkage, *Annals of Statistics*, vol. 26, no. 3, pp. 879–921.

Donoho, D. L., Johnstone, I. M., Kerkyacharian, G. and Ricard, D. (1995). Wavelet shrinkage: asymptopia? (with discussion), *Journal of the Royal Statistical Society: Series B*, vol. 57, pp. 301–337.

Fisz, M. (1955). The limiting distribution of a function of two independent random variables and its statistical application, *Colloquium Mathematicum*, vol. 3, pp. 138–146.

Freeman, M. F. and Tukey, J. W. (1950). Transformations related to the angular and the square root, *The Annals of Mathematical Statistics*, vol. 21, no. 4, pp. 607–611.

Gandy, A. and Jensen, U. (2004). A non-parametric approach to software reliability, *Applied Stochastic Models in Business and Industry*, vol. 20, no. 1, pp. 3–15.

Goel, A. L. and Okumoto, K. (1979). Time-dependent error-detection rate model for software reliability and other performance measures, *IEEE Transactions on Reliability*, vol. 28, no. 3, pp. 206–211.

Grossmann, A. and Morlet, J. (1984). Decomposition of Hardy Functions into Square Integrable Wavelets of Constant Shape, *SIAM Journal on Mathematical Analysis*, vol. 15, no. 4, pp. 723–736.

Haar, A. (1910). Zur theorie der orthogonalen funktionen-systeme, *Mathematische Annalen*, vol. 69, pp. 331–371.

Ishii, T., Fujiwara, T. and Dohi, T. (2008). Bivariate extension of discrete software reliability modeling with number of test cases, *International Journal of Reliability, Quality and Safety Engineering*, vol. 15, no. 1, pp. 1–17.

Jeske, D. R. and Pham, H. (2001). On the maximum likelihood estimates for the Goel-Okumoto software reliability model, *The American Statistician*, vol. 55, no. 3, pp. 219–222.

Kuo, L. and Yang, T. Y. (1996). Bayesian computation for nonhomogeneous Poisson processes in software reliability, *Journal of the American Statistical Association*, vol. 91, pp. 763–773.

Lyu, M. R. (ed.) (1996). *Handbook of Software Reliability Engineering*, McGraw-Hill, New York.

Mallat, S. G. (1989). A theory for multiresolution signal decomposition: the wavelet representation, *IEEE Transactions on Pattern Analysis and Machine Intelligence*, vol. 11, no. 7, pp. 674–693.

Meyer, Y. (1993). *Wavelets: Algorithms and Applications*, SIAM, Philadelphia.

Musa, J. D., Iannino, A. and Okumoto, K. (1987). *Software Reliability, Measurement, Prediction, Application*, McGraw-Hill, New York.

Nason, G. P. (1996). Wavelet shrinkage using cross-validation, *Journal of the Royal Statistical Society: Series B*, vol. 58, pp. 463–479.

Nayak, T. K., Bose, S. and Kundu, S. (2008). On inconsistency of estimators of parameters of non-homogeneous Poisson process models for software reliability, *Statistical and Probability Letters*, vol. 78, no. 14, pp. 2217–2221.

Ohishi, K., Okamura, H. and Dohi, T. (2009). Gompertz software reliability model: estimation algorithm and empirical validation, *Journal of Systems and Software*, vol. 82, no. 3, pp. 535–543.

Okamura, H., Grottke, M., Dohi, T. and Trivedi, K. S. (2007). Variational Bayesian approach for interval estimation of NHPP-based software reliability models, *Proceedings of the 37th Annual IEEE/IFIP International Conference on Dependable Systems and Networks* (DSN'07), pp. 698–707, IEEE CS Press.

Okamura, H., Murayama, A. and Dohi, T. (2004). EM algorithm for discrete software reliability models: a unified parameter estimation method, *Proceedings of the 8th IEEE International Symposium on High Assurance Systems Engineering*, (HASE'04), pp. 219–228, IEEE CS Press.

Okamura, H., Murayama, A. and Dohi, T. (2006) A unified parameter estimation algorithm for discrete software reliability models, *Opsearch*, vol. 42, no. 4, pp. 355–377.

Pham, H. (2000). *Software Reliability*, Springer, Singapore.

Shibata, K., Rinsaka, K. and Dohi, T. (2007). Dynamic software reliability modeling with discrete-test metrics; how good is it?, *International Journal of Industrial Engineering*, vol. 14, no. 4, pp. 332–339.

Sofer, A. and Miller, D. R. (1991). A non-parametric software reliability growth model, *IEEE Transactions on Reliability*, vol. 40, no. 3, pp. 329–337.

Tada, D., Xiao, X. and Yamamoto, H. (2016). Wavelet shrinkage estimation using unbiased inverse transformation for software reliability assessment, *Proceedings of the 7th Asia-Pacific International Symposium on Advanced Reliability and Maintenance Modeling* (APARM'16), pp. 493–500.

Wang, Z., Wang, J. and Liang, X. (2007). Non-parametric estimation for NHPP software reliability models, *Journal of Applied Statistics*, vol. 34, no. 1, pp. 107–119.

Xiao, X. (2015). NHPP-based software reliability model with Marshall-Olkin failure time distribution, *IEICE Transactions on Fundamentals*, vol. E98-A, no. 10, pp. 2060–2068.

Xiao, X. and Dohi, T. (2009). Wavelet-based approach for estimating software reliability, *Proceedings of 20th International Symposium on Software Reliability Engineering* (ISSRE'09), pp. 11–20, IEEE CS Press.

Xiao, X. and Dohi, T. (2012). A comparative study of data transformations for wavelet shrinkage estimation with application to software reliability assessment, *Advances in Software Engineering*, vol. 2012, Article ID 524636, 9 pages.

Xiao, X. and Dohi, T. (2012a). Software failure time data analysis via wavelet-based approach, *IEICE Transactions on Fundamentals*, vol. E95-A, no. 9, pp. 1490–1497.

Xiao, X. and Dohi, T. (2013). A study on applying extreme value distribution to NHPP-based SRM, *Information*, vol. 16, no. 1(B), pp. 575–580.

Xiao, X. and Dohi, T. (2013a). On the role of Weibull-type distributions in NHPP-based software reliability modeling, *International Journal of Performability Engineering*, vol. 9, no. 2, pp. 123–132.

Xiao, X. and Dohi, T. (2013b). Wavelet shrinkage estimation for non-homogenous Poisson process based software reliability models, *IEEE Transactions on Reliability*, vol. 62, no. 1, pp. 211–225.

Xiao, X. and Dohi, T. (2013c). Estimating software intensity function based on translation-invariant Poisson smoothing approach, *IEEE Transactions on Reliability*, vol. 62, no. 4, pp. 930–945.

Xiao, X., Okamura, H. and Dohi, T. (2012). NHPP-based software reliability models using equilibrium distribution, *IEICE Transactions on Fundamentals*, vol. E95-A, no. 5, pp. 894–902.

Yamada, S. and Osaki, S. (1985). Discrete software reliability growth models, *Applied Stochastic Models and Data Analysis*, vol. 1, no.1, pp. 65–77.

Yamada, S., Osaki, S. and Narihisa, H. (1984). Software reliability growth modeling with number of test runs, *Transactions of the IEICE of Japan*, vol. E67-E, no.2, pp. 79–83.

Zhao, M. and Xie, M. (1996). On maximum likelihood estimation for a general non-homogeneous Poisson process, *Scandinavian Journal of Statistics*, vol. 23, pp. 597–607.

Chapter 3

Dependability Analysis Tool Considering the Optimal Data Partitioning in a Mobile Cloud

Yoshinobu Tamura[1] and Shigeru Yamada[2]

[1] *Graduate School of Sciences and Technology for Innovation,*
Yamaguchi University

[2] *Graduate School of Engineering,*
Tottori University

1   Introduction

Software reliability has been mainly focused on the testing-phase under the software development process. However, many software are updated via the internet network at present. Then, the structure of software have been changed from hour to hour. Therefore, it is important to manage the operational phase of software. Also, the cloud computing with big data is known as a next-generation software service paradigm. There are some interesting research papers in terms of the cloud computing, cloud service, mobile clouds, and cloud performance evaluation [Suo et al. (2013); Khalifa and Eltoweissy (2013)].

At present, many software services based on the cloud computing with big data are used by many users. In the past, many software reliability growth models (SRGM's) [Yamada (2013); Lyu (1996); Kapur et al. (2011)] have been applied to assess the reliability for quality management and testing-progress control of software development. However, the effective methods of software reliability assessment considering the cloud computing under the influence of big data have been only few presented. We focus on the reliability assessment for the cloud computing with big data.

Considering the management of cloud computing, OSS (Open Source Software) such as OpenStack and Eucalyptus are frequently used in the cloud computing from the standpoint of the unified management of data, low cost, easily-maintenance, and easily-operation. The database software such as Hadoop and NoSQL is embedded with the cloud software such as OpenStack because of the cloud computing with big data. The relationship between database software and cloud software. The cloud software perform in cooperation with the database software in the environment of cloud computing with big data. Then, the amount of traffic data with the relationship among the cloud software and database one also becomes large in the environment. Considering the software failure in the whole environment of cloud computing, it is important to assess the software failure occurred in database software as well as one occurred in cloud software. As an example, it means the data traffic failure in case of the failure on "NameNode" replaced between "Client" and "DataNode", e.g., it is not the failure of cloud software.

Considering the dependency relationship among main software components in cloud computing, we propose the method of system-wide reliability assessment based on the jump diffusion process model considering the big data on cloud computing. Also, it is necessary to grasp the relationship between the cloud-based data and the contents data on the database software. Then, we consider the status of the data partitioning between the cloud-based data and the contents data. The proposed method will be useful for the software managers to assess the reliability of the characteristics of big data on cloud computing. In particular, we describe the dependability as several noises included in the model. Moreover, it is very important in terms of software management for us to decide for the optimal length of the maintenance period for big data on cloud computing. We propose the optimal maintenance problem based on the jump diffusion model. Considering the amount of noise in the sample path as the stability requirement, we find the optimum maintenance time by minimizing the total expected software cost. Furthermore, we analyze actual data to show numerical examples of the dependability optimization. Especially, the dependability analysis tool for mobile cloud is developed in this paper. Also, a set of actual software fault data is analyzed in order to show numerical illustrations of application software of dependability analysis tool. Then, this paper shows that the developed dependability analysis tool can assist the improvement of quality for a cloud computing.

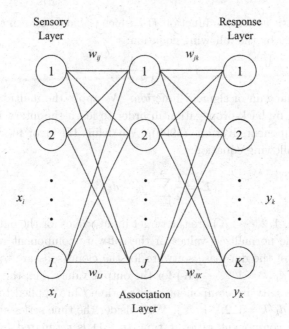

Fig. 1 Structure of our neural network.

2 Estimation of Software Component Ratio Based on Neural Network

The structure of the neural networks in this paper is shown in Figure 1. Let $w_{ij}^1(i = 1, 2, \cdots, I; j = 1, 2, \cdots, J)$ be the connection weights from i-th unit on the sensory layer to j-th unit on the association layer, $w_{jk}^2(j = 1, 2, \cdots, J; k = 1, 2, \cdots, K)$ denote the connection weights from j-th unit on the association layer to k-th unit on the response layer. Moreover, $x_i(i = 1, 2, \cdots, I)$ represent the normalized input values of i-th unit on the sensory layer, and $y_k(k = 1, 2, \cdots, K)$ are the output values. We apply the actual software component ratio of the database software for the cloud software per unit time to the input values $x_i(i = 1, 2, \cdots, I)$.

The input-output rules of each unit on each layer are given by

$$h_j = f\left(\sum_{i=1}^{I} w_{ij}^1 x_i\right), \tag{1}$$

$$y_k = f\left(\sum_{j=1}^{J} w_{jk}^2 h_j\right), \tag{2}$$

where a logistic activation function $f(\cdot)$ which is widely-known as a sigmoid function given by the following equation:

$$f(x) = \frac{1}{1 + e^{-\theta x}}, \tag{3}$$

where θ is the gain of sigmoid function. We apply the multi-layered neural networks by back-propagation in order to learn the interaction among software components[Karnin (1990)]. We define the error function in Eq. (2) by the following equation:

$$E = \frac{1}{2} \sum_{k=1}^{K} (y_k - d_k)^2, \tag{4}$$

where $d_k(k = 1, 2, \cdots, K)$ are the target input values for the output values. We apply the normalized values of the software component ratio $d_t(t = 2, 3, \cdots, K)$ of the database software for the cloud software to the target input values $d_k(k = 1, 2, \cdots, K)$ for the output values, i.e., the normalized values of the software component ratio at time t are applied to the target input values $d_k(k = 1, 2, \cdots, K)$. We consider the time series analysis that the software component ratio at time $(t + 1)$ is estimated by using the software component ratios until time t.

3 Jump Diffusion Process Modeling

Let $N(t)$ be the cumulative number of faults detected by operation time t $(t \geq 0)$. Suppose that $N(t)$ takes on continuous real values. Since latent faults in the software are detected and eliminated during the operation phase, $N(t)$ gradually increases as the operational procedures go on. Thus, under common assumptions for software reliability growth modeling, the following linear differential equation can be formulated:

$$\frac{dN(t)}{dt} = b(t)\{a - N(t)\}, \tag{5}$$

where $b(t)$ is the software fault-detection rate at operation time t and a non-negative function, and a means the initial number of faults latent in the environment on cloud computing. Then, we consider the big data in order to assess the reliability for cloud computing. We extend to the following stochastic differential equation modeling considering Brownian motions[Arnold (1974)]:

$$\frac{dN(t)}{dt} = \{b(t) + \sigma\nu(t)\}\{a - N(t)\}, \tag{6}$$

where σ is a positive constant representing a magnitude of the irregular fluctuation, and $\nu(t)$ a standardized Gaussian white noise. We extend to the following stochastic differential equation of an Itô type[Wong (1971); Yamada et al. (1994)]:

$$dN(t) = \left\{ b(t) - \frac{1}{2}\sigma^2 \right\} \{a - N(t)\}dt + \sigma\{a - N(t)\}dW(t), \qquad (7)$$

where $W(t)$ is a one-dimensional Wiener process which is formally defined as an integration of the white noise $\nu(t)$ with respect to time t. Then, the Wiener processes, $W(t)$, is a Gaussian process. By using Itô's formula, we can obtain the solution under the initial condition $N(0) = 0$ as follows:

$$N(t) = a\left[1 - \exp\left\{ -\int_0^t b(s)ds - \sigma W(t) \right\} \right]. \qquad (8)$$

Using solution process $N(t)$, we can derive several software reliability measures. Moreover, we define the software fault-detection rate per fault in case of $b(t)$ defined as:

$$b(t) \simeq \frac{b^2 t}{1 + bt}, \qquad (9)$$

where b the fault-detection rate per fault obtained from the delayed S-shaped SRGM, based on a nonhomogeneous Poisson process (NHPP). Then, we can obtain the expected number of detected faults as follows:

$$E[N(t)] = a\left\{ 1 - (1 + bt)\exp\left(-bt + \frac{\sigma^2}{2}t \right) \right\}. \qquad (10)$$

Therefore, the numbers of remaining faults are obtained as follows:

$$R(t) = a(1 + bt)\exp\left\{ -bt - \sigma W(t) \right\}. \qquad (11)$$

Moreover, the jump term can be added to the proposed stochastic differential equation model in order to incorporate the irregular state of the influence from the database software handling the big data. Then, the jump-diffusion process[Merton (1976)] is given as follows:

$$dN_j(t) = \left\{ b - \frac{1}{2}\sigma^2 \right\} \{a - N_j(t)\}dt + \sigma\{a - N_j(t)\}dW(t)$$
$$+ d\left\{ \sum_{i=1}^{M_t(\lambda)} (V_i - 1) \right\}, \qquad (12)$$

where $M_t(\lambda)$ is a Poisson point process with parameter λ at operation time t. Also, $M_t(\lambda)$ means the number of occurred jumps where λ is the jump rate. $M_t(\lambda)$, $W(t)$, and V_i are assumed to be mutually independent. Moreover, V_i is the i-th jump range.

By using Itô's formula, the solution of the former equation can be obtained as follows:

$$N_j(t) = a\left[1 - (1 + bt)\exp\left\{-bt - \sigma W(t) - \sum_{i=1}^{M_t(\lambda)} \log V_i\right\}\right]. \quad (13)$$

Then, the number of remaining faults is given as follows:

$$R_j(t) = a(1 + bt)\exp\left\{-bt - \sigma W(t) - \sum_{i=1}^{M_t(\lambda)} \log V_i\right\}. \quad (14)$$

4   Parameter Estimation

4.1   *Method of Maximum-likelihood*

In this section, the estimation method of unknown parameters a, b, and σ in Eq. (8) is presented. The joint probability distribution function of the process $N(t)$ is denoted as

$$P(t_1, y_1;\ t_2, y_2;\ \cdots;\ t_K, y_K)$$
$$\equiv \Pr[N(t_1) \leq y_1,\ \cdots,\ N(t_K) \leq y_K | N(t_0) = 0]. \quad (15)$$

The probability density of Eq. (15) is denote as

$$p(t_1, y_1;\ t_2, y_2;\ \cdots;\ t_K, y_K)$$
$$\equiv \frac{\partial^K P(t_1, y_1;\ t_2, y_2;\ \cdots;\ t_K, y_K)}{\partial y_1 \partial y_2 \cdots \partial y_K}. \quad (16)$$

Since $N(t)$ takes on continuous values, the likelihood function, l, for the observed data $(t_k, y_k)(k = 1, 2, \cdots, K)$ is constructed as follows:

$$l = p(t_1, y_1;\ t_2, y_2;\ \cdots;\ t_K, y_K). \quad (17)$$

For convenience in mathematical manipulations, the following logarithmic likelihood function is used:

$$L = \log l. \quad (18)$$

The maximum-likelihood estimates a^*, b^*, and σ^* are the values making L in Eq. (18) maximize. These can be obtained as the solutions of the following simultaneous likelihood equations[Yamada et al. (1994)]:

$$\frac{\partial L}{\partial a} = \frac{\partial L}{\partial b} = \frac{\partial L}{\partial \sigma} = 0. \quad (19)$$

4.2   *Estimation of Jump-diffusion Parameters*

Generally, it is difficult to estimate the jump-diffusion parameters of stochastic differential equation model because of the complicated likelihood function, mixed distribution, etc. The estimation methods of jump-diffusion parameters are proposed by several researchers. However, the effective method of estimation has only a few presented. We focus on the estimation methods performed in two stages[Honoré (1998)]. A genetic algorithm (GA) in order to estimate the jump-diffusion parameters of the proposed model is used in this section. The procedure of GA algorithm is given in the following[Holland (1975)].

It is assumed that the proposed jump-diffusion model includes the parameters λ, μ, and τ. The parameters μ and τ mean the parameters included in i-th jump range V_i. In this paper, we assume that the parameter μ means the software component ratio of the database software for the cloud software. Then, the jump-diffusion parameters λ and τ are estimated as follows:

Step. 1 The initial individuals are randomly generated. Also, the set of initial individual is converted to the binary digit.

Step. 2 Two parental individuals are selected, and new individuals are produced by the crossover recombination.

Step. 3 The value of fitness is calculated from the evaluated value of each individual. The following value of fitness as the error between the estimated and the actual values is defined in this paper:

$$\min_{\boldsymbol{\theta}} \ F_i(\boldsymbol{\theta}),$$

$$F_i = \sum_{i=0}^{K} \left\{ N_j(i) - y_i \right\}^2, \tag{20}$$

where $N_j(i)$ is the number of detected faults at operation time i in the proposed jump-diffusion model, y_i the number of actual detected faults. Also, $\boldsymbol{\theta}$ means the set of parameters λ and τ.

Step. 4 Step.2 and Step.3 are continued until reaching the specific size.

The jump-diffusion parameters λ and τ are estimated by using above mentioned steps.

5 Optimal Maintenance Time for Mobile Cloud

We find the optimum maintenance time based on the total expected software maintenance cost in this section. Several optimal software release problems considering software development process have been proposed by several researchers[Yamada and Osaki (1985)]. However, optimal software release problems for mobile cloud have not been proposed. Therefore, we propose the maintenance cost models based on our models proposed in Section 3, and discuss the optimal maintenance problem minimizing the total expected maintenance cost.

It is interesting for the software developers to predict and estimate the time when we should stop operation in order to maintain a cloud computing system efficiently. Hence, we discuss the determination of software maintenance times minimizing the total software cost.

We define the following cost parameters:

c_1: the fixing cost per fault during the operation,
c_2: the cost per unit time during the operation,
c_3: the maintenance cost per fault after the maintenance.

Then, the software cost in the operation of mobile cloud can be formulated as:

$$C_1(t) = c_1 N(t) + c_2 t. \tag{21}$$

Also, the software maintenance cost after the maintenance of mobile cloud is represented as follows:

$$C_2(t) = c_3 R(t). \tag{22}$$

Consequently, from Eqs.(21) and (22), the total software maintenance cost is given by

$$C(t) = C_1(t) + C_2(t). \tag{23}$$

The optimum maintenance time t^* is obtained by minimizing $C(t)$ in Eq.(23).

6 Dependability Analysis Tool

The specification requirement of the dependability analysis tool for mobile cloud are shown as follows:

1. This tool should be operated by clicking the mouse button and typing on the keyboard to input the data through GUI system.

2. Open source Apache Flex SDK[Flex.org–Adobe Flex Developer Resource (2016)] should be used to implement the program. This tool is developed as a stand-alone Adobe AIR application on Windows, Unix, and Mac OS X operating system. Also, this tool operates as Web application.

3. This tool treats the proposed jump diffusion models for mobile cloud, and illustrate the software component ratio and the sample path of estimated number of remaining faults as software reliability assessment measures, and the sample path of total software cost.

The procedures of dependability analysis built into the developed software for mobile cloud are shown as follows:

1. This tool processes the data file in terms of the software fault-detection count data in the operating-phase of mobile cloud for reliability analysis.

2. The data set obtained from the operation phase is analyzed.

3. This tool estimates the unknown parameters included in the proposed jump diffusion models.

4. This tool illustrates the software component ratio and the sample path of estimated number of remaining faults as software reliability assessment measures.

6. We focus on optimal software release problems based on the proposed models for the mobile cloud. Especially, the sample path of total software cost and the optimal software maintenance time minimizing the cost for the proposed models are plotted.

This tool is composed of several function components such as fault analysis, estimation of unknown parameters, graphical representation of fault data, and results of estimation.

7 Numerical Examples

The OSS is closely watched from the point of view of the cost reduction and the quick delivery. There are several open source projects in the area of cloud computing. In particular, we focus on Hadoop[The Apache Software Foundation (2016)] and OpenStack[The OpenStack project (2016)] in order to evaluate the performance of our methods. In this paper, we show numerical examples by using the data sets for Hadoop and OpenStack as OSS of mobile cloud. The data used in this paper are collected in the bug tracking system on the website of Hadoop and OpenStack open source project.

The estimated software component ratio is useful for the software managers to review the allocation of man-hour cost for the database software and the cloud software. Figure 2 shows the estimated software component ratio based on the cumulative numbers of detected faults. The sample path of the estimated number of remaining faults is shown in Figure 3. From Figure 3, we confirm that the sample path is dispersed in the early operating phase as the interesting aspect of mobile cloud, i.e., our model can cover the component collision status in the confusion period of mobile cloud[Tamura and Yamada (2014)].

Moreover, we focus on the optimum release problem. We show the numerical examples based on the optimal maintenance problems which are discussed in Section 5. Figure 4 is shown the sample path of the estimated total software cost. From Figure 4, we can find that the optimum maintenance time is derived as $t^* = 153.3$ days. Then, the total expected software cost is 1049.2. Therefore, this means that the condition of mobile cloud software will be ensured perfect preserving by making a maintenance at 153.3 days from the beginning of operation. Considering the noise, the optimum software maintenance time is about $t^* = 200$ days.

8 Performance Illustrations of Developed Application Software

For examples of reliability analysis, the main screen of the developed tool are shown in Figure 5. Also, Figure 6 shows the estimated software component ratio. The estimated number of remaining faults is shown in Figure 7. Moreover, Figure 8 is shown the estimated total software cost.

It is difficult to assess the operating-phase of mobile cloud by using these conventional software tools because of the other SRGM's are used in the other tools, i.e., these SRGM's used in the conventional tools are not appropriate to the mobile cloud. The developed tool is considered the characteristics of mobile cloud. Therefore, it is useful for software managers of mobile cloud to understand the debugging progress in operation-phase of mobile cloud by using a software dependability analysis tool without knowing the details of the process of the fault data analysis.

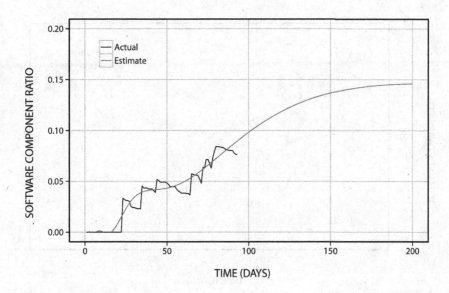

Fig. 2 Estimated software component ratio based on the cumulative numbers of detected faults.

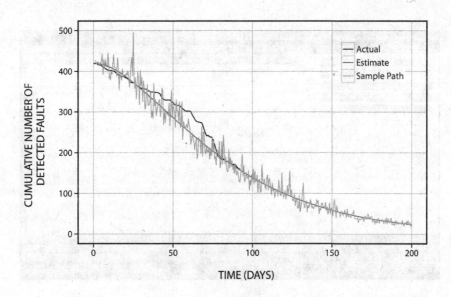

Fig. 3 Sample path of estimated number of remaining faults.

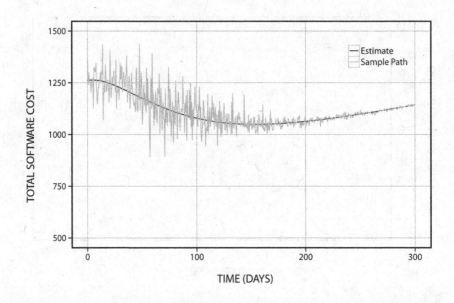

Fig. 4   Estimated total software cost.

Fig. 5   Main screen of the developed tool.

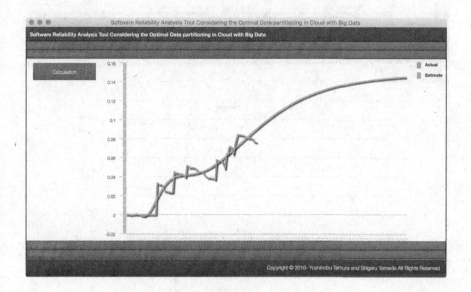

Fig. 6   Estimated estimated software component ratio.

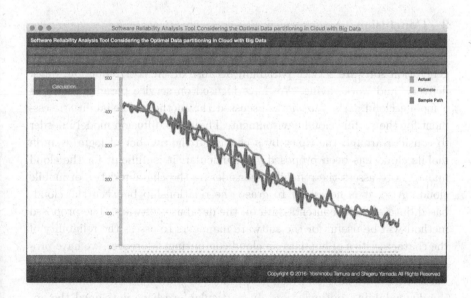

Fig. 7   Estimated number of remaining faults.

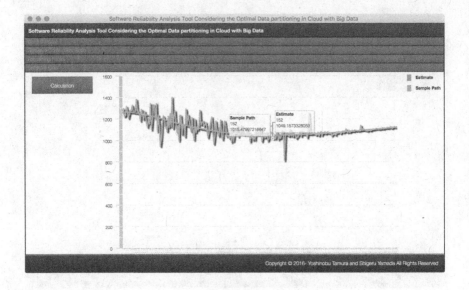

Fig. 8   Estimated total software cost.

9 . Conclusion

A cloud OSS such as OpenStack is now attracting attention as the next-generation software service paradigm because of the cost reduction, quick delivery, and work saving. We have focused on service paradigm such as a mobile cloud. Also, we have discussed the method of reliability assessment for the mobile cloud environment. The jump diffusion model in order to consider around the times by a change in the number of login users in mobile cloud has been proposed. In particular, it is difficult for the cloud managers to assess the reliability considering the characteristics of mobile cloud. Also, it is necessary to grasp the relationship between the cloud-based data and the contents data on the database software. The proposed method will be useful for the software managers to assess the reliability of the characteristics of big data on cloud computing. Moreover, we have proposed the optimal maintenance problem based on the jump diffusion model. Furthermore, we have analyzed actual data to show numerical examples of the dependability optimization. In particular, we have developed the application software for reliability analysis based on the proposed method. Then, several performance examples of the developed application software have shown in order to quantitatively analyze software reliability for the mobile cloud. Our method and tool may be useful as one of the methods of dependability assessment for the mobile cloud with big data.

Acknowledgments

This work was supported in part by the Telecommunications Advancement Foundation in Japan, the Okawa Foundation for Information and Telecommunications in Japan, and the JSPS KAKENHI Grant No. 15K00102 and No. 16K01242 in Japan.

References

Suo, H., Liu, Z., Wan, J., and Zhou, K. (2013). "Security and privacy in mobile cloud computing," *Proceedings of the 9th International Wireless Communications and Mobile Computing Conference*, 655–659.

Khalifa, A. and Eltoweissy, M. (2013). "Collaborative autonomic resource management system for mobile cloud computing," *Proceedings of the Fourth International Conference on Cloud Computing, GRIDs, and Virtualization*, 115–121.

Yamada S. (2013). *Software Reliability Modeling: Fundamentals and Applications*, Springer–Verlag, Tokyo/Heidelberg.

Lyu, M.R. ed. (1996). *Handbook of Software Reliability Engineering*, IEEE Computer Society Press, Los Alamitos, CA.

Kapur, P.K., Pham, H., Gupta, A., and Jha, P.C. (2011). *Software Reliability Assessment with OR Applications*, Springer–Verlag, London.

Karnin, E.D. (1990). "A simple procedure for pruning back-propagation trained neural networks," *IEEE Transactions on Neural Networks*, **1**, 239-242.

Arnold, L. (1974). *Stochastic Differential Equations-Theory and Applications*, John Wiley & Sons, New York.

Wong, E. (1971). *Stochastic Processes in Information and Systems*, McGraw-Hill, New York.

Yamada, S., Kimura, M., Tanaka, H., and Osaki, S. (1994). "Software reliability measurement and assessment with stochastic differential equations," *IEICE Transactions on Fundamentals*, **E77–A**, 1, 109–116.

Merton, R.C. (1976). "Option pricing when underlying stock returns are discontinous," *Journal of Financial Economics*, **3**, 125–144.

Honoré, P. (1998). "Pitfalls in estimating jump-diffusion models," Working Paper Series 18, University of Aarhus, School of Business.

Holland, J.H. (1975). *Adaptation in Natural and Artificial Systems*, University of Michigan Press.

Yamada S. and Osaki S. (1985). "Cost-reliability optimal software release policies for software systems," *IEEE Transactions on Reliability*, **R–34**, 5, 422–424.

Yamada, S. and Osaki, S. (1987). "Optimal software release policies with simultaneous cost and reliability requirements," *European Journal of Operational Research*, **31**, 1, 46–51.

Flex.org–Adobe Flex Developer Resource (2016). Adobe Systems Incorporated, `http://flex.org/`

The Apache Software Foundation (2016). Apache Hadoop, `http://hadoop.apache.org/`

The OpenStack project (2016). OpenStack, `http://www.openstack.org/`

Tamura Y. and Yamada S. (2014). "Optimization analysis based on stochastic differential equation model for cloud computing," *International Journal of Reliability, Quality and Safety Engineering*, **21**, 4, 1–13.

Chapter 4

Interval Estimation of Software Reliability and Shipping Time Based on a Discretized NHPP Model

Shinji Inoue and Shigeru Yamada

Department of Social Management Engineering,
Tottori University

1 Introduction

Optimal software release problems [Yamada and Osaki (1985)] are known as interesting topics for estimating optimal software shipping time in terms of total software cost. The total software cost is formulated by a software reliability growth model [Yamada and Osaki (1985); Musa et al. (1987); Pham (2000); Yamada (2013)] and by assuming actual debugging environment in the testing and operational phases. The software reliability growth model enables us to describe the software failure-occurrence or fault-detection phenomenon observed in the testing-phase and the operational phase by using a stochastic modeling approach. A lot of total software cost models have been proposed so far for matching realistic total software cost. For examples, Pham and Zhang (1999) proposed a total software cost model with consideration of time to remove errors, cost of removing each error during the testing-phase, cost of removing error during warranty period, and risk cost due to software failure-occurrence, and derived optimal software release policies for estimating the cost-optimal software release time. Gokhale (2003) formulated the total software cost model considering with the fault correction to provide realistic predictions of software release time and the cost. Huang and Lin (2010) proposed an nonhomogeneous Poisson process (NHPP) model with a change of fault-detection rate in the testing-phase by using a testing compression factor,

61

and formulated a total software cost. A two-dimensional expected total software cost model was proposed [Kapur et al. (2012)] to estimate optimal testing time and testing resource expenditure by using two-dimensional (or bivariate) software reliability growth model [Inoue and Yamada (2008)], in which the software reliability growth process depends on the testing-time and testing-effort factors.

However, most of optimal software release time estimation approaches including the researches above use a point estimation method. Considering an practical situation, we encourage software development managers to use the interval estimation method. It is more useful to provide optimal software release time-interval rather than optimal release time-point and the point estimation method for the optimal software release time has a possibility of mismatched estimation. In the point estimation, it does not reflect an actual situation or the true value of the optimal software release time point when we do not obtain a sufficient number of software reliability data (sampling data), such as fault-counting or software failure-occurrence time data. Needless to say, we should use the interval estimation method in software reliability measurement/assessment based on a software reliability growth model in such situation. The interval estimation needs to derive a probability distribution function for the estimator of interest. However, it is very difficult to derive the probability distribution function analytically. That means, it is not easy to derive some useful information for the statistical inference on software reliability assessment and optimal software release time even if we use the approximation approach assuming a large number of samples. For overcoming problems above, Kimura and Fujiwara (2006, 2010) discussed a bootstrap software reliability assessment method for an incomplete gamma function-based software reliability growth model. Kaneishi and Dohi (2010) discussed a parametric bootstrap method for software reliability assessment based on continuous-time NHPP models.

We discuss another bootstrapping approach for an NHPP model by using a discretized NHPP model. Concretely speaking, we apply a nonparametric bootstrap method for obtaining probability distributions of parameters and software reliability assessment measures by using a discretized NHPP model, which conserves the basic property of the continuous-time NHPP model and have good prediction and fitting performance for the actual data Inoue and Yamada (2006, 2010) because the discretized model has consistency with discrete fault count data collection activities. Especially, as one of our main interest, we discuss an interval estimation approach for cost-optimal software release time by following our nonparametric bootstrapping approach. And, we discuss three types of bootstrap confidence intervals, such as basic, standard normal, and percentile bootstrap confidence intervals, for interval estimation of the model parameters, software reliability assessment measures, and cost-optimal software release time. Finally, we show numerical examples of our bootstrap approach by using actual fault-count data, and show results of interval estimations for the parameters, software reliability assessment measures, and cost-optimal software release time based on the notion of the bootstrap confidence intervals.

2   Optimal Software Release Problem

Software developing managers have a great interest in how to develop a reliable software product economically and when to release the software system to the customers or market. As a well-known issue being related to the software development management, optimal software release problems Yamada and Osaki (1985) are known as interesting topics for estimating optimal software shipping time in terms of the total software cost. Generally, the total software cost is formulated by a software reliability growth model, which describes the software reliability growth process and characterize the software failure-occurrence or the software fault-detection phenomenon in the testing-phase and operational phases mathematically. We briefly discuss the total software cost and the deriving process of cost-optimal software release time minimizing the total software cost when we apply an exponential software reliability growth model, which has the simplest model structure and is widely-used in a practical field.

2.1   *Exponential Software Reliability Growth Model*

An exponential software reliability growth model Goel and Okumoto (1979) is well-known as the continuous-time NHPP model, in which the stochastic property of the software failure-occurrence or software fault-detection phenomenon is assumed to be the continuous-time NHPP Osaki (1992); Ross (1997); Trivedi (2002):

$$\Pr\{N(t) = x \mid N(0) = 0\} = \frac{\{\Lambda(t)\}^x}{x!} \exp[-\Lambda(t)]$$
$$(t \geq 0, x = 0, 1, 2, \cdots), \tag{1}$$

where $\Pr\{A\}$ means the probability of event A, $\{N(t), t \geq 0\}$ is a stochastic process representing the cumulative number of faults detected up to testing-time t, $\Lambda(t)$ is a mean value function of the continuous-time NHPP in Eq. (1). $\Lambda(t)$ also represents the expected cumulative number of faults detected up to testing-time t. Now we define that $\Lambda(t) \equiv H(t)$ is the mean value function following the exponential software reliability growth model, in which $H(t)$ is characterized by the following differential equation:

$$\frac{\mathrm{d}H(t)}{\mathrm{d}t} = \beta\{\omega - H(t)\} \qquad (\omega > 0, \ \beta > 0), \tag{2}$$

where ω the expected total number of potential faults to be detected in an infinitely long duration or the expected initial fault content, and β the fault detection rate per one fault. Eq. (2) is developed by the basic assumption that the expected number of faults detected at testing-time t is proportional to the current expected number of faults in a program and the fault-detection rate is constant over the testing-period. Solving the differential equation in Eq. (2) with respect to $H(t)$, we have

$$\Lambda(t) \equiv H(t) = \omega\{1 - \exp[-\beta t]\} \qquad (\omega > 0, \ \beta > 0). \tag{3}$$

2.2 *Optimal Software Release Time*

The cost-optimal software release time means the testing-termination time minimizing the total software cost formulated by a software reliability growth model. For formulating the total software cost, we define the following cost parameters:

c_1 : debugging cost per one fault in the testing-phase.

c_2 : debugging cost per one fault in the operational phase,

where $c_1 < c_2$.

c_3 : testing cost per unit time.

Suppose that T is the testing termination time or the software release time and T_{LC} the length of the software life cycle measured from the test beginning. By using the cost parameters, we can formulate the expected total software cost $C(T)$ as

$$C(T) = c_1\Lambda(T) + c_2\{\Lambda(T_{LC}) - \Lambda(T)\} + c_3T$$
$$= (c_1 - c_2)\Lambda(T) + c_2\Lambda(T_{LC}) + c_3T. \tag{4}$$

From Eq. (4), the cost-optimal software release time T^* is derived from

$$\frac{\mathrm{d}C(T)}{\mathrm{d}T} = -(c_2 - c_1)\omega\beta e^{-\beta T} + c_3 = 0, \tag{5}$$

if we assume Eq. (3). Then, we have

$$T^* = \frac{1}{\beta} \log \frac{\omega\beta(c_2 - c_1)}{c_3}. \tag{6}$$

From Eq. (6), we can estimate the cost-optimal software release time based on the point estimation method. As we show in Eq. (6), most of approaches for estimating optimal software release time follow the point estimation method. However, we encourage software development managers to use the interval estimation method because it is more useful to provide optimal release time-interval rather than optimal release time-point when we consider the practical situation. And, when we cannot obtain a sufficient number of software reliability data (sampling data), such as fault-counting or software failure-occurrence time data, for estimating parameters of a software reliability growth model, the point estimation method for the optimal software release time has a possibility of mismatched estimation, which does not reflect real situation or the true value of the cost-optimal software release time. Therefore, we discuss an interval estimation approach for the cost-optimal software release time based on a nonparametric bootstrap method via a discretized software reliability growth model. The nonparametric bootstrap method does not need to assume the underlying probability distribution function for the sampling data.

3   Discretized NHPP Model

The discretized NHPP model is used for applying a nonparametric bootstrap method to the interval estimations of the software reliability measurement and cost-optimal software release time. Now, we introduce the aspect of a discretized NHPP model by focusing on a discretized exponential software reliability growth model Inoue and Yamada (2006, 2010). Define a discrete counting process $\{N_n, n = 0, 1, 2, \cdots\}$ representing the cumulative number of faults detected up to n-th testing-period. And we can say that the discrete conuting process $\{N_n, n = 0, 1, 2, \cdots\}$ follows a discrete-time NHPP Yamada and Osaki (1985); Fries and Sen (1996); Huang et al. (2003) if the discrete stochastic process has the following property:

$$\Pr\{N_n = x \mid N_0 = 0\} = \frac{\{\Lambda_n\}^x}{x!} \exp[-\Lambda_n] \qquad (n, x = 0, 1, 2, \cdots). \qquad (7)$$

In Eq. (7), $\Pr\{A\}$ means the probability of event A, Λ_n is a mean value function of the discrete-time NHPP. The mean value function, Λ_n, also represents the expected cumulative number of faults detected up to the n-th testing-period.

Let $\Lambda_n \equiv H_n$ denote a mean value function following a discretized exponential software reliability growth model. The discretized exponential software reliability growth model is derived from the following difference equation:

$$H_{n+1} - H_n = \delta\beta(\omega - H_n), \tag{8}$$

which is the discrete analog of the differential equation of the corresponding continuous-time exponential software reliability growth model in Eq. (2). Regarding the discretization method, we use the Hirota's bilinearization methods Hirota (1979); Satoh (2000); Satoh and Yamada (2001, 2002) for conserving the property of the continuous-time exponential software reliability growth model. Solving the above integrable difference equation in Eq. (8), we can obtain an exact solution H_n in Eq. (8) as

$$\Lambda_n \equiv H_n = \omega\left[1 - (1 - \delta\beta)^n\right] \qquad (\omega > 0, \ \beta > 0), \tag{9}$$

where δ represents the constant time-interval. As $\delta \to 0$, Eq. (9) converges to the exact solution of the original continuous-time exponential software reliability growth model in Eq. (3) which is derived by the differential equation in Eq. (2).

The discretized exponential software reliability growth model in Eq. (9) has two parameters, ω and β, which have to be estimated by using actual data. The parameter estimations of ω and β, $\widehat{\omega}$ and $\widehat{\beta}$, can be obtained by the following procedure using the method of least-squares. First of all, if we observe fault counting data $(n, y_n)(n = 1, 2, \cdots, N)$, where y_n represents the cumulative number of faults detected up to the n-th testing-period, we derive the following regression equation from Eq. (8):

$$C_n = \alpha_0 + \alpha_1 D_n, \tag{10}$$

where

$$\begin{cases} C_n = H_{n+1} - H_n \equiv y_{n+1} - y_n \\ D_n = H_n \equiv y_n \\ \alpha_0 = \delta\omega\beta \\ \alpha_1 = -\delta\beta. \end{cases} \tag{11}$$

Based on the regression analysis, we can estimate $\widehat{\alpha}_0$ and $\widehat{\alpha}_1$, which are the estimations of α_0 and α_1 in Eq. (10). Then, the parameter estimations, $\widehat{\omega}$ and $\widehat{\beta}$, can be obtained as

$$\begin{cases} \widehat{\omega} = -\widehat{\alpha}_0/\widehat{\alpha}_1 \\ \widehat{\beta} = -\widehat{\alpha}_1/\delta, \end{cases} \tag{12}$$

respectively. C_n in Eq. (10) is independent of δ because δ is not used in calculating C_n as showing Eq. (11). Hence, we can obtain the same parameter estimates $\widehat{\omega}$ and $\widehat{\beta}$, respectively, when we choose any constant value of δ Inoue and Yamada (2006, 2010).

Software reliability assessment measures are useful in quantitative software reliability assessment based on the software reliability growth model. We discuss the discrete versions of the expected number of remaining faults and the software reliability function, which are well-known software reliability assessment measures. The discrete version of the expected number of remaining faults, M_n, represents the expected number of undetected faults in the software system at arbitrary testing-period. Then, we have

$$M_n \equiv \mathrm{E}[N_\infty - N_n] = \omega - \Lambda_n = \omega(1 - \delta\beta)^n, \tag{13}$$

if we assume that N_n follows a discrete-time NHPP with mean value function H_n in Eq. (9). The discrete software reliability function, $R(n, h)$, is defined as the probability that a software failure does not occur in the time-interval $(n, n + h]$ $(h = 1, 2, \cdots)$ given that the testing has been going up to the n-th testing-priod. Then, we have

$$R(n, h) \equiv \Pr\{N_{n+h} - N_n = 0 \mid N_n = x\} = \exp[-\{\Lambda_{n+h} - \Lambda_n\}]$$
$$= \exp[-H_h(1 - \delta\beta)^n]. \tag{14}$$

4   Nonparametric Bootstrap Method

It is very difficult or complex to identify probability distribution functions of parameters and reliability assessment measures of a software reliability growth model analytically. Therefore, we apply a nonparametric bootstrap method Efron (1979) to conducting simulation-based interval estimations for the estimates of the model parameters, software reliability assessment measures, and cost-optimal software release time by using the discretized NHPP model. Further, we discuss three types of bootstrap confidence intervals, such as basic, standard normal, and percentile bootstrap confidence interval estimation methods, for the interval estimations.

4.1   *Bootstrap Method*

Our bootstrap method for software reliability measurement and estimating optimal software release time follows the following procedure:

Step 1   Estimate α_0 and α_1 in Eq. (10) by following the linear regression scheme with observed data $(n, y_n)(n = 1, 2, \cdots, N)$. And we indicate $\widehat{\alpha}_0$ and $\widehat{\alpha}_1$ as $\widehat{\alpha}_{0(0)}$ and $\widehat{\alpha}_{1(0)}$, respectively.

Step 2   Calculate the residual errors, $\widehat{d}_i$, at each observation points by
$$\widehat{d}_i = C_i - (\widehat{\alpha}_{0(0)} + \widehat{\alpha}_{1(0)} D_i)$$
$$(i = 1, 2, \cdots, N - 1).$$

Step 3   Construct an empirical distribution function $\widehat{F}$ by assuming the residual errors $\widehat{d}_i$ follows the independent and identical probability distribution and by putting mass $1/(N - 1)$ at each ordered point $\{\widehat{d}_{[1]}, \widehat{d}_{[2]}, \cdots, \widehat{d}_{[N-1]}\}$ (see Figure 1).

Step 4   Set the total number of iteration B and let $b(b = 1, 2, \cdots, B)$ be the iteration count.

Step 5   Generate a bootstrap sample for the residual errors, $\widehat{\boldsymbol{d}}_{(b)}^* = \{\widehat{d}_{b,1}^*, \widehat{d}_{b,2}^*, \cdots, \widehat{d}_{b,N-1}^*\}$ by sampling with replacement from $\widehat{F}$.

Step 6   Generate a bootstrap sample,
$$\boldsymbol{z}_{(b)}^* = \{(y_1, C_{b,1}^*), (y_2, C_{b,2}^*), \cdots, (y_{N-1}, C_{b,N-1}^*)\}, \text{ by}$$
$$C_{b,i}^* = \widehat{\alpha}_{0(0)} + \widehat{\alpha}_{1(0)} D_i + \widehat{d}_{b,i}^*.$$

Step 7   Estimate $\alpha_{0(b)}^*$ and $\alpha_{1(b)}^*$ from the bootstrap sample $\boldsymbol{z}_{(b)}^*$.

Step 8   Calculate model parameters in Eq. (9), $\widehat{\omega}_{(b)}^*$ and $\widehat{\delta\beta}_{(b)}^*$, by the following equations:
$$\widehat{\omega}_{(b)}^* = -\frac{\widehat{\alpha}_{0(b)}^*}{\widehat{\alpha}_{1(b)}^*},$$
$$\widehat{\delta\beta}_{(b)}^* = -\widehat{\alpha}_{1(b)}^*.$$

Step 9   Calculate a software reliability assessment measure $h(\widehat{\boldsymbol{\tau}}_{(b)}^*)$ and cost-optimal software release time $T^*(\widehat{\boldsymbol{\tau}}_{(b)}^*)$, where $\widehat{\boldsymbol{\tau}}_{(b)}^* = \{\widehat{\omega}_{(b)}^*, \widehat{\beta}_{(b)}^*\}$.

Step 10   Let $b = b + 1$ and go back to **Step 5** if $b < B$.

Step 11   We have B samples for $\widehat{\omega}$, $\widehat{\beta}$, $h(\widehat{\boldsymbol{\tau}}_{(b)}^*)$, and $T^*(\widehat{\boldsymbol{\tau}}_{(b)}^*)$.

Finally, we calculate the standard deviations of $\widehat{\omega}$ and $\widehat{\beta}$, a software reliability assessment measure $h(\widehat{\boldsymbol{\tau}}_{(b)}^*)$, and the cost-optimal software release time $T^*(\widehat{\boldsymbol{\tau}}_{(b)}^*)$, respectively. For examples, the standard deviation and the mean for the cost-optimal software release time, $T^*(\widehat{\boldsymbol{\tau}}_{(b)}^*)$, are derived as

$$SD[T^*(\widehat{\boldsymbol{\tau}}_{(b)}^*)] = \sqrt{\frac{1}{B-1} \sum_{b=1}^{B} \{T^*(\widehat{\boldsymbol{\tau}}_{(b)}^*) - \overline{T^*(\widehat{\boldsymbol{\tau}}_{(b)}^*)}\}^2}, \qquad (15)$$

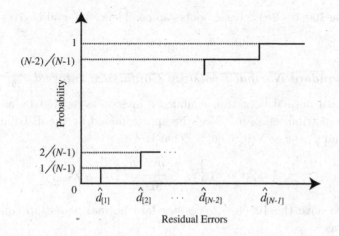

Fig. 1   Empirical distribution function $\widehat{F}$ of the residual errors $\widehat{d}_i$.

$$\bar{T}^*(\widehat{\tau}^*_{(b)}) = \frac{1}{B} \sum_{b=1}^{B} T^*(\widehat{\tau}^*_{(b)}), \tag{16}$$

respectively, by the Monte Carlo approximation.

5   Bootstrap Confidence Intervals

We discuss the following three typical bootstrap confidence intervals Rizzo (2008): basic, standard normal, and percentile bootstrap confidence intervals. Let θ be parameter of interest.

5.1   *Basic Bootstrap Confidence Interval*

A basic bootstrap confidence interval is developed by using the quantile of the distribution of $\widehat{\theta}^* - \widehat{\theta}$, where θ^* is the bootstrap statistic. We can approximate the α and $(1-\alpha)$ quantile denoting v_α and $v_{1-\alpha}$, respectively, of the distribution of $\widehat{\theta} - \theta$ by $\widehat{\theta}^*_{[B\alpha]} - \widehat{\theta}$ and $\widehat{\theta}^*_{[B(1-\alpha)]} - \widehat{\theta}$. Then,

$$1 - 2\alpha = \Pr\{v_\alpha \le \widehat{\theta} - \theta \le v_{1-\alpha}\}$$
$$= \Pr\{\widehat{\theta} - v_{1-\alpha} \le \theta \le \widehat{\theta} - v_\alpha\}$$
$$= \Pr\{2\widehat{\theta} - \widehat{\theta}^*_{[B(1-\alpha)]} \le \theta \le 2\widehat{\theta} - \widehat{\theta}^*_{[B\alpha]}\}.$$

Thus, the $100(1 - 2\alpha)\%$ basic bootstrap confidence interval is given by

$$[2\widehat{\theta} - \widehat{\theta}^*_{[B(1-\alpha)]}, 2\widehat{\theta} - \widehat{\theta}^*_{[B\alpha]}]. \tag{17}$$

5.2 *Standard Normal Bootstrap Confidence Interval*

A standard normal bootstrap confidence interval is derived by assuming that the distribution of $\widehat{\theta} - \theta$ can be approximated by the distribution of $\widehat{\theta}^* - \widehat{\theta}$ and $\widehat{\theta}^* - \widehat{\theta} \sim N(0, \mathrm{SD}[\widehat{\theta}]^2)$. That is,

$$1 - 2\alpha = \Pr\left\{ z_\alpha \leq \frac{\widehat{\theta}^* - \widehat{\theta}}{\mathrm{SD}[\widehat{\theta}]} \leq z_{1-\alpha} \right\}.$$

Thus, we have the $100(1 - 2\alpha)\%$ standard normal bootstrap confidence interval as

$$[\widehat{\theta} - z_{1-\alpha}\mathrm{SD}[\widehat{\theta}], \widehat{\theta} - z_\alpha\mathrm{SD}[\widehat{\theta}]], \tag{18}$$

where z_α is $\Phi^{-1}(1 - 2\alpha)$. For example, $z_{0.025} = 1.96$.

5.3 *Percentile Bootstrap Confidence Interval*

A percentile bootstrap confidence interval is calculated from the empirical cumulative distribution function consisted by the bootstrap iteration value: $\widehat{\theta}^*_{(1)}, \widehat{\theta}^*_{(2)}, \cdots, \widehat{\theta}^*_{(B)}$. The $100(1 - 2\alpha)\%$ percentile bootstrap confidence interval is calculated by

$$[\widehat{\theta}^*_{[B\alpha]}, \widehat{\theta}^*_{[B(1-\alpha)]}], \tag{19}$$

where $\widehat{\theta}^*_{[B\alpha]}$ represents the α quantile of the empirical cumulative distribution.

6   Numerical Examples

We show numerical examples for our nonparametric bootstrapping software reliability assessment method based on the discretized exponential software reliability growth model. We apply the following data: $(n, y_n)(n = 1, 2, \cdots, 25; y_{25} = 136)$ Inoue and Yamada (2008) and we set the total number of iteration $B = 2000$. Actually, it is known that we need to set the number of iteration $B = 1000 \sim 2000$ for obtaining a bootstrap distribution of a parameter of interest.

We first obtain $\widehat{\alpha}_{0(0)} = 15.8586$ and $\widehat{\alpha}_{1(0)} = -0.1133109$ by the linear regression scheme from the actual data. Following the procedure of our non-parametric bootstrapping software reliability assessment method, we have 2000 bootstrap samples $\{z^*_{(1)}, z^*_{(2)}, \cdots, z^*_{(2000)}\}$. Needless to say, we obtain bootstrap samples for ω and β as $\{\widehat{\tau}^*_{(1)}, \widehat{\tau}^*_{(2)}, \cdots, \widehat{\tau}^*_{(2000)}\}$. Figures 2 and 3 show the histograms for the bootstrap samples $\widehat{\omega}^*_{(b)}$ and $\widehat{\beta}^*_{(b)}$ to see the their probability distributions, respectively. And we have bootstrap samples for the software reliability assessment measures, such as the expected number of remaining fault at the termination time of the testing, $\widehat{M}^*_{25(b)}$, and the software reliability, $\widehat{R}^*_{(b)}(25, 1)$, respectively. These bootstrap samples of $\widehat{M}^*_{25(b)}$ and $\widehat{R}^*_{(b)}(25, 1)$ are calculated by

$$\widehat{M}^*_{25(b)} = \frac{\widehat{\alpha}^*_{0(b)}}{\widehat{\alpha}^*_{1(b)}}(1 + \widehat{\alpha}^*_{1(b)})^{25} \tag{20}$$

$$\widehat{R}^*_{(b)}(25, 1) = \exp\left[\frac{\widehat{\alpha}^*_{0(b)}}{\widehat{\alpha}^*_{1(b)}}\left\{1 - (1 + \widehat{\alpha}^*_{1(b)})^1\right\}(1 + \widehat{\alpha}^*_{1(b)})^n\right], \tag{21}$$

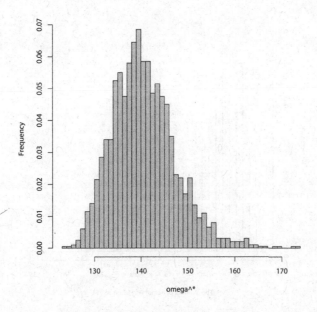

Fig. 2   Bootstrap distribution of $\widehat{\omega}$.

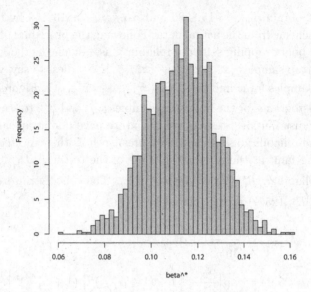

Fig. 3   Bootstrap distribution of $\widehat{\beta}$.

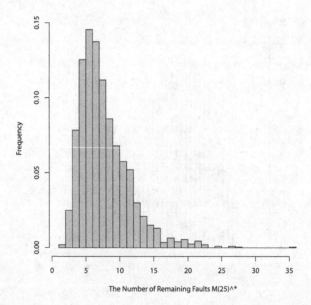

Fig. 4   Bootstrap distribution of the expected number of remaining faults at $n = 25$, $\widehat{M}_{25}$.

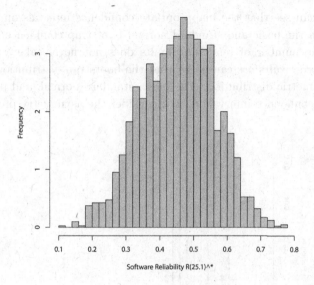

Fig. 5   Bootstrap distribution of software reliability, $\widehat{R}(25,1)$.

Table 1   Results of interval estimations.

	BCI	Lower	Upper
$\widehat{\omega}$	Basic	124.5319	150.7172
	Standard Normal	126.6071	153.3058
	Percentile	129.1957	155.381
$\widehat{\beta}$	Basic	0.08620381	0.143164
	Standard Normal	0.08487927	0.1417426
	Percentile	0.08345792	0.1404181
$\widehat{M}_{25}$	Basic	-3.613981	10.87824
	Standard Normal	-0.3191112	14.16454
	Percentile	2.967196	17.45941
$\widehat{R}(25,1)$	Basic	0.253525	0.6808198
	Standard Normal	0.2416769	0.6710921
	Percentile	0.2319492	0.659244

(BCI: Bootstrap Confidence Interval)

from Eqs. (13) and (14), respectively. Figures 4 and 5 show histograms of the bootstrap samples for $M_{25(b)}^{*}$ and $R_{(b)}^{*}(25,1)$, respectively. Table 1 shows the results of interval estimations for $\widehat{\omega}$, $\widehat{\beta}$, $\widehat{M}_{25}$, and $\widehat{R}(25,1)$, respecitvely, with the 5% significance level ($\alpha = 0.025$) based on the basic, standard normal, and percentile bootstrap confidence intervals. From Table 1, we can see that the inappropriate confidence intervals on $\widehat{M}_{25}$ are obtained in the basic and standard normal bootstrap confidence intervals because the number of remaining faults does not never take a negative value. These results are caused by that the bootstrap distribution of $\widehat{M}_{25}$ is an asymmetric distribution. The basic, standard normal, and percentile bootstrap confidence intervals do not consider the asymmetry property of

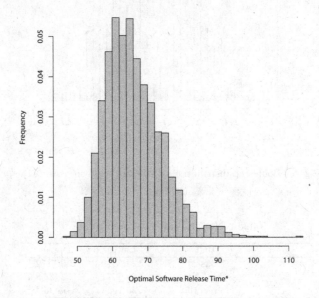

Fig. 6 Bootstrap distribution of the cost-optimal software release time, $\widehat{T}^*$, in a case $c_1 = 1$, $c_2 = 2$, and $c_3 = 0.01$.

Table 2   Results of interval estimations for the cost-optimal software release time.

c_1	c_2	c_3	Basic BCI		Standard Normal BCI		Percentile BCI	
			Lower	Upper	Lower	Upper	Lower	Upper
1	2	0.001	57.31584	100.8694	63.84933	106.8573	69.83729	113.3908
1	4	0.001	63.53389	112.4563	70.89792	119.1999	77.64143	126.5639
1	8	0.001	68.32952	121.3927	76.334	128.719	83.66033	136.7235
1	16	0.001	72.64316	129.4309	81.22366	137.2816	89.0743	145.8621
1	2	0.01	44.28341	76.59158	49.0754	80.98939	53.47321	85.78137
1	4	0.01	50.50146	88.17119	56.12453	93.33136	61.2847	98.95443
1	8	0.01	55.29709	97.10756	61.5609	102.8503	67.3036	109.1141
1	16	0.01	59.61074	105.1458	66.45077	111.4126	72.71756	118.2526

(BCI: Bootstrap Confidence Interval)

the bootstrap distribution. In most cases, the probability distribution of an estimator follows an asymmetric distribution and the accuracy is influenced by the bias and skewness of the distribution. However, the results of interval estimations based on the percentile bootstrap have appropriate results, which do not take negative values, because the percentile bootstrap confidence interval uses the bootstrap samples themselves.

Regarding the interval estimation of the cost-optimal software release time, Figure 6 shows a histogram for the bootstrap samples $T^*_{(b)}(\widehat{\tau}^*_{(b)})$ when $c_1 = 1$, $c_2 = 2$, and $c_3 = 0.01$. In Figure 6, the bootstrap sample of the cost-optimal software release time $T^*(\widehat{\tau}^*_{(b)})$ can be obtained by

$$T^*(\widehat{\tau}^*_{(b)}) = \frac{1}{\widehat{\delta\beta}^*_{(b)}} \log \frac{\widehat{\omega}^*_{(b)} \widehat{\delta\beta}^*_{(b)} (c_2 - c_1)}{c_3}. \tag{22}$$

Now, we suppose that $c_1 = 1$ to consider the relative software costs. Table 2 shows the results of interval estimations for the cost-optimal software release time by following the basic, standard normal, and percentile bootstrap confidence intervals. From Table 2, we can see that the lower and upper bounds of the optimal software release time are becoming large as the values of c_2 and c_3 are getting large. And we have the same consideration in Table 1, that is, it might be better to use the percentile bootstrap confidence interval because the bootstrap distribution of the cost-optimal software release time in Figure 6 is a asymmetric distribution.

7 Concluding Remarks

We discussed a nonparametric bootstrap method for interval estimations of software reliability and cost-optimal software release time based on a discretized NHPP model. And we discussed three types of bootstrap confidence interval estimation methods, such as basic, standard normal, and percentile bootstrap confidence intervals, for interval estimations of model parameters, several software reliability assessment measures, and cost-optimal software release time. Further, we showed numerical examples for our approach by using actual data. We have confirmed that our bootstrap approach yielded simulation-based probability distributions of model parameters, software reliability assessment measures, and cost-optimal software release time without deriving these probability distributions analytically. In fact, it is known that it is almost impossible to derive a probability distribution for parameters in NHPP models Kaneishi and Dohi (2010) and the point estimation leads mismatched estimation when the number of sampling data is not sufficiently large. These problems relate to the practical application of quantitative software reliability measurement/assessment based on a software reliability growth model. The bootstrap method overcomes such problems by simulation or resampling approach. Especially, bootstrap interval estimation for optimal software release time is very useful for planning software release time and quantifying the risk of mismatched estimation. Further, our nonparametric bootstrap method via a discretized software reliability growth model does not need to give a underlying probability distribution function for the sampling data when we generate a bootstrap sample. Our basic idea of the nonparametric bootstrap method can be applied to other software reliability growth models whose parameters can be estimated by using the method of least-squares, and can be obviously applied to other discretized NHPP models Inoue and Yamada (2006, 2010, 2003).

References

Efron, B. (1979). Bootstrap methods: another look at the jackknife, *The Annals of Statistics*, **7**, 1, pp. 1–26.

Fries, A. and Sen, A. (1996). A survey of discrete reliability-growth models, *IEEE Transactions on Reliability*, **45**, 4, pp. 582–603.

Gokhale, S.S. (2003). Optimal software release time incorporating fault correction, *Proceedings of the 28th Annual NASA Goddard Software Engineering Workshop*, pp. 175–184.

Goel, A.L. and Okumoto, K. (1979). Time-dependent error-detection rate model for software reliability and other performance measures, *IEEE Transactions on Reliability*, **R-28**, 3, pp. 206–211.

Hirota, R. (1979). Nonlinear partial difference equations. V. Nonlinear equations reducible to linear equations, *Journal of the Physical Society of Japan*, **46**, 1, pp. 312–319.

Huang, C.Y. and Lin, C.T. (2010). Analysis of software reliability modeling considering testing compression factor and failure-to-fault relationship, *IEEE Transactions on Computers*, **59**, 2.

Huang, C.Y., Lyu, M.R. and Kuo, S.Y. (2003). A unified scheme of some nonhomogeneous Poisson process models for software reliability estimation, *IEEE Transactions on Software Engineering*, **29**, 3, pp. 261–269.

Inoue, S. and Yamada, S. (2003). NHPP modeling based on discrete statistical data analysis models for software reliability assessment, *Proceedings of the International Workshop on Reliability and Its Applications*, pp. 138–143.

Inoue, S. and Yamada, S. (2006). Discrete software reliability assessment with discretized NHPP models, *Computers & Mathematics with Applications: An International Journal*, **51**, 2, pp. 161–170.

Inoue, S. and Yamada, S. (2008). Two-dimensional software reliability assessment with testing-coverage, *Proceedings of the Second IEEE International Conference on Secure System Integration and Reliability Improvement* (SSIRI 2008), pp. 150–157.

Inoue, S. and Yamada, S. (2010). Integrable difference equations for software reliability assessment and their applications, *International Journal of Systems Assurance Engineering and Management*, **1**, 1, pp. 2–7.

Kaneishi, T. and Dohi, T. (2010). Parametric bootstraping for assessing software reliability measures," *Proceedings of the 17th IEEE Pacific Rim International Symposium on Dependable Computing*, pp. 1–9.

Kapur, P.K., Pham, H., Aggarwal, A.G. and Kaur, G. (2012). Two dimensional multi-release software reliability modeling and optimal release planning, *IEEE Transactions on Reliability*, **61**, 3, pp. 758–768.

Kimura, M. and Fujiwara, T. (2006) *A study on bootstrap confidence intervals of software reliability measures based on an incomplete gamma function model* in *Advanced Reliability Modeling II*, T. Dohi and W.Y. Yun (Eds.), World Scientific, pp. 419–426.

Kimura, M. and Fujiwara, T. (2010). *A bootstrap software reliability assessment method to squeeze out remaining faults* in *Advances in Computer Science and Information Technology*, T.H. Kim and H. Adeli (Eds.), Springer-Verlag, Berlin Heidelberg, pp. 435–446.

Musa, J.D., Iannio, D. and Okumoto, K. (1987). *Software Reliability: Measurement, Prediction, Application*. McGraw-Hill, New York.

Osaki, S. (1992). *Applied Stochastic System Modeling*. Springer-Verlag, Berlin, Heidelberg.

Pham, H. (2000). *Software Reliability*. Springer-Verlag, Singapore.

Pham, H. and Zhang, X. (1999). A software cost model with warranty and risk costs. *IEEE Transactions on Computers*, **48**, 1, pp. 71–75.

Rizzo, M.L. (2008). *Statistical Computing with R*, Chapman and Hall/CRC, Boca Raton.

Ross, S.M. (1997). *Introduction to Probability Models*. (Sixth Edition), Academic Press, San Diego.

Satoh, D. (2000). A discrete Gompertz equation and a software reliability growth model, *IEICE Transactions on Information and Systems*, **E83-D**, 7, pp. 1508–1513.

Satoh, D. and Yamada, S. (2001). Discrete equations and software reliability growth models, *Proceedings of the 12th IEEE International Symposium on Software Reliability Engineering*, pp. 176–184.

Satoh, D. and Yamada, S. (2002). Parameter estimation of discrete logistic curve models for software reliability assessment, *Japan Journal of Industrial and Applied Mathematics*, **19**, 1, pp. 39–54.

Trivedi, K.S. (2002). *Probability and Statistics with Reliability, Queueing and Computer Science*. (Second ed.), John Wiley & Sons, New York.

Yamada, S. (2013). *Software Reliability Modeling —Fundamentals and Applications —*, Springer-Verlag, Tokyo.

Yamada, S. and Osaki, S. (1985). Cost-reliability optimal release policies for software systems, *IEEE Transactions on Reliability*, **R-34**, 5, pp. 422–424.

Yamada, S. and Osaki, S. (1985). Discrete software reliability growth models, *Journal of Applied Stochastic Models and Data Analysis*, **1**, 1, pp. 65–77.

Yamada, S. and Osaki, S. (1985). Software reliability growth modeling: Models and applications, *IEEE Transactions on Software Engineering*, **SE-11**, 12, pp. 1431–1437.

Chapter 5

Confidence Intervals in Optimal Checkpoint Placement

Shunsuke Tokumoto[1], Tadashi Dohi[1], Hiroyuki Okamura[1]
and Won Young Yun[2]

[1] *Department of Information Engineering,*
Hiroshima University,

[2] *Department of Industrial Engineering,*
Pusan National University

1 Introduction

System failures in large scaled computer systems can lead to a huge economic and/or critical social loss. Checkpointing and rollback recovery is a
commonly used solution for improving the dependability of computer systems, and is regarded as a low-cost environment diversity technique from
the standpoint of fault-tolerant computing. Especially, when the file system
to write and/or read data is designed in terms of preventive and proactive
fault management, checkpoint generations can back up occasionally or periodically the significant data or processes on the primary medium to safe
secondary media, and can play a significant role to limit the amount of data
processing for the recovery actions after system failures occur. If checkpoints are frequently taken, a larger overhead by checkpointing itself will
be incurred. Conversely, if checkpoints are seldom placed, a larger recovery
overhead after a system failure will be required. Hence, it is important
to determine the optimal checkpoint sequence taking account of the trade-
off between two kinds of overhead factors above. Since the system failure
phenomenon under uncertainty is described by a probability distribution,
called the system failure time distribution, the optimal checkpoint sequence
should be determined based on any stochastic model [Nicola (1995)].

Since the seminal contribution by Young (1974), a huge number of checkpoint placement problems have been discussed by many authors. In general checkpoint placement models can be classified into two categories; periodic checkpoint placement model and aperiodic checkpoint placement model. The former denotes the checkpoint placement at a constant interval periodically, the latter the one at a non-constant time sequence aperiodically. When the checkpoint is placed so as to maximize the steady-state system availability or minimize the expected system overhead for centralized file systems, it is well known that the periodic checkpoint placement is the best strategy in almost all cases if the system failure time is exponentially distributed with constant failure rate. On the other hand, if the system failure time possesses the increasing failure rate property, *i.e.* the system failure rate increases as the operation time elapses, under some specific cost functions, the optimal checkpoint interval becomes a decreasing sequence [Duda (1983); Okamura *et al.* (2006); Ozaki *et al.* (2004, 2006, 2009); Toueg and Babaoğlu (1984)]. In other words, the checkpoint placement problem with periodic checkpoint interval can be regarded as a simpler optimization problem with single decision variable than that with aperiodic checkpoint sequence which leads to a much complex non-linear optimization problem with multiple decision variables.

Another important issue to apply the checkpoint placement to real file system operations is the statistical estimation problem, because the system failure time distribution and its parameters are unknown in common cases. As mentioned in the next section, almost all checkpoint placement models implicitly assume the complete knowledge on the system failure time distribution and the failure rate in the exponential failure time distribution in aperiodic and periodic checkpointing, respectively. Dohi *et al.* (1999) propose a non-parametric estimation method of the optimal periodic checkpoint interval when the system failure data are given but the corresponding failure time distribution is unknown. Ozaki *et al.* (2004; 2006) introduce the notion of another non-parametric estimation of the system failure time distribution and derive approximately some distribution-free checkpoint placement algorithms by means of min-max principle. Kobayashi and Dohi (2005) give a Bayesian estimation algorithm to seek the optimal checkpoint interval sequentially under the assumption that the system failure time is given by the two-parameter Weibull distribution. It is surprising to know that there are very a few works to deal with the statistical estimation problems of the checkpoint placement in spite of their significance in practice.

Recently, Tokumoto *et al.* (2012) derive a parametric confidence interval of the optimal periodic checkpoint interval under the assumption that the system failure time obeys the exponenetial distribution with unknown failure rate. Based on the similar idea to the bootstrap confidence interval of optimal age replacement policy by Tokumoto *et al.* (2014), they give both point estimate and interval estimate of the cost optimal periodic checkpoint interval. More specifically, they obtain the confidence interval and equivalently the probability distribution of an estimator of the optimal checkpoint interval from the complete sample of system failure time. Since in general it is difficult to obtain analytically the exact probability distribution of an estimator of the optimal checkpoint interval minimizing the expected system overhead, it is a primising approach to apply the parametric bootstrap method, and to obtain the probability distribution and its associated higher moments of the optimal checkpoint interval estimator. Bootstrapping is introduced by Efron (1981; 1985) to derive estimates of standard errors and confidence intervals for complex estimators of complex parameters of the distribution, such as percentile points. In the modern statistics, bootstrapping is a major computer-intensive approach to statistical inference based on resampling methods, and is the practice of estimating properties of an estimator by measuring those properties when sampling from an approximating distribution.

In this article we summarize the confidence interval approach to the optimal checkpoint placement by Tokumoto *et al.* (2012) and complement their results through comprehensive numerical illustrations. More precisely, we develop a novel approach to derive statistical estimates of the optimal checkpoint interval which minimizes the expected system overhead in the Young's model [Young (1974)] without analytical approximations from the frequentist (non-Bayesian) standpoint, and estimate the system failure rate by two well-known estimators; maximum likelihood estimator with consistency and unbiased estimator. Then we calculate the probability distributions, 95% confidence interval, median, variance, skewness and kurtosis of the optimal checkpoint interval estimator. We also investigate the statistical properties on estimators of the corresponding minimum expected system overhead. The resulting confidence-based checkpoint placement scheme enables us to learn the outside environment on the file system operation, and leads to the more robust decision making on the checkpoint placement. In numerical examples, we perform the Monte Carlo simulation and calculate the above statistics of the confidence-based optimal checkpoint placement. We also examine asymptotic properties of the confidence-based optimal checkpointing scheme, as the number of system failure time under observation increases. Finally, the article is concluded with some remarks.

2　Related Work

In the existing literature on the optimal checlpoint placement, it is assumed that the system failure time distribution is completely known. Chandy (1975), Chandy *et al.* (1975), Elnozahy *et al.* (2002), Gelenbe and De-rochette (1978), Gelenbe (1979), Gelenbe and Hernandez (1990), Grassi *et al.* (1992), Kulkarni *et al.* (1990), L'Ecuyer and Malenfant (1988), Lohman and Muckstadt (1977), Nocola and van Spanje (1990), Tanwawi and Ruschitzka (1984) consider a variety of optimal checkpoint placememe-ment models under different model assumptions, but the underlying system failure time is assumed to be the exponential. Baccelli (1981), Dohi *et al.* (1997; 2000; 2002), Goes and Sumita (1995), Sumita *et al.* (1989) introduce the more general assumption that the system failure time follows a general distribution, and extend a few existing checkpoint placement models with periodic checkpoint interval. An aperiodic checkpoint placement model is first considered by Toueg and Babaoğlu (1984) under a specific mod-eling assumption. Duda (1983) independently considers a checkpointing scheme on program execution time under the general failure time distribu-tion assumption. Lin *et al.* (2001) apply a variational calculus approach to approximate the optimal aperiodic checkpoint sequence. Okamura *et al.* (2006) and Ozaki *et al.* (2009) develop a dynamic programing algorithm and a fixed point algorithm, respectively, to calculate the optimal aperi-odic checkpoint sequence efficiently. For a comprehensive survey on the aperiodic checkpoint placement algorithms see [Hiroyama *et al.* (2013)].

Apart from the classiscal availability modeling with checkpointing, application-oriented checkpoint placemenet models are considered by sev-eral authors. Soliman and Elmaghraby (1998) propose a hybrid check-pointing model in time warp distributed simulation. Vaidya (1997; 1999) consider stochastic models to investigate effects on checkpoint latency and staggered consistent checkpointing. Ziv and Bruck (1997) develop an on-line algorithm for checkpoint placement. As mentioned in the previous section, the statistical estimation problem is an important issue to design the optimal checkpoint placement scheme with actual data of system fail-ure times observed in the testing phase. When the system failure time distribution is unknown, a non-parametric approach by Dohi *et al.* (1999) is straightforward but useful. However, since this is based on the complete sample of system failure time, it is needed to observe a sufficiently large number of data in the testing phase. A semi-parametric Bayesian estimation by Kobayashi and Dohi (2005) is also a promising approach to derive the predictive distribution of the optimal checkpoint interval estimator. Unfortunately, the computation cost of this method is expensive and the applicability is rather limitted in terms of the checkpoint modeling. Okamura *et al.* (2004) propose a reinforcement learning algorithm, called *Q*-learning, for the well-known Vaidya's model [Vaidya (1997)]. It can be regarded as an on-line non-parametric method to estimate the optimal checkpoint interval, but the convergence speed to the real optimal solution is very slow. The distribution-free algorithms by Ozaki *et al.* (2004; 2006) can be applied to the pessimistic situation where neither system failure time distribution nor system failure time data are available.

In this article, we suppose that the system failure time data are given under the exponentially distributed system failure time distribution [Young (1974)]. In this case, the maximum likelihood estimator or the unbiased estimator is commonly used to estimate the system failure rate from the underlying failure time data. Based on these two point estimators, we derive a parametric confidence interval of the optimal periodic checkpoint interval such as 95% two-sided confidence intervals. Bootstrap method is introduced by Efron (1981; 1985) to derive estimates of standard errors and confidence intervals for complex estimators of complex parameters of the distribution, but nowaday there are several variations [Jeng and Meeker (2000); Jeng *et al.* (2005)]. In general, bootstrapping is categorized into two types; resampling-based method and simulation-based method. In the reference by Tokumoto *et al.* (2012), only the simulation-based bootstrap method is used, where the underlying system failure time data is generated through a Monte Calro simulation with the estimated exponential distribution. Based on the puseudo random variates generated by the simulation, we get an estimate of the optimal checkpoint interval maximizing the expected system overhead with the plug-in estimate of system failure rate, and at the same time the probability distribution of the estimator as a randdom variable. In addition to the simulation-based bootstrap, we also apply the resampling-based bootstrap which is much more standard in statistics. The procedure employed leads to the derivation of the higher moments of the optimal checkpoint interval estimator and the confidence intervals. Because the statistical estimation error always occurs in practice, the resulting confidence-based approach is useful to make a consistent decision making for checkpoint placement in computer systems.

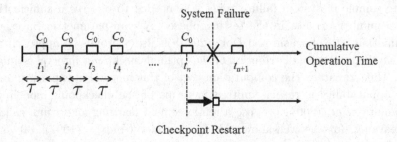

Fig. 1   Configuration of the optimal checkpoint placement.

3   Checkpoint Placement Model

3.1   *Model Description*

Consider a simple file system with sequential checkpointing over an infinite time horizon. The system operation starts at time $t_0 = 0$, and the checkpoint (CP) is sequentially placed at time $\{t_1, t_2, \cdots, t_k, \cdots\}$. At each CP, t_k $(k = 1, 2, \cdots)$, all the file data on the main memory is saved to a safe secondary medium like CD-Rom, where the cost (time overhead) c_0 (> 0) is needed per each CP placement. It is assumed that the system operation stops during the checkpointing and the file system is not deteriorated. System failure occurs according to an absolutely continuous and non-decreasing probability distribution function $F(t)$ having finite mean $1/\lambda$ (> 0), which depends on the cumulative system operation time excluded the checkpointing period. Upon a system failure, a rollback recovery is done immediately where the file data saved at the last CP creation is used.

Next, a checkpoint restart is performed and the file data is recovered to the state just before the system failure point. The time length required for the checkpoint restart is given by the function $L(\cdot)$, which depends on the system failure time and is assumed to be differentiable and increasing. More specifically, suppose that the recovery function is an affine function of the time interval between the begin of the last checkpointing before system failure and the system failure time, *i.e.*, $L(t - t_k) = a_0(t - t_{k-1}) + b_0$, $(t > t_{k-1}, k = 1, 2, \cdots)$, where a_0 (> 0) and b_0 (> 0) are constants. The first term a_0 denotes the constant restart time needed per unit of time passed since the last checkpointing, and the second term b_0 is a fixed time associated with the CP restart. Throughout this article, it is assumed that no failure occurs during the recovery period with probability one. We define the time interval from $t = 0$ to the completion time of recovery operation from the system failure as one cycle. The same cycle repeats again and again over an infinite time span. Figure 1.1 depicts a possible realization of the above CP model.

Then the expected system overhead is formulated by

$$C(t_1, t_2, \ldots) = \sum_{n=0}^{\infty} \int_{t_n}^{t_{n+1}} \left\{ c_0(n+1) + a_0(x - t_n) + b_0 \right\} dF(x)$$

$$= c_0(n+1) + \sum_{n=0}^{\infty} \int_{t_n}^{t_{n+1}} \left\{ a_0(x - t_n) + b_0 \right\} dF(x), \quad (1)$$

where $t_0 = 0$ for notational convenience. When $F(x)$ is the exponential distribution, $F(x) = 1 - \exp(-\lambda x)$, it is well known that the resulting CP interval is reduced to constant, *i.e.*, $t_{n+1} - t_n = \tau \ (> 0)$ (constant). From this fact, the expected system overhead is given, as a function of τ, by

$$C(\tau) = \sum_{n=0}^{\infty} \int_{n\tau}^{(n+1)\tau} \left\{ c_0(n+1) + a_0(x - n\tau) + b_0 \right\} dF(x). \quad (2)$$

Differentiating $C(\tau)$ with respect to τ and setting equal to zero imply the first order considtion of optimality:

$$\exp(c_0\lambda) - \lambda\tau - \exp(-\lambda\tau) = 0 \quad (3)$$

Hence the unique solution τ^* of the above non-linear equation yields the optimal CP interval minimizing the expected system overhead for given λ.

3.2   *Parameter Estimation*

Let $X_1, X_2, \ldots, X_n$ denote n system failure times, which are non-negative random variables. Given n system failure time data $x_1, x_2, \ldots, x_n$ as the realizations of $X_i \ (i = 1, 2, \ldots, n)$, the most well-known technique to estimate the model parameter λ and its associated optimal checkpoint interval is the maximum likelihood estimation. For the above data set, define the likelihood function

$$\mathcal{L}(\lambda; X_1, X_2, \ldots, X_n) = \Pi_{i=1}^{n} \lambda \exp(-\lambda X_i)$$

$$= \lambda^n \exp(-\lambda \sum_{i=1}^{n} X_i). \quad (4)$$

By solving the likelihood equation

$$\frac{\partial \mathcal{L}(\lambda; X_1, X_2, \ldots, X_n)}{\partial \lambda} = 0, \quad (5)$$

we obtain the maximum likelihood estimator:

$$\Lambda_1 = \frac{n}{\sum_{i=1}^{n} X_i} \tag{6}$$

as the inverse of arithmetic mean of X_i $(i = 1, 2, \ldots, n)$. It is known that the estimator in Eq.(6) is biased, *i.e.*, for the real (but unknown) λ, it turns out that $E[\Lambda_1] = (n/(n-1))\lambda \neq \lambda$, although it possesses statistical consistency, $\Pr\{|\Lambda_1 - \lambda| > \epsilon\} \to 0$ as $n \to \infty$, and obeys asymptotically the normal distribution with mean λ and variance λ^2/n. We call this consistent estimator *Estimator 1*. On the other hand, it is easy to obtain an unbiased estimator by introducing the genomic control:

$$\Lambda_2 = \frac{n-1}{\sum_{i=1}^{n} X_i}, \tag{7}$$

which is an unbiased estimator, *i.e.*, $E[\Lambda_2] = \lambda$, and is called *Estimator 2* in this article.

For the checkpoint placement problem, an estimator of the optimal checkpoint interval τ^* is defined by $\hat{\tau}_k^*$ $(k = 1, 2)$, which are the minimizers of the expected system overhead $C(\tau|\lambda = \hat{\lambda}_k)$, where $\hat{\lambda}_k$ are the realization of the random variables Λ_k and can be derived from the replacement of X_i by the system failure time data x_i. These plug-in estimates, $\hat{\tau}_k^* = \hat{\tau}_k^*(x_1, x_2, \ldots, x_n)$ $(k = 1, 2)$, are also called Estimate 1 $(k = 1)$ and Estimate 2 $(k = 2)$ in this article, and are expected to work well in the sense of expectation. However, our concern is the probability distributions of Estimator 1 and Estimator 2, $\hat{\tau}_k^*(X_1, X_2, \ldots, X_n)$ $(k = 1, 2)$, which are the random variables. It is mentioned previously that Λ_1 is normally distributed random variable with mean λ and variance λ^2/n for unknown λ. But this cannot be applied to the interval estimation of the random variable $\hat{\tau}_k^*(X_1, X_2, \ldots, X_n)$ $(k = 1, 2)$. In the next section, we develop the bootstrap (BS) estimator of the optimal checkpoint interval.

4   Bootstrap Confidence Intervals

The statistical bootstrap is a combination of data resampling and replication of estimation. Let $X_1, \cdots X_n$ be the samples from the exponential distribution function $F(x)$ with mean λ, and consider the mean value of a function $h(\cdot)$ of the random samples such as

$$E_F[h(X_1, \cdots, X_n)] = \int \cdots \int h(x_1, \cdots, x_n) \prod_{i=1}^{n} dF(x_i). \tag{8}$$

It is not always possible to obtain the closed form of the above quantity for an arbitrary function $h(\cdot)$. The intuitive and simplest method is the well-known Monte Carlo approximation of $E_F[h(X_1, \cdots, X_n)]$. First, we generate n pseudo random numbers from the exponential distribution $F(x)$ and repeat the procedure m times to get

$$x(i) = \{x_1(i), \cdots, x_n(i), \ i = 1, 2, \cdots, m\}. \tag{9}$$

Then we replace Eq.(8) by

$$E_F[h(X_1, \cdots, X_n)] \approx \frac{\sum_{i=1}^{m} h(x_1(i), \cdots, x_n(i))}{m}. \tag{10}$$

From the large number's law, as $m \to +\infty$, it is evident that the approximation error approaches to zero. In this way, if the underlying probability distribution is completely known, the Monte Carlo simulation can be used to generate the realizations of random samples. On the other hand, even if the underlying probability distribution is unknown, it is possible to resample the data with replacement. This is called the bootstrap sampling. For the purpose of CP placement, we replicate m system failure time data sets from the underlying system failure time data, $t_1, \ldots, t_n$, by means of the sampling-based method. Let T_{ki}^* be the random sample data of t_i at k-th ($= 1, 2, \cdots, m$) sampling. For the parametric estimation, we first obtain m estimates of $\hat{\lambda}_k$ for m re-sampled data sets for Estimator $k = 1, 2$. In this article we take the following two bootstraping (BS) methods to replicate the data sets.

(i) Simulation-based method (BS 1): Based on an estimator, $\hat{\lambda}_1$ or $\hat{\lambda}_2$, with the original failure time data t_i ($i = 1, 2, \ldots, n$), we generate the exponential pseudo random time sequence T_{ji}^* at j-th simulation, where $j = 1, 2, \ldots, m$ and $i = 1, 2, \ldots, n$. Then we obtain m point estimates for $\hat{\lambda}_1$ or $\hat{\lambda}_2$.

(ii) Resampling-based method (BS 2): Next we consider the sampling-based method. Given the underlying system failure time data t_i ($i = 1, 2, \ldots, n$), we sample exactly n replicated data with replacement randomly. Let T_{ji}^* be the system failute time after removing all the identical (tie) data at the j-th resampling. Then, we have the bootstrap sample t_{ji}^* ($i = 1, 2, \ldots, N_j^*, j = 1, 2, \ldots, m$) and call this BS 2, where N_j^* denotes the number of data for T_{ji}^* ($i = 1, 2, \ldots, N_j^*$). Based on m BS 2 samples, we obtain the probability distribution of an estimator, $\hat{\lambda}_1$ or $\hat{\lambda}_2$.

Let $\hat{\boldsymbol{\lambda}}_k$ be a vector with m estimates of $\hat{\lambda}_k$ ($k = 1, 2$). Based on $\hat{\boldsymbol{\lambda}}_k$, we construct an empirical distribution for the estimator Λ_k. More specifically, let $\hat{\lambda}_{(1k)} \leq \hat{\lambda}_{(2k)} \leq \ldots \leq \hat{\lambda}_{(mk)}$ be the ordered complete sample from the random variable Λ_k. Then the empirical distribution function G_{mk} corresponding to the sample estimates $\hat{\lambda}_{jk}$ ($k = 1, 2; j = 1, 2, \ldots, m$) is given by

$$G_{mk}(\lambda) = \begin{cases} j/m \text{ for } \hat{\lambda}_{jk} \leq \lambda < \hat{\lambda}_{(j+1)k}, \\ 1 \quad \text{for} \quad \hat{\lambda}_{mk} \geq \lambda \end{cases} \tag{11}$$

for $k = 1, 2$. It is well known that the above empirical distribution approaches to the probability distribution of an estimator Λ_k ($k = 1, 2$) as $m \to \infty$. From the empirical distribution of Λ_k, we can obtain not only the mean $\mathrm{E}[\Lambda_k] \approx \sum_{j=1}^m \hat{\lambda}_{(jk)}/m$ and its higher moments, but also the bootstrap percentile confidence interval with significance level $\alpha \in (0, 1)$, so we do not need to apply any approximation such as the normal percentile interval. Then the two sided $100(1 - \alpha)\%$ confidence interval $[\underline{\lambda}_k, \overline{\lambda}_k]$ is given so as to satisfy $\underline{\lambda}_k = \sup\{\lambda \geq 0; G_{km}(\lambda) = 1 - \alpha\}$ (LCL) and $\overline{\lambda}_k = \inf\{\lambda \geq 0; G_{km}(\lambda) = \alpha\}$ (UCL). The similar approach can be taken to the optimal CP interval and its associated minimum expected system overhead. In the following section, we estimate the probability distributions of the BS estimators (BS1 and (BS 2) with two different point estimation methods (Estimator 1 and Estimator 2) for $\hat{\tau}_k^*$ ($k = 1, 2$) and $C(\hat{\tau}_k^*)$.

5   Numerical Examples

We compute the optimal CP interval and its associated expected system overhead through the Monte Carlo simulation. Under the assumption that the system failure time is exponentially distributed with rate $\lambda = 1/30$, we generate 100 pseudo random variates as the system failure time data available in the testing phase, where the other model parameters are given by $a_0 = 0.50$, $b_0 = 1.00$ and $c_0 = 0.01$. If the system failure time is completely known, the (real) optimal CP interval and its associated minimum expected system overhead are given by $\tau^* = 1.10215$ and $C(\tau^*) = 1.55108$, respectively, in this example. Based on 100 system failure time data, we estimate model parameters $\hat{\lambda}_1 = 0.0310$ and $\hat{\lambda}_2 = 0.0307$ by means of two estimators in Eqs. (6) and (7), respectively. Hence, the corresponding estimates of the pair of $(\tau_k^*, C(\tau_k^*))$ to $\hat{\lambda}_1$ and $\hat{\lambda}_2$ are given by $(\tau_1^*, C(\tau_1^*)) = (1.14202, 1.57101)$ and $(\tau_2^*, C(\tau_2^*)) = (1.14774, 1.57387)$, respectively, for Estimators $\hat{\lambda}_1$ and $\hat{\lambda}_1$.

Table 1
Statistics of estimators of the optimal CP interval via BS1 with Estimate 1.

n	Estimate 1	mean	median	variance	skewness	kurtosis	95% confidence interval
10	1.17941	1.18658	1.18553	0.03533	0.12365	2.92703	[0.83190, 1.56937]
15	1.23472	1.26184	1.25816	0.02647	0.13202	2.93567	[0.95136, 1.58872]
20	1.19436	1.21402	1.21234	0.01845	0.11161	3.07511	[0.95438, 1.48638]
25	1.17873	1.19682	1.19580	0.01424	0.08074	2.95429	[0.96613, 1.43812]
30	1.16610	1.18182	1.18082	0.01123	0.09139	2.91581	[0.98088, 1.39363]
35	1.22289	1.25079	1.25048	0.01091	0.03246	2.89461	[1.04658, 1.45741]
40	1.22686	1.25871	1.25703	0.00961	0.07472	2.92502	[1.07123, 1.45162]
45	1.19485	1.21853	1.21705	0.00806	0.02642	2.96878	[1.04457, 1.39152]
50	1.18173	1.20237	1.20079	0.00691	0.09930	3.00084	[1.04251, 1.36848]
55	1.17060	1.19045	1.19012	0.00640	0.04953	2.99640	[1.03706, 1.35024]
60	1.16420	1.18341	1.18357	0.00574	0.03456	3.02339	[1.03838, 1.33214]
65	1.13311	1.14676	1.14675	0.00507	0.05429	2.95468	[1.00846, 1.28753]
70	1.11322	1.12364	1.12304	0.00446	0.09767	2.99065	[0.99730, 1.25897]
75	1.13610	1.14947	1.14899	0.00436	0.06201	2.97671	[1.02234, 1.28101]
80	1.12453	1.13654	1.13562	0.00410	0.07261	3.07455	[1.01382, 1.26447]
85	1.11948	1.13118	1.13046	0.00379	0.02398	3.05018	[1.01222, 1.25113]
90	1.12059	1.13230	1.13177	0.00353	0.09662	3.06869	[1.01833, 1.25119]
95	1.13371	1.14753	1.14713	0.00332	0.00744	2.98113	[1.03557, 1.26183]
100	1.14202	1.15700	1.15635	0.00334	0.05742	2.98170	[1.04514, 1.27209]

Table 2
Statistics of estimators of the expected system overhead via BS1 with Estimate 1.

n	Estimate 1	mean	median	variance	skewness	kurtosis	95% confidence interval
10	1.58971	1.59329	1.59277	0.00883	0.12365	2.92703	[1.41595, 1.78468]
15	1.61736	1.63092	1.62908	0.00662	0.13202	2.93567	[1.47568, 1.79436]
20	1.59718	1.60701	1.60617	0.00461	0.11161	3.07511	[1.47719, 1.74319]
25	1.58937	1.59841	1.59790	0.00350	0.08074	2.95429	[1.48307, 1.71906]
30	1.58305	1.59091	1.59041	0.00281	0.09139	2.91581	[1.48307, 1.69682]
35	1.61145	1.62539	1.62524	0.00273	0.03247	2.89460	[1.52329, 1.72871]
40	1.61343	1.62936	1.62851	0.00240	0.07472	2.92502	[1.53561, 1.72581]
45	1.59743	1.60927	1.60853	0.00202	0.02642	2.96878	[1.52228, 1.69576]
50	1.59087	1.60118	1.60040	0.00173	0.09930	3.00084	[1.52125, 1.68424]
55	1.58530	1.59523	1.59506	0.00160	0.04953	2.99640	[1.51853, 1.67512]
60	1.58210	1.59171	1.59179	0.00144	0.03456	3.02339	[1.51919, 1.66607]
65	1.56656	1.57338	1.57338	0.00127	0.05430	2.95468	[1.50423, 1.64376]
70	1.55661	1.56182	1.56152	0.00112	0.09767	2.99065	[1.49865, 1.62948]
75	1.56805	1.57473	1.57450	0.00109	0.06201	2.97671	[1.51117, 1.64051]
80	1.56226	1.56827	1.56781	0.00102	0.07261	3.07455	[1.50691, 1.63224]
85	1.55974	1.56559	1.56523	0.00095	0.02398	3.05018	[1.50611, 1.62557]
90	1.56030	1.56615	1.56588	0.00088	0.09662	3.06869	[1.50917, 1.62560]
95	1.56686	1.57377	1.57357	0.00083	0.00745	2.98113	[1.51778, 1.63091]
100	1.57101	1.57850	1.57817	0.00084	0.05742	2.98171	[1.52257, 1.63604]

Table 3
Statistics of estimators of the optimal CP interval via BS2 with Estimate 1.

n	Estimate 1	mean	median	variance	skewness	kurtosis	95% confidence interval
10	1.17941	1.07847	0.98230	0.05051	0.20677	1.53830	[0.75528, 1.45142]
15	1.23472	1.18028	1.18130	0.28623	-0.24135	2.57538	[0.83543, 1.47063]
20	1.19436	1.15055	1.14900	0.01722	-0.15091	2.53651	[0.89568, 1.38282]
25	1.17873	1.14524	1.14534	0.01184	-0.15620	2.56978	[0.92802, 1.33964]
30	1.16610	1.13807	1.13961	0.00931	-0.13723	2.69201	[0.94377, 1.31597]
35	1.22289	1.20097	1.20409	0.00754	-0.20532	2.88184	[1.02047, 1.36021]
40	1.22686	1.20868	1.21036	0.00608	-0.15127	2.88622	[1.05258, 1.35416]
45	1.19485	1.17789	1.17975	0.00535	-0.14554	2.85535	[1.02849, 1.31554]
50	1.18173	1.16643	1.16865	0.00447	-0.15646	2.87540	[1.02986, 1.29148]
55	1.17060	1.15611	1.15813	0.00391	-0.14437	2.90981	[1.03195, 1.27308]
60	1.16420	1.15075	1.15177	0.00335	-0.12627	2.80294	[1.03462, 1.25946]
65	1.13311	1.12038	1.12171	0.00319	-0.16743	2.95619	[1.00566, 1.22674]
70	1.11322	1.10116	1.10221	0.00285	-0.16077	2.86360	[0.99292, 1.19992]
75	1.13610	1.12512	1.12530	0.00260	-0.09550	2.91209	[1.02640, 1.22333]
80	1.12453	1.11412	1.11531	0.00240	-0.14914	2.89025	[1.02640, 1.20640]
85	1.11948	1.10931	1.11029	0.00220	-0.09514	2.83781	[1.01605, 1.19742]
90	1.12059	1.11162	1.11275	0.00201	-0.16173	2.94363	[1.02098, 1.19584]
95	1.13371	1.12539	1.12591	0.00188	-0.11984	2.93532	[1.03755, 1.20757]
100	1.14202	1.13450	1.13489	0.00173	-0.12778	2.91371	[1.04874, 1.21266]

Table 4
Statistics of estimators of the expected system overhead via BS2 with Estimate 1.

n	Estimate 1	mean	median	variance	skewness	kurtosis	95% confidence interval
10	1.58971	1.53924	1.49115	0.01263	0.20677	1.53830	[1.37764, 1.72571]
15	1.61736	1.59014	1.59065	0.00716	-0.24135	2.57538	[1.41772, 1.73532]
20	1.59718	1.57527	1.57450	0.00430	-0.15091	2.53650	[1.44784, 1.69141]
25	1.58937	1.57262	1.57267	0.00296	-0.15620	2.56978	[1.46401, 1.66982]
30	1.58305	1.56903	1.56980	0.00233	-0.13723	2.69201	[1.47188, 1.65899]
35	1.61145	1.60049	1.60205	0.00189	-0.20532	2.88184	[1.51023, 1.68011]
40	1.61343	1.60434	1.60518	0.00152	-0.15127	2.88623	[1.52629, 1.67708]
45	1.59743	1.58894	1.58988	0.00134	-0.14554	2.85535	[1.51424, 1.65777]
50	1.59087	1.58322	1.58433	0.00112	-0.15646	2.87540	[1.51493, 1.64574]
55	1.58530	1.57805	1.57907	0.00098	-0.14436	2.90981	[1.51597, 1.63654]
60	1.58210	1.57537	1.57588	0.00084	-0.12627	2.80294	[1.51731, 1.62973]
65	1.56656	1.56019	1.56085	0.00080	-0.16743	2.95619	[1.50283, 1.61337]
70	1.55661	1.55058	1.55110	0.00071	-0.16077	2.86360	[1.49646, 1.59996]
75	1.56805	1.56256	1.56265	0.00065	-0.09550	2.91208	[1.51320, 1.61166]
80	1.56226	1.55706	1.55766	0.00060	-0.14914	2.89025	[1.50784, 1.60320]
85	1.55974	1.55466	1.55514	0.00055	-0.09514	2.83781	[1.50803, 1.59871]
90	1.56030	1.55581	1.55638	0.00050	-0.16173	2.94364	[1.51049, 1.59792]
95	1.56686	1.56270	1.56295	0.00047	-0.11984	2.93532	[1.51878, 1.60378]
100	1.57101	1.56725	1.56744	0.00043	-0.12778	2.91371	[1.52437, 1.60633]

Table 5
Statistics of estimators of the optimal CP interval via BS1 with Estimate 2.

n	Estimate 2	mean	median	variance	skewness	kurtosis	95% confidence interval
10	1.24285	1.25040	1.24930	0.03925	0.12253	2.92192	[0.87653, 1.65390]
15	1.27782	1.30589	1.30208	0.02836	0.13202	2.93567	[0.98451, 0.16443]
20	1.22521	1.24539	1.24366	0.01942	0.11160	3.07511	[0.97900, 1.52482]
25	1.20290	1.22136	1.22032	0.01483	0.08074	2.95430	[0.98592, 1.46764]
30	1.18592	1.20191	1.20089	0.01161	0.09139	2.91581	[0.99754, 1.41734]
35	1.24065	1.26895	1.26864	0.01123	0.03246	2.89461	[1.06176, 1.47859]
40	1.24240	1.27466	1.27296	0.00986	0.07472	2.92502	[1.08478, 1.47003]
45	1.20828	1.23223	1.23073	0.00825	0.02642	2.96878	[1.05630, 1.40718]
50	1.19366	1.21450	1.21291	0.00705	0.09930	3.00084	[1.05302, 1.38230]
55	1.18133	1.20136	1.20102	0.00652	0.04953	2.99640	[1.04655, 1.36263]
60	1.17397	1.19334	1.19350	0.00584	0.03456	3.02339	[1.04708, 1.34333]
65	1.14188	1.15563	1.15562	0.00515	0.05429	2.95468	[1.01626, 1.29749]
70	1.12121	1.13171	1.13110	0.00452	0.09767	2.99065	[1.00445, 1.26801]
75	1.14370	1.15716	1.15669	0.00442	0.06201	2.97671	[1.02918, 1.28960]
80	1.13158	1.14367	1.14274	0.00415	0.07261	3.07455	[1.02017, 1.27241]
85	1.12609	1.13786	1.13713	0.00384	0.02398	3.05018	[1.01819, 1.25852]
90	1.12683	1.13860	1.13807	0.00357	0.09662	3.06869	[1.02400, 1.25816]
95	1.13969	1.15358	1.15318	0.00336	0.00745	2.98113	[1.04102, 1.26848]
100	1.14774	1.16280	1.16214	0.00338	0.05742	2.98170	[1.05037, 1.27846]

Table 6
Statistics of estimators of the expected system overhead via BS1 with Estimate 2.

n	Estimate 2	mean	median	variance	skewness	kurtosis	95% confidence interval
10	1.62143	1.62520	1.62465	0.00982	0.12366	2.92707	[1.43826, 1.82695]
15	1.63891	1.65295	1.65104	0.00709	0.13202	2.93567	[1.49226, 1.82212]
20	1.61261	1.62269	1.62183	0.00485	0.11160	3.07511	[1.48950, 1.76241]
25	1.60145	1.61068	1.61016	0.00371	0.08074	2.95429	[1.49296, 1.73382]
30	1.59296	1.60095	1.60044	0.00290	0.09139	2.91581	[1.49877, 1.70867]
35	1.62032	1.63447	1.63432	0.00281	0.03246	2.89460	[1.53088, 1.73930]
40	1.62120	1.63733	1.63648	0.00246	0.07472	2.92502	[1.54239, 1.73502]
45	1.60414	1.61611	1.61537	0.00206	0.02642	2.96878	[1.52815, 1.70359]
50	1.59683	1.60725	1.60646	0.00176	0.09930	3.00084	[1.52651, 1.69115]
55	1.59067	1.60068	1.60051	0.00163	0.04953	2.99640	[1.52328, 1.68131]
60	1.58698	1.59667	1.59675	0.00146	0.03456	3.02339	[1.52354, 1.67166]
65	1.57094	1.57782	1.57781	0.00129	0.05430	2.95468	[1.50813, 1.64875]
70	1.56060	1.56585	1.56555	0.00113	0.09767	2.99065	[1.50223, 1.63401]
75	1.57185	1.57858	1.57834	0.00111	0.06201	2.97671	[1.51459, 1.64480]
80	1.56579	1.57183	1.57137	0.00104	0.07261	3.07455	[1.51009, 1.63620]
85	1.56304	1.56893	1.56856	0.00096	0.02398	3.05018	[1.50910, 1.62926]
90	1.56342	1.56930	1.56903	0.00089	0.09662	3.06869	[1.51200, 1.62908]
95	1.56985	1.57679	1.57659	0.00084	0.00745	2.98113	[1.52051, 1.63424]
100	1.57387	1.58140	1.58107	0.00084	0.05742	2.98171	[1.52518, 1.63923]

Table 7
Statistics of estimators of the optimal CP interval via BS2 with Estimate 2.

n	Estimate 2	mean	median	variance	skewness	kurtosis	95% confidence interval
10	1.24285	1.17600	1.07593	0.05975	0.27383	1.71007	[0.81994, 1.60336]
15	1.27782	1.24819	1.24856	0.03197	-0.19739	2.61185	[0.88539, 1.56069]
20	1.22521	1.19899	1.19678	0.18668	-0.12112	2.56164	[0.93373, 1.44508]
25	1.20290	1.18320	1.18312	0.01261	-0.13516	2.58237	[0.95973, 1.38482]
30	1.18592	1.16927	1.17073	0.00982	-0.11925	2.70047	[0.97089, 1.35415]
35	1.24065	1.22900	1.23218	0.00789	-0.18852	2.88330	[1.04459, 1.39202]
40	1.24240	1.23331	1.23472	0.00634	-0.13700	2.89121	[1.07470, 1.38185]
45	1.20828	1.17306	1.17490	0.00403	-0.13524	2.91227	[1.04755, 1.29196]
50	1.19366	1.16618	1.16716	0.00344	-0.11842	2.80189	[1.04883, 1.27658]
55	1.18133	1.13422	1.13546	0.00326	-0.16091	2.95843	[1.01839, 1.24209]
60	1.17397	1.11376	1.11477	0.00291	-0.15564	2.86568	[1.00477, 1.21399]
65	1.14188	1.13422	1.13546	0.00326	-0.16091	2.95843	[1.01839, 1.24209]
70	1.12121	1.11376	1.11477	0.00291	-0.15564	2.86568	[1.00477, 1.21399]
75	1.14370	1.13712	1.13723	0.00265	-0.08837	2.90974	[1.03726, 1.23689]
80	1.13158	1.12526	1.12649	0.00245	-0.14553	2.89161	[1.02605, 1.21867]
85	1.12609	1.11973	1.12064	0.00224	-0.09157	2.83959	[1.02592, 1.20908]
90	1.12683	1.12147	1.12257	0.00204	-0.15705	2.94194	[1.02994, 1.20656]
95	1.13969	1.13483	1.13534	0.00191	-0.11615	2.93587	[1.04654, 1.21737]
100	1.14774	1.14353	1.14388	0.00175	-0.12460	2.91529	[1.05707, 1.22236]

Table 8
Statistics of estimators of the expected system overhead via BS2 with Estimate 2.

n	Estimate 2	mean	median	variance	skewness	kurtosis	95% confidence interval
10	1.62143	1.58800	1.53796	0.01494	0.27553	1.71848	[1.40997, 1.80168]
15	1.63891	1.62410	1.62428	0.00799	-0.19739	2.61185	[1.44270, 1.78035]
20	1.61261	1.59950	1.59839	0.00467	-0.12112	2.56164	[1.46686, 1.72254]
25	1.60145	1.59160	1.59156	0.00315	-0.13516	2.58237	[1.47986, 1.69241]
30	1.59296	1.58464	1.58537	0.00246	-0.11925	2.70047	[1.48545, 1.67708]
35	1.62032	1.61450	1.61609	0.00197	-0.18852	2.88330	[1.52229, 1.69601]
40	1.62120	1.61665	1.61736	0.00158	-0.13700	2.89121	[1.53735, 1.69092]
45	1.60414	1.59954	1.60054	0.00139	-0.13373	2.86442	[1.52375, 1.66972]
50	1.59683	1.59264	1.59356	0.00115	-0.14740	2.88103	[1.52323, 1.65672]
55	1.59067	1.58653	1.58745	0.00101	-0.13524	2.91227	[1.52378, 1.64598]
60	1.58698	1.58309	1.58358	0.00086	-0.11842	2.80189	[1.52442, 1.63829]
65	1.57094	1.56711	1.56773	0.00082	-0.16091	2.95843	[1.50920, 1.62105]
70	1.56060	1.55688	1.55738	0.00073	-0.15564	2.86568	[1.50239, 1.60699]
75	1.57185	1.56856	1.56862	0.00066	-0.08837	2.90974	[1.51863, 1.61844]
80	1.56579	1.56263	1.56324	0.00061	-0.14553	2.89161	[1.51303, 1.60933]
85	1.56304	1.55987	1.56032	0.00056	-0.09157	2.83959	[1.51296, 1.60454]
90	1.56342	1.56074	1.56128	0.00051	-0.14705	2.94194	[1.51497, 1.60328]
95	1.56985	1.56741	1.56767	0.00048	-0.11615	2.93586	[1.52327, 1.60869]
100	1.57387	1.57177	1.57194	0.00044	-0.12460	2.91528	[1.52853, 1.61118]

Next, we generate two kinds of BS samples. For each bootstrap method, we generate $m = 10,000$ BS samples and obtain the estimates, $\hat{\lambda}_{1,j}$ and $\hat{\lambda}_{2,j}$, for $k = 1,2$ and $j = 1,2,\ldots,10,000$. Using these estimates, we calculate $(\tau_{k,j}^*, C(\tau_{k,j}^*))$ ($k = 1,2$, $j = 1,2,\ldots,10,000$) and the empirical distribution, mean, median, variance, skewness and kurtosis. In Tables 1 to 8 we present the point estimate, BS mean, BS median, variance, skewness and kurtosis of $(\hat{\tau}_k^*, C(\hat{\tau}_k^*))$, $(k = 1,2)$ with BS 1 and BS 2 for varying the number of system failure time data. As the sample size of system failure time decreases, the variance increases and the 95% confidence interval length also becomes longer. In both cases on Estimator 1 and Estimator 2, the skewness and kurtosis get closed to 0 and 3 enough, respectively, so that the both estimators can be asymptotically approximated by the normal distributions. Again, focusing on the case of $n = 100$, Figures 2 and 3 show the empirical probability density functions of $(\hat{\tau}_k^*, C(\hat{\tau}_k^*))$, $(k = 1,2)$,

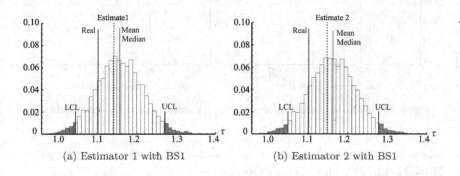

(a) Estimator 1 with BS1   (b) Estimator 2 with BS1

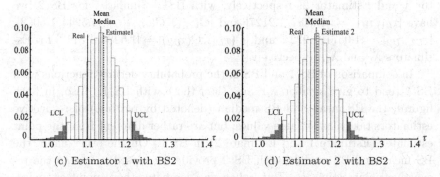

(c) Estimator 1 with BS2   (d) Estimator 2 with BS2

Fig. 2 Bootstrap confidence intervals of the optimal CP interval.

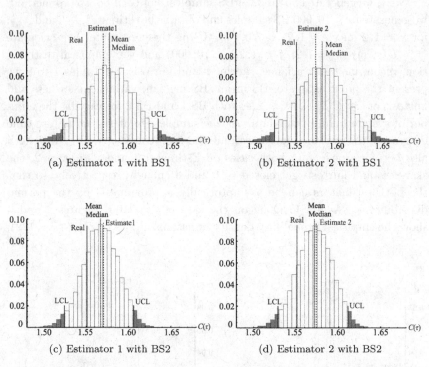

Fig. 3   Bootstrap confidence intervals of the minimum expected system overhead.

where the pair of LCL and UCL in Figs. 2and 3 are given by $[\tau_{L1}, \tau_{U1}] =$ [1.04514, 1.27209] and $[C(\tau_{L1}), C(\tau_{U1})] = [1.52257, 1.63604]$, $[\tau_{L2}, \tau_{U2}] =$ [1.05037, 1.27846] and $[C(\tau_{L2}), C(\tau_{U2})] == [1.52518, 1.63923]$ for Estimator 1 and Estimator 2, respectively, with BS1. Similarly, for BS 2, we have $[\tau_{L1}, \tau_{U1}] = [1.0487, 1.2127]$ and $[C(\tau_{L1}), C(\tau_{U1})] = [1.5244, 1.6063]$, $[\tau_{L2}, \tau_{U2}] = [1.0571, 1.2224]$ and $[C(\tau_{L2}), C(\tau_{U2})] = [1.5285, 1.6112]$ for Estimators $\hat{\lambda}_1$ and $\hat{\lambda}_1$, respectively.

In comparison of BS 1 and BS 2, the probability density functions with BS 2 tend to give smaller variance than those with BS 1. Also, in both figures, the BS mean and BS median (denoted by red line) of respective estimators take almost same values, but are rather different from the point estimates (Estimate 1 and Estimate 2) in BS 1. On the other hand, the BS mean and BS median with BS 2 provide the closed values to the respective point estimates. But, when one compares those point estimates with the real solutions, it turns out that the statistical estimation methods employed here do not work well. This is because the number of system failure time data is not still enough to get the accurate estimates, though the measurement of $n = 100$ test data seems to be quite expensive from the practical point of view. Even in this example, our confidence intervals of the optimal CP interval and its associated expected system overhead allow us the probabilistic interpretation in the sense of confidence limits. Throughout this example, it can be seen that all the point estimates provided here overestimate the real optimal CP interval and the corresponding expected system overhead. Our suggestion from the lessons learned is to control the significance level α so as to include the real solutions in the two-sided confidence intervals and to assess the estimation error as a risk in the software fault management with checkpointing.

Next, our concern is the asymptotic properties of the proposed BS estimates. In Figs. 4 and 5, we plot the asymptotic behaviors of estimators of the optimal CP interval and its associated expected system overhead with Estimator 1 and Estimator 2, respectively. As the number of sample (sys-

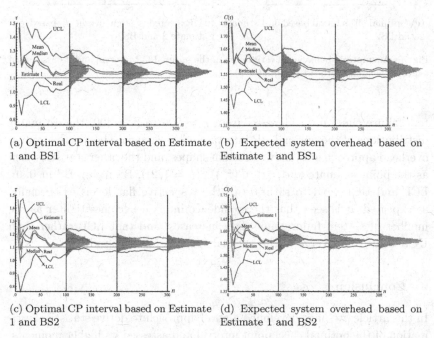

(a) Optimal CP interval based on Estimate 1 and BS1

(b) Expected system overhead based on Estimate 1 and BS1

(c) Optimal CP interval based on Estimate 1 and BS2

(d) Expected system overhead based on Estimate 1 and BS2

Fig. 4 Asymptotic behavior of estimators of the optimal CPt interval and its associated expectedsystem overhead (Estimator 1).

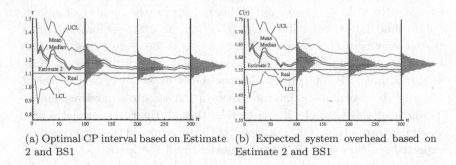

(a) Optimal CP interval based on Estimate 2 and BS1

(b) Expected system overhead based on Estimate 2 and BS1

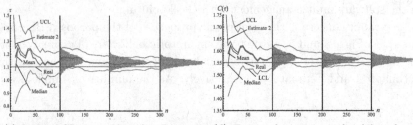

(c) Optimal CP interval based on Estimate 2 and BS2

(d) Expected system overhead based on Estimate 2 and BS2

Fig. 5   Asymptotic behavior of estimators of the optimal CP interval and its associated expected system overhead (Estimator 2).

tem failure time) data increases from $n = 200$ to $n = 300$, the estimator distributions of the optimal CP interval and its associated expected system overhead approach gradually to certain shapes, and the other statistics such as the point estimate (*i.e.*, $(\hat{\tau}_k^*, C(\hat{\tau}_k^*))$, $(k = 1, 2)$), BS mean, BS median, LCL and UCL tend to saturate to the respective flat levels. Especially, as expected, it is seen that the confidence interval becomes tighter as the number of system failure time data increases, and that LCL rather than UCL tends to converge to the optimal solution faster as well.

6   Conclusion

In this article, we have developed a novel approach to derive statistical estimation of the optimal checkpoint interval and assessed its higher moments. More concretely, we have applied two bootstrap methods; simulation-based method and sampling-based methods, and derived the confidence intervals of the optimal checkpoint interval and irs associated expected system overhead. Throughout simulation experiments, it has be seen that the sampling-based method could give smaller variance than the simulation-based method, and that the significance level α should be controled so as to include the real solutions in the two-sided confidence intervals. We have also examined asymptotic properties of the proposed interval estimates of the optimal checkpoint interval. We have confirmed that the bootstrap-based point estimates, mean, median, lower confidence limit and and

upper confidence limit tended to saturate to the respective flat levels, and that the confidence interval of the optimal checkpoint interval became tighter as the number of system failure time data increased.

In the future study, we will apply the same techniques to the other type of checkpoint placement problems. Also, we will improve the resulting confidence interval estimates by applying a sophisticated bias correction technique, such as *BCa technique*.

References

Baccelli, F. (1981). Analysis of s service facility with periodic checkpointing, *Acta Informatica*, vol. 15, pp. 67–81.

Chandy, K. M. (1975). A survey of analytic models of roll-back and recovery strategies, *Computer*, vo. 8, no. 5, pp. 40–47.

Chandy, K. M., Browne, J. C. Dissly, C. W. and Uhrig, W. R. (1975). Analytic models for rollback and recovery strategies in database systems, *IEEE Transactions on Software Engineering*, vol. SE-1, no. 1, pp. 100–110.

Dohi, T., Aoki, T., Kaio, N. and Osaki, S. (1997). Computational aspects of optimal checkpoint strategy in fault-tolerant database management, *IEICE Transactions on Fundamentals of Electronics, Communications and Computer Sciences (A)*, vol. E80-A, no. 10, 2006–2015.

Dohi, T., Kaio, N. and Osaki, S. (1999). Optimal checkpointing and rollback strategies with media failures: statistical estimation algorithms, *Proceedings of The 1999 Pacific Rim International Symposium on Dependable Computing (PRDC-1999)*, pp. 161–168, IEEE CPS.

Dohi, T., Kaio, N. and Osaki, S. (2000). The optimal age-dependent checkpoint strategy for a stochastic system subject to general failure mode, *Journal of Mathematical Analysis and Applications*, vol. 249, pp. 80–94.

Dohi, T., Kaio, N. and Trivedi, S. (2002). Availability models with age dependent-checkpointing, *Proceedings of The 21st Symposium on Reliable Distributed Systems* (SRDS-2002), pp. 130–139, IEEE CPS.

Duda, A. (1983). The effects of checkpointing on program execution time, *Information Processing Letters*, vol. 16, no. 5, pp. 221–229.

Efron, B. (1981). Censored data and the bootstrap," *Journal of the American Statistical Association*, vol. 76, pp. 312–319.

Efron, B. (1985). Bootstrap confidence intervals for a class of parameter problems, *Biometrika*, vol. 72, pp. 45–58.

Elnozahy, E. N., Alvisi, L., Wang, Y. M. and Johnson, D. B. (2002). A survey of rollback-recovery protocols in message-passing systems, *ACM Computing Survey*, vol. 34, no. 3, pp. 375–408.

Gelenbe, E. and Derochette, D. (1978). Performance of rollback recovery systems under intermittent failures, *Communications of the ACM*, vol. 21, no, 6, pp. 493–499.

Gelenbe, E. (1978). On the optimum checkpoint interval, *Journal of the ACM*, vol. 26, no. 2, pp. 259–270.

Gelenbe, E. and Hernandez, M. (1990). Optimum checkpoints with age dependent failures, *Acta Informatica*, vol. 27, pp. 519–531.

Goes, P. B. and Sumita, U. (1995). Stochastic models for performance analysis of database recovery control, *IEEE Transactions on Computers*, vol. C-44, no. 4, pp. 561–576.

Grassi, V., Donatiello, L. and Tucci, S. (1992). On the optimal checkpointing of critical tasks and transaction-oriented systems, *IEEE Transactions on Software Engineering*, vol. SE-18, no. 1, pp. 72–77.

Hiroyama, S., Dohi, T. and Okamura, H. (2013). Aperiodic checkpoint placement algorithms – survey and comparison –, *Journal of Software Engineering and Applications*, vol. 6, no. 4A, pp. 41–53.

Jeng, S.-L. and Meeker, W. Q. (2000). Comparisons of approximate confidence interval procedures for type I censored data, *Technometrics*, vol. 42, no. 2, pp. 135–150.

Jeng, S.-L., Lahiri, S. N. and Meeker, W. Q. (2005). Asymptotic properties of bootstrapped likelihood ratio statistics for time censored data, *Statistica Sinica*, vol. 15, pp. 35–57.

Kobayashi, N. and Dohi, T. (2005). Bayesian perspective of optimal checkpoint placement, *Proceedings of The 9th IEEE International Symposium on High Assurance Systems Engineering (HASE-2005)*, pp. 143–159, IEEE CPS.

Kulkarni, V. G., Nicola, V. F. and Trivedi, K. S. (1990). Effects of checkpointing and queueing on program performance, *Stochastic Models*, vol. 6, no. 4, pp. 615–6480.

L'Ecuyer, P. and Malenfant, J. (1988). Computing optimal checkpointing strategies for rollback and recovery systems, *IEEE Transactions on Computers*, vol. C-37, no. 4, pp. 491–496.

Ling, Y., Mi, J. and Lin, X. (2001). A variational calculus approach to optimal checkpoint placement, *IEEE Transactions on Computers*, vol. 50, no. 7, pp. 699–707.

Lohman, G. M. and Muckstadt, J. A. (1977). Optimal policy for batch operations: backup, checkpointing, reorganization and updating, *ACM Transactions on Database Systems*, vol. 2, no. 3, pp. 209–222.

Nicola, V. F. (1995). Checkpointing and modeling of program execution time, *Software Fault Tolerance* (ed. by Lyu, M. R.), pp. 167–188, John Wiley & Sons, New York.

Nicola, V. F. and van Spanje, J. M. (1990). Comparative analysis of different models of checkpointing and recovery, *IEEE Transactions on Software Engineering*, vol. SE-16, no. 8, pp. 807–821.

Okamura, H., Nishimura, Y. and Dohi, T. (2004). A dynamic checkpointing scheme based on reinforcement learning, *Proceedings of The 2004 Pacific Rim International Symposium on Dependable Computing* (PRDC-2004), pp. 151–158, IEEE CPS.

Okamura, H., Iwamoto, K. and Dohi, T. (2006). A DP-based optimal checkpointing algorithm for real-time appications, *International Journal of Reliability, Quality and Safety Engineering*, vol. 13, no. 4, pp. 323–340.

Ozaki, T., Dohi, T., Okamura, H. and Kaio, N. (2004). Min-max checkpoint placement under incomplete information, *Proceedings of The 2004 International Conference on Dependable Systems and Networks (DSN-2004)*, pp. 721–730, IEEE CPS.

Ozaki, T., Dohi, T., Okamura, H. and Kaio, N. (2006). Distribution-free checkpoint placement algorithms based on min-max principle, *IEEE Transactions on Dependable and Secure Computing*, vol. 3, no. 2, pp. 130–140.

Ozaki, T., Dohi, T. and Kaio, N. (2009). Numerical computation algorithms for sequential checkpoint placement, *Performance Evaluation*, vol. 66, pp. 311–326.

Soliman, H. M. and Elmaghraby, A. S. (1998). An analytical model for hybrid checkpointing in time warp distributed simulation, *IEEE Transactions on Parallel and Distributed Systems*, vol. 9, no. 10, pp. 947–951.

Sumita, U., Kaio, N. and Goes, P. B. (1989). Analysis of effective service time with age dependent interruptions and its application to optimal rollback policy for database management, *Queueing Systems*, vol. 4, pp. 193–212.

Tantawi, A. N. and Ruschitzka, M. (1984). Performance analysis of checkpointing strategies, *ACM Transactions on Computer Systems*, vol. 2, no. 2, pp. 123–144.

Tokumoto, S., Dohi, T. and Yun, W. Y. (2012). Towards development of risk-based checkpointing scheme via parametric bootstrapping, *Proceedings of The 2012 Workshop on Dependable Transportation/Recent Advances in Software Dependability* (WDTS-RASD 2012), pp. 50–55, IEEE CPS.

Tokumoto, S., Dohi, T. and Yun, W. Y. (2014). Bootstrap confidence interval of optimal age replacement policy, *International Journal of Reliability, Quality and Safety Engineering*, vol. 21, no. 4, pp. 98–115.

Toueg, S. and Babaoğlu, Ö. (1984). On the optimum checkpoint selection problem, *SIAM Journal of Computing*, vol. 13, no. 3, pp. 630–649.

Vaidya, N. H. (1997). Impact of checkpoint latency on overhead ratio of a checkpointing scheme, *IEEE Transactions on Computers*, vol. C-46, no. 8, pp. 942–947.

Vaidya, N. H. (1999). Staggered consistent checkpointing, *IEEE Transactions on Parallel and Distributed Systems*, vol. 10, no. 7, pp. 694–702.

Ziv, A. and Bruck, J. (1997). An on-line algorithm for checkpoint placement, *IEEE Transactions on Computers*, vol. C-46, no. 9, pp. 976–985.

Young, J. W. (1974). A first order approximation to the optimum checkpoint interval, *Communications of ACM*, vol. 17, no. 9, pp. 530–531.

PART 2
Reliability Analysis

Chapter 6

Importance Measures for a Binary State System

Fumio Ohi

Institute of Consumer Sciences and Human Life,
Kinjo Gakuin University

1 Introduction

Some notions of importance measures for a system have been proposed
and played a crucial role in our decision making to decide which component should be preferentially maintained to improve the systems reliability
performance. The basic notions of importance measures are structure and
Birnbaum importance measures, [Birnbaum (1968, 1969)], criticality importance measures, [Bisanovic, Hajro and Samardzic (2013); Espiritu, Coit and
Prakash (2007)], and Barlow and Proschan's importance measure, [Barlow
and Proschan (1974b)], all of which are based on the concept of critical
state vector. Fussel-Vesely's importance measure [Fussel (1975)] and risk
achievement and reduction worth [Vesely, Davis, Denning and Saltos (1983);
Cheok, Parry and Sherry (1998)] also play important roles in reliability decision making. See Fussel (1975), Vesely, Davis, Denning and Saltos (1385)
and Cheok, Parry and Sherry (1998). These importance measures have
been summarised by Kuo and Zhu (2012), where we can find various definitions of importance measures which based on the fruits of structural
and probabilistic studies of binary state systems. [Meng (1996)], where
Birnbaum and Fussel-Vesely's importance measures are examined and some
stochastic properties are shown, basing on the decomposition of the space
of the state vectors. Many authors have studied about binary state systems
and these studies have been summarised by Barlow and Proschan (1975).

For the pioneering work, see [Mine (1959)], [Birnbaum and Esary (1968)], [Birnbaum, Esary and Saunder (1961)], [Esary and Proschan (1963)].

Systems and their components, however, could practically take many intermediate performance levels between perfectly functioning and complete failure states, and furthermore several states sometime can not be compared with each other. Mathematical studies about multi-state systems with totally ordered state spaces have been performed by many authors [Barlow and Wu (1978)],[El-Neweihi, Proschan and Sethurman (1978)],[Natvig (1982)],[Ohi and Nishida (1983)], [Ohi and Nishida (1984a)], [Ohi and Nishida (1984b)],[Ohi (2010)]. Huang, Zuo and Fang (2003) have extended a binary state consecutive k-out-of-n system. Natvig (2011), Lisnianski and Levitin (2003), Lisnianski, Frenkel and Ding (2010) have summarised the work performed so far, and we may find examples of practical applications of multi-state models. Levitin (2004, 2005, 2008) have extensively applied the universal generating functionUGFmethod for solving reliability problems of multi-state systems and showed its effectiveness. UGF method was first proposed by Ushakov (1987, 2000) as a stochastic evaluation method of multi-state systems, and is especially thought to be effective for the stochastic analysis of a system hierarchically composed of modules like series-parallel or parallel-series systems. Ohi (2014a) has generally given stochastic upper and lower bounds for system's stochastic performances via a modular decomposition, which are convenient for systems designers and analysts. Furthermore, a model of partially ordered state spaces is required for the reliability analysis in a situation that we can not say for two states which state is good or not. Such a model has been recently examined and some useful stochastic evaluation methods have been proposed [Levitin (2013), Yu, Koren and Guo, (1994) Ohi (2012, 2013, 2014b, 2015)]. Studies about notions of importance measures for a multi-state system, however, are not seen so much. We have some works by Levitin and Lisnianski (1999), Levitin, Podofilini and Zio (2003), Natvig (2011) which are from the practical point of view.

Levitin and Lisnianski (1999) and Levitin, Podofillinib and Zio (2003) have considered generalised concepts of importance measures and demonstrated numerical examples calculated by universal generating functions. Natvig (2011) has proposed generalisations of Birnbaum importance and Barlow and Proschan's importance measures to multi-state cases, which were applied to the performance analysis of an offshore gas pipeline system. These proposed importance measures incorporate the effect of the maintenance into itself.

This paper aims at summarising the importance measures of binary state systems and presents a few new results about the importance measures for binary state systems.

In this paper, we show stochastic formulations of Birnbaum, criticality, Fussel-Vesely's importance measures and risk achievement and reduction worth and examine mutual relations among them with an intention to extend them to the multi-state case. We especially show the consistency of the magnitude relations of Birnbaum, criticality and Fussel-Vesely's importance measures for a series-parallel system which is well observed system's structure in a practical situation. This consistency tells us that we may use any of Birnbaum, criticality or Fussel-Vesely's importance measure for judging the importance of the series-parallel systems components. The former two importance measures are basically defined on the basis of the set of critical state vectors, which are somewhat different from the minimal path and cut vectors, but may be derived from these minimal and cut vectors. We show a basic algorithm for the derivation. The Fussel-Vesely's importance measure, however, is different from the former two measures and is defined on the basis of minimal path and cut vectors. It is clearly shown that the Fussel-Vesely's importance measure is given by relaxing the conditions for the definition of Birnbaum importance measure.

We also propose a new importance measure which is more restricted than Fussel-Vesely's importance measure, called the restricted Fussel-Vesely's importance measure. This measure is defined to be the probability of the set of particular types of minimal path and cut vectors and, in this sense, is easily calculated and so may be used as a kind of convenience tool.

We prove that the chain rule of multiplication via a modular decomposition holds for Birnbaum, Fussel-Vesely's and criticality importance measures, but not for the restricted Fussel-Vesely's importance measure, which is shown by a counter example.

We also examine the risk achievement and reduction worth which are, along with Fussel-Vesely's importance measure, used as a probabilistic safety assessment method of nuclear power plants [Shimada (2004)].

2 Notations

In this paper we use the following notations. Finite sets $C = \{1, 2, \cdots, n\}$, Ω_i $(i \in C)$ and S are respectively the set of the components, the state space of the i-th component and the state space of the system. φ is a mapping from the product ordered set $\Omega_C = \prod_{i \in C} \Omega_i$ to S, called a structure function of the system. The precise definition of a multi-state system is presented in Definition 6.1.

1) $\{\, x : A; B\,\}$ and $\{\, x : A, B\,\}$ are the same set of all the element x which satisfies the conditions A and B.

2) The backslash $\backslash$ denotes the difference between two sets A and B as $A\backslash B = \{x : x \in A, x \notin B\}$.

3) $|A|$ is the cardinal number of the set A.

4) $\boldsymbol{P}(A|B)$ is the conditional probability of the event A with respect to the event B.

5) For $A \subseteq C$, $\Omega_A = \prod_{i \in A} \Omega_i$ is the product set of Ω_i $(i \in A)$. When $\boldsymbol{P}$ is a probability on Ω_C, $\boldsymbol{P}^A$ is the restriction of $\boldsymbol{P}$ to Ω_A.

6) $\otimes$ means the product probability.

7) An element $\boldsymbol{x}$ of Ω_C is precisely written as $\boldsymbol{x} = (x_1, \cdots, x_n)$, where $x_i \in \Omega_i$ $(i = 1, \cdots, n)$.

8) Letting $\{B_j : 1 \leq j \leq m\}$ be a partition of $A \subseteq C$, for $\boldsymbol{x}_j \in \prod_{i \in B_j} \Omega_i$ $(1 \leq j \leq m)$, $\boldsymbol{x} = (\boldsymbol{x}_1, \cdots, \boldsymbol{x}_m)$ is an element of Ω_A such that $P_{B_j}\boldsymbol{x} = \boldsymbol{x}_j$. Then for every $\boldsymbol{x} \in \Omega_A$ $(A \subseteq C)$, $\boldsymbol{x} = (\boldsymbol{x}^{B_1}, \cdots, \boldsymbol{x}^{B_m})$, where $\boldsymbol{x}^{B_j} = P_{B_j}(\boldsymbol{x})$ $(j = 1, \cdots, m)$. P_{B_j} is the projection mapping from Ω_A to Ω_{B_j}. For example, when $C = \{1, 2, 3, 4, 5\}, A = \{1, 2, 3, 4\}, B_1 = \{1, 3\}, B_2 = \{2, 4\}, (x_1, x_3) \in \Omega_1 \times \Omega_3$ and $(x_2, x_4) \in \Omega_2 \times \Omega_4$, $((x_1, x_3), (x_2, x_4)) = (x_1, x_2, x_3, x_4)$ is an element of Ω_A and $(x_1, x_2, x_3, x_4)^{B_1} = (x_1, x_3)$, $(x_1, x_2, x_3, x_4)^{B_2} = (x_2, x_4)$.

9) For $\boldsymbol{x} \in \Omega_A$ $(A \subseteq C)$, $(k_i, \boldsymbol{x})$ $(i \in A)$ denotes the state of the component i in the state vector $\boldsymbol{x}$ to be k. The symbol $(\cdot_i, \boldsymbol{x})$ denotes a state vector of $\Omega_{A\backslash\{i\}}$ by deleting x_i from the original $\boldsymbol{x} \in \Omega_A$ or a state vector $\boldsymbol{x} \in \Omega_{A\backslash\{i\}}$ attached with the empty i-th coordinate. We are sure that there is no confusion for which $(\cdot_i, \boldsymbol{x})$ means. When $A = C$, for $i \in C$,

$$(\cdot_i, \boldsymbol{x}) = (x_1, \cdots, x_{i-1}, \cdot, x_{i+1}, \cdots, x_n).$$

For a subset $U \subseteq \Omega_{A\backslash\{i\}}$ $(i \in A)$ and $k \in \Omega_i$,

$$\{k_i\} \times U = \{(k_i, \boldsymbol{x})|(\cdot_i, \boldsymbol{x}) \in U\}.$$

10) Every order is commonly denoted by the symbol $\leq$. $a \leq b$ means b is greater than or equal to a. $a < b$ means $a \leq b$ and $a \neq b$. Then, for $\boldsymbol{x}, \boldsymbol{y} \in \Omega_C$, $\boldsymbol{x} \leq \boldsymbol{y}$ means $\forall i \in C, x_i \leq y_i$, and $\boldsymbol{x} < \boldsymbol{y}$ means $\forall i \in C, x_i \leq y_i$ and $\exists j \in C, x_j \neq y_j$.

11) For a subset A of S, $\varphi^{-1}(A)$ is the inverse image of A with respect to φ, i.e., $\varphi^{-1}(A) = \{\boldsymbol{x} : \varphi(\boldsymbol{x}) \in A\}$. When the bracket is cumbersome, it is dropped as $\varphi^{-1}A$ without any confusion.

12) For an element x of an ordered set W, intervals $[x, \rightarrow)$ and $(\leftarrow, x]$ on W are defined as

$$[x, \rightarrow) = \{y \in W : x \leqq y\}, \quad (\leftarrow, x] = \{y \in W : y \leqq x\}.$$

$MI(W)$ and $MA(W)$ denote the set of all the minimal and maximal elements of the finite ordered set W, respectively. An element $x \in W$ is called minimal (maximal), when there is no $y \in W$ such that $y < x$ $(x < y)$.

3 Preliminary Definitions and Theorems

Our examinations of importance measures in this paper are performed for the binary state systems. We, however, present a definition of a system in a context of multi-state system having the totally ordered state spaces, since we aim at generalisation of these importance concepts to the multi-state case in future. The multi-state concepts presented in this section were first proposed and examined precisely under different conditions on the state spaces of components and the system in the work of Ohi and Nishida (1983, 1984a, 1984b) and Ohi (2013, 2014a, 2014b, 2015).

Definition 6.1. (Definition of a multi-state system) A multi-state system is a triplet $\left(\prod_{i \in C} \Omega_i, S, \varphi\right)$ satisfying the following conditions.

(i) $C = \{1, 2, \cdots, n\}$ denotes a set of the components consisting the system.

(ii) Ω_i $(i \in C)$ and S are finite totally ordered sets, which denote the state space of the component i and the system. We assume the cardinal numbers of the state spaces are greater than or equal to 2, i.e., $|\Omega_i| \geqq 2$, $|S| \geqq 2$, which means that the stat spaces include the perfectly failure and operating states.

(iii) φ is a surjection from the product ordered set $\prod_{i \in C} \Omega_i$ to S, which is called a structure function and denotes the inner structure of the system.

When a multi-state system $\left(\prod_{i \in C} \Omega_i, S, \varphi\right)$ satisfies $|\Omega_i| = 2$ $(i \in C)$, $|S| = 2$, the system is called a binary state system.

Definition 6.2. (Increasing system) A system φ is called an incureasing system, when the following condition is satisfied.

$$\forall \boldsymbol{x}, \forall \boldsymbol{y} \in \Omega_C \text{ such that } \boldsymbol{x} \leqq \boldsymbol{y}, \ \varphi(\boldsymbol{x}) \leqq \varphi(\boldsymbol{y}).$$

The increasing notion means that the system does not deteriorate by improving the components' states.

Theorem 6.1. For an increasing system (Ω_C, S, φ), the following equivalent relations hold.

$$\varphi(\boldsymbol{x}) = s \iff \begin{cases} \exists \boldsymbol{a} \in MI\left(\varphi^{-1}[s, \rightarrow)\right), \ \boldsymbol{x} \geqq \boldsymbol{a}, \\ \forall t \text{ such that } t > s, \ \forall \boldsymbol{b} \in MI\left(\varphi^{-1}[t, \rightarrow)\right), \ \boldsymbol{x} \ngeqq \boldsymbol{b}, \end{cases}$$

$$\varphi(\boldsymbol{x}) \geqq s \iff \exists \boldsymbol{a} \in MI\left(\varphi^{-1}[s, \rightarrow)\right), \ \boldsymbol{x} \geqq \boldsymbol{a}. \tag{1}$$

By Theorem 6.1, we have the equality

$$\boldsymbol{x} \in \Omega_C, \quad \varphi(\boldsymbol{x}) = \max\{ t \mid \exists \boldsymbol{a} \in MI\left(\varphi^{-1}[t, \rightarrow)\right), \ \boldsymbol{x} \geqq \boldsymbol{a} \},$$

which means that the structure function φ is uniquely determined by the family $\left\{MI\left(\varphi^{-1}[s, \rightarrow)\right)\right\}_{s \in S}$ or $\left\{MA\left(\varphi^{-1}(\leftarrow, s]\right)\right\}_{s \in S}$. In the binary case, $MI\left(\varphi^{-1}[1, \rightarrow)\right) = MI\left(\varphi^{-1}(1)\right)$ and $MA\left(\varphi^{-1}(\leftarrow, 0]\right) = MA\left(\varphi^{-1}(0)\right)$ are the sets of the minimal path and cut vectors, respectively, and so Theorem 6.1 is an extension of it to the multi-state case that a binary state system is uniquely determined by minimal path sets or minimal cut sets.

Definition 6.3. (Relevant property) Suppose (Ω_C, S, φ) to be a system.

(i) component $i \in C$ of the system is called relevant when the following condition is satisfied.

$\forall k$ and $\forall l \in \Omega_i$ such that $k \neq l$, $\exists(\cdot_i, \boldsymbol{x}) \in \Omega_{C \setminus \{i\}}$, $\varphi(k_i, \boldsymbol{x}) \neq \varphi(l_i, \boldsymbol{x})$.

(ii) When all the components are relevant, the system is called to be relevant.

If a system φ is not relevant, we have

$\exists i \in C, \ \exists k, \exists l \in \Omega_i$ such that $k \neq l$, $\forall(\cdot_i, \boldsymbol{x})$, $\varphi(k_i, \boldsymbol{x}) = \varphi(l_i, \boldsymbol{x})$,

which means that these two states k and l have the same contribution to the system's performance and may be merged into one state, and then we have a relevant system equivalent to the original non-relevant system.

Theorem 6.2. For an increasing and relevant system (Ω_C, S, φ), we have

(i) $\forall i \in C, \ \forall k \in \Omega_i, \ \exists s \in S, \ \exists \boldsymbol{x} \in MI(\varphi^{-1}(s)), \ x_i = k,$

(ii) $\forall i \in C, \ \forall k \in \Omega_i, \ \exists s \in S, \ \exists \boldsymbol{x} \in MA(\varphi^{-1}(s)), \ x_i = k.$

Theorem 6.2 tells us that every state of every component is an element of some minimal and maximal state vectors. The proof of the theorem needs the assumption that all the state spaces are totally ordered sets. When the state spaces are not necessarily totally ordered sets, the theorem does not generally hold.

Definition 6.4. (Normal property) Let (Ω_C, S, φ) be a system.
   (i) The system is called minimally normal if

$$\forall s \in S, \; MI\left(\varphi^{-1}[s, \rightarrow)\right) = MI\left(\varphi^{-1}(s)\right).$$

   (ii) The system is called maximally normal if

$$\forall s \in S, \; MA\left(\varphi^{-1}(\leftarrow, s]\right) = MA\left(\varphi^{-1}(s)\right).$$

   (iii) When the system is minimally and maximally normal, the system is simply called normal.

In this paper, an increasing, relevant and normal system is called a coherent system.

Definition 6.5. (Modular decomposition) A partition $\{A_1, \cdots, A_m\}$ of C is called a modular decomposition of a coherent system (Ω_C, S, φ), when there exist coherent systems $(\Omega_{A_j}, S_j, \chi_j)$ $(j = 1, \cdots, m)$ and $\left(\prod_{j=1}^{m} S_j, S, \psi\right)$ such that

$$\boldsymbol{x} \in \Omega_C, \; \varphi(\boldsymbol{x}) = \psi\left(\chi_1\left(\boldsymbol{x}^{A_1}\right), \cdots, \chi_m\left(\boldsymbol{x}^{A_m}\right)\right).$$

In the binary state case, all the state spaces on the modular decomposition are assumed to be binary state systems.

Theorem 6.3. (Modular decomposition and minimal state vectors) When a coherent system φ has a modular decomposition χ_i $(i = 1, \cdots, n)$ and ψ, for every $s \in S$, we have

$$MI\left(\varphi^{-1}(s)\right) = \bigcup_{(s_1, \cdots, s_m) \in MI(\psi^{-1}(s))} \prod_{j=1}^{m} MI\left(\chi_j^{-1}(s_j)\right),$$

$$MA\left(\varphi^{-1}(s)\right) = \bigcup_{(s_1, \cdots, s_m) \in MA(\psi^{-1}(s))} \prod_{j=1}^{m} MA\left(\chi_j^{-1}(s_j)\right).$$

Theorem 6.3, which is proved by crucially using the normal property, plays an important role to give the chain rule of multiplication for Birnbaum and criticality importance measures [Ohi (2014a)(2014b)(2015)].

In this paper, we mainly treat the binary state systems and then do not take care of the normal property, since the binary state system is automatically normal.

4   Binary State Case

In this section we examine importance measures of a component of a binary state system (Ω_C, S, φ). $\boldsymbol{P}$ is assumed to be a probability on Ω_C which denotes joint stochastic performance of the components.

4.1   *Critical State Vectors and Decomposition*

A critical state vector of component i is a state vector $(\cdot_i, \boldsymbol{x}) \in \Omega_{C \setminus \{i\}}$ which satisfies
$$\varphi(1_i, \boldsymbol{x}) = 1, \ \varphi(0_i, \boldsymbol{x}) = 0.$$
We write $C_\varphi(i)$ as the set of all the critical state vectors of the component i as follows.
$$C_\varphi(i) = \{(\cdot_i, \boldsymbol{x}) : \varphi(1_i, \boldsymbol{x}) = 1, \varphi(0_i, \boldsymbol{x}) = 0\}. \tag{2}$$
A state vector of $C_\varphi(i)$ means a circumstance where the state of the component i critically determines the state of the system, in other words, the state of the system, 0 or 1, is determined solely by the state of the component i, 0 or 1, respectively.

We define two more sets as
$$NC_\varphi(i;1) = \{(\cdot_i, \boldsymbol{x}) : \varphi(0_i, \boldsymbol{x}) = 1\}, \tag{3}$$
$$NC_\varphi(i;0) = \{(\cdot_i, \boldsymbol{x}) : \varphi(1_i, \boldsymbol{x}) = 0\}. \tag{4}$$
NC stands for "non critical". For example, $(\cdot_i, \boldsymbol{x}) \in NC_\varphi(i;1)$ is not a critical state vector of component i, since $\varphi(0_i, \boldsymbol{x}) = \varphi(1_i, \boldsymbol{x}) = 1$ by the increasing property of the system.

Using $C_\varphi(i)$, $NC_\varphi(i;1)$ and $NC_\varphi(i;0)$, we may have the following decompositions.
$$\Omega_C = (\Omega_i \times C_\varphi(i)) \cup (\Omega_i \times NC_\varphi(i;0)) \cup (\Omega_i \times NC_\varphi(i;1)), \tag{5}$$
$$\varphi^{-1}(1) = (\{1_i\} \times C_\varphi(i)) \cup (\Omega_i \times NC_\varphi(i;1)), \tag{6}$$
$$\varphi^{-1}(0) = (\{0_i\} \times C_\varphi(i)) \cup (\Omega_i \times NC_\varphi(i;0)). \tag{7}$$
Using the minimal and maximal state vectors, we may have another decompositions as the following.
$$\varphi^{-1}(1) = \{1_i\} \times C_\varphi(i)$$
$$\cup \, \Omega_i \times \{(\cdot_i, \boldsymbol{x}) : \exists \boldsymbol{b} \in MI\left(\varphi^{-1}(1), i, 1\right), \boldsymbol{b} \leq (1_i, \boldsymbol{x}); \varphi(0_i, \boldsymbol{x}) = 1\}$$
$$\cup \, \Omega_i \times \{(\cdot_i, \boldsymbol{x}) : \forall \boldsymbol{b} \in MI\left(\varphi^{-1}(1), i, 1\right), \boldsymbol{b} \nleq (1_i, \boldsymbol{x}); \varphi(0_i, \boldsymbol{x}) = 1\}, \tag{8}$$
$$\varphi^{-1}(0) = \{0_i\} \times C_\varphi(i)$$
$$\cup \, \Omega_i \times \{(\cdot_i, \boldsymbol{x}) : \exists \boldsymbol{a} \in MA\left(\varphi^{-1}(0), i, 0\right), (0_i, \boldsymbol{x}) \leq \boldsymbol{a}; \varphi(1_i, \boldsymbol{x}) = 0\}$$
$$\cup \, \Omega_i \times \{(\cdot_i, \boldsymbol{x}) : \forall \boldsymbol{a} \in MA\left(\varphi^{-1}(0), i, 0\right), (0_i, \boldsymbol{x}) \ngeq \boldsymbol{a}; \varphi(1_i, \boldsymbol{x}) = 0\}, \tag{9}$$

where

$$MI\left(\varphi^{-1}(1), i, 0\right) = \{x : x \in MI\left(\varphi^{-1}(1)\right), x_i = 0\}, \tag{10}$$

$$MI\left(\varphi^{-1}(1), i, 1\right) = \{x : x \in MI\left(\varphi^{-1}(1)\right), x_i = 1\}, \tag{11}$$

$$MA\left(\varphi^{-1}(0), i, 0\right) = \{x : x \in MA\left(\varphi^{-1}(0)\right), x_i = 0\}, \tag{12}$$

$$MA\left(\varphi^{-1}(0), i, 1\right) = \{x : x \in MA\left(\varphi^{-1}(0)\right), x_i = 1\}. \tag{13}$$

These sets and decompositions are used in the sequel for examinations of importance measures and their monotone properties.

We finally in this section show relationships among $C_\varphi(i)$, $NC_\varphi(i; 1)$, $NC_\varphi(i; 0)$, $MI\left(\varphi^{-1}(1), i, 0\right)$, $MI\left(\varphi^{-1}(1), i, 1\right)$, $MA\left(\varphi^{-1}(0), i, 0\right)$ and $MA\left(\varphi^{-1}(0), i, 1\right)$ as the following theorem, of which proof is easy and is omitted here.

Theorem 6.4. We have the following relations about maximal and minimal state vectors.

$$MI\left(\varphi^{-1}(1), i, 0\right) = \{0_i\} \times MI(NC_\varphi(i; 1)), \tag{14}$$

$$MI\left(\varphi^{-1}(1), i, 1\right) = \{1_i\} \times MI(C_\varphi(i)), \tag{15}$$

$$MA\left(\varphi^{-1}(0), i, 0\right) = \{0_i\} \times MA(C_\varphi(i)), \tag{16}$$

$$MA\left(\varphi^{-1}(0), i, 1\right) = \{1_i\} \times MA(NC_\varphi(i; 0)). \tag{17}$$

4.2 *Birnbaum Importance Measure*

Definition 6.6. (Birnbaum importance measure) The Birnbaum importance measure of the component $i \in C$ is defined to be the following probability.

$$IB_\varphi(i) = \boldsymbol{P}^{C \setminus \{i\}}\left(C_\varphi(i)\right), \quad i \in C. \tag{18}$$

The Birnbaum importance measure denotes the probability of the occurrence of the circumstances where the state of the component i critically contribute to the system's state.

When the components are stochastically independent, the Birnbaum importance measure, also called the reliability importance, is defined from the sensitivity analysis point of view as

$$IB_\varphi(i) = \frac{\partial h(p_1, \cdots, p_n)}{\partial p_i} = h(1_i, \boldsymbol{p}) - h(0_i, \boldsymbol{p}), \tag{19}$$

where h is the reliability function of the system φ, for the definition [Barlow and Proschan (1975)]. The right hand side of (19) is stochastically

$\boldsymbol{P}^{C\backslash\{i\}}\left(C_{\varphi}(i)\right)$. The formulation (18) is more general than (19) in the sense of that (18) does not require the independence assumption.

When the probability $\boldsymbol{P}$ is uniform, the Birnbaum importance measure comes to be

$$IB_{\varphi}(i) = \boldsymbol{P}^{C\backslash\{i\}}\left(C_{\varphi}(i)\right) = \frac{1}{2^{n-1}}|C_{\varphi}(i)|,$$

which is called a structural importance measure of the component i.

Critical state vectors are determined by the minimal state vectors (also called as the minimal path vectors) of $\varphi^{-1}(1)$ and the maximal state vectors (also called as minimal cut vectors) of $\varphi^{-1}(0)$.

Theorem 6.5. (Determination of $C_{\varphi}(i)$) For a state vector $\boldsymbol{x} \in \Omega_C$, $(\cdot_i, \boldsymbol{x})$ is a critical state vector of the component i if and only if

$$\exists \boldsymbol{b} \in MI\left(\varphi^{-1}(1)\right), \ \exists \boldsymbol{a} \in MA\left(\varphi^{-1}(0)\right), \ (\cdot_i, \boldsymbol{b}) \leqq (\cdot_i, \boldsymbol{x}) \leqq (\cdot_i, \boldsymbol{a}). \quad (20)$$

For these $\boldsymbol{b}$ and $\boldsymbol{a}$, $b_i = 1$ and $a_i = 0$ hold by the increasing property of φ.

Proof. (Proof of if part) Supposing (20) to hold for a state vector $\boldsymbol{x} \in \Omega_{C\backslash\{i\}}$, we have

$$(0_i, \boldsymbol{a}) \geqq (0_i, \boldsymbol{x}), \ (1_i, \boldsymbol{x}) \geqq (1_i, \boldsymbol{b}),$$

and then $\varphi(0_i, \boldsymbol{x}) = 0$ and $\varphi(1_i, \boldsymbol{x}) = 1$ follows, which means the state vector $\boldsymbol{x}$ is a critical state vector of the component i.

(Proof of only if part) Let $\boldsymbol{x} \in \Omega_{C\backslash\{i\}}$ be a critical state vector. Since $\varphi(0_i, \boldsymbol{x}) = 0$ and $\varphi(1_i, \boldsymbol{x}) = 1$ hold, then

$$\exists \boldsymbol{b} \in MI\left(\varphi^{-1}(1)\right), \ \exists \boldsymbol{a} \in MA\left(\varphi^{-1}(0)\right), \ (1_i, \boldsymbol{x}) \geqq \boldsymbol{b}, \ \boldsymbol{a} \geqq (0_i, \boldsymbol{x})$$

holds and we have

$$(\cdot_i, \boldsymbol{a}) \geqq (\cdot_i, \boldsymbol{x}) \geqq (\cdot_i, \boldsymbol{b}).$$

If $b_i \neq 1$ or $a_i \neq 0$, then $\boldsymbol{a} \geq \boldsymbol{b}$ holds and contradicts to $\varphi(\boldsymbol{a}) = 0$ and $\varphi(\boldsymbol{b}) = 1$. ∎

From Theorem 6.5, we may have a basic algorithm to have the critical state vectors as the following steps.

Step.1. Set

$$MI \times MA_{\varphi}(i) = \{ \ (\boldsymbol{b}^{C\backslash\{i\}}, \boldsymbol{a}^{C\backslash\{i\}}) \ : \ (\cdot_i, \boldsymbol{a}) \geqq (\cdot_i, \boldsymbol{b}),$$
$$\boldsymbol{b} \in MI\left(\varphi^{-1}(1)\right), \ \boldsymbol{a} \in MA\left(\varphi^{-1}(0)\right) \ \}.$$

Step.2. For $(\boldsymbol{b}^{C\backslash\{i\}}, \boldsymbol{a}^{C\backslash\{i\}}) \in MI \times MA_{\varphi}(i)$, set

$$\boldsymbol{X}_{\varphi}(i, \boldsymbol{b}, \boldsymbol{a}) = \{ \ (\cdot_i, \boldsymbol{x}) \ : \ (\cdot_i, \boldsymbol{a}) \geqq (\cdot_i, \boldsymbol{x}) \geqq (\cdot_i, \boldsymbol{b}) \ \}.$$

Step.3. Then the critical state vectors of the component i are given by

$$C_\varphi(i) = \bigcup_{(b,a) \in MI \times MA_\varphi(i)} X_\varphi(i, b, a).$$

Example 6.1. (Application of the algorithm to a bridge system) In this example, we demonstrate the algorithm by applying it to the bridge system given in Figure 1. The minimal path and cut vectors are given as

$$MI\left(\varphi^{-1}(1)\right) = \{(1,0,0,1,0),(1,0,1,0,1),(0,1,1,1,0),(0,1,0,0,1)\},$$
$$MA\left(\varphi^{-1}(0)\right) = \{(0,0,1,1,1),(0,1,0,1,0),(1,0,0,0,1),(1,1,1,0,0)\}.$$

Following the algorithm, we have the critical state vectors of the component 1 as follows.

Step.1.
$$MI \times MA_\varphi(1) = \Big\{\left((1,0,0,1,0)^{\{2,3,4,5\}}, (0,0,1,1,1)^{\{2,3,4,5\}}\right),$$
$$\left((1,0,0,1,0)^{\{2,3,4,5\}}, (0,1,0,1,0)^{\{2,3,4,5\}}\right),$$
$$\left((1,0,1,0,1)^{\{2,3,4,5\}}, (0,0,1,1,1)^{\{2,3,4,5\}}\right)\Big\}.$$

Step.2.
$$X_\varphi\left(1, \left((1,0,0,1,0)^{\{2,3,4,5\}}, (0,0,1,1,1)^{\{2,3,4,5\}}\right)\right)$$
$$= \{(\cdot_i, x) : (0,0,1,0) \le x \le (0,1,1,1)\}$$
$$= \{(0,0,1,0),(0,1,1,0),(0,0,1,1),(0,1,1,1)\},$$
$$X_\varphi\left(1, \left((1,0,0,1,0)^{\{2,3,4,5\}}, (0,1,0,1,0)^{\{2,3,4,5\}}\right)\right)$$
$$= \{(\cdot_i, x) : (0,0,1,0) \le x \le (1,0,1,0)\}$$
$$= \{(0,0,1,0),(1,0,1,0)\},$$
$$X_\varphi\left(1, \left((1,0,1,0,1)^{\{2,3,4,5\}}, (0,0,1,1,1)^{\{2,3,4,5\}}\right)\right)$$
$$= \{(\cdot_i, x) : (0,1,0,1) \le x \le (0,1,1,1)\}$$
$$= \{(0,1,0,1),(0,1,1,1)\}.$$

Step.3. the critical set of the component 1 is given as
$$C_\varphi(1) = \{(0,0,1,0),(0,1,1,0),(0,0,1,1),$$
$$(0,1,1,1),(1,0,1,0),(0,1,0,1)\}.$$

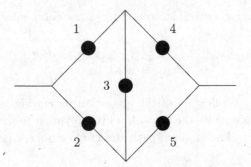

Fig. 1   Figure of bridge system.

4.3   *Criticality Importance Measure*

By the total probability theorem, we may decompose the Birnbaum importance measure (18) of the component i to the following.

$$\boldsymbol{P}^{C\backslash\{i\}}\left(C_\varphi(i)\right) = \boldsymbol{P}\left(\{1_i\} \times C_\varphi(i)\right) + \boldsymbol{P}\left(\{0_i\} \times C_\varphi(i)\right)$$
$$= \boldsymbol{P}\left(\{1_i\} \times C_\varphi(i) \mid \varphi = 1\right) \cdot \boldsymbol{P}(\varphi = 1)$$
$$+\boldsymbol{P}\left(\{0_i\} \times C_\varphi(i) \mid \varphi = 0\right) \cdot \boldsymbol{P}(\varphi = 0), \quad (21)$$

where we notice that for example

$$\{1_i\} \times C_\varphi(i) = \{\, (1_i, \boldsymbol{x}) : \boldsymbol{x} \in C_\varphi(i) \,\},$$

and so

$$\{1_i\} \times C_\varphi(i) \subseteqq \{\varphi = 1\}. \quad (22)$$

Taking separately the terms in the right hand side of (21), we have the following definition of the two kinds of criticality importance measures of the component i.

Definition 6.7. (Criticality importance measure) The criticality importance measures of the component i is defined by the following two conditional probabilities called criticality reliability importance measure and criticality failure importance measure, respectively.

$$IC_\varphi(i; 1) = \boldsymbol{P}\left(\{1_i\} \times C_\varphi(i) \mid \varphi = 1\right), \quad (23)$$
$$IC_\varphi(i; 0) = \boldsymbol{P}\left(\{0_i\} \times C_\varphi(i) \mid \varphi = 0\right). \quad (24)$$

The conditional probability (24) is usually called the criticality importance measure.

When the components are stochastically independent, we may have the following differential calculation

$$IC_\varphi(i; 1) = \frac{\partial \log h(\boldsymbol{p})}{\partial \log p_i} = \frac{p_i}{h(\boldsymbol{p})} \times \frac{\partial h(\boldsymbol{p})}{\partial p_i}, \tag{25}$$

which is the criticality reliability importance (23). And it is also easy to have

$$IC_\varphi(i; 0) = \frac{\partial \log(1 - h(\boldsymbol{p}))}{\partial \log q_i} = \frac{q_i}{1 - h(\boldsymbol{p})} \times \frac{\partial h(\boldsymbol{p})}{\partial p_i},$$

which is the criticality failure importance (24).

When the components are stochastically independent, i.e., the probability $\boldsymbol{P}$ is the product probability of $\boldsymbol{P}^i$ ($i \in C$), noticing the inclusion relation (22), we have

$$\boldsymbol{P}(\{1_i\} \times C_\varphi(i) \mid \varphi = 1) = \boldsymbol{P}^{C \setminus \{i\}}(C_\varphi(i)) \cdot \frac{\boldsymbol{P}^{\{i\}}(1)}{\boldsymbol{P}(\varphi = 1)}, \tag{26}$$

$$\boldsymbol{P}(\{0_i\} \times C_\varphi(i) \mid \varphi = 0) = \boldsymbol{P}^{C \setminus \{i\}}(C_\varphi(i)) \cdot \frac{\boldsymbol{P}^{\{i\}}(0)}{\boldsymbol{P}(\varphi = 0)}, \tag{27}$$

which are summarised as the following theorem.

Theorem 6.6. When the components are stochastically independent, we have the following relations among Birnbaum and the criticality importance measures component $i \in C$ as

$$IC_\varphi(i; 1) = IB_\varphi(i) \times \frac{\boldsymbol{P}^{\{i\}}(1)}{\boldsymbol{P}(\varphi = 1)},$$

$$IC_\varphi(i; 0) = IB_\varphi(i) \times \frac{\boldsymbol{P}^{\{i\}}(0)}{\boldsymbol{P}(\varphi = 0)}.$$

$\boldsymbol{P}^{\{i\}}(1)/\boldsymbol{P}(\varphi = 1)$ means the ratio between the reliabilities when the system is composed of only one component i and when the system is composed of n components including the component i with a structure. We can not say uniquely whether this quantity is smaller or greater than 1. When the system φ is a series system, this quantity is greater than 1 and is smaller than 1 for a parallel system.

Using the decompositions (6) and (7), we have the reliability and unreliability of the system as the following.

$$\boldsymbol{P}(\varphi = 1) = \boldsymbol{P}^{\{i\}}(1) \cdot \boldsymbol{P}^{C \setminus \{i\}}(C_\varphi(i)) + \boldsymbol{P}^{C \setminus \{i\}}(NC_\varphi(i; 1)),$$

$$\boldsymbol{P}(\varphi = 0) = \boldsymbol{P}^{\{i\}}(0) \cdot \boldsymbol{P}^{C \setminus \{i\}}(C_\varphi(i)) + \boldsymbol{P}^{C \setminus \{i\}}(NC_\varphi(i; 0)).$$

Then with Theorem 6.6, we have

$$IC_\varphi(i;1) = \frac{\boldsymbol{P}^{\{i\}}(1) \cdot IB_\varphi(i)}{\boldsymbol{P}^{\{i\}}(1) \cdot IB_\varphi(i) + \boldsymbol{P}^{C\backslash\{i\}}(NC_\varphi(i;1))},$$

$$IC_\varphi(i;0) = \frac{\boldsymbol{P}^{\{i\}}(0) \cdot IB_\varphi(i)}{\boldsymbol{P}^{\{i\}}(0) \cdot IB_\varphi(i) + \boldsymbol{P}^{C\backslash\{i\}}(NC_\varphi(i;0))}.$$

Hence the next theorem about the monotonic properties of $IC_\varphi(i;1)$ and $IC_\varphi(i;0)$ hold.

Theorem 6.7. When the components are stochastically independent, the criticality reliability importance measure of the component i, $IC_\varphi(i;1)$, is increasing in the reliability $\boldsymbol{P}^{\{i\}}(1)$ of the component, and the criticality failure importance measure, $IC_\varphi(i;0)$, is increasing in the unreliability $\boldsymbol{P}^{\{i\}}(0)$ of the component.

4.4　*Restricted Fussel–Vesely's Importance Measure*

Restricted Fussel-Vesely's importance measures are defined, basing on $MA\left(\varphi^{-1}(0)\right)$, the set of all the minimal cut vectors, and $MI\left(\varphi^{-1}(1)\right)$, the set of all the minimal path vectors.

Definition 6.8. (Restricted Fussel-Vesely's importance measures) Restricted Fussel-Vesely's importance measures of the component i is defined in the following two ways.

$$IRFV_\varphi(i;0) = \boldsymbol{P}\left(MA(\varphi^{-1}(0),i,0) \mid \varphi = 0\right) = \frac{P(MA(\varphi^{-1}(0),i,0))}{\boldsymbol{P}(\varphi = 0)},$$

$$IRFV_\varphi(i;1) = \boldsymbol{P}\left(MI(\varphi^{-1}(1),i,1) \mid \varphi = 1\right) = \frac{P(MI(\varphi^{-1}(1),i,1))}{\boldsymbol{P}(\varphi = 1)},$$

where we notice the notions from (10) to (13).

$IRFV_\varphi(i;0)$ denotes the probability that the component i's failure contributes critically to the failure of the system through a maximal state vector of $MA\left(\varphi^{-1}(0)\right)$. $IRFV_\varphi(i;1)$ similarly denotes the probability that the component i's operation contributes critically to the system's operation through a minimal state vector of $MI\left(\varphi^{-1}(1)\right)$.

Using Theorem 6.4, the decompositions (6) and (7), when the components are stochastically independent, we have the following equations of

$IRFV_\varphi(i; 0)$ and $IRFV_\varphi(i; 1)$ as

$$IRFV_\varphi(i; 0) = \frac{\boldsymbol{P}^{\{i\}}(0) \cdot \boldsymbol{P}^{C \setminus \{i\}}\left(MA\left(C_\varphi(i)\right)\right)}{\boldsymbol{P}^{\{i\}}(0) \cdot IB_\varphi(i) + \boldsymbol{P}^{C \setminus \{i\}}(NC_\varphi(i; 0))},$$

$$IRFV_\varphi(i; 1) = \frac{\boldsymbol{P}^{\{i\}}(1) \cdot \boldsymbol{P}^{C \setminus \{i\}}\left(MI\left(C_\varphi(i)\right)\right)}{\boldsymbol{P}^{\{i\}}(1) \cdot IB_\varphi(i) + \boldsymbol{P}^{C \setminus \{i\}}(NC_\varphi(i; 1))}.$$

Then, we have monotonic properties of the restricted Fussel-Vesely's importance measures.

Theorem 6.8. The components are supposed to be stochastically independent. For every component i, the restricted Fussel-Vesely's importance measure $IRFV_\varphi(i; 0)$ and $IRFV_\varphi(i; 1)$ are increasing in the unreliability $\boldsymbol{P}^{\{i\}}(0)$ and the reliability $\boldsymbol{P}^{\{i\}}(1)$ of component i, respectively.

4.5   Fussel–Vesely's Importance Measure

For the definition of Fussel-Vesely's importance measure, we introduce the following sets.

$$FV(\varphi^{-1}(0), i, 0) = \left\{ (\cdot_i, \boldsymbol{x}) : \exists \boldsymbol{a} \in MA(\varphi^{-1}(0), i, 0), (0_i, \boldsymbol{x}) \leqq \boldsymbol{a} \right\}, \quad (28)$$

$$FV(\varphi^{-1}(1), i, 1) = \left\{ (\cdot_i, \boldsymbol{x}) : \exists \boldsymbol{b} \in MI(\varphi^{-1}(1), i, 1), \boldsymbol{b} \leqq (1_i, \boldsymbol{x}) \right\}. \quad (29)$$

For example, for $(\cdot_i, \boldsymbol{x}) \in FV(\varphi^{-1}(0), i, 0)$, $(0_i, \boldsymbol{x}) \leqq \boldsymbol{a}$ holds for some $\boldsymbol{a} \in MA(\varphi^{-1}(0), i, 0)$ and so $a_i = 0$ and the component i is included in the minimal cut set $C_0(\boldsymbol{a}) = \{j : a_j = 0\}$ which satisfies the inclusion relation $C_0(\boldsymbol{a}) \subseteq C_0((0_i, \boldsymbol{x}))$. Then the conditional probability $\boldsymbol{P}\left(\{0_i\} \times FV(\varphi^{-1}(0), i, 0) \mid \varphi = 0\right)$ denotes the probability that a minimal cut set which contains component i fails under the condition of the system's failure. Thus, considering the dual case, Fussel-Vesely's importance measure can be considered in two ways.

Definition 6.9. (Fussel-Vesely's importance measure) Fussel-Vesely's importance measure of the component i is defined in the following two ways.

$$IFV_\varphi(i; 0) = \boldsymbol{P}\left(\{0_i\} \times FV(\varphi^{-1}(0), i, 0) \mid \varphi = 0\right), \quad (30)$$

$$IFV_\varphi(i; 1) = \boldsymbol{P}\left(\{1_i\} \times FV(\varphi^{-1}(1), i, 1) \mid \varphi = 1\right). \quad (31)$$

The first and second defined importance measures are called Fussel-Vesely's failure and reliability importance measures, respectively.

When the components are stochastically independent, using the decompositions (6) and (7), the Fussel-Vesely's importance measures come to be

$$IFV_\varphi(i;0) = \frac{\boldsymbol{P}^{\{i\}}(0) \cdot \boldsymbol{P}^{C\backslash\{i\}}\left(FV\left(\varphi^{-1}(0),i,0\right)\right)}{\boldsymbol{P}^{\{i\}}(0) \cdot IB_\varphi(i) + \boldsymbol{P}^{C\backslash\{i\}}(NC_\varphi(i;0))},$$

$$IFV_\varphi(i;1) = \frac{\boldsymbol{P}^{\{i\}}(1) \cdot \boldsymbol{P}^{C\backslash\{i\}}\left(FV\left(\varphi^{-1}(1),i,1\right)\right)}{\boldsymbol{P}^{\{i\}}(1) \cdot IB_\varphi(i) + \boldsymbol{P}^{C\backslash\{i\}}(NC_\varphi(i;1))},$$

which show us monotonic properties of Fussel-Vesely's importance measures.

Theorem 6.9. When the components are stochastically independent, for every component i, Fussel-Vesely's importance measures $IFV_\varphi(i;0)$ and $IFV_\varphi(i;1)$ are increasing in $\boldsymbol{P}^{\{i\}}(0)$ and $\boldsymbol{P}^{\{i\}}(1)$, respectively.

4.6 Relationship between Fussel–Vesely's and Criticality Importance Measures

Noticing that for $\boldsymbol{x} \in MA\left(\varphi^{-1}(0),i,0\right)$, $\varphi(1_i,\boldsymbol{x}) = 1$ holds and Theorem 6.5, we have the following inclusion relations.

$$MA\left(\varphi^{-1}(0),i,0\right) \subseteq \{0_i\} \times C_\varphi(i) \subseteq \{0_i\} \times FV\left(\varphi^{-1}(0),i,0\right), \quad (32)$$
$$MI\left(\varphi^{-1}(1),i,1\right) \subseteq \{1_i\} \times C_\varphi(i) \subseteq \{1_i\} \times FV\left(\varphi^{-1}(1),i,1\right), \quad (33)$$

from which we have the following theorem about the inequalities among importance measures.

Theorem 6.10. We have the following inequalities between restricted Fussel-Vesely's and criticality importance measures.

$$IRFV_\varphi(i;0) \leqq IC_\varphi(i;0) \leqq IFV_\varphi(i;0),$$
$$IRFV_\varphi(i;1) \leqq IC_\varphi(i;1) \leqq IFV_\varphi(i;1).$$

The next theorem gives us a sufficient condition for the restricted Fussel-Vesely's and the criticality importance measures to be coincident with each other.

Theorem 6.11. The restricted Fussel-Vesely's and the criticality importance measures are coincident with each other, when the following condition holds.

$$\forall \boldsymbol{b} \in MI\left(\varphi^{-1}(1),i,1\right) \text{ such that } b_i = 1,$$
$$\{(\cdot_i,\boldsymbol{a}) : (\cdot_i,\boldsymbol{b}) \leqq (\cdot_i,\boldsymbol{a}), \ \boldsymbol{a} \in MA\left(\varphi^{-1}(0),i,0\right)\} = \phi \text{ or } \{(\cdot_i,\boldsymbol{b})\}, \quad (34)$$

which is equivalent to

$$\forall a \in MA\left(\varphi^{-1}(0), i, 0\right),$$

$$\{(\cdot_i, b) : (\cdot_i, b) \leqq (\cdot_i, a), \ b \in MI\left(\varphi^{-1}(1), i, 1\right)\} = \phi \text{ or } \{(\cdot_i, a)\}. \quad (35)$$

Proof. From (34), we have

$$MI \times MA(i) = \{(b^{C\backslash\{i\}}, a^{C\backslash\{i\}}) : (\cdot_i, b) \leqq (\cdot_i, a),$$

$$b \in MI\left(\varphi^{-1}(1), i, 1\right), \ a \in MA\left(\varphi^{-1}(0), i, 0\right)\}$$

$$= \{(a, a) : (1_i, a) \in MI\left(\varphi^{-1}(1), i, 1\right), \ (0_i, a) \in MA\left(\varphi^{-1}(0), i, 0\right)\},$$

and then from Theorem 6.5,

$$C_\varphi(i) = \{(\cdot_i, a) : (1_i, a) \in MI\left(\varphi^{-1}(1)\right), \ (0_i, a) \in MA\left(\varphi^{-1}(0)\right)\},$$

and furthermore

$$\{1_i\} \times C_\varphi(i) = MI\left(\varphi^{-1}(1), i, 1\right),$$

$$\{0_i\} \times C_\varphi(i) = MA\left(\varphi^{-1}(0), i, 0\right).$$

Hence it is proved that the restricted Fussel-Vesely's and the criticality importance measures are coincident with each other. ∎

We may not generally state a sufficient condition for Fussel-Vesely's and the criticality importance measures to be coincident with each other. From the definition, $FV\left(\varphi^{-1}(0), i, 0\right)$ necessarily includes $(\cdot_i, \mathbf{0})$. Then the including relation $(\cdot_i, \mathbf{0}) \in C_\varphi(i)$ is necessary for the equality $FV\left(\varphi^{-1}(0), i, 0\right) = C_\varphi(i)$ to hold, and so from Theorem 6.5,

$$(1_i, \mathbf{0}) \in MI\left(\varphi^{-1}(1), i, 1\right),$$

which denotes that the component i is connected to a module constructed of the other $n - 1$ components in Figure 2. Hence we may say that if the system is parallel,

$$C_\varphi(i) = FV\left(\varphi^{-1}(0), i, 0\right) = FV\left(\varphi^{-1}(1), i, 1\right) = (\cdot_i, \mathbf{0}),$$

and we also have

$$C_\varphi(i) = FV\left(\varphi^{-1}(0), i, 0\right) = FV\left(\varphi^{-1}(1), i, 1\right) = (\cdot_i, \mathbf{1}),$$

when the system is series.

As an apparent relation, we have the following equality.

$$C_\varphi(i) = FV\left(\varphi^{-1}(0), i, 0\right) \cap FV\left(\varphi^{-1}(1), i, 1\right).$$

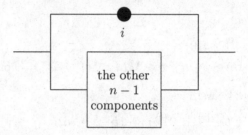

Fig. 2   Component i is connected to the module constructed of the other $n-1$ components.

4.7   *Examples*

Example 6.2. (Series System) For a series system φ, it is usually known that

$$MI\left(\varphi^{-1}(1)\right) = \{\ (1,\cdots,1)\ \},\ MA\left(\varphi^{-1}(0)\right) = \{\ (0_i,1),\ i=1,\cdots,n\ \}.$$

For the unique $\mathbf{1} \in MI\left(\varphi^{-1}(1)\right)$,

$$\{(\cdot_i,\boldsymbol{a}) : (\cdot_i;\mathbf{1}) \leqq (\cdot_i,\boldsymbol{a}),\ \boldsymbol{a}\in MA\left(\varphi^{-1}(0)\right)\ \} = \{\ (\cdot_i,\mathbf{1})\},$$

which means that the condition (34) is satisfied, and then the restricted Fussel-Vesely's and criticality importance condition of any component of the series system are coincident with each other. Noticing

$$C_\varphi(i) = FV\left(\varphi^{-1}(0),i,0\right) = FV\left(\varphi^{-1}(1),i,1\right) = \{(\cdot_i,\mathbf{1})\},$$

each importance measure is precisely given as the following. Birnbaum importance measure is

$$IB_\varphi(i) = \boldsymbol{P}^{C\setminus\{i\}}\left(C_\varphi(i)\right) = \boldsymbol{P}^{C\setminus\{i\}}\left\{(\cdot_i,\mathbf{1})\right\}.$$

Criticality importance measures are

$$IC_\varphi(i;1) = \boldsymbol{P}(\{1_i\}\times C_\varphi(i)\mid\varphi=1) = \frac{\boldsymbol{P}\left(\{1_i\}\times C_\varphi(i)\right)}{\boldsymbol{P}\left(\varphi=1\right)} = \frac{\boldsymbol{P}\left(\{\mathbf{1}\}\right)}{\boldsymbol{P}\left(\{\mathbf{1}\}\right)} = 1,$$

$$IC_\varphi(i;0) = \boldsymbol{P}(\{0_i\}\times C_\varphi(i)\mid\varphi=0) = \frac{\boldsymbol{P}\left(\{0_i\}\times C_\varphi(i)\right)}{\boldsymbol{P}\left(\varphi=0\right)} = \frac{\boldsymbol{P}\left(\{(0_i,1)\}\right)}{\boldsymbol{P}\left(\varphi=0\right)},$$

which are coincident with the restricted Fussel-Vesely's and Fussel-Vesely's importance measures, and shows us that the criticality importance measure $\boldsymbol{P}(\{1_i\}\times C_\varphi(i)\mid\varphi=1)$ does not work for a series system.

When the components are independent with each other, denoting the reliability and unreliability of each component as the following,

$$\boldsymbol{P}^{\{i\}}\{1\} = p_i,\ \boldsymbol{P}^{\{i\}}\{0\} = q_i = 1-p_i,\ i=1,\cdots,n,$$

the importance measures are given as

$$IB_\varphi(i) = \prod_{j=1,\ j\neq i}^{n} p_j, \tag{36}$$

$$IFV_\varphi(i;1) = IRFV_\varphi(i;1) = IC_\varphi(i;1) = 1, \tag{37}$$

$$IFV_\varphi(i;0) = IRFV_\varphi(i;0) = IC_\varphi(i;0) = \frac{q_i \prod_{j=1,\ j\neq i}^{n} p_j}{1 - \prod_{j=1}^{n} p_j}. \tag{38}$$

For inequalities among the importance measures of a series system, noting

$$\frac{q_i}{1 - \prod_{j=1}^{n} p_j} = \frac{1 - p_i}{1 - \prod_{j=1}^{n} p_j} \leq 1,$$

we have the following chain of inequalities among the importance measures.

$$IFV_\varphi(i;0) = IRFV_\varphi(i;0) = IC_\varphi(i;0)$$
$$\leq IB_\varphi(i)$$
$$\leq IFV_\varphi(i;1) = IRFV_\varphi(i;1) = IC_\varphi(i;1) = 1.$$

For consistency among magnitude relationships of the importance measures, from (36) and (38), we have the following equivalent relations for different components k and l.

$$\frac{q_k \prod_{j=1,\ j\neq k}^{n} p_j}{1 - \prod_{j=1}^{n} p_j} \leq \frac{q_l \prod_{j=1,\ j\neq l}^{n} p_j}{1 - \prod_{j=1}^{n} p_j} \iff p_k \geq p_l,$$

$$\prod_{j=1,\ j\neq k}^{n} p_j \leq \prod_{j=1,\ j\neq l}^{n} p_j \iff p_l \leq p_k.$$

Then the following inequalities are equivalent.

$$IB_\varphi(k) \leq IB_\varphi(l),$$
$$IC_\varphi(k;0) \leq IC_\varphi(l;0),$$
$$IRFV_\varphi(k;0) \leq IRFV_\varphi(l;0),$$
$$IFV_\varphi(k;0) \leq IFV_\varphi(l;0).$$

Hence for a series system, we may use any importance measure except (37) for the importance evaluation of components.

Example 6.3. (Parallel System) A parallel system is a dual of a series system, and then by using (35), we may easily have that the Fussel-Vesely's and criticality importance measures are coincident with each other, and are given as the following. Noticing

$$C_\varphi(i) = \{(\cdot_i, \mathbf{0})\},$$

Birnbaum importance measure is given as follows.

$$IB_\varphi(i) = \boldsymbol{P}^{C\backslash\{i\}}\left(C_\varphi(i)\right) = \boldsymbol{P}^{C\backslash\{i\}}\{(\cdot_i, \boldsymbol{0})\}.$$

Criticality importance measures are

$$IC_\varphi(i;1) = \boldsymbol{P}(\{1_i\} \times C_\varphi(i) \mid \varphi = 1) = \frac{\boldsymbol{P}\left(\{1_i\} \times C_\varphi(i)\right)}{\boldsymbol{P}\left(\varphi = 1\right)} = \frac{\boldsymbol{P}\left(\{(1_i, \boldsymbol{0})\}\right)}{\boldsymbol{P}(\varphi = 1)},$$

$$IC_\varphi(i;0) = \boldsymbol{P}(\{0_i\} \times C_\varphi(i) \mid \varphi = 0) = \frac{\boldsymbol{P}\left(\{0_i\} \times C_\varphi(i)\right)}{\boldsymbol{P}\left(\varphi = 0\right)} = 1,$$

which are coincident with the restricted Fussel-Vesely's and Fussel-Vesely's importance measure.

The examinations about inequalities and consistency of magnitude relationships for a parallel system are performed similarly to the case of a series system by the duality between the two systems.

Example 6.4. (*k*-out-of-*n*:*G* System) The structure function of a *k*-out-of-*N*:*G* system is defined as

$$\boldsymbol{x} \in \Omega_C, \ \varphi(\boldsymbol{x}) = \begin{cases} 1, & \sum_{i=1}^{n} x_i \geq k, \\ 0, & \sum_{i=1}^{n} x_i \leq k - 1. \end{cases}$$

Then the set of the critical state vectors of the component i is given as

$$C_\varphi(i) = \{(\cdot_i, \boldsymbol{x}) : \sum_{j=1, j\neq i}^{n} x_j = k - 1\},$$

and then

$$\{1_i\} \times C_\varphi(i) = MI\left(\varphi^{-1}(1), i, 1\right) = \{\boldsymbol{x} : \sum_{j=1, j\neq i}^{n} x_j = k - 1, \ x_i = 1\},$$

$$\{0_i\} \times C_\varphi(i) = MA\left(\varphi^{-1}(0), i, 0\right) = \{\boldsymbol{x} : \sum_{j=1, j\neq i}^{n} x_j = k - 1, \ x_i = 0\}.$$

Hence the restricted Fussel-Vesely's and criticality importance measures are coincident with each other and are given as

$$IC_\varphi(i;1) = IRFV_\varphi(i;1) = \frac{\boldsymbol{P}\left(\{1_i\} \times C_\varphi(i)\right)}{\boldsymbol{P}(\varphi = 1)},$$

$$IC_\varphi(i;0) = IRFV_\varphi(i;0) = \frac{\boldsymbol{P}\left(\{0_i\} \times C_\varphi(i)\right)}{\boldsymbol{P}(\varphi = 0)}.$$

The Birnbaum importance measure is given as

$$IB_\varphi(i) = \boldsymbol{P}^{C\backslash\{i\}}\left(C_\varphi(i)\right).$$

Fussel-Vesely's importance measures are given as follows.

$$FV\left(\varphi^{-1}(1), i, 1\right) = \left\{(\cdot_i, \boldsymbol{x}) \middle| \sum_{j=1, j \neq i}^{n} x_j \geq k - 1 \right\},$$

$$FV\left(\varphi^{-1}(0), i, 0\right) = \left\{(\cdot_i, \boldsymbol{x}) \middle| \sum_{j=1, j \neq i}^{n} x_j \leq k - 1 \right\},$$

$$IFV_\varphi(i; 1) = \frac{\boldsymbol{P}\left(\{1_i\} \times FV\left(\varphi^{-1}(1), i, 1\right)\right)}{\boldsymbol{P}(\varphi = 1)},$$

$$IFV_\varphi(i; 0) = \frac{\boldsymbol{P}\left(\{0_i\} \times FV\left(\varphi^{-1}(0), i, 0\right)\right)}{\boldsymbol{P}(\varphi = 0)}.$$

When the components are stochastically independent, we have the following equations for components 1 and 2,

$$\boldsymbol{P}\left(\{1_1\} \times C_\varphi(1)\right) - \boldsymbol{P}\left(\{1_2\} \times C_\varphi(2)\right)$$

$$= (p_1 q_2 - q_1 p_2) \cdot \boldsymbol{P}^{C \setminus \{1,2\}} \left\{ (x_3, \cdots, x_n) : \sum_{j=3}^{n} x_j = k - 1 \right\},$$

$$\boldsymbol{P}\left(\{0_1\} \times C_\varphi(1)\right) - \boldsymbol{P}\left(\{0_2\} \times C_\varphi(2)\right)$$

$$= (q_1 p_2 - p_1 q_2) \cdot \boldsymbol{P}^{C \setminus \{1,2\}} \left\{ (x_3, \cdots, x_n) : \sum_{j=3}^{n} x_j = k - 2 \right\}.$$

Noticing that the restriction of the component numbers to 1 and 2 does not lose the generality, we have the following relations between magnitude relations of the criticality importance measures of the components i and j, under the assumption that $0 < p_i < 1$, $i = 1, \cdots, n$,

$$\boldsymbol{P}\left(\{1_i\} \times C_\varphi(i)\right) > \boldsymbol{P}\left(\{1_j\} \times C_\varphi(j)\right)$$
$$\Longleftrightarrow \boldsymbol{P}\left(\{0_i\} \times C_\varphi(i)\right) < \boldsymbol{P}\left(\{0_j\} \times C_\varphi(j)\right),$$

which means that the two kinds of criticality importance measures show an inverse tendency in the case of the k-out-of-n:G system except the parallel ($k = 1$) or the series ($k = n$) case.

Importance measures of a series-parallel system is discussed in the section 4.9 after examinations of importance measures via a modular decomposition.

4.8   *Modular Decomposition and Importance Measures*

In this section, we examine if the chain law of multiplication via a modular decomposition may hold for each importance measure.

For a binary state system (Ω_C, S, φ), we suppose that a modular decomposition $\{A_1, \cdots, A_m\}$ is given, i.e., there exist binary state systems $\left(\prod_{i \in A_j} \Omega_i, S_j, \chi_j\right), j = 1, \cdots, m$ and $\left(\prod_{j=1}^m S_j, S, \psi\right)$ such that

$$\forall \boldsymbol{x} \in \Omega_C, \; \varphi(\boldsymbol{x}) = \psi\left(\chi_1\left(\boldsymbol{x}^{A_1}\right), \chi_2\left(\boldsymbol{x}^{A_2},\right), \cdots, \chi_m\left(\boldsymbol{x}^{A_m}\right)\right). \tag{39}$$

Furthermore, a probability $\boldsymbol{P}$ is assumed to be given on Ω_C. $\boldsymbol{P}^{A_j}$ is the restriction of $\boldsymbol{P}$ to Ω_{A_j} and $\boldsymbol{P}$ is the product probability of $\boldsymbol{P}^{A_j}, j = 1, \cdots, m$, so to say,

$$\boldsymbol{P} = \otimes_{j=1}^m \boldsymbol{P}^{A_j}, \tag{40}$$

which means that the modules are stochastically independent. $\chi_j \circ \boldsymbol{P}^{A_j}$ is the image probability of $\boldsymbol{P}^{A_j}$ on S_j by χ_j $(j = 1, \cdots, m)$, $\otimes_{j=1}^m \chi_j \circ \boldsymbol{P}^{A_j}$ is the product probability on $\prod_{j=1}^m S_j$, and $\psi \circ \left(\otimes_{j=1}^m \chi_j \circ \boldsymbol{P}^{A_j}\right)$ is the image probability of $\otimes_{j=1}^m \chi_j \circ \boldsymbol{P}^{A_j}$ on S by ψ. By the equality (39), the following equality holds.

$$\varphi \circ \boldsymbol{P} = \psi \circ \left(\otimes_{j=1}^m \chi_j \circ \boldsymbol{P}^{A_j}\right). \tag{41}$$

We notice that the importance measures of the component i in the system φ is defined with respect to the probability $\boldsymbol{P}$ on Ω_C, the importance measures of the component i in the system χ_{j_i} is defined with respect to the probability $\boldsymbol{P}^{A_{j_i}}$, and the importance measures of the modules A_{j_i} in the system ψ is defined with respect to the probability $\otimes_{j=1}^m \chi_j \circ \boldsymbol{P}^{A_j}$, where j_i is the index of the module which contains the component i. In the sequel of this section, we consider the importance measures of the component 1 and module 1 contains the component 1 without loss of generality.

We remark for the minimal path and cut vectors of the binary state system, the following relations hold,

$$MI\left(\varphi^{-1}(1)\right) = \bigcup_{(s_1, \cdots, s_m) \in MI(\psi^{-1}(1))} \prod_{j=1}^m MI\left(\chi_j^{-1}(s_j)\right), \tag{42}$$

$$MA\left(\varphi^{-1}(0)\right) = \bigcup_{(s_1, \cdots, s_m) \in MA(\psi^{-1}(0))} \prod_{j=1}^m MA\left(\chi_j^{-1}(s_j)\right), \tag{43}$$

and from which we have the next relationships about the critical state vectors.

Lemma 6.1. The following equalities hold for the component 1 and the module 1.

$$C_\varphi(1) = C_{\chi_1}(1) \times (\chi_2, \cdots, \chi_m)^{-1}(C_\psi(1)), \tag{44}$$

$$\{1_1\} \times C_\varphi(1) = \{1_1\} \times C_{\chi_1}(1) \times (\chi_2, \cdots, \chi_m)^{-1}(C_\psi(1)), \tag{45}$$

$$\{0_1\} \times C_\varphi(0) = \{0_1\} \times C_{\chi_1}(1) \times (\chi_2, \cdots, \chi_m)^{-1}(C_\psi(1)), \tag{46}$$

$$MI\left(\varphi^{-1}(1), 1, 1\right) = \bigcup_{(1_1, s_2, \cdots, s_m) \in MI(\psi^{-1}(1))} MI\left(\chi_1^{-1}(1), 1, 1\right)$$
$$\times \prod_{j=2}^m MI\left(\chi_j^{-1}(s_j)\right), \tag{47}$$

$$MA\left(\varphi^{-1}(0), 1, 0\right) = \bigcup_{(0_1, s_2, \cdots, s_m) \in MA(\psi^{-1}(0))} MA\left(\chi_1^{-1}(0), 1, 0\right)$$
$$\times \prod_{j=2}^m MA\left(\chi_j^{-1}(s_j)\right), \tag{48}$$

$$FV\left(\varphi^{-1}(1), 1, 1\right) = FV\left(\chi^{-1}(1), 1, 1\right)$$
$$\times (\chi_2, \cdots, \chi_m)^{-1}\left(FV\left(\psi^{-1}(1), 1, 1\right)\right), \tag{49}$$

$$FV\left(\varphi^{-1}(1), 1, 0\right) = FV\left(\chi^{-1}(1), 1, 0\right)$$
$$\times (\chi_2, \cdots, \chi_m)^{-1}\left(FV\left(\psi^{-1}(1), 1, 0\right)\right). \tag{50}$$

Proof. We prove only (47) and (49), since (48) and (50) are proved similarly, and the proof of (44), (45) and (46) are easy.
(Proof of (47)) For x of the right hand side of (47),

$$x_1 = 1, \ x^{A_1} \in MI\left(\chi_1^{-1}(1)\right), \ x^{A_j} \in MI\left(\chi_j^{-1}(s_j)\right), \ j = 2, \cdots, m,$$

then

$$(1_1, s_2, \cdots, s_m) \in MI\left(\psi^{-1}(1)\right).$$

Hence by (42), x is an element of the left hand side of (47).
For x of the left hand side of (47), by (42)

$$\exists (s_1, s_2, \cdots, s_m) \in MI\left(\psi^{-1}(1)\right), \ x^{A_j} \in MI\left(\chi_j^{-1}(s_j)\right), \ j = 1, \cdots, m.$$

Noticing $1 \in A_1$ and $x_1 = 1$, we have

$$(1_1, x^{A_1}) \in MI\left(\chi_1^{-1}(s_1)\right).$$

If $s_1 = 0$, then $MI\left(\chi_1^{-1}(0)\right) = \{\mathbf{0}^{A_1}\}$ holds and contradicts to $x_1 = 1$. Thus $s_1 = 1$.

(Proof of (49))   Noticing (47), we have

$$FV\left(\varphi^{-1}(1), 1, 1\right) = \bigcup_{\mathbf{b}\in MI(\varphi^{-1}(1),1,1)} \{(\cdot_1, \boldsymbol{x}) : \mathbf{b} \leqq (1_1, \boldsymbol{x})\}$$

$$= \bigcup_{(1_1,\boldsymbol{s})\in MI(\psi^{-1}(1))} \bigcup_{\mathbf{b}\in MI(\chi_1^{-1}(1),1,1)\times\prod_{j=2}^{m} MI(\chi_j^{-1}(s_j))} \{(\cdot_1, \boldsymbol{x}) : \mathbf{b} \leqq (1_1, \boldsymbol{x})\}$$

$$= FV\left(\chi_1^{-1}(1), 1, 1\right)$$

$$\times \bigcup_{(1_1,\boldsymbol{s})\in MI(\psi^{-1}(1))} \bigcup_{\mathbf{b}^{C\backslash A_1}\in\prod_{j=2}^{m} MI(\chi_j^{-1}(s_j))} \{\boldsymbol{x}^{C\backslash A_1} : \boldsymbol{b}^{C\backslash A_1} \leqq \boldsymbol{x}^{C\backslash A_1}\} \quad (51)$$

$$= FV\left(\chi_1^{-1}(1), 1, 1\right) \times (\chi_2, \chi_3, \cdots, \chi_m)^{-1}\left(FV\left(\psi^{-1}(1), 1, 1\right)\right). \quad (52)$$

Noticing

$$FV\left(\psi^{-1}(1), 1, 1\right) = \{(\cdot_1, \boldsymbol{t}) : \exists \boldsymbol{s} \in MI\left(\psi^{-1}(1), 1, 1\right), \ \boldsymbol{s} \leqq (1_1, \boldsymbol{t})\},$$

the equality (52) is proved as follows.

$$(\boldsymbol{x}^{A_2}, \cdots, \boldsymbol{x}^{A_m}) \in (\chi_2, \cdots, \chi_m)^{-1}\left(FV(\psi^{-1}(1), 1, 1)\right)$$
$$\Longleftrightarrow \left(\chi_2\left(\boldsymbol{x}^{A_2}\right), \cdots, \chi_m\left(\boldsymbol{x}^{A_m}\right)\right) \in FV\left(\psi^{-1}(1), 1, 1\right)$$
$$\Longleftrightarrow \exists \boldsymbol{s} \in MI\left(\psi^{-1}(1), 1, 1\right), \ \boldsymbol{s} \leqq \left(1_1, \chi_2\left(\boldsymbol{x}^{A_2}\right), \cdots, \chi_m\left(\boldsymbol{x}^{A_m}\right)\right)$$
$$\Longleftrightarrow \exists \boldsymbol{s} \in MI\left(\psi^{-1}(1), 1, 1\right), \ s_1 = 1, \ s_2 \leqq \chi_2\left(\boldsymbol{x}^{A_2}\right), \cdots, s_m \leqq \chi_m\left(\boldsymbol{x}^{A_m}\right)$$
$$\Longleftrightarrow \exists \boldsymbol{s} \in MI\left(\psi^{-1}(1), 1, 1\right), \exists \boldsymbol{b}_j \in MI\left(\chi_j^{-1}(s_j)\right), \boldsymbol{b}_j \leqq \boldsymbol{x}^{A_j}, j = 2, \cdots, m$$
$$\Longleftrightarrow \left(\boldsymbol{x}^{A_1}, \cdots, \boldsymbol{x}^{A_m}\right) \in \text{ the set of (51)},$$

and then the proof of (49) is terminated. ∎

Taking probabilities of the equalities (44), (45), (46), (49) and (50) in Lemma 6.1, we have the following theorem about the chain rule of multiplication of the importance measures, of which proof is easy by noticing the independence assumption (40) and the equality (41), and then omitted.

Theorem 6.12. Under the independence assumption of the component, for BirnbaumFussel-Vesely's and the criticality importance measures, we have the following chain rule of multiplication via a modular decomposition, where we suppose without loss of generality that component 1 belongs to module A_1.

$$\boldsymbol{P}^{C\backslash\{1\}}\left(C_\varphi(1)\right) = \boldsymbol{P}^{A_1\backslash\{1\}}\left(C_{\chi_1}(1)\right) \times \otimes_{j=2}^{m} \chi_j \circ \boldsymbol{P}^{A_j}\left(C_\psi(1)\right), \qquad (53)$$

$$\boldsymbol{P}\left(\{1_1\} \times C_\varphi(1) \mid \varphi = 1\right) = \frac{\boldsymbol{P}^{A_1}\left(\{1_1\} \times C_{\chi_1(1)}\right)}{\boldsymbol{P}^{A_1}(\chi_1 = 1)}$$
$$\cdot \frac{\otimes_{j=1}^{m}\chi_j \circ \boldsymbol{P}^{A_j}\left(\{1_1\} \times C_\psi(1)\right)}{\otimes_{j=1}^{m}\chi_j \circ \boldsymbol{P}^{A_j}(\psi = 1)}, \qquad (54)$$

$$\boldsymbol{P}\left(\{0_1\} \times C_\varphi(1) \mid \varphi = 0\right) = \frac{\boldsymbol{P}^{A_1}\left(\{0_1\} \times C_{\chi_1(1)}\right)}{\boldsymbol{P}^{A_1}(\chi_1 = 0)}$$
$$\cdot \frac{\otimes_{j=1}^{m}\chi_j \circ \boldsymbol{P}^{A_j}\left(\{0_1\} \times C_\psi(1)\right)}{\otimes_{j=1}^{m}\chi_j \circ \boldsymbol{P}^{A_j}(\psi = 0)}, \qquad (55)$$

$$\boldsymbol{P}(\{1_1\} \times FV\left(\varphi^{-1}(1), 1, 1 \mid \varphi = 1\right) = \frac{\boldsymbol{P}^{A_1}\left(\{1_1\} \times FV\left(\chi_1^{-1}(1), 1, 1\right)\right)}{\boldsymbol{P}^{A_1}(\chi_1 = 1)}$$
$$\cdot \frac{\otimes_{j=1}^{m}\chi_j \circ \boldsymbol{P}^{A_j}\left(\{1_1\} \times FV\left(\psi^{-1}(1), 1, 1\right)\right)}{\otimes_{j=1}^{m}\chi_j \circ \boldsymbol{P}^{A_j}(\psi = 1)}, \qquad (56)$$

$$\boldsymbol{P}(\{0_1\} \times FV\left(\varphi^{-1}(0), 1, 0 \mid \varphi = 0\right) = \frac{\boldsymbol{P}^{A_1}\left(\{0_1\} \times FV\left(\chi_1^{-1}(0), 1, 0\right)\right)}{\boldsymbol{P}^{A_1}(\chi_1 = 0)}$$
$$\cdot \frac{\otimes_{j=1}^{m}\chi_j \circ \boldsymbol{P}^{A_j}\left(\{0_1\} \times FV\left(\psi^{-1}(0), 1, 0\right)\right)}{\otimes_{j=1}^{m}\chi_j \circ \boldsymbol{P}^{A_j}(\psi = 0)}. \qquad (57)$$

The equality (53) shows us

$$IB_\varphi(1) = IB_{\chi_1}(1) \cdot IB_\psi(1),$$

and (54) and (55) tell us that

$$IC_\varphi(1;1) = IC_{\chi_1}(1;1) \cdot IC_\psi(1;1),$$
$$IC_\varphi(1;0) = IC_{\chi_1}(1;0) \cdot IC_\psi(1;0).$$

For Fussel-Vesely's importance measure, we have from (56) and (57)

$$IFV_\varphi(1;1) = IFV_{\chi_1}(1;1) \cdot IFV_\psi(1;1),$$
$$IFV_\varphi(1;0) = IFV_{\chi_1}(1;0) \cdot IFV_\psi(1;0).$$

For the restricted Fussel-Vesely's importance measures, we easily know from (47) and (48) that such a chain rule does not generally hold. An example is given in the following.

Example 6.5. We consider a series-parallel system as shown in Figure 3, of which structure function may be written as

$$\varphi(x_1, x_2, x_3, x_4, x_5) = \psi(\chi_1(x_1, x_2), \chi_2(x_3, x_4, x_5)),$$

$$\psi(s_1, s_2) = \min(s_1, s_2),$$

$$\chi_1(x_1, x_2) = \max\{\ x_1, x_2\ \},$$

$$\chi_2(x_3, x_4, x_5) = \max\{\ x_3, x_4, x_5\ \}.$$

This formula of the structure function tells us that the system is composed of two modules connected in a series form, and the modules are parallel systems.

The restricted Fussel-Vesely's importance measure of the module A_1 in the system $(S_1 \times S_2, S, \psi)$ is

$$\otimes_{j=1}^{2} \chi_j \circ \boldsymbol{P}^{A_j} \left\{ \{(s_1, s_2) : (s_1, s_2) \in MI\left(\psi^{-1}(1)\right),\ s_1 = 1\} \mid \psi = 1 \right\} = 1, \tag{58}$$

the restricted Fussel-Vesely's importance measure of the component 1 in the system $(\Omega_{A_1}, S_1, \chi_1)$ is

$$\frac{\boldsymbol{P}^{A_1}\left\{\boldsymbol{x}^{A_1} : \boldsymbol{x}^{A_1} \in MI\left(\chi_1^{-1}(1)\right),\ x_1 = 1\right\}}{\boldsymbol{P}^{A_1}(\chi_1 = 1)} = \frac{\boldsymbol{P}^{A_1}\{(1,0)\}}{\boldsymbol{P}^{A_1}(\chi_1 = 1)}, \tag{59}$$

the restricted Fussel-Vesely's importance measure of the component 1 in the system (Ω_C, S, φ) is

$$\frac{\boldsymbol{P}\{\ \boldsymbol{x}\ ;\ \boldsymbol{x} \in MI\left(\varphi^{-1}(1)\right),\ x_1 = 1\ \}}{\boldsymbol{P}(\varphi = 1)} \tag{60}$$

$$= \frac{\boldsymbol{P}\{(1,0,1,0,0),(1,0,0,1,0),(1,0,0,0,1)\}}{\boldsymbol{P}(\varphi = 1)}$$

$$= \frac{\boldsymbol{P}^{A_1}\{(1,0)\} \cdot \boldsymbol{P}^{A_2}\{(1,0,0),(0,1,0),(0,0,1)\}}{\boldsymbol{P}(\varphi = 1)}$$

$$= \frac{\boldsymbol{P}^{A_1}\{(1,0)\}}{\boldsymbol{P}^{A_1}(\chi_1 = 1)} \cdot \frac{\boldsymbol{P}^{A_1}(\chi_1 = 1) \cdot \boldsymbol{P}^{A_2}\{(1,0,0),(0,1,0),(0,0,1)\}}{\boldsymbol{P}(\varphi = 1)}, \tag{61}$$

then clearly we have

$$(58) \times (59) = \frac{\boldsymbol{P}^{A_1}\{(1,0)\}}{\boldsymbol{P}^{A_1}(\chi_1 = 1)} \neq (61),$$

which shows us that the chain rule via modular decomposition does not hold for the restricted Fussel-Vesely's importance measure.

The critical state vectors of the component 1 is given as

$$C_\varphi(1) = \{(\cdot_1, 0, 1, 1, 1), (\cdot_1, 0, 1, 1, 0), (\cdot_1, 0, 1, 0, 1), (\cdot_1, 0, 0, 1, 1),$$

$$(\cdot_1, 0, 1, 0, 0), (\cdot_1, 0, 0, 1, 0), (\cdot_1, 0, 0, 0, 1)\},$$

which tells us the criticality and the restricted Fussel-Vesely's importance measures are not generally coincident with each other for a series-parallel system.

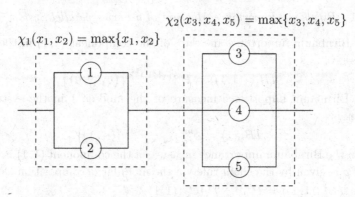

Fig. 3 A series-parallel system, where components 1 and 2 compose a parallel system and components 3, 4 and 5 compose another parallel system.

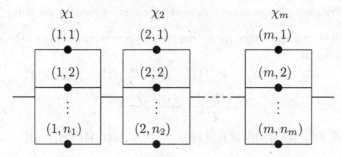

Fig. 4 A series-parallel system composed of components doubly indexed as (i, j), where i is the number of the module and j is the number of the component in the module i.

4.9 *Importance Measures of a Series-parallel System*

The chain rule of multiplication has been shown to hold for Birnbaum, criticality and Fussel-Vesely's importance measures but not for the restricted Fussel-Vesely's importance measure as shown in Example 6.5.

In this section, we calculate the importance measures for a series-parallel system φ, of which structure function is given as the following, and examine the consistency of the magnitude relations of them. The system is given by Figure 4, and is considered to have a modular decomposition $\{A_i\}_{i=1,\cdots,m}$, where $A_i = \{(i, 1), \cdots, (i, n_i)\}$ and each module is a parallel system. The organising structure ψ is a series system. The components are assumed to be stochastically independent.

4.9.1   *Birnbaum Importance Measure of a Series-parallel System*

The Birnbaum importance measure of the component $(1,1)$ in the system χ_1 is given as

$$IB_{\chi_1}((1,1)) = P^{A_1 \setminus \{(1,1)\}} \left\{ \left(\cdot_{(1,1)}, \mathbf{0} \right) \right\}.$$

The Birnbaum importance measure of the module 1 in the system ψ is given as

$$IB_{\psi}(1) = \otimes_{j=2}^{m} \chi_j \circ P^{A_j} \left\{ (\cdot_1, \mathbf{1}) \right\}.$$

Then the Birnbaum importance measure of the component $(1,1)$ in the system φ is given by the chain rule via the modular decomposition as follows.

$$\begin{aligned}
IB_{\varphi}((1,1)) &= P^{C \setminus \{(1,1)\}} \left(C_{\varphi}((1,1)) \right) \\
&= P^{A_1 \setminus \{(1,1)\}} \left\{ \left(\cdot_{(1,1)}, \mathbf{0} \right) \right\} \times \otimes_{j=2}^{m} \chi_j \circ P^{A_j} \left\{ (\cdot_1, \mathbf{1}) \right\} \\
&= IB_{\chi_1}((1,1)) \times IB_{\psi}(1).
\end{aligned}$$

4.9.2   *Criticality Importance Measure of a Series-parallel System*

The criticality importance measures of the component $(1,1)$ in the system χ_1 are given as

$$\begin{aligned}
IC_{\chi_1}((1,1);1) &= P^{A_1} \{ \{ 1_{(1,1)} \} \times C_{\chi_1}((1,1)) \mid \chi_1 = 1 \} \\
&= \frac{P^{A_1} \{ (1_{(1,1)}, \mathbf{0}) \}}{P^{A_1}(\chi_1 = 1)}, \\
IC_{\chi_1}((1,1);0) &= P^{A_1} \{ \{ 0_{(1,1)} \} \times C_{\chi_1}((1,1)) \mid \chi_1 = 0 \} \\
&= 1.
\end{aligned}$$

The criticality importance measures of the module A_1 in the system ψ are given as

$$\begin{aligned}
IC_{\psi}(1;1) &= \otimes_{j=1}^{m} \chi_j \circ P^{A_j} \{ \{ 1_1 \} \times C_{\psi}(1) \mid \psi = 1 \} \\
&= 1, \\
IC_{\psi}(1;0) &= \otimes_{j=1}^{m} \chi_j \circ P^{A_j} \{ \{ 0_1 \} \times C_{\psi}(1) \mid \psi = 0 \} \\
&= \frac{\otimes_{j=1}^{m} \chi_j \circ P^{A_j} \{ (0_1, \mathbf{1}) \}}{\otimes_{j=1}^{m} \chi_j \circ P^{A_j}(\psi = 0)}.
\end{aligned}$$

Then the criticality importance measures of the component $(1,1)$ in the system φ are given by the chain rule as follows.

$$IC_{\varphi}((1,1);1) = IC_{\chi_1}((1,1);1) \cdot IC_{\psi}(1;1) = \frac{P^{A_1} \{ (1_{(1,1)}, \mathbf{0}) \}}{P^{A_1}(\chi_1 = 1)},$$

$$IC_{\varphi}((1,1);0) = IC_{\chi_1}((1,1);0) \cdot IC_{\psi}(1;0) = \frac{\otimes_{j=1}^{m} \chi_j \circ P^{A_j} \{ (0_1, \mathbf{1}) \}}{\otimes_{j=1}^{m} \chi_j \circ P^{A_j}(\psi = 0)}.$$

4.9.3 Fussel–Vesely's Importance Measure of a Series-parallel System

Reminding Theorem 6.12, Examples 6.2 and 6.3 telling us that Fussel-Vesely's and criticality importance measures of a component of a series or parallel system are coincident with each other, we have Fussel-Vesely's importance measures of component $(1,1)$ in the system φ a follows.

$$IFV_\varphi((1,1);1) = IFV_{\chi_1}((1,1);1) \cdot IFV_\psi(1;1) = \frac{P^{A_1}\{(1_{(1,1)}, \mathbf{0})\}}{P^{A_1}(\chi_1 = 1)},$$

$$IFV_\varphi((1,1);0) = IFV_{\chi_1}((1,1);0) \cdot IFV_\psi(1;0) = \frac{\otimes_{j=1}^m \chi_j \circ P^{A_j}\{(0_1, 1)\}}{\otimes_{j=1}^m \chi_j \circ P^{A_j}(\psi = 0)}.$$

4.9.4 Consistency of Magnitude Relations of Birnbaum, Criticality and Fussel–Vesely's Importance Measures

From the above results, for the components $(1,1)$ and $(1,2)$ in the same module A_1, we have the consistency between magnitude relations of the importance measures as the following inequalities are equivalent with each other.

$$IB_\varphi((1,1)) \leqq IB_\varphi((1,2)),$$
$$IC_\varphi((1,1);1) \leqq IC_\varphi((1,2);1),$$
$$IC_\varphi((1,1);0) \leqq IC_\varphi((1,2);0),$$
$$IFV_\varphi((1,1);1) \leqq IFV_\varphi((1,2);1),$$
$$IFV_\varphi((1,1);0) \leqq IFV_\varphi((1,2);0).$$

Furthermore for the components $(1,1)$ and $(2,1)$, we have the similar consistency as the equivalent relation between the following inequalities.

$$IB_\varphi((1,1)) \leqq IB_\varphi((2,1)),$$
$$IC_\varphi((1,1);1) \leqq IC_\varphi((2,1);1),$$
$$IC_\varphi((1,1);0) \leqq IC_\varphi((2,1);0),$$
$$IFV_\varphi((1,1);1) \leqq IFV_\varphi((2,1);1),$$
$$IFV_\varphi((1,1);0) \leqq IFV_\varphi((2,1);0).$$

In other words, the first consistency follows from the consistency in a parallel system and the second from the consistency in a series system. Then, for every series-parallel system, the consistency of magnitude relation of Birnbaum and criticality importance measures ahold, and then we may use whichever importance measure. This assertion is still true for a system which is hierarchically composed of series and parallel modules.

4.9.5 *Restricted Fussel–Vesely's Importance Measures of a Series-parallel System*

The restricted Fussel-Vesely's importance measure should be directly calculated, since the chain rule via the modular decomposition does not hold for this importance measure.

Since the system considered in this section is a series-parallel system given in Figure 3, the following equalities are clear.

$$MI_\varphi((1,1),1) = \{\ \boldsymbol{x}\ ;\ x_{(1,1)} = 1, x_{(1,j)} = 0\ (j = 2, \cdots, n_1),$$
$$\boldsymbol{x}^{A_k} \in MI\left(\chi_k^{-1}(1)\right)\ (k = 2, \cdots, m)\ \},$$
$$MA_\varphi((1,1),0) = \left\{\left(\boldsymbol{0}^{A_1}, \boldsymbol{1}^{C\backslash\{A_1\}}\right)\right\},$$

where $\boldsymbol{x}^{A_k} \in MI\left(\chi^{-1}(1)\right)$ is of the following pattern,

$$x_{(k,l)} = 1\ (1 \leqq \exists l \leqq n_k)\ \text{and}\ x_{(k,j)} = 0\ (1 \leqq \forall j \leqq n_k,\ j \neq l),$$

since the module χ_k is a parallel system. $\boldsymbol{P}\left(MI_\varphi((1,1),1)\right)$ is given as follows.

$$\boldsymbol{P}\left(MI_\varphi((1,1),1)\right) = p_{(1,1)} \prod_{j=2}^{n_1} q_{(1,j)} \cdot \boldsymbol{P}^{C\backslash\{A_1\}}\left(\prod_{k=2}^{n_1} MI\left(\chi_k^{-1}(1)\right)\right),$$

and furthermore

$$\boldsymbol{P}\left(MI_\varphi((1,2),1)\right) = p_{(1,2)} \prod_{j=1,j\neq 2}^{n_1} q_{(1,j)} \cdot \boldsymbol{P}^{C\backslash\{A_1\}}\left(\prod_{k=2}^{n_1} MI\left(\chi_k^{-1}(1)\right)\right),$$

$$\boldsymbol{P}\left(MI_\varphi((2,1),1)\right) = p_{(2,1)} \prod_{j=2}^{n_2} q_{(2,j)} \cdot \boldsymbol{P}^{C\backslash\{A_2\}}\left(\prod_{k=1,k\neq 2}^{n_1} MI\left(\chi_k^{-1}(1)\right)\right).$$

Then we have the following equivalent relations.

$$\boldsymbol{P}\left(MI_\varphi((1,1),1)\right) \leqq \boldsymbol{P}\left(MI_\varphi((1,2),1)\right)$$
$$\Longleftrightarrow p_{(1,1)} \cdot q_{(1,2)} \leqq q_{(1,1)} \cdot p_{(1,2)}$$
$$\Longleftrightarrow q_{(1,2)} \leqq q_{(1,1)}$$
$$\Longleftrightarrow \boldsymbol{P}^{A_1\backslash\{(1,1)\}}\{(\cdot_{(1,1)}, \boldsymbol{0})\} \leqq \boldsymbol{P}^{A_1\backslash\{(1,2)\}}\{(\cdot_{(1,2)}, \boldsymbol{0})\}.$$

Noticing that the above examination about the components $(1,1)$, $(1,2)$ and $(2,1)$ does not lose the generality, the above equivalent relations generally mean that for two components in a same module, the magnitude relations of the importance measures are coincident with each other. For two components in different modules, however, we may not clearly say if the consistency between the magnitude relation between the restricted Fussel-Vesely's and another importance measures holds or not.

We remark here that the condition of Theorem 6.11 does not hold when $m \geqq 2$.

4.10 Risk Achievement and Reduction Worth

Not only Fussel-Vesely's importance measure but also Risk achievement worth which has been proposed by Vesely, et al. (1983) is a practically important and used as a probabilistic safety assessment method of nuclear power plants [Shimada (2004)].

The risk achievement worth of component i is given as the following.

$$\frac{P^{C\setminus\{i\}}\left\{x \in \Omega_{C\setminus\{i\}} : \varphi(0_i, x) = 0\right\}}{P\left\{x \in \Omega_C : \varphi(x) = 0\right\}} = \frac{P^{C\setminus\{i\}}\left(C_\varphi(i) \cup NC_\varphi(i;0)\right)}{P\{\varphi = 0\}}.$$

The numerator of the definition means the unreliability of the system when the component i is permanently failed, and the denominator is the unreliability of the overall system φ. Noticing that the unreliability means the risk of the system, then the ratio denotes a degree of an increase or a decrease of the system's risk triggered by the failure of the component i. We should notice that the probability in the denominator is the one on Ω_C and the probability in the numerator is on $\Omega_{C\setminus\{i\}}$, and then the above fractional formula is not a conditional probability and seems not to have a consistency.

If we replace the numerator by $P\left\{(0_i, x) \in \Omega_C : \varphi(0_i, x) = 0\right\}$, we may have alternative definition of risk achievement worth as follows.

$$\frac{P\left\{(0_i, x) \in \Omega_C : \varphi(0_i, x) = 0\right\}}{P\left\{x \in \Omega_C : \varphi(x) = 0\right\}} = P\{(0_i, x) \in \Omega_C : \varphi(0_i, x) = 0 \mid \varphi = 0\}.$$

For example, when the system is a series system, the risk achievement worth is given as

$$\frac{1}{P\{\varphi = 0\}},$$

which is constant and independent of the failure probability of component i. The alternative one is as

$$\frac{q_i}{P\{\varphi = 0\}},$$

which is the risk achievement worth with the failure probability of component i built in it.

We may think that the alternative risk achievement worth is better than the original risk achievement worth, but practical examination of the new measure is remained for future work.

We may furthermore consider a notion dual to the risk achievement worth, which is defined as the following.

$$\frac{P\left\{x \in \Omega_C : \varphi(x) = 0\right\}}{P^{C\setminus\{i\}}\left\{x \in \Omega_{C\setminus\{i\}} : \varphi(1_i, x) = 0\right\}},$$

which is called risk reduction worth.

5   Conclusion

In this paper, summarising the importance measures of binary state systems components, Birnbaum, criticality, Fussel-Vesely's and restricted Fussel-Vesely's importance measures, we have presented a few new results about the importance measures.

We especially have shown the consistency of the magnitude relations of Birnbaum, criticality and Fussel-Vesely's importance measures for a series-parallel system which is well observed system's structure in a practical situation. This consistency tells us that we may use any of Birnbaum, criticality or Fussel-Vesely's importance measure for judging the importance of the series-parallel systems components.

The former two importance measures are defined on the basis of the set of critical state vectors, which are somewhat different from the minimal path and cut vectors, but may be derived from these minimal and cur vectors. We have shown a basic algorithm for the derivation of the critical state vectors. The Fussel-Vesely's importance measure, however, is different from the former two measures and is defined on the basis of minimal path and cut vectors. It is clearly shown that the Fussel-Vesely's importance measure is given by relaxing the conditions for the definition of critical state vectors. Then it has been shown that restricted Fussel-Vesely's, Birnbaum, the criticality, Fussel-Vesely's importance measures and the risk achievement and reduction worth are defined hierarchically along with the relaxation of the conditions in each definition.

We have proposed a new importance measure called the restricted Fussel-Vesely's importance measure. This measure is easily calculated from minimal cut and path vectors and so may be used as a kind of convenience tool. However, it is remained for future work how to use practically the measure.

We have proved that the chain rule of multiplication via a modular decomposition holds for Birnbaum, Fussel-Vesely's and criticality importance measures.

When we consider an extension of these importance measures to the multi-state case, the most important point is how to define the concept corresponding to the critical state vector. This problem has been already solved, but the extension of criticality and Fussel-Vesely's importance measures is remained for future work. Furthermore, the issue how to incorporate stochastic dynamical properties of components and systems into a importance measure is also remained for future work.

References

Barlow, R.E. and Proschan, F.(1975). *Statistical Theory of Reliability and Life Testing*, HOLT, Rinehart and Winston, New York.

Barlow, R.E. and Wu, A.S.(1978). "Coherent systems with multistate components, " *Mathematics of Operations Research*, **3**, 275–281.

Barlow, R.E. and Proschan, F.(1974b). "Importance of system components and fault tree events, " *Stochastic Processes and their Applications*, **3**, 153–173.

Bisanovic, S., Hajro,M. and Samardzic, M.(2013). "Component criticality importance measures in thermal power plants design, " *International Journal of Electric, Energetic, Electronic and Communication Engineering*, **7**, No.3.

Birnbaum, Z.W., Esary, J.D. and Saunder, S.C.(1961). "Multi-component systems and structures and their reliability, " *Technometrics*, **3**, 55–77.

Birnbaum, Z.W. and Esary, J.D.(1968). "Modules of coherent binary systems, " *SIAM J. Appl. Math.*, **13**, 444–462.

Birnbaum, Z.W.(1968). "On the importance of different components in a multi-component system, " *Technical Report of University of Washington*, No.54.

Birnbaum, Z.W.(1969). "On the Importance of different components in a multi-component system," in *Multivariate Analysis-II*, Krishnaiah, P.R.(ed.) Academic Press, New York, 581–592.

Bodin, L.D.(1970). "Approximations to system reliability using a modular decomposition, " *Technometorics*, **12**, 335–344.

Cheok, M.C., Parry, G.W. and Sherry, R.R.(1998). "Use of importance measures in risk-informed regulatory applications, " *Reliability Engineering and System Safety*, **60**, 213–226.

Esary, J.D. and Proschan, F.(1963). "Coherent structures of non-identical components, " *Technometrics*, **5**, 191–209.

Espiritu, J., Coit, D. and Prakash, U.(2007). "Component criticality importance measures for the power industry, " *Electric Power Systems Research*, **77**, 407–420.

Fussel, J.B.(1975). "How to hand calculate system reliability and safety characteristics, " *IEEE Transactions on Reliability*, **R-24(3)**, 69–174.

Griffith, E.S.(1980). "Multistate Reliability Models, " *Journal of Applied Probability*, **17**, 735–744.

Huang, J., Zuo, M.J. and Fang, Z.(2003). "Multi-state consecutive-k-out-of-n systems," *IIE Transactions*, **35**, 527–534.

Kuo, W. and Zhu, X.(2012). *Importance Measures in Reliability, Risk, and Optimisation, Principles and Applications*, John Wiley and Sons, Ltd, Publication.

Levitin, G. and Lisnianski, A.(1999). "Importance and sensitivity analysis of multi-state systems using the universal generating function method, " *Reliability Engineering and System Safety*, **65**, 271–282.

Lisnianski, A. and Levitin, G.(2003). *Multi-State Systems Reliability. Assessment, Optimization and Applications*, World Scientific.

Levitin, G., Podofilini, L. and Zio, E.(2003). "Generalised importance measures for multi-state elements based on performance level restrictions, " *Reliability Engineering and System Safety*, **82**, 287–298.

Levitin, G.(2004). "A Universal Generating Function Approach for the Analysis of Multi-state Systems with Dependent Elements," *Reliability Engineering and System Safety*, **84**, 285–292.

Levitin, G.(2005). *The Universal Generating Function in Reliability Analysis and Optimization*, Springer-Verlag.

Levitin, G.(2008). "A Universal Generating Function in the Analysis of Multi-state Systems, " in *Handbook of Performability Engineering*, Misra, K.B.(ed.), Springer-Verlag, chapter 29, 447–463.

Levitin, G.(2013). "Multi-state vector-k-out-of-n systems, "*IEEE Transactions on Reliability*, **62**(3), 648–657.

Lisnianski, A., Frenkel, I. and Ding, Y.(2010). *Multi-state System Reliability Analysis and Optimization for Engineers and Industrial Managers*, Springer.

Meng, F.C.(1996). "Comparing the Importance of System Components by Some Structural Characteristics, " *IEEE Transactions on Reliability*, **45**(1), 59–65.

Mine, H.(1959). "Reliability of physical system, " *IRE Special Supplement*, **CT-6**, 138–151.

Natvig, B.(2011). *Multistate Systems Reliability Theory with Applications*, Wiley.

Natvig, B.(1982). "Two Suggestions of How to Define a Multistate Coherent System, " *Adv. Appl. Prob.*, **14**, 434–455.

El-Neweihi, E., Proschan, F. and Sethurman, J.(1978). "Multistate coherent systems, " *J. Appl. Probability*, **15**, 675–688.

Ohi, F. and Nishida, T.(1983). "Generalized multistate coherent systems, " *J. Japan Statist. Soc.*, **13**, 165–181.

Ohi, F. and Nishida, T.(1984a). "On Multistate Coherent Systems, " *IEEE Transactions on Reliability*, **R-33**, 284–288.

Ohi, F. and Nishida, T.(1984b). "Multistate Systems in Reliability Theory, " *Stochastic Models in Reliability Theory, Lecture Notes in Economics and Mathematical Systems* 235, Springer-Verlag, 12–22.

Ohi, F.(2010). "Multistate Coherent Systems, " In *Stochastic Reliability Modeling, Optimization and Applications*, Nakamura S, Nakagawa T (eds), World Science, 3–34.

Ohi, F.(2012). "Multi-State Coherent Systems and Modules – Basic Properties –," in *ADVANCED reliability and maintenance modeling V, Basis of Reliability Analysis, Nanjing, China, 1-3 November 2012/12/02*, Mc Grow Hill Education, Taiwan, 374–381.

Ohi, F.(2013). "Lattice Set Theoretic Treatment of Multi-state Coherent Systems," *Reliability Engineering and System Safety*, **116**, 86–90.

Ohi, F.(2014a). "Steady-State Bounds for Multi-state Systems' Reliability via Modular Decompositions," *Applied Stochastic Models in Business and Industry*, **31**, 307–324, JUNE.

Ohi, F.(2014b). "Stochastic Bounds for Multi-state Coherent Systems via Modular Decompositions - Case of Partially Ordered State Spaces -," in *AD-*

VANCED reliability and maintenance modeling VI, Basis of Reliability Analysis, Hokkaido, Japan, 21-23 August, Mc Grow Hill Education, Taiwan, 357–364.

Ohi, F.(2015). "Stochastic evaluation methods of multi-state systems via modular decompositions - A case of partially ordered states -," in the *Proceedings of The Ninth International Conference on Mathematical Methods in Reliability: Theory, Methods and Applications (MMR2015)*, 545–552.

Shimada, Y.(2004). "A Probabilistic Safety Assessment Approach toward Identification of Information on Safety Significant Adverse Events at Overseas Nuclear Power Plants, " *INSS journal,* **11**, 87–94.

Ushakov, I.(1987). "Optimal Standby Problem and a Universal Generating Function, " *Soviet Journal Computer and System Science*, **25**, 61–73.

Ushakov, I.(2000). "The Method of Generalized Generating Functions, " *European Journal of Operations Research*, **125**(2), 316–323.

Vesely, W.E., Davis, T.C., Denning, R.S. and Saltos, N.(1983). "Measures of Risk Importance And Their Applications, " *NUREG/CR-3385, BMI-2103, RX.*

Yu, K., Koren, I. and Guo, Y.(1994). "Generalized Multistate Monotone Coherent Systems, " *IEEE Transactions on Reliability*, **43**, 242–250.

Chapter 7

Proposal of Calculation Method for Reliability of Toroidal Connected-$(1,2)$-or-$(2,1)$-out-of-(m,n):F Lattice System with Markov Chain

Taishin Nakamura[1], Hisashi Yamamoto[1], Takashi Shinzato[2]
Xiao Xiao[1] and Tomoaki Akiba [3]

[1] *Faculty of System Design,*
Tokyo Metropolitan University,

[2]*Mori Arinori Center for Higher Education and Global Mobility,*
Hitotsubashi University,

[3]*Faculty of Social Systems Science,*
Chiba Institute of Technology

1 Introduction

A linear (circular) consecutive-k-out-of-n:F system consists of n components arranged linearly (circularly). This system fails if and only if at least k consecutive components fail. Salvia and Lasher (1990) extended consecutive-k-out-of-n:F system to two-dimensional system, which is called the consecutive-k^2-out-of-n^2:F system. Boehme et al. (1992) have generalized the consecutive-k^2-out-of-n^2:F system and defined a linear (circular) connected-X-out-of-(m,n):F lattice system.

This linear system consists of $m \times n$ components arranged in m rows and n columns. The parameter X means failure conditions of the system. In this paper, we consider a connected-$(1,2)$-or-$(2,1)$-out-of-(m,n):F lattice system, which is a special case of connected-X-out-of-(m,n):F lattice system. The system fails if and only if there exist at least 2 consecutive failed components on each row or each column. For the connected-$(1, 2)$-or-$(2, 1)$-out-of-(m, n):F lattice system, previous researches [Yamamoto (1996); Higashiyama (2002); Yamamoto et al. (2008); Nakamura et al.] have provided some calculating methods for reliability evaluation. They focused on linear systems (rectangle) or circular systems (cylinder). However, there are practical systems which cannot be evaluated by existing system models because they have a specific shape. Therefore, we consider a toroidal system.

Example 7.1. (High-speed electron accelerator system in the acceleration experiment of a synchrotron): We consider a high-speed electron accelerator system in the acceleration experiment of a synchrotron. Magnetic field generating apparatuses are located in lattice patterns as a torus. Even if one magnetic field generating apparatus fails, the high-speed electron accelerator system is working. However, the accelerator system fails if and only if two adjacent magnetic field generating apparatuses simultaneously fail. This is because the acceleration control of charged particles may not be working well.

In this paper, we consider the toroidal system, which is called a toroidal connected-$(1, 2)$-or-$(2, 1)$-out-of-(m, n):F lattice system (Tor/(m, n):F system) [Nakamura et al. (2016)]. The purpose of this study is to develop a method for calculating the reliability of Tor/(m, n):F system. So as to calculate it efficiently, we use the finite Markov chain embedding approach and we closed-formulas for the reliability of Tor/(m, n):F system in the special cases. Furthermore, we compare our proposed method with the exhaustive enumeration method in order to verify the effectiveness of the proposed method using numerical experiments.

2   Previous Study

For the consecutive-k-out-of-n:F system, many studies in the past decades have proposed various calculation methods like the combinatorial approach, the recursive equation, etc. However the Markov chain embedded approach, simply called Markov approach, which was first employed by Fu and Hu (1987) and summarized by Zhao et al. (2011), has recently attracted a lot of attention of researchers because of its calculation effectiveness. In this paper, we apply the method to the reliability evaluation of Tor/(m, n):F system.

Next, we introduce Markov approach for the linear consecutive-k-out-of-n:F system [Fu and Hu (1987)]. We propose the calculation method based on Markov approach[Fu and Hu (1987)]. We denote j-th component from the left of the linearly arranged components by component j. For $j = 1, 2, \cdots, n$, let p_j be reliability of component j and q_j be unreliability of component j, where $p_j + q_j = 1$. Then, we consider Markov chain $K(j)$ defined on a state space $\mathcal{S} = \{0, 1, \cdots, k\}$, for $j = 1, 2, \cdots, n$. In the consecutive-k-out-of-n:F system, $K(j) \in \{0, 1, \cdots, k - 1\}$ represents the number of consecutive failed components from component j toward component 1 when the consecutive-k-out-of-j:F system works. For example, $K(j) = i$ means that component j is failed, component $j - 1$ is failed, $\cdots$, component $j - i + 1$ is failed, component $j - i$ is working and there are more than or equal to k consecutive failed components between component 1 and component $j - i - 1$. In particular, $K(j) = 0$ means that component j is working and there are more than or equal to k consecutive failed components between component 1 and component $j - 1$. When $K(j)$ takes k, there are more than or equal to k consecutive failed components from component j, that is, the consecutive-k-out-of-j:F system fails.

For $j = 1, 2, \cdots, n$, we denote $m_{rs}^{(j)}$ by the transition probability from state r to state s and it is given by:

$$m_{rs}^{(j)} = Pr\{K(j) = s | K(j - 1) = r\}, \tag{1}$$

where $r, s \in \mathcal{S}$. We can rewrite Eq. (1) into the following form:

$$m_{rs}^{(j)} = \begin{cases} p_j & \text{if}(r, s) \in \{(1, 1), (2, 1), \cdots, (k, 1)\}, \\ q_j & \text{if}(r, s) \in \{(1, 2), (2, 3), \cdots, (k, k + 1)\}, \\ 1 & \text{if}(r, s) \in \{(k + 1, k + 1)\}, \\ 0 & \text{otherwise.} \end{cases} \tag{2}$$

Then, the transition probability matrix is

$$\Lambda^{(j)} = \left(m_{rs}^{(j)}\right) \in \mathbf{R}^{(k+1) \times (k+1)}. \tag{3}$$

As a result, the reliability of the linear consecutive-k-out-of-n:F system ($R(n)$) can be expressed as

$$R(n) = (\vec{\pi}_0)^{\mathrm{T}} \prod_{j=1}^{n} \Lambda^{(j)} \vec{u}, \tag{4}$$

where $\vec{\pi}_0 = (1, 0, 0, \cdots, 0) \left(\in \mathbf{R}^{(k+1)}\right)$ means the initial column vector, and $\vec{u} = (1, 1, \cdots, 1, 0) \left(\in \mathbf{R}^{(k+1)}\right)$.

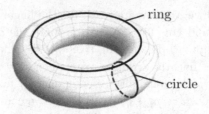

Fig. 1   Definition of circle and ring.

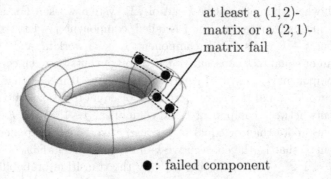

Fig. 2   Example of Tor/(m, n):F system failure.

Zhao et al. (2011) applied Accelerated Scan Finite Markov Chain Imbedding (AS-FMCI) to this method. AS-FMCI can decrease the number of matrix multiplications. Consequently, they can calculate the system reliability faster. In particular, assuming all components are i.i.d., we can employ Fast-Matrix-Power Algorithm, which is used by Lin (2004). This algorithm achieves logarithmic running time. In this study, by utilizing the Markov approach [Fu and Hu (1987)], we develop the calculation method based on Markov approach.

3   Reliability of Tor/(m, n):F System

In this section, according to Nakamura et al. (2016), we define the reliability of Tor/(m, n):F system. The components in this system are described using the intersections of m circles and n rings, where "circle" and "ring" are shown in Fig. 1. This system fails if and only if at least consecutive components pair simultaneously fails, that is, failure patterns are two consecutive components in a ring, shortly (1,2)-matrix, or two consecutive components in a circle, shortly (2,1)-matrix, as shown in Fig. 2.

In this paper, we denote the component located at i-th circle and j-th ring by component(i, j). For $i = 0, 1, \cdots, m$ and $j = 0, 1, \cdots, n$, let x_{ij} be component state of component (i, j) as follows:

$$x_{ij} = \begin{cases} 0 \text{ if component } (i, j) \text{ is working,} \\ 1 \text{ if component } (i, j) \text{ is failed.} \end{cases} \tag{5}$$

For convenience'sake, $x_{i0} = x_{in}$ for $i = 1, 2, \cdots, m$ and $x_{0j} = x_{mj}$ for $j = 1, 2, \cdots, n$. Here, we define the binary variable Y_{mn} and Z_{mn}, respectively as follows:

$$Y_{mn} \equiv \prod_{i=1}^{m} \prod_{j=1}^{n} (1 - x_{i-1,j} \cdot x_{ij}), \tag{6}$$

$$Z_{mn} \equiv \prod_{i=1}^{m} \prod_{j=1}^{n} (1 - x_{i,j-1} \cdot x_{ij}). \tag{7}$$

Then, let $R(m, n)$ be the reliability of Tor/(m, n):F system, and it is defined by:

$$R(m, n) \equiv Pr\{Y_{mn} \cdot Z_{mn} = 1\}, \tag{8}$$

where $Y_{mn} \cdot Z_{mn} = 1$ means that Tor/(m, n):F system is working. In the following sections, we will assume that

1) Each component and the entire system can only be in one of two states: working or failed.
2) Each of the components operates s-independently.
3) All components reliabilities are given.

4   Proposal of Method for Calculating Reliability of Tor/(m, n):F System

In this section, we describe the method for calculating the reliability of Tor/(m, n):F system based on Markov approach. The basic idea in Markov approach is based on the idea of Nakamura et al., which was proposed Markov approach for the reliability of the circular connected-$(1, 2)$-or-$(2, 1)$-out-of-(m, n):F lattice system (Cir/(m, n):F system) with identical components. As stated in the preceding section, Fu and Hu (1987) determine the state space by the length of the latest consecutive failure. On the other hand, Nakamura et al. determine it by the number of failed components and their positions in one circle. In order to calculate the reliability of

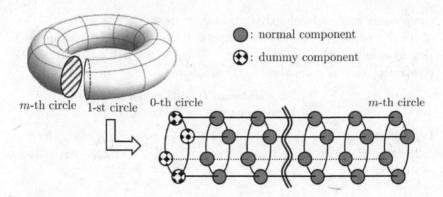

Fig. 3   Tor/(m,n):F system and a special Cir/$(m+1,n)$:F system made a cut between 1-st circle and m-th circle.

Tor/(m,n):F system, we present Markov approach when components are independent and not necessarily identical.

We explain basic ideas for our proposed methods. First, we make a cut in the Tor/(m,n):F system between 1-st circle and m-th circle. In order to bond 1-st circle and m-th circle later, we add virtually n components $(0,1),(0,2),\cdots,(0,n)$ as dummy components in 0-th circle. Note that component $(0,j)$ and component (m,j) are coincident for $j = 1, 2, \cdots, n$; $x_{0j} = x_{mj}$. As a result, we regard this system as Cir/$(m+1,n)$:F system as shown in Fig. 3. However, this system differs from an ordinary Cir/$(m+1,n)$:F system because 0-th circle should be coincident with m-th circle. Second, we need to calculate the reliability of the special Cir/$(m+1,n)$:F system in which component states in both edge circles are consistent. Note that Tor/(m,n):F system can be be expressed by the above special Cir/$(m+1,n)$:F systems. Finally, we can obtain the reliability of Tor/(m,n):F system by summing up these reliabilities.

We consider Markov chain $\{K(i); i = 1, 2, \cdots, m\}$ defined on a state space $\mathcal{S}$. The state space is comprised uniquely of circle states in this system. We can transform state vector of the i-th circle component $(\vec{x}_i)$ into state numbers (S_i) as follows:

$$S_i = 1 + \sum_{j=1}^{n} 2^{j-1} x_{ij}, \qquad (9)$$

where the state of the i-th circle is described by the n-dimensional vector $\vec{x}_i = (x_{i1}, x_{i2}, \cdots, x_{in}) \in \{0,1\}^n$. For example, if $n = 3$ and $\vec{x}_i = (0,0,0)$, then $S_i = 1$, and if $\vec{x}_i = (0,0,1)$, then $S_i = 5$. Consequently, we can change a binary-coded from $\vec{x}_i$ to a decimal number S_i in Eq. (9). Hence,

$K(i)$ presents the number of failed components and their positions in i-th circle when the special $\text{Cir}/(i, n)$:F system works. In other words, $K(i) = a$ means that special $\text{Cir}/(i, n)$:F system works and the state of i-th circle is a.

Next, we consider the transition from the state of the $(i-1)$-th circle to the state of the i-th circle. For $a = 1, 2, \cdots, 2^n$ and $b = 1, 2, \cdots, 2^n$, let $m_{ba}^{(i)}$ denote the probability that makes a transition from state a in the $(i-1)$-th circle to state b in the i-th circle. The probability is given by:

$$m_{ba}^{(i)} = Pr\left\{\{K(i) = b\} \cap \{\text{sub-cir}/(2, n)\text{:F system is working}\} \\ \mid \{K(i-1) = a\}\right\}, \quad (10)$$

where $a = 1 + \sum_{j=1}^{n} 2^{j-1} x_{i-1,j}$, $b = 1 + \sum_{j=1}^{n} 2^{j-1} x_{i,j}$. The sub-cir$/(2, n)$:F system in Eq. (10) consists of $(i-1)$-th circle and i-th circle and it fails if and only if there exist at least 2 consecutive failed components. When the sub-cir$/(2, n)$:F system consisting of $(i-2)$-th circle and $(i-1)$-th circle is working, whether or not the sub-cir$/(2, n)$:F system consisting of $(i-1)$-th circle and i-th circle is failed is determined by the state of the $(i-1)$-th circle and the state of the i-th circle. Hence, Eq. (10) holds. For $i = 1, 2, \cdots, m$ and $j = 1, 2, \cdots, n$, let p_{ij} be reliability of component (i, j) and q_{ij} be unreliability of component (i, j), where $p_{ij} + q_{ij} = 1$. Accordingly, we can rewrite Eq. (10) as

$$m_{ba}^{(i)} = \prod_{k=1}^{n} p_{ik}^{(1-x_{ik})} q_{ik}^{x_{ik}} \times \phi(\vec{x}_i, \vec{x}_{i-1}), \quad (11)$$

where

$$\phi(\vec{x}_i, \vec{x}_{i-1}) = \prod_{j=1}^{n} [(1 - x_{ij} \cdot x_{i-1,j})(1 - x_{ij} \cdot x_{i,j-1})(1 - x_{i-1,j} \cdot x_{i-1,j-1})],$$

and $\phi(\vec{x}_i, \vec{x}_{i-1})$ presents the state of the sub-cir$/(2, n)$:F system, namely, if the system is working, it takes 1 and if the system is failed, it takes 0. From Eq. (11), the transition probability matrix is given by:

$$M^{(i)} = \left(m_{ba}^{(i)}\right) \in \mathbf{R}^{2^n \times 2^n}. \quad (12)$$

If there are at least 2 consecutive failed components in i-th circle; $\prod_{j=1}^{n}(1 - x_{i,j-1} \cdot x_{ij}) = 0$, then all of the elements in the corresponding S_i-th row in $M^{(i)}$ are zero. Similarly, if there are at least 2 consecutive failed components in $(i-1)$-th circle, then all of the elements in the corresponding S_{i-1}-th column in $M^{(i)}$ are zero. Thus, we can reduce the dimension of the transition probability matrix$\left(M^{(i)}\right)$ by deleting any rows or columns with all zero values and increase the efficiency of the computation. Then, let $M_{part}^{(i)}$ be a partial transition probability matrix and we can get it by eliminating any rows or columns with all zero values from the original transition probability matrix $(M^{(i)})$. For example, when $n = 3$, the transition probability matrix is

$$M^{(i)} = \begin{pmatrix} p_{i,1}p_{i,2}p_{i,3} & p_{i,1}p_{i,2}p_{i,3} & p_{i,1}p_{i,2}p_{i,3} & 0 & p_{i,1}p_{i,2}p_{i,3} & 0\ 0\ 0 \\ q_{i,1}p_{i,2}p_{i,3} & 0 & q_{i,1}p_{i,2}p_{i,3} & 0 & q_{i,1}p_{i,2}p_{i,3} & 0\ 0\ 0 \\ p_{i,1}q_{i,2}p_{i,3} & p_{i,1}q_{i,2}p_{i,3} & 0 & 0 & p_{i,1}q_{i,2}p_{i,3} & 0\ 0\ 0 \\ 0 & 0 & 0 & 0 & 0 & 0\ 0\ 0 \\ p_{i,1}p_{i,2}q_{i,3} & p_{i,1}p_{i,2}q_{i,3} & p_{i,1}p_{i,2}q_{i,3} & 0 & 0 & 0\ 0\ 0 \\ 0 & 0 & 0 & 0 & 0 & 0\ 0\ 0 \\ 0 & 0 & 0 & 0 & 0 & 0\ 0\ 0 \\ 0 & 0 & 0 & 0 & 0 & 0\ 0\ 0 \end{pmatrix}. \tag{13}$$

In Eq. (13), the 4,6,7 and 8-th rows and columns have only zero values. Thus, by eliminating elements from the original transition probability matrix $(M^{(i)})$, the partial transition probability matrix $M_{part}^{(i)}$ is obtained as

$$M_{part}^{(i)} = \begin{pmatrix} p_{i,1}p_{i,2}p_{i,3} & p_{i,1}p_{i,2}p_{i,3} & p_{i,1}p_{i,2}p_{i,3} & p_{i,1}p_{i,2}p_{i,3} \\ q_{i,1}p_{i,2}p_{i,3} & 0 & q_{i,1}p_{i,2}p_{i,3} & q_{i,1}p_{i,2}p_{i,3} \\ p_{i,1}q_{i,2}p_{i,3} & p_{i,1}q_{i,2}p_{i,3} & 0 & p_{i,1}q_{i,2}p_{i,3} \\ p_{i,1}p_{i,2}q_{i,3} & p_{i,1}p_{i,2}q_{i,3} & p_{i,1}p_{i,2}q_{i,3} & 0 \end{pmatrix}. \tag{14}$$

Next, we calculate the reliability of the special Cir/$(m+1,n)$:F system that each component state in both edge circles are consistent. By summing these reliabilities, we can obtain the reliability of Tor/(m,n):F system. Let $R(m,n)$ be the reliability of Tor/(m,n):F system. Here, since it can be expressed by trace of the m-th power of transition probability matrix, we propose a theorem for obtaining the reliability of Tor/(m,n):F system.

Theorem 7.1.

$$R(m,n) = \mathrm{Tr}\left(\prod_{i=1}^{m} M_{part}^{(i)}\right), \tag{15}$$

where $M_{part}^{(i)} \in \mathbf{R}^{C(n) \times C(n)}$, and $C(n)$, the dimension of the partial transition probability matrix, is determined as follows:
For $j = 4, 5, \cdots, n$,

$$C(j) = C(j-1) + C(j-2), \tag{16}$$

with the boundary conditions $C(2) = 3$ and $C(3) = 4$.

Proof. First, we will prove Eq. (16). Let $R_j^C(p)$ be the reliability of a circular consecutive-2-out-of-j:F system with common component reliability p. Then, Lin (2004) provided the following recursive equation for $R_j^C(p)$ for $j = 3, 4, \cdots, n$,

$$R_j^C(p) = pR_{j-1}^C(p) + pqR_{j-2}^C(p). \tag{17}$$

If $p = q = \frac{1}{2}$, all possible system states occur with equal probability. Hence, from Eq. (17), the number of working systems in a circular consecutive-2-out-of-j:F system is equal to $C(j) = 2^j R_j^C(1/2)$ [Cowell (2015)]. Thus, from Eq. (17), we can prove Eq. (16). Note that the boundary conditions $C(2) = 3$ and $C(3) = 4$ were obtained from Lin (2004).

Next, we define $F(h, l)$ by the reliability of a special Cir/$(m + 1, n)$:F system in which the state of the 0-th circle is l and the state of the m-th circle is h, where $l, h \in \mathcal{S} = \{1, 2, \cdots, 2^n\}$. Then, we obtain $F(h, l)$ as follows:

$$F(h, l) = (\vec{\pi}_m(h))^{\mathrm{T}} \left(\prod_{i=1}^m M^{(i)} \right) \vec{\pi}_0(l), \tag{18}$$

where $\vec{\pi}_0(l)^{\mathrm{T}} = (0, \cdots, 0, 1, 0, \cdots, 0) \in \mathbf{R}^{2^n}$ means the initial column vector which has the element 1 at the l-th position and the others are zero and $\vec{\pi}_m(h)^{\mathrm{T}} = (0, \cdots, 0, 1, 0, \cdots, 0) \in \mathbf{R}^{2^n}$ means the final column vector which has the element 1 at the h-th position and the others are zero. Then, $F(h, l)$ corresponds exactly to the reliability of the special Cir/$(m+1, n)$:F system whose state of 0-th circle is h and state of m-th circle is l. Note that for Tor/(m, n):F system, 0-th circle is coincident with m-th circle, namely, $h = l$ in Eq. (18). Hence, we can obtain the reliability of Tor/(m, n):F system by summing the reliabilities of the special Cir/$(m + 1, n)$:F systems as follows:

$$R(m, n) = \sum_{h=1}^{2^n} F(h, h) = \sum_{h=1}^{2^n} (\vec{\pi}_m(h))^{\mathrm{T}} \left(\prod_{i=1}^m M^{(i)} \right) \vec{\pi}_0(h). \tag{19}$$

If there are 2 consecutive failed components in m-th circle (0-th circle), then the reliabilities of the special Cir/$(m+1, n)$:F systems are equal to 0. Hence, we only have to sum the reliabilities of the special Cir/$(m + 1, n)$:F systems whose m-th circle (0-th circle) has no 2 consecutive failed components. Here, we denote a set of states numbers of the working systems in a circle by $\mathcal{S}_w$ and it is given by:

$$\mathcal{S}_w = \left\{ s \mid s = 1 + \sum_{j=1}^n 2^{j-1} x_j, (x_{j-1} \cdot x_j) = 0 (j = 1, 2, \cdots, n) \right\},$$

$$\tag{20}$$

where $x_0 = x_n$. Then, Eq. (19) can be written as

$$R(m,n) = \sum_{h \in \mathcal{S}_w} (\vec{\pi}_m(h))^{\mathrm{T}} \left(\prod_{i=1}^{m} M^{(i)} \right) \vec{\pi}_0(h)$$

$$= \sum_{h \in \mathcal{S}_w} (\vec{\pi}_m(h))^{\mathrm{T}} \left(\prod_{i=1}^{m} M_{part}^{(i)} \right) \vec{\pi}_0(h). \tag{21}$$

Note that the rows and the columns with all zero values do not affect matrix multiplications. Since Eq. (21) means the sum of the elements on the diagonal from the upper left to the lower right of the matrix multiplication $\left(\prod_{i=1}^{m} M_{part}^{(i)} \right)$. Theorem 7.1 has been proved. ∎

Next, we present closed-formulas for the reliability of Tor/$(m,3)$:F system and Tor/$(m,4)$:F system with identical components by using the proposed method.

Corollary 7.1. If $p_{i,1} = p_{i,2} = p_{i,3} = p$ and $q_{i,1} = q_{i,2} = q_{i,3} = q$ for $i = 1, 2, \cdots, m$, then

$$R(m,3) = 2 \left(-p^2 q \right)^m + \left(\frac{1}{2} p^2 \left(1 + q - \alpha \right) \right)^m + \left(\frac{1}{2} p^2 \left(1 + q + \alpha \right) \right)^m,$$

where $\alpha = \sqrt{p^2 + 8pq + 4q^2}$.

Proof. We present the partial transition probability matrix in the case of $n = 3$ in Eq. (14). If all components are i.i.d., then $M_{part}^{(1)} = M_{part}^{(2)} = \cdots = M_{part}^{(m)} = M_{part}$. Thus, M_{part} can be obtained from Eq. (14) as follows:

$$M_{part} = \begin{pmatrix} p^3 & p^3 & p^3 & p^3 \\ p^2 q & 0 & p^2 q & p^2 q \\ p^2 q & p^2 q & 0 & p^2 q \\ p^2 q & p^2 q & p^2 q & 0 \end{pmatrix}. \tag{22}$$

From the eigenvalue equation of Eq. (22), we can obtain four eigenvalues $\lambda_1, \lambda_2, \lambda_3 and \lambda_4$ as follows:

$$\lambda_1 = -p^2 q,$$
$$\lambda_2 = -p^2 q,$$
$$\lambda_3 = \frac{1}{2} p^2 \left(1 + q - \sqrt{p^2 + 8pq + 4q^2} \right),$$
$$\lambda_4 = \frac{1}{2} p^2 \left(1 + q + \sqrt{p^2 + 8pq + 4q^2} \right).$$

As is well known, the trace of a matrix is equal to the sum of its eigenvalues, that is,

$$R(m,3) = \text{Tr}\left((M_{part})^m\right)$$
$$= (\lambda_1)^m + (\lambda_2)^m + (\lambda_3)^m + (\lambda_4)^m. \tag{23}$$

Therefore, Corollary 7.1 has been proved. ∎

Corollary 7.2. If $p_{i,1} = p_{i,2} = p_{i,3} = p_{i,4} = p$ and $q_{i,1} = q_{i,2} = q_{i,3} = q_{i,4} = q$ for $i = 1, 2, \cdots, m$, then

$$R(m,4) = 2\left(-p^3 q\right)^m + \left(-\frac{1}{2}p^2 q\left(1 + \sqrt{p^2 + 6pq + q^2}\right)\right)^m$$
$$+ \left(-\frac{1}{2}p^2 q\left(1 - \sqrt{p^2 + 6pq + q^2}\right)\right)^m + (\beta_1)^m + (\beta_2)^m + (\beta_3)^m, \tag{24}$$

where β_1, β_2 and β_3 are the solutions to the following characteristic equation:

$$x^3 + \left(-p^4 - 3p^3 q - p^2 q^2\right)x^2 + \left(-p^7 q + p^6 q^2 + p^5 q^3\right)x + p^9 q^3 = 0. \tag{25}$$

Proof. When $n = 4$, M_{part} can be obtained by using Theorem 7.1 as follows:

$$M_{part} = \begin{pmatrix} p^4 & p^4 & p^4 & p^4 & p^4 & p^4 & p^4 \\ p^3 q & 0 & p^3 q & p^3 q & 0 & p^3 q & p^3 q \\ p^3 q & p^3 q & 0 & p^3 q & p^3 q & p^3 q & 0 \\ p^3 q & p^3 q & p^3 q & 0 & 0 & p^3 q & p^3 q \\ p^2 q^2 & 0 & p^2 q^2 & 0 & 0 & p^2 q^2 & p^2 q^2 \\ p^3 q & p^3 q & p^3 q & p^3 q & p^3 q & 0 & 0 \\ p^2 q^2 & p^2 q^2 & 0 & p^2 q^2 & p^2 q^2 & 0 & 0 \end{pmatrix}. \tag{26}$$

From the eigenvalue equation of Eq. (26), we can obtain the characteristic equation as follows:

$$p^{20}q^8 - 2p^{18}q^6 x + p^{16}q^8 x + p^{16}q^4 x^2 - 4p^{15}q^5 x^2 - 6p^{14}q^6 x^2$$
$$+4p^{13}q^3 x^3 + 3p^{12}q^4 x^3 - 4p^{11}q^5 x^3 - 2p^{10}q^6 x^3 + 6p^{10}q^2 x^4$$
$$+12p^9 q^3 x^4 + 5p^8 q^4 x^4 + 4p^7 qx^5 + 8p^6 q^2 x^5$$
$$+4p^5 q^3 x^5 + p^4 q^4 x^5 + p^4 x^6 - x^7 = 0,$$
$$\left(p^3 q + x\right)^2 \left(p^5 q^3 - p^3 qx - p^2 q^2 x - x^2\right)$$
$$+ \left(p^9 q^3 - p^7 qx - p^6 q^2 x + p^5 q^3 x - p^4 x^2 - 3p^3 qx^2 - p^2 q^2 x^2 + x^3\right) = 0. \tag{27}$$

Then, seven eigenvalues $\lambda_1, \lambda_2, \cdots, \lambda_7$ are

$$\lambda_1 = -p^3 q,$$
$$\lambda_2 = -p^3 q,$$
$$\lambda_3 = -\frac{1}{2}p^2 q \left(1 + \sqrt{p^2 + 6pq + q^2}\right),$$
$$\lambda_4 = -\frac{1}{2}p^2 q \left(1 - \sqrt{p^2 + 6pq + q^2}\right),$$

and $\lambda_5, \lambda_6, \lambda_7$ are the solutions of the following characteristic equation.

$$x^3 + \left(-p^4 - 3p^3 q - p^2 q^2\right) x^2 + \left(-p^7 q + p^6 q^2 + p^5 q^3\right) x + p^9 q^3 = 0.$$

Thus,

$$\begin{aligned} R(m,4) &= \text{Tr}\left((M_{part})^m\right) \\ &= (\lambda_1)^m + (\lambda_2)^m + (\lambda_3)^m + (\lambda_4)^m + (\lambda_5)^m + (\lambda_6)^m + (\lambda_7)^m. \end{aligned}$$
(28)

Therefore, Corollary 7.2 has been proved. ∎

5 Evaluation

In this section, we evaluate our proposed method for calculating the reliability of Tor/(m,n):F system. First, we consider the complexity of computing. Since the state space $\mathcal{S}$ has at most 2^n elements, the complexity of computing $R(m,n)$ is $O(m2^n)$. Second, we consider memory requirements for the proposed method. Since the dimension of the partial transition probability matrix is at most $2^n \times 2^n$, the maximum memory required is $O(2^{2n})$. Eqs. (6) and (7) show that the number of circle (m) and the number of ring (n) are symmetric. If we replace m and n, we can obtain the same value as the system reliability. Accordingly, by utilizing the symmetry, we can calculate it more effectively.

Next, we investigate the computation time for obtaining the reliability of Tor/(m,n):F system in order to compare with the exhaustive enumeration method. All experiments were executed using a Windows 10, Intel Core i5, 3.20GHz, 8GB and MATLAB R2016a. In the numerical experiments, component reliabilities are given as follows:

$$p_{ij} = \begin{cases} 0.99 \text{ if } (i+j) \text{ is even,} \\ 0.95 \text{ if } (i+j) \text{ is odd,} \end{cases}$$
(29)

for $i = 1, 2, \cdots, m$ and $j = 1, 2, \cdots, n$. Table 1 shows the comparison of the computation time of our proposed method with the exhaustive enumeration

Table 1   Comparison of computation time (sec.)

(m, n)	(3,3)	(4,4)	(10,10)	(14,14)	(18,18)
Enumeration method	0.04	21.54	N/A	N/A	N/A
Proposed method	0.03	0.04	0.07	1.96	146.74
System reliability	0.989	0.985	0.912	0.835	0.743

Table 2   Computation time when $m = 500$ (sec.)

n	7	9	11	13	15
Proposed method	0.125	0.382	1.941	13.095	101.071

Table 3   Computation time when $n = 12$ (sec.)

m	100	300	500	700	900
Proposed method	1.128	3.073	4.886	6.78	8.576

method. eN/Af in the table means that computation time is larger than 1800 seconds. As shown in Table 1, the exhaustive enumeration method took about 21 seconds for the reliability of Tor/(4, 4):F system, because all states must be checked. On the other hand, our proposed method took 0.04 seconds. Thus, our proposed method is more effective than the exhaustive enumeration method in terms of computation time.

Next, in Table 2, we show results for systems fixed m, and in Table 3, we show results for systems fixed n. Tables 2 and 3 clearly indicate that our proposed method is effective, especially for systems with large m. However, even if we interchange parameter m and parameter n, the changed system remains essentially the same . Hence, if the smaller value of the circle or ring is m, our proposed method is effective when the number of circle is large or the number of ring is large.

6 Conclusion

In this paper, so as to evaluate the toroidal system, we consider the toroidal connected-$(1, 2)$-or-$(2, 1)$-out-of-(m, n):F lattice system. We have proposed a calculating method based on Markov chain for the reliability of Tor/(m, n):F system. We showed that the reliability of Tor/(m, n):F system is obtained by summing the reliabilities of special Cir/$(m + 1, n)$:F systems whose both edge circles are consistent. The basic idea of the proposed method is based on the idea of Nakamura et al. In order to compare our proposed method with the exhaustive enumeration method, we performed numerical experiments. In practice, the numerical experiments showed that the proposed method was more efficient than the exhaustive enumeration method. In addition, we derived closed-formulas for the reliability of Tor/(m, n):F system in the special cases.

In our future work, in order to calculate the reliability of Tor/(m, n):F system more efficiently, we will apply the proposed method to Accelerated Scan Finite Markov Chain Imbedding (AS-FMCI) (2011).

References

Salvia, A. A. and Lasher, W. C. (1990). "2-dimensional consecutive-k-out-of-n:F models," *IEEE Transactions on Reliability*, **R–39**, 3, 382–385.

Boehme, T. K., Kossow, A. and Preuss, W. (1992). "A generalization of consecutive-k-out-of-n:F system," *IEEE Transactions on Reliability*, **R–41**, 3, 451–457.

Yamamoto, H. (1996). "Reliability of a connected-(r_1, s_1)-or-(r_2, s_2)-or-..-or-(r_k, s_k)-out-of-(m, n):F lattice system," *Microelectronics Reliability*, **36**, 2, 151–168.

Higashiyama, Y. (2002). "A recursive method for computing the reliability of circular consecutive 2-out-of-(m, n):F system," *International Journal of Reliability, Quality and Safety Engineering*, **9**, 3, 229–235.

Yamamoto, H., Akiba, T., Nagatsuka, H. and Moriyama, Y. (2008). "Recursive algorithm for the reliability of a connected-$(1, 2)$-or-$(2, 1)$-out-of-(m, n):F lattice system," *European Journal of Operational Research*, **188**, 3, 854–864.

Nakamura, T., Yamamoto, H., Shinzato, T., Xiao, X. and Akiba, T. "Reliability of a circular connected-$(1, 2)$-or-$(2, 1)$-out-of-(m, n):F lattice system with identical components," (submitted to IEICE Transactions).

Nakamura, T., Yamamoto, H., Shinzato, T., Akiba, T. and Xiao, X. "Reliability of a toroidal connected-$(1, 2)$-or-$(2, 1)$-out-of-(m, n):F lattice system," *Proceedings of the 7th Asia-Pacific International Symposium on Advanced Reliability and Maintenance Modeling (APARM 2016)*, 399–406.

Fu, J. C. and Hu, B. (1987). "On reliability of a large consecutive-k-out-of-n:F system with $(k-1)$-step Markov Dependence," *IEEE Transactions on Reliability*, **R–36**, 1, 75–77.

Zhao, X., Cui, L., Zhao, W. and Liu, F. (2011). "Exact Reliability of a Linear Connected-(r, s)-out-of-(m, n):F System," *IEEE Transactions on Reliability*, **R–60**, 3, 689–698.

Lin, M.-S. (2004). "An $O(k^2 \cdot \log(n))$ algorithm for computing the reliability of consecutive-k-out-of-n:F systems," *IEEE Transactions on Reliability*, **R–53**, 1, 3–6.

Cowell, S. (2015). "A Formula for the Reliability of a d-Dimensional Consecutive-k-out-of-n:F System," *International Journal of Combinatorics*, Article ID 140909.

Chapter 8

Some Reliability Properties of n-Component Parallel/Series Systems with Interdependent Failures

Mitsuhiro Kimura[1], Shuhei Ota[2], and Shogo Abe[1]

[1] *Department of Industrial & Systems Engineering,*
Hosei University,

[2] *Graduate School of Hosei University*

1 Introduction

Reliability analysis of parallel, series, parallel-series, and network systems has drawn great interest of a lot of researchers so far, as one of the fundamental aspects of reliability assessment issues. Thus there are many publications on this topic in the literature. For instance, Carhart (1953) is one of the oldest contributions. This paper surveyed the reliability analysis for series and parallel systems which are constructed by identical components. Also, Creveling (1956) and Moore and Shannon (1956) dealt with more complex systems like series-parallel and network systems. Zelen (1964) well summarized the reliability analysis for redundant systems including such systems. Most of these researches assumed that the lifetimes of the components are statistically independent. However, it is natural that the researchers began to focus on the dependent failure-occurrence phenomena which might be possible to be observed in the actual situations.

One of the modeling frameworks for interdependent failure-occurrence environment is to employ copula functions. In particular, FGM (Farlie-Gumbel-Morgenstern) copula is widely-known since it is comparatively easy to model the dependent failure-occurrence characteristics. Hence in this chapter, we investigate and present several reliability-related properties of parallel [Ota and Kimura (2016)] and series systems which consist of n components based on the FGM copula.

This chapter consists of the following sections. After exhibiting the notation for the mathematical description, we introduce the EFGM copula and mention its several important properties on the constant parameters included in the formulas in Section 3. We used the term EFGM copula instead of FGM copula by considering its history. A brief explanation about this is also described in Section 3. Section 4 investigates an MTTF and variance of the lifetime of n-component parallel and series systems, respectively. Several numerical illustrations of the results are presented in Section 5. Finally we conclude our study in the last Section 6.

1.1 *Notation*

The followings are the definitions of variables, symbols, and abbreviations.

n : Total number of components which construct a multi-component system ($n \geq 2$)

i : Index number of i-th component ($i = 1, 2, \ldots, n$)

u_i : i-th real-valued variable defined on $[0, 1]$ (This may be considered as a realization of a $[0, 1]$ uniform distribution)

X_i : Random variable representing a lifetime of the i-th component

x_i : Realization of X_i

$F_i(x_i)$: Cumulative distribution function of X_i, i.e. $F_i(x_i) = \Pr[X_i \leq x_i]$

$\bar{F}_i(x_i)$: Survival function, namely, $\bar{F}_i(x_i) = 1 - F_i(x_i)$

$\Gamma(n)$: Gamma function of n

CDF : Cumulative distribution function

PDF : Probability density function

$E[X]$: Expectation of a random variable X

$\text{Var}[X]$: Variance of a random variable X

$\overline{\mathbf{R}}$: Extended real line $[-\infty, \infty]$

$\text{Ran}F$: Range of F

2 Sklar's Theorem

The mathematical foundation of copula modeling owes the Sklar's theorem. Here we briefly introduce the theory described in the Nelsen's book [Nelsen (2007)][1].

---

[1]See, p. 18 in [Nelsen (2007)].

Let $H(x,y)$ be a joint distribution function with margins F and G. Then there exists a copula C such that for all x, y in $\overline{\mathbf{R}}$,

$$H(x,y) = C(F(x), G(y)). \qquad (1)$$

If F and G are continuous, the C is unique; otherwise, C is uniquely determined on $\mathrm{Ran}F \times \mathrm{Ran}G$. Conversely, if C is a copula and F and G are distribution functions, then the function H defined by Eq. (1) is a joint distribution function with margins F and G.

For further mathematical formulations and their theoretical deployment to a multivariate version, refer to [Nelsen (2007)] and [Jaworski (2010)] for instance.

3   Eyraud–Farlie–Gumbel–Morgenstern Copula

We start with the mathematical formulation of an Eyraud-Farlie-Gumbel-Morgenstern copula (for short, EFGM copula) [Jaworski (2010)]. It is widely known that this type of copula has several attractive properties. Probably, the paper [Eyraud (1936)] firstly showed a mathematical form of a bivariate exponential distribution in the year of 1936. Unfortunately, since this first contribution by Eyraud has been the forgotten work, a lot of papers call it FGM copula. Therefore, by considering its origin, we use the term EFGM copula instead of FGM copula in the rest of this chapter. Such a brief historical background is mentioned [Johnson (1987)]. After the work by Eyraud, many successive and related researches have been known (e.g., [Morgenstern (1956); Farlie (1960); Gumbel (1960); Pathak and Vellaisamy (2016); Lai and Xie (2006)]). Numbers of researches on a bivariate distribution of this type and also the EFGM copula have been deeply investigated so far. The papers [Johnson and Kotz (1975); Cambanis (1977)] deployed it to n-variate distribution for example, and also Mari and Kotz (2001) showed some properties of n-variate EFGM distribution with Weibull marginals. Recently, these works have been referred from the view point of copula distributions (e.g., [Jaworski (2010); Pathak and Vellaisamy (2016); Nelsen (2007)]). Looking into the research [Mari and Kotz (2001)], our research results presented in this chapter are related to their results, however, we can show the closed form of several reliability characteristics of the n-component parallel and series systems under the dependent failure-occurrence environment, and explain some complicated properties of the dependence parameters. Also, Eryilmaz (2011) provided a generalization of the modeling framework of multi-component systems by copulas, and discussed the method of parameters estimation.

Under the modeling methodology of EFGM copula, the copula function denoted by C of n variables can be expressed by

$$C(u_1, u_2, \ldots, u_n) = \left\{ \prod_{i=1}^{n} u_i \right\} \left(1 + \sum_{S \in \mathscr{S}} \alpha_S \prod_{j \in S} (1 - u_j) \right). \qquad (2)$$

Equation (2) contains $2^n - n - 1$ constant parameters denoted by α_S. The set $\mathscr{S}$ consists of the subsets which are all combinations of at least two elements of the index number set $\{1, 2, \ldots, n\}$. The set S represents an element of $\mathscr{S}$, and j is an index number belongs to S.

3.1 Dependence Parameters

From Eq. (2), we obtain

$$\frac{\partial^n C(u_1, u_2, \ldots, u_n)}{\partial u_1 \partial u_2 \cdots \partial u_n} \equiv c(u_1, u_2, \ldots, u_n)$$

$$= 1 + \sum_{S \in \mathscr{S}} \alpha_S \prod_{j \in S} (1 - 2u_j). \qquad (3)$$

The value of each constant parameter α_S has to be restricted so as to satisfy the inequality $c(u_1, u_2, \ldots, u_n) \geq 0$ for all u_i's $(i = 1, 2, \ldots, n)$. More specifically, in the case of $n = 2$, we have the following formulas.

$$C(u_1, u_2) = u_1 u_2 (1 + \alpha_{\{1,2\}}(1 - u_1)(1 - u_2)), \qquad (4)$$

$$c(u_1, u_2) = 1 + \alpha_{\{1,2\}}(1 - 2u_1)(1 - 2u_2). \qquad (5)$$

From Eq. (5), we have

$$1 + \alpha_{\{1,2\}}(1 - 2u_1)(1 - 2u_2) \geq 0. \qquad (6)$$

In order to find the range of $\alpha_{\{1,2\}}$, we investigate the following four cases, i.e., $(u_1, u_2) = (0, 0), (0, 1), (1, 0),$ and $(1, 1)$ for the necessary and sufficient conditions for Eq. (6). Therefore they yield

$$\left. \begin{array}{c} 1 + \alpha_{\{1,2\}} \geq 0 \\ 1 - \alpha_{\{1,2\}} \geq 0 \end{array} \right\}. \qquad (7)$$

Hence the appropriate range of $\alpha_{\{1,2\}}$ is given by

$$-1 \leq \alpha_{\{1,2\}} \leq 1. \qquad (8)$$

In the case of $n = 3$, since $\mathscr{S} = \{\{1,2\}, \{1,3\}, \{2,3\}, \{1,2,3\}\}$, we have

$$
\begin{aligned}
C(u_1, u_2, u_3) = u_1 u_2 u_3 \Big[& 1 + \alpha_{\{1,2\}}(1 - u_1)(1 - u_2) \\
& + \alpha_{\{1,3\}}(1 - u_1)(1 - u_3) + \alpha_{\{2,3\}}(1 - u_2)(1 - u_3) \\
& + \alpha_{\{1,2,3\}}(1 - u_1)(1 - u_2)(1 - u_3) \Big].
\end{aligned}
\tag{9}
$$

By following the same manner, the constant parameters $\alpha_{\{1,2\}}$, $\alpha_{\{1,3\}}$, $\alpha_{\{2,3\}}$, and $\alpha_{\{1,2,3\}}$ have to hold the following conditions (e.g., [Johnson and Kotz (1975)]).

$$
\left.
\begin{aligned}
1 + \alpha_{\{1,2\}} + \alpha_{\{1,3\}} + \alpha_{\{2,3\}} &\geq |\alpha_{\{1,2,3\}}| \\
1 + \alpha_{\{1,2\}} - \alpha_{\{1,3\}} - \alpha_{\{2,3\}} &\geq |\alpha_{\{1,2,3\}}| \\
1 - \alpha_{\{1,2\}} + \alpha_{\{1,3\}} - \alpha_{\{2,3\}} &\geq |\alpha_{\{1,2,3\}}| \\
1 - \alpha_{\{1,2\}} - \alpha_{\{1,3\}} + \alpha_{\{2,3\}} &\geq |\alpha_{\{1,2,3\}}|
\end{aligned}
\right\}.
\tag{10}
$$

Thus for example, if $\alpha_{\{123\}} = 1$, the other parameters are fixed to $\alpha_{\{12\}} = \alpha_{\{13\}} = \alpha_{\{23\}} = 0$. On the contrary, if $\alpha_{\{12\}} = \alpha_{\{13\}} = \alpha_{\{23\}} = 0$, then $-1 \leq \alpha_{\{123\}} \leq 1$. These conditions which are structured as Eq. (10) become complex when n is large.

In order to simplify the modeling, we introduce another constant parameter θ_k, where $k = |S|$ of α_S. Therefore in the case of $n = 3$, Eq. (9) can be contracted as

$$
\begin{aligned}
C(u_1, u_2, u_3) = u_1 u_2 u_3 \Big[& 1 + \theta_2\big((1 - u_1)(1 - u_2) + (1 - u_1)(1 - u_3) \\
& + (1 - u_2)(1 - u_3)\big) + \theta_3(1 - u_1)(1 - u_2)(1 - u_3) \Big].
\end{aligned}
\tag{11}
$$

Hence Eq. (10) is also reduced to

$$
\left.
\begin{aligned}
1 + 3\theta_2 &\geq |\theta_3| \\
1 - \theta_2 &\geq |\theta_3|
\end{aligned}
\right\}.
\tag{12}
$$

Figure 1 illustrates the region of (θ_2, θ_3) satisfying Eq. (12). As seen in the figure, it should be noted that the conditions $-1 \leq \theta_2 \leq 1$ and $-1 \leq \theta_3 \leq 1$ do not hold. If $\theta_3 = 0$, then $-1/3 \leq \theta_2 \leq 1$. Moreover, if one further assumes $\theta_2 = \theta_3 = \theta$, the possible range of θ is restricted to $-1/4 \leq \theta \leq 1/2$. Note that there exists an appropriate range of θ_k in each modeling.

One advantage of employing a copula function as a framework of describing a multi-variate distribution incorporating dependency among the random variables is that the variable u_i can be replaced with an appropriate continuous CDF, because $u_i = F_i(x_i)$ $(i = 1, 2, \ldots, n)$.

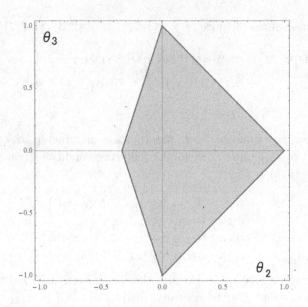

Fig. 1   Region of (θ_2, θ_3) $(n = 3)$.

4   Reliability Assessment of n-Component Systems Under Dependent Failure-Occurrence Environment

We presume that the lifetime distribution of the i-th component is an identical exponential distribution. That is, the marginal distribution function is presented by $F_i(x_i) \equiv F(x_i) = 1 - \exp[-\lambda x_i]$ $(\lambda > 0)$.

4.1   Parallel System with Interdependent Failures

We can derive the CDF of the lifetime of n-component parallel system, $\Pr[\max\{X_1, X_2, \ldots, X_n\} \equiv X_{\max} \le x] \equiv F_{\max}(x)$, as

$$F_{\max}(x) = F(x)^n \left(1 + \sum_{k=2}^{n} \binom{n}{k} \theta_k \bar{F}(x)^k \right), \tag{13}$$

from Eq. (2) via the simplification of the constant parameters. If $n = 3$, PDF of $X_{\max}$, namely, $f_{\max}(x)$ can be written as follows.

$$f_{\max}(x) = 3F(x)^2 f(x) \{ 1 + \theta_2 (1 - F(x))(3 - 5F(x))$$
$$+ \theta_3 (1 - F(x))^2 (1 - 2F(x)) \}. \tag{14}$$

The region of (θ_2, θ_3) satisfying $f_{\max}(x) \ge 0$ for all x is depicted in Figure 2.

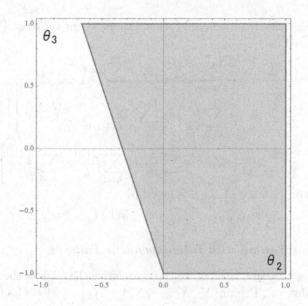

Fig. 2   Region of (θ_2, θ_3) for the 3-component parallel system.

From Eq. (13), the MTTF of an n-component parallel system can be obtained as

$$E[X_{\max}] = \mathrm{MTTF}_{\max}(n) = \frac{1}{\lambda}\Big[H(n) - \sum_{k=2}^{n} \frac{J(k)}{k}\theta_k\Big], \qquad (15)$$

where $H(n)$ describes a partial sum of the harmonic series

$$H(n) = \sum_{i=1}^{n} \frac{1}{i}, \qquad (16)$$

and

$$J(k) = \binom{n}{n-k}\Big/\binom{n+k}{k}. \qquad (17)$$

Note that if all of the components are mutually independent, the MTTF can be given by

$$\mathrm{MTTF}(n) = \frac{1}{\lambda}H(n), \qquad (18)$$

(e.g., [Nakagawa and Yun (2011)]). Hence we can understand that if the system operates under the positively-dependent failure-occurrence environment (i.e., $\theta_k > 0$ $(k = 2, 3, \ldots, n)$), the achieved MTTF declines from the design MTTF under the assumption of the independence.

From Eq. (13), the moment of second order about the origin, $M_{\max}^{(2)}(n)$, can be derived as

$$M_{\max}^{(2)}(n) = -\frac{2}{\lambda^2}\left[\sum_{k=2}^{n}\frac{1}{k^2}\binom{n}{k}\theta_k + \sum_{r=1}^{n}\frac{1}{r^2}\binom{n}{r}(-1)^r\right.$$

$$\left. + \sum_{k=2}^{n}\binom{n}{k}\theta_k\left\{\sum_{r=1}^{n}\frac{1}{(k+r)^2}\binom{n}{r}(-1)^r\right\}\right]$$

$$= \frac{1}{\lambda^2}\left[H(n)^2 + \sum_{i=1}^{n}\frac{1}{i^2} - 2\sum_{k=2}^{n}\frac{J(k)}{k}\theta_k\sum_{r=0}^{n}\frac{1}{k+r}\right]. \qquad (19)$$

Therefore the variance of $X_{\max}$ is given by

$$\mathrm{Var}[X_{\max}] = M_{\max}^{(2)}(n) - \mathrm{MTTF}_{\max}(n)^2. \qquad (20)$$

4.2   Series System with Interdependent Failures

By following the same fashion, we can also derive the CDF of the minimum of n variables, i.e., $\Pr[\min\{X_1, X_2, \ldots, X_n\} \equiv X_{\min} \leq x] = F_{\min}(x)$, as

$$F_{\min}(x) = 1 - \bar{F}(x)^n\left(1 + \sum_{k=2}^{n}\binom{n}{k}(-1)^k\theta_k F(x)^k\right), \qquad (21)$$

from Eq. (2) with reducing the number of the dependence parameters.

If $n = 3$, PDF of $X_{\min}$, $f_{\min}(x)$ can be obtained as

$$f_{\min}(x) = 3(1 - F(x))^2 f(x)\{1 - \theta_2(2 - 5F(x))F(x)$$

$$+ \theta_3(1 - 2F(x))F(x)^2\}. \qquad (22)$$

The region of (θ_2, θ_3) which satisfies $f_{\min}(x) \geq 0$ for all x is illustrated in Fig. 3.

MTTF is given by

$$E[X_{\min}] = \mathrm{MTTF}_{\min}(n) = \frac{1}{n\lambda} + \frac{1}{\lambda}\sum_{k=2}^{n}\binom{n}{k}\theta_k(-1)^k\sum_{r=0}^{k}\binom{k}{r}(-1)^r\frac{1}{n+r}$$

$$= \frac{1}{\lambda}\left\{\frac{1}{n} + \sum_{k=2}^{n}(-1)^k\frac{J(k)}{n}\theta_k\right\}. \qquad (23)$$

Moment of second order about the origin, denoted by $M_{\min}^{(2)}(n)$ can be obtained as

$$M_{\min}^{(2)}(n) = \frac{2}{n^2\lambda^2} + 2\sum_{k=2}^{n}\binom{n}{k}\theta_k(-1)^k\sum_{r=0}^{k}\binom{k}{r}(-1)^r\frac{1}{\lambda^2(n+r)^2}. \qquad (24)$$

Therefore the variance of $X_{\min}$ can be calculated by

$$\mathrm{Var}[X_{\min}] = M_{\min}^{(2)}(n) - \mathrm{MTTF}_{\min}(n)^2. \qquad (25)$$

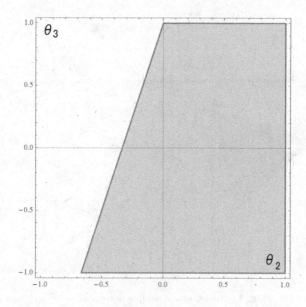

Fig. 3   Region of (θ_2, θ_3) for 3-component series system.

5   Numerical Illustrations

5.1   *Basic Behavior of EFGM Copula with Exponential Marginals*

At first, we are interested in the behavior of EFGM copula with exponential marginals. The CDF of the bivariate case is given by

$$\Pr[X_1 \leq x_1, X_2 \leq x_2] = (1 - e^{-\lambda x_1})(1 - e^{-\lambda x_2})(1 + \theta_2 e^{-\lambda x_1} e^{-\lambda x_2}). \quad (26)$$

Therefore, the PDF which is expressed by $f(x_1, x_2)$ is derived as

$$f(x_1, x_2) = \lambda^2 e^{-\lambda x_1} e^{-\lambda x_2} + \theta_2 \{ 4\lambda^2 e^{-2\lambda x_1} e^{-2\lambda x_2}$$
$$- 2\lambda^2 e^{-\lambda x_1} e^{-2\lambda x_2} - 2\lambda^2 e^{-2\lambda x_1} e^{-\lambda x_2} + \lambda^2 e^{-\lambda x_1} e^{-\lambda x_2} \}. \quad (27)$$

We depict the behavior of Eq. (27) in Fig. 4 with $\lambda = 1$ and $\theta_2 = 0$. This histogram was obtained by simulation density plot of 10000 data points for 50×50 bins. This is a 2-dimensional independent bivariate exponential density, since we set $\theta_2 = 0$ in this histogram. On the other hand, when X_1 and X_2 are dependent, the shape of joint density changes of course. Figures 5 and 6 illustrate two simulated densities in order to compare with Fig. 4. Figure 5 ($\theta_2 = 1$) can be characterized by, for example, the joint density $f(x_1, x_2)$ takes larger value if both values are smaller (near by zero), and

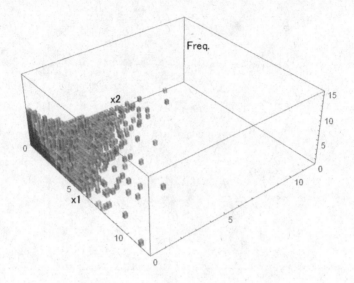

Fig. 4   Histogram of sample density ($\theta_2 = 0$).

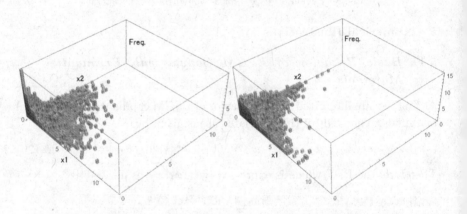

Fig. 5   Sample density ($\theta_2 = 1$).   Fig. 6   Sample density ($\theta_2 = -1$).

the shape of 'edge' of density can be seen like a convex curve from the birds-eye view, since X_1 and X_2 tend to take slightly closer values theoretically. On the contrary, the opposite characteristics can be seen by observing Fig. 6.

In general, from the view point of reliability analysis taking account of the dependent failure-occurrence environment, it can be considered natural that the value of each θ_k $(k = 2, 3, \ldots, n)$ is non-negative. Hence in the rest of this chapter, we perform the reliability analysis and the character-istics investigation under the assumption of $\theta_k \geq 0$ $(k = 2, 3, \ldots, n)$. It is intuitively understandable that the MTTF of parallel systems gets smaller when θ_k is positive. This fact can be confirmed by Eq. (15), since $J(k)$ is a decreasing sequence. On the other hand, in the case of series systems, the MTTF of the system becomes larger if the term

$$\sum_{k=2}^{n} (-1)^k J(k) \theta_k \tag{28}$$

is positive (Eq. (23)).

5.2 *Relationship with Rank Correlation Indices*

We additionally mention two correlation indices between two variates, namely, Kendall's τ and Spearman's ρ. Both correlation indices are known as non-parametric ones, and these can be expressed by utilizing a copula function. On the rank correlation property of two variates of a copula, the following facts are widely known [Nelsen (2007)].

Kendall's τ can be obtained by

$$\tau = 4 \int_0^1 \int_0^1 C(u_1, u_2) c(u_1, u_2) du_1 du_2 - 1. \tag{29}$$

In the case of EFGM copula, we have

$$\tau = \frac{2}{9} \theta_2. \tag{30}$$

On the other hand, Spearman's ρ is given by

$$\rho = 12 \int_0^1 \int_0^1 \left[C(u_1, u_2) - u_1 u_2 \right] du_1 du_2$$

$$= \frac{1}{3} \theta_2, \tag{31}$$

based on the EFGM copula. Note that these indices are free from the selection of marginal distributions of the copula. This is greatly related to the fact that a copula function can separately treat the concept of 'coupling' and the selection of the marginal distributions. Also considering the range of θ_2 is $-1 \leq \theta_2 \leq 1$, we understand that the EFGM copula cannot describe the strong dependence, that is, $-2/9 \leq \tau \leq 2/9$ and $-1/3 \leq \rho \leq 1/3$, respectively.

Table 1 Coefficients of θ_k of Parallel Systems.

	$k = 2$	$k = 3$	$k = 4$	$k = 5$	$k = 6$
$n = 2$	$\frac{1}{12}$	–	–	–	–
$n = 3$	$\frac{3}{20}$	$\frac{1}{60}$	–	–	–
$n = 4$	$\frac{1}{5}$	$\frac{4}{105}$	$\frac{1}{280}$	–	–
$n = 5$	$\frac{5}{21}$	$\frac{5}{84}$	$\frac{5}{504}$	$\frac{1}{1260}$	–
$n = 6$	$\frac{15}{56}$	$\frac{5}{63}$	$\frac{1}{56}$	$\frac{1}{385}$	$\frac{1}{5544}$

As n increases in a column, the value increases. As k increases in a row, the value rapidly decreases.

5.3 Parallel System with Interdependent Failures

We now focus on the values of the coefficients of dependence parameters θ_k $(k = 2, 3, \ldots, n)$, denoted by $J(k)/k$ in Eq. (15). Table 1 shows several coefficients of θ_k. We can see that the coefficient of θ_k with the smaller index number k becomes significantly larger than other coefficients of θ_k as the number of components, n, becomes large. In other words, the value of θ_k with the larger index number k does not contribute to reduce the MTTF by the possibility of dependent failure occurrences.

Another finding from Table 1 is that these values in Table 1 correspond to the values of the coefficients which appear in a certain approximation method of the difference equation theory (e.g., [Fornberg (1988); Gorski and Szmigielski (1998)]). In addition, an alternative form of $J(k)/k$ can be described by

$$\frac{J(k)}{k} = \binom{n}{k} \frac{\Gamma(k)\Gamma(n+1)}{\Gamma(n+k+1)} = \binom{n}{k} B(k, n+1), \qquad (32)$$

where $B(a, b)$ is the beta function.

Here we assume $\theta \equiv \theta_k$ $(k = 2, 3, \ldots, n)$ for more simplicity. Several behaviors of CDF and PDF are shown in Figs. 7 and 8, respectively ($\lambda = 1$).

Figure 8 suggests that the PDF shows a bimodal shape when both of θ and n become large. Figures 9 and 10 represent the hazard rate function and MTTF, respectively. In Fig. 9, when θ is large, the shape of the hazard rate depicts characteristic behavior as seen in Fig. 8. It is also represented that the more stronger dependence reduces the MTTF in Fig. 10.

Variance of the lifetime $X_{\max}$ is illustrated in Fig. 11 ($\lambda = 1$). In the case of $\theta = 0$, it converges to $\pi^2/6$ as $n \to \infty$.

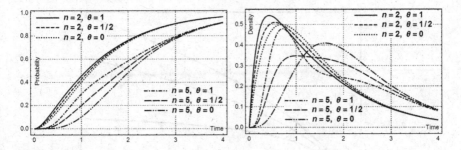

Fig. 7   Behaviors of CDF.   Fig. 8   Behaviors of PDF.

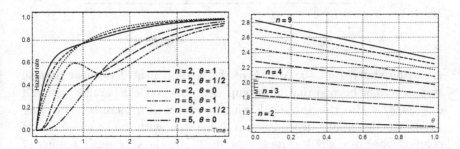

Fig. 9   Behaviors of hazard rate.   Fig. 10   Behaviors of MTTF.

5.3.1   *Decrement of MTTF*

As shown in Fig. 10, the dependent failure-occurrence environment has a harmful influence on the parallel system in the sense of the decrement of MTTF. For example, if one has designed an n-component parallel system under the expectation of the independent failure-occurrence environment, he/she would be betrayed if the actual operation environment induces the interdependent failures. Therefore we calculate the value of dependence parameter which spoils the amount of MTTF of one component out of n-component parallel system by using the following equation.

$$\text{MTTF}(n-1) = \text{MTTF}_{\max}(n), \tag{33}$$

where $\text{MTTF}(n-1)$ is derived by Eq. (18). Solving Eq. (33) with respect to θ analytically, we have

$$\theta(n) = 1/\left[n\left(\frac{H(n)}{2} - \frac{n}{n+1}\right)\right]. \tag{34}$$

Table 2 is a summary of the relation between n ($n \geq 5$) and θ. $n \geq 5$ is needed to satisfy the condition $\theta \leq 1$. In this table, for example,

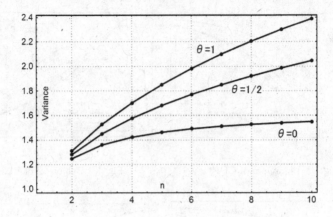

Fig. 11 Variance of $X_{\max}$ $(\theta = 1, 1/2, 0)$.

it can be stated that the MTTF of the 5-component dependent parallel system cannot beyond that of 4-component independent parallel system if $\theta \geq 24/37$. Also this threshold value decreases as n increases. In other words, the potentially-dependent parallel system with the large number of components can easily lose its design MTTF by the very small amount of dependency which is represented by θ.

Table 2 Threshold value of θ which spoils MTTF of n-independent-component parallel system.

$n = 5$	6	7	8	9	10
$\theta = \frac{24}{37}$	$\frac{140}{309}$	$\frac{20}{59}$	$\frac{630}{2369}$	$\frac{560}{2593}$	$\frac{5544}{30791}$
$=0.6487$	$=0.4531$	$=0.3390$	$=0.2660$	$=0.2160$	$=0.1801$

For instance, if $\theta \geq 24/37$, $\mathrm{MTTF}(4) \geq \mathrm{MTTF}_{\max}(5)$.

5.4 *Series System with Interdependent Failures*

Here, we investigate several characteristics of an n-component series system with interdependent failures by following the same manner to the previous section. Table 3 presents the coefficients of θ_k $(k = 2, 3, \ldots, 6)$, that is, $J(k)/n$. The same behavior except for the factor of $(-1)^k$ is observed by comparing Table 1. Therefore, we can understand that the MTTF of a series system under the interdependent failure-occurrence environment gets longer than that of the case of independent-component series system if the positive dependence [Eryilmaz and Tank (2012)] is possible.

Table 3   Coefficients of θ_k of Series Systems.

	$k = 2$	$k = 3$	$k = 4$	$k = 5$	$k = 6$
$n = 2$	$\frac{1}{12}$	–	–	–	–
$n = 3$	$\frac{1}{10}$	$-\frac{1}{60}$	–	–	–
$n = 4$	$\frac{1}{10}$	$-\frac{1}{35}$	$\frac{1}{280}$	–	–
$n = 5$	$\frac{2}{21}$	$-\frac{1}{28}$	$\frac{1}{126}$	$-\frac{1}{1260}$	–
$n = 6$	$\frac{5}{56}$	$-\frac{5}{126}$	$\frac{1}{84}$	$-\frac{1}{462}$	$\frac{1}{5544}$

As n increases in a column, the value increases. As k increases in a row, each absolute value rapidly decreases.

In addition, corresponding to Eq. (32), it is obvious that

$$\frac{J(k)}{n} = \binom{n-1}{k-1}\frac{\Gamma(k)\Gamma(n+1)}{\Gamma(n+k+1)} = \binom{n-1}{k-1}B(k, n+1). \qquad (35)$$

Several behaviors of CDF and PDF based on Eq. (21) are shown in Figs. 12 and 13, respectively ($\lambda = 1$). Different from the parallel system, these curves seem unimodal.

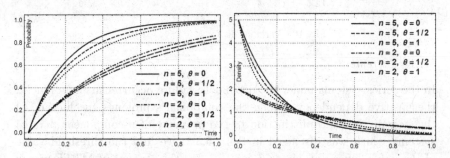

Fig. 12   Behaviors of CDF.   Fig. 13   Behaviors of PDF.

Figures 14 and 15 show the hazard functions and MTTF respectively ($\lambda = 1$). It is interesting that the hazard rate temporarily drops at the early stage of the life time. It can be confirmed that the MTTF increases when the degree of positive dependence becomes high.

Variance of the lifetime $X_{\min}$ is illustrated in Fig. 16. It converges to 0 as $n \rightarrow \infty$.

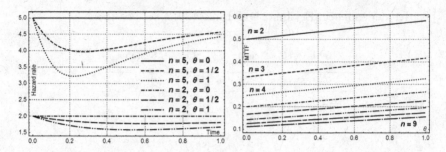

Fig. 14   Behaviors of hazard rate.   Fig. 15   Behaviors of MTTF.

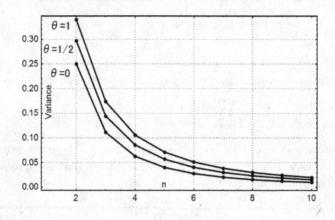

Fig. 16   Variance of $X_{\max}$ ($\theta = 1, 1/2, 0$).

5.4.1   *Increment of MTTF*

In the series systems under the dependent failure-occurrence environment, the positive dependency among the components prolongs the lifetime of the system. In contradistinction to the property of n-component parallel systems which was discussed in Sec. 5.3.1, we find the threshold value of the dependence parameter θ, which gains the amount of MTTF of one component out of an n-component series system. By solving the following equation

$$\text{MTTF}(n - 1) = \text{MTTF}_{\min}(n), \tag{36}$$

with respect to θ, we obtain the relation as

$$\theta(n) = \frac{2(n + 1)}{(n - 1)^2}. \tag{37}$$

Table 4 consists of several numerical results. By the same reason to the case of Table 2, $n \geq 5$ is required.

Table 4 Threshold value of θ which gains MTTF of $(n-1)$-independent-component series system.

$n = 5$	6	7	8	9	10
$\theta = \frac{3}{4}$	$\frac{14}{25}$	$\frac{4}{9}$	$\frac{18}{43}$	$\frac{5}{16}$	$\frac{22}{81}$
=0.75	=0.56	=0.4444	=0.3673	=0.3125	=0.2716

For example, if $\theta \geq 3/4$, $\mathrm{MTTF}(4) \leq \mathrm{MTTF}_{\min}(5)$.

6 Conclusion

This study has presented several reliability-related properties of n-component systems under the assumption that the components may fail dependently. We restricted the structure of n-component systems into the parallel and series systems, respectively. As a modeling framework, EFGM copula has attractive characteristics, and it is comparatively easy for doing mathematical manipulations. As a result, it was confirmed that there exist several complex conditions among the dependence parameters. By using the simplification for many constant parameters, we derived the closed forms of MTTF and variance of the systems. In order to illustrate the characteristics of two kinds of n-component systems, several numerical examples were shown. We have already obtained the results for k-out-of-n, and a certain kind of network systems by using the same methodology. We are now preparing the results of the investigation.

For future study, we would like to analyze the actual lifetime data on the real structure of n-component systems by using our EFGM copula models in order to perform the precise reliability assessment.

Acknowledgments

This study is partially supported by JSPS KAKENHI Grant Number 15k01208.

References

Carhart, R. R. (1953). "A survey of the current status of the electronic reliability problem,"*Rand Corporation Research Memorandum*, RM-1131.

Creveling, C. J. (1956). "Increasing the reliability of electronic equipment by the use of redundant circuits,"*Proceedings of the IRE*, Vol. 44, Issue 4, pp. 509-515.

Moore, E. F. and Shannon, C. E. (1956). "Reliable circuits using less reliable relays," *Journal of the Franklin Institute*, Vol. 262, Issue 3, pp. 191-208.

Zelen, M. ed. (1964). *Statistical Theory of Reliability*, University of Wisconsin Press, Wisconsin.

Ota, S. and Kimura, M. (2016). "A Study on the MTTF of Parallel Systems Under Dependent Failure-occurrence Environment," Jun, K. M., Kimura, M., and Cui, L.-R. (eds.), Advanced Reliability and Maintenance Modeling VII, McGraw-Hill, Taiwan, pp. 423-429.

Nelsen, R. B. (2007). *An Introduction to Copulas*, Springer.

Jaworski, P. (eds.) (2010). *Copula Theory and Its Applications*, Lecture Notes in Statistics – Proceedings (198), Springer.

Eyraud, H. (1936). "Les principes de la mesure des correlations," *Ann Univ Lyon Series A*, Vol. 1, pp. 30-47.

Johnson, M. E. (1987). *Multivariate Statistical Simulation: A Guide to Selecting and Generating Continuous Multivariate Distributions*, John Wiley & Sons, Inc.

Morgenstern, D. (1956). "Einfache Beispiele zweidimensionaler Verteilungen," *Mitteislingsblatt für Mathematische Statistik*, Vol. 8, pp. 234-235.

Farlie, D. J. (1960). "The Performance of Some Correlation Coefficients for a General Bivariate Distribution," *Biometrika*, Vol. 47, pp. 307-323.

Gumbel, E. J. (1960). "Bivariate Exponential Distributions," *Journal of the American Statistical Association*, Vol. 55, Issue 292, pp. 698-707.

Pathak, A. K. and Vellaisamy, P. (2016). "A note on generalized Farlie-Gumbel-Morgenstern copulas," *Journal of Statistical Theory and Practice*, Vol. 10, No. 1, pp. 40-58, DOI:10.1080/15598608.2015.1064838.

Lai, C.-D. and Xie, M. (2006). *Stochastic Ageing and Dependence for Reliability*, Springer.

Johnson, N. L. and Kotz, S. (1975). "On Some Generalized Farlie-Gumbel-Morgenstern Distributions," *Communications in Statistics*, Vol. 4, pp. 415-427.

Cambanis, S. (1977). "Some Properties and Generalization of Multivariate Eyraud-Gumbel-Morgenstern Distributions," *Journal of Multivariate Analysis*, Vol. 7, pp. 551-559.

Mari, D. D. and Kotz, S. (2001). *Correlation and Dependence*, Imperial College Press, London.

Eryilmaz, S. (2011). "Estimation in coherent reliability systems through copulas," *Reliability Engineering and System Safety*, Vol. 96, pp. 564-568.

Nakagawa, T. and Yun, W. Y. (2011). "Note on MTTF of a parallel system," *International Journal of Reliability, Quality and Safety Engineering*, Vol. 18, Issue 1, pp. 43-50.

Fornberg, B. (1988). "Generation of finite difference formulas on arbitrarily spaced grids," *Journal of Mathematics of Computation*, Vol. 51, No. 184, pp. 699-706 (1988).

Górski, A. Z. and Szmigielski, J. (1998). "On pairs of difference operators satisfying: [D,X]=Id," *Journal of Mathematical Physics*, Vol. 39, pp. 545-568.

Eryilmaz, S. and Tank, F. (2012). "On reliability analysis of a two-dependent-unit series system with a standby unit," *Applied Mathematics and Computation*, Vol. 218, Issue 15, pp. 7792-7797.

Chapter 9

Common-cause Failure Analysis in Probabilistic Risk Assessment

Tetsushi Yuge and Shigeru Yanagi

Department of Electrical and Electronic Engineering,
National Defense Academy

1 Introduction

Redundant structures are commonly used in practical systems to improve their reliability. Ensuring the independence between components is particularly important when a redundant structure is installed in a system; the existence of dependence invalidates the effect of redundancy. In reliability and risk analysis, the treatment of dependence in the identification and quantification of failure/accident sequences is referred to as dependent failure (DF) analysis. The two event A and B are said to be dependent if

$$\Pr(A \wedge B) = \Pr(A) \Pr(B|A) \neq \Pr(A) \Pr(B). \tag{1}$$

Many authors have developed extensive lists of categories of dependent failure. One of the more comprehensive classification is that by Watson and Edwards (1979).

DF analysis is extremely important in probabilistic risk assessment (PRA) studies because dependence tends to increase the frequency of multiple concurrent failures and is often a major cause of system low reliability [NRC (1983)]. In fact, the primary cause of the Fukushima Daiichi nuclear disaster is considered to be the complete power loss due to the simultaneous failures of the emergency diesel generators following the tsunami[IAEA (2011)]. Several terms have been used to describe specific types of DF. Following the classification, DFs are classified into three groups by the extent of dependence[NRC (1983)].

- Type 1. Common-cause initiating events, also called external events: external and internal events that have the potential for initiating a plant transient and increase the probability of failure in multiple systems. Examples include fires, floods, earthquake, aircraft crashes, loss of off-site power.
- Type 2. Inter-system dependences: event or failure causes that create interdependences among the probabilities of failure for multiple systems.
- Type 3. Inter-component dependences: event or failure causes that result in a dependence among the probabilities of failure for multiple components or subsystems.

There are several subtypes in Type 2 and 3.

- Type 2A(3A). Functional dependences: dependences among systems (components) that follow from the plant design philosophy, system capabilities and limitations.
- Type 2B(3B). Shared equipment dependences: dependences of multiple systems (components) on the same components, subsystems.
- Type 2C(3C). Physical interactions: similar to common-cause initiators, that do not necessarily cause an initiating event but increase the probability of multiple system (component) failures occurring at the same time.
- Type 2D(3D). Human-interaction dependences: dependences introduced by human actions, including errors and commission.

Subtypes C and D are also called as common-cause failure (CCF). In this paper we incorporate CCF as a representative DF into system analysis.

Figure 1 shows a procedure of CCF analysis[NRC (1983, 1998)]. The first step of CCF analysis is to understand the system and to identify the root causes, the coupling factors and the common-cause component group (CCCG). The CCCG is a set of components whose CCF contributes significantly to the system unreliability. Qualitative and quantitative screenings are adopted to determine the CCCG in a system.

The next step is CCF modeling and analysis. There are two fundamentally different approaches for incorporating CCF into system analysis: explicit and implicit methods[NRC (1998)]. In the explicit method, each CCF is modeled as a common-cause basic event (CCBE) in the system fault tree or reliability block diagram, appearing as repeated inputs to all components within the CCCG. Boolean reduction is performed to handle

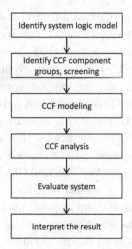

Fig. 1   Procedure of CCF analysis[Yuge et al. (2016)].

these events, and quantification uses the CCBE probabilities. In the implicit method, the effect of CCF and the shared causes are modeled as a combined basic event. This method implies that CCF modeling methods such as the β-factor model, MGL model and α-factor model are used to quantify the failure probabilities of CCBEs and the CCCG. Most models assume that the CCBEs have constant rates of occurrence, leading to variants of multivariate exponential distribution[Vasely (1977); Dhillon and Anude (1994)]. In principle, implicit methods can completely cover CCFs if sufficient failure data regarding the CCFs are available, but sometime large uncertainties arise because of insufficient data.

The final step of CCF analysis is quantitative analysis of the system. The probability of failure of the whole system is quantified using fault tree or event tree methods. The results are interpreted and used to take preventive measures to increase system reliability/safety.

CCF modeling is at the heart of CCF analysis and the implicit approach has mainly been studied. Almost all the models used in the implicit approach assume symmetry principle [NRC (1983, 1998); Dhillon and Anude (1994); Vaurio (1994)]. The components in the target CCCG/system have the same constant failure rate, and all combinations of k out of n components failing have the same occurrence probability. This assumption reduces the computational load and makes it possible to incorporate CCF into system analysis. However, the assumption limits the CCF to within the CCCG boundaries, meaning that a CCCG does not include components of a different type in the same system or components belonging to more than one system. If we need to analyze CCFs beyond these boundaries, i.e., in the case of intersystem CCFs or external events such as earthquakes, we cannot take this approach, and the explicit approach is the only effective method. However, even if we take the explicit approach, estimating the failure probabilities of a CCBE remains a difficult problem. To evaluate the failure probability of a CCCG using the CCBE probabilities, independence between CCBEs and a rare event approximation are usually adopted [NRC (1983); Dhillon and Anude (1994); Chae and Clark (1986)]. The probability of a combined event involving several CCBEs is given as a product of the CCBE probabilities. The rare event approximation is a truncation of high-order cutsets. However, the effectiveness and accuracy of this assumption or approximation have not been clearly verified.

In Section 2, we discuss the system failure probability when the failure probabilities of CCBEs are known. A k-out-of-n structure is focused on to formulate the system failure probability. The conventional implicit technique is employed. The failure probabilities assuming independence between CCBEs and with the rare event approximation have been provided in [NRC (1998)] for some specific k-out-of-n systems. We first expand the results in [NRC (1998)] and formulate the system failure probability for a general k-out-of-n system. We present an efficient algorithm for calculating the probability without the rare event approximation. We also provide algorithms to enumerate minimal cut sets (MCs) and to calculate the system failure probability using the MCs. These methods can be applied to systems with non-identical components. Such systems are referred to asymmetric systems. The formulation and algorithms enable us to obtain the failure probability only assuming independence between CCBEs and to verify the effect of the assumption by comparison with the exact solution in numerical examples. Note that Section 2 is a reprint of Yuge and Yanagi (2015) with permission (Copyright ©2006 IEICE).

In Section 3, we consider a multivariate exponential distribution (MVE) to evaluate the failure probability/reliability of a system. Marshall and Olkin considered the independent exponential shock model called Marshall-Olkin type shocks[Marchall and Olkin (1967); Vasely (1977)]. They derived the joint survival function (MVE) of the system and some of its properties[Marchall and Olkin (1967)]. In recent years, numerous papers dealing with extensions of Marshall-Olkin distributions have appeared. However, the Marshall-Olkin model is not yet a commonly used mathematical model in the field of risk analysis, even though it has been considered to be a suitable model for CCF analysis in the field of statistics. One of the reasons for this is the difficulty of formulating the system reliability or unreliability for various system structures such as a k-out-of-n system using this model. In an earlier study, Bayramoglu and Ozkut considered the system reliability of a k-out-of-n system subjected to Marshall-Olkin type shocks[Bayramoglu and Ozkut (2015)]. They assumed two types of shocks, one destroying only one component and the other destroying all components simultaneously. Yuge et al. also consider the reliability of a k-out-of-n system[Yuge et al. (2016)]. They extend Bayramoglu and Ozkut's model and consider all combinations of components in a system as shocks, i.e., $2^n - 1$ shocks. They formulated the system reliability and numerically compare the results with those obtained using the conventional α-factor model[Yuge et al. (2016)]. In Section 3, we introduce the result (Copyright ©2016 Elsevier B.V.).

2 CCF Modeling by α-Factor Method

We introduce an α-factor method [NRC (1998)] as a representative CCF modeling method. Then, we expand the idea to non-i.i.d system in Section 2.1.

Let consider a CCCG with $m(m = 1, 2, \ldots)$ components. When all components are i.i.d, we denote λ_k as a failure rate of CCBE involving failures of $k(k = 1, 2, \ldots, m)$ components in the CCCG, where, λ_1 is defined as a failure rate that a component fails solely. Then, α_k is defined as a probability that when a CCBE occurs in the CCCG, it involves failures of k components. In other words,

$$\alpha_k = \frac{\binom{m}{k}\lambda_k}{\sum_{i=1}^{m}\binom{m}{i}\lambda_i}. \tag{2}$$

The total failure rate λ_T of a component in CCCG is

$$\lambda_T = \sum_{k=1}^{m}\binom{m-1}{k-1}\lambda_k. \tag{3}$$

Using Eqs.(2) and (3), we can see that the basic event probabilities can be written as a function of λ_T and the α_k as follows:

$$\lambda_k = \frac{1}{\binom{m-1}{k-1}}\alpha_k\lambda_T. \tag{4}$$

Event statistics are used to develop estimates of CCF model parameter α_k. For example, if the total number of failure events involving failures of k components in a system with m i.i.d. components n_k is collected, then α_k can be estimated using the following maximum likelihood estimator;

$$\hat{\alpha}_k = \frac{n_k}{\sum_{j=1}^m n_j}. \tag{5}$$

After obtaining λ_k, the probability that any k components fail by a CCF at time t, $Q_k(t)$ is obtained as follows:

$$Q_k(t) = 1 - exp(-\lambda_k t). \tag{6}$$

The description of Q_k means $Q_k(t)$ in the rest of this paper.

2.1 α Parameters for Non-i.i.d. System

The α-factor method in the previous section has an assumption that a CCCG consists of i.i.d. components. This assumption is reasonable in many systems and has the advantage of reducing the number of parameters that are required to quantify the system failure probabilities. However, considering the treatment without the assumption of symmetry is also important to extend the capability of the analysis. To describe the α parameters and CCBE failure rates in a non-i.i.d. system, the following notations are used:

- A_i : component i $(i = 1, \ldots, m)$
- X : set of components $\{A_1, \ldots, A_m\}$
- $Y^{(k)}$: set of subset of X where the number of elements in the subset is k $(k = 1, 2, \ldots, m)$
- $Y_j^{(k)}$: the j-th element $(j = 1, 2, \ldots, \binom{m}{k})$ of $Y^{(k)}$ that corresponds to a CCBE involving k components
- λ_{iT} : a total failure rate of component A_i
- $\alpha_j^{(k)}$: ratio of a CCF corresponding to a CCBE $Y_j^{(k)}$

Note that the number of CCF parameters $\alpha_j^{(k)}$ corresponds to the sum of the cardinality of $Y^{(k)}$ and is given by $2^m - 1$. Parameter $\alpha_j^{(k)}$ is estimated by extending Eq.(5) to

$$\hat{\alpha}_{ij}^{(k)} = \frac{n_{ij}^{(k)}}{\sum_{k=1}^m \sum_j n_{ij}^{(k)}}, \tag{7}$$

where $n_{ij}^{(k)}$ is the number of observed failure events corresponding to $Y_{ij}^{(k)}$. The failure rate of $Y_j^{(k)}$ denoted by $\lambda_j^{(k)}$ can be written as

$$\lambda_j^{(k)} = \alpha_j^{(k)} \hat{\lambda}_j^{(k)}, \tag{8}$$

where

$$\hat{\lambda}_j^{(k)} = \sum_{A_i \in Y_j^{(k)}} \lambda_i T,$$

which represents a total failure rate of components in $Y_j^{(k)}$. Then, the failure probability $Q_j^{(k)}$ that all components in $Y_j^{(k)}$ fail can be represented as follows

$$Q_j^{(k)} = 1 - exp\left(-\hat{\lambda}_j^{(k)} t\right). \tag{9}$$

2.2 System Failure Probability

In this section, we introduce the solution using the implicit method and formulate the system failure probability for a k-out-of-n system (k-out-of-n:G system, to be precise). As an example, consider the 2-out-of-3 system composed of components A, B and C discussed in [NRC (1998)]. We assume a complete combination for CCBEs, i.e., C_{AB}, C_{AC}, C_{BC} and C_{ABC}, where $C_{i_1 i_2 \ldots i_j}$ denotes a CCBE involving components $i_1, i_2 \ldots i_j$. The MCs of the system are $\{C_A, C_B\}$, $\{C_A, C_C\}$, $\{C_B, C_C\}$, $\{C_{AB}\}$, $\{C_{AC}\}$, $\{C_{BC}\}$ and $\{C_{ABC}\}$, where C_A, C_B and C_C represent the events of the single independent failure of each component. The Boolean representation of the system failure is

$$S = C_A C_B + C_A C_C + C_B C_C + C_{AB} + C_{AC} + C_{BC} + C_{ABC}. \tag{10}$$

If the probabilities of the single independent failures and CCBEs are given, the probability of the system failure can be derived using the inclusion-exclusion principle. However, using the rare event approximation, the probability of system failure is given by

$$P(S) = P(C_A)P(C_B) + P(C_A)P(C_C) + P(C_B)P(C_C)$$
$$+ P(C_{AB}) + P(C_{AC}) + P(C_{BC}) + P(C_{ABC}). \tag{11}$$

It is common practice in risk and reliability analysis to assume that the probabilities of similar events involving similar components in a redundant system are the same. In Eq.(11), it is assumed that $P(C_A) = P(C_B) = P(C_C) = Q_1$, $P(C_{AB}) = P(C_{AC}) = P(C_{BC}) = Q_2$ and $P(C_{ABC}) = Q_3$. With this assumption of symmetry, the probability of system failure can be written as

$$P(S) = 3Q_1^2 + 3Q_2 + Q_3. \tag{12}$$

Note that the probabilities given by Eqs.(11) and (12) are not the exact values. In addition to the rare event approximation and the assumption of symmetry, the independence between CCBEs is assumed in Eq.(11). Actually, there is some dependence between CCBEs. For instance, C_A and C_{AB} never occur simultaneously. Although the assumption of independence is substantial and more serious than the other assumptions, such modeling is common in risk analysis because no other effective modeling techniques have been developed. Hence, we also assume independence in this paper and verify the error caused by the assumption.

Failure probabilities such as that given by Eq.(12) are listed in [NRC (1998)] for some simple and frequently encountered k-out-of-n systems, i.e., $2 \leq n \leq 5$, $1 \leq k \leq n$. However, obtaining the failure probabilities of a relatively large k-out-of-n system without the assumption of symmetry or the rare event approximation is tedious and requires considerable effort. Efficient procedures for obtaining the failure probability of a general k-out-of-n system with and without the rare event approximation are presented in the following sections.

2.3　*CCF Modeling without Rare Event Approximation*

Let us consider a k-out-of-n system composed of identical components where Q_i is defined as the probability of a CCBE involving CCF of i components ($1 \leq i \leq n$). Note that Q_1 is the probability of an independent failure and $Q_0 = 1 - \sum_{i=1}^{n} Q_i$. Strictly, Q_0 is not the reliability of a component because of the dependence between CCBEs. However, on the basis of independence assumption, Q_0 is treated as a reliability in this paper. Let $\boldsymbol{x} = (x_0, x_1, \ldots, x_n)$ be an $n+1$ dimensional vector representing the state of the system, where x_0 is the number of working components and x_i ($i \geq 1$) is the number of CCBEs involving i specific components. Namely, state $\boldsymbol{x} = (x_0, x_1, \ldots, x_n)$ means that the system has x_0 working components, x_1 independently failed components, x_2 sets of two components that failed simultaneously due to CCF, ..., and x_n set of n components that failed as a result of CCF involving all n components. Here, x_i has the constraint $\sum_{i=1}^{n} i x_i \leq n$, and we assume that a component failed by an arbitrary failure mode never fails due to other failure mode. The distribution for a system in state $\boldsymbol{x}$ is similar to the multinomial distribution with n categories. The differences from the multinomial distribution are the weighted constraint and the dependence among the categories. The constraint can be formulated by considering the concept of repeated combination. The probability x is given by

$$\Pr(x) = \frac{n!}{\prod_{i=0}^{n} x_i!(i!)^{x_i}} Q_0^{x_0} Q_1^{x_1} \cdots Q_j^{x_n}. \tag{13}$$

Hence, the probability that j $(1 \leq j \leq n)$ components fail in an n-component system is given by

$$P_n(j) = \sum_{X_j} \frac{n!}{\prod_{i=0}^{j} x_i!(i!)^{x_i}} Q_0^{x_0} Q_1^{x_1} \cdots Q_j^{x_j} = n! \sum_{X_j} \prod_{i=0}^{j} \frac{Q_i^{x_i}}{x_i!(i!)^{x_i}}, \tag{14}$$

where the sum is performed for $X_j = \{x | \ x_0 = n - j, \sum_{i=1}^{j} i x_i = j\}$.

As a special case, if $j = 1$,

$$P_n(1) = nQ_0^{n-1}Q_1. \tag{15}$$

Using Eq.(14), the solution for the failure probability $F_{k/n}$ of a k-out-of-n system can be derived as

$$F_{k/n} = \sum_{j=0}^{k-1} P_n(n - j). \tag{16}$$

For example, when $n = 4$, $X_4 = \{(0, 4, 0, 0, 0), (0, 2, 1, 0, 0), (0, 1, 0, 1, 0), (0, 0, 0, 0, 1), (0, 0, 2, 0, 0)\}$. Then, from Eq.(14),

$$P_4(4) = Q_1^4 + 6Q_1^2 Q_2 + 4Q_1 Q_3 + Q_4 + 3Q_2^2.$$

In the same way,

$$P_4(3) = 4Q_0 Q_1^3 + 12Q_0 Q_1 Q_2 + 4Q_0 Q_3,$$
$$P_4(2) = 6Q_0^2 Q_1^2 + 6Q_0^2 Q_2,$$
$$P_4(1) = 4Q_0^3 Q_1.$$

Substituting these probabilities into Eq.(16), $F_{k/4}$ $(k = 1, \ldots, 4)$ can be derived.

2.4 State Enumeration Algorithm

The procedure in Section 2.3 gives the failure probability of k-out-of-n systems only with the assumption of independence. Although this procedure is very simple, much effort is required to obtain the set of cut vectors, X_j. The following algorithm gives an efficient procedure for obtaining X_j.

Step 0. Input n and k. Prepare an $(n + 1)$-dimensional vector $x= (x_0, x_1, \ldots, x_n)$. Set $x= (n, 0, \ldots, 0)$, which corresponds to X_0. Set $j=1$.

Step 1. $x_0 = n - j$. Increase one or more $x_i, i = 1, \ldots, j$ up to j. In this increment, one increase of x_i is counted with i among j. Create all the vectors that satisfy $x_0 = n - j$ and $\sum_{i=1}^{n} i x_i = j$.

Step 2. The enumerated vectors are the elements of X_j. If $j = n$, stop. Otherwise, set $j = j + 1$ and $\boldsymbol{x} = (n, 0, \ldots, 0)$ and go to Step 1.

2.4.1   Asymmetric Systems

Let us rewrite $Q_j^{(k)}$ in Section 2.1 as $Q_{i_1 i_2 \ldots i_k}^{(k)}$ to specify the components in $Y_j^{(k)}$, where $Y_j^{(k)}$ consists of $A_{i_1}, A_{i_2}, \ldots, A_{i_k}$, and $Q_i^{(0)}$ is the probability that component A_i is working. The system failure probability is obtained by identifying the components within the CCBE. For example, $P_4(4)$ in Section 2.3 is

$$
\begin{aligned}
P_4(4) =\ & Q_1^{(1)} Q_2^{(1)} Q_3^{(1)} Q_4^{(1)} + Q_{12}^{(2)} Q_3^{(1)} Q_4^{(1)} + Q_{13}^{(2)} Q_2^{(1)} Q_4^{(1)} + Q_{14}^{(2)} Q_2^{(1)} Q_3^{(1)} \\
& + Q_{23}^{(2)} Q_1^{(1)} Q_4^{(1)} + Q_{24}^{(2)} Q_1^{(1)} Q_3^{(1)} + Q_{34}^{(2)} Q_1^{(1)} Q_2^{(1)} + Q_{123}^{(3)} Q_4^{(1)} + Q_{124}^{(3)} Q_3^{(1)} \\
& + Q_{134}^{(3)} Q_2^{(1)} + Q_{234}^{(3)} Q_1^{(1)} + Q_{1234}^{(4)} + Q_{12}^{(2)} Q_{34}^{(2)} + Q_{13}^{(2)} Q_{24}^{(2)} + Q_{14}^{(2)} Q_{23}^{(2)}.
\end{aligned}
$$

In general, Eq.(14) can be written as

$$
P_n(j) = \sum_{X_j} \sum_{S_k} \prod_{j_1, j_2, \ldots, j_i \in S_k} Q_{j_1, j_2, \ldots, j_i}^{(i)}, \tag{17}
$$

where $\boldsymbol{x} = \{x_0, x_1, \ldots, x_n\} \in X_j$ and S_k $(k = 1, 2, \ldots, \sum_i x_i)$ is a subset of $\boldsymbol{N} = \{1, 2, \ldots, n\}$ having i elements that satisfies $\bigcap_k S_k = 0$ and $\bigcup_k S_k = \boldsymbol{N}$.

2.5   Rare Event Approximation

It is common, particularly in risk analysis, to use the rare event approximation to reduce the effort required for quantification. The rare event approximation is one of the truncation methods and gives an upper bound for the system failure probability as the sum of MC probabilities. The approximated probability can be easily calculated when all the MCs are obtained. Therefore, the problem is to obtain the MCs (the combinations of CCBEs and their numbers) for a k-out-of-n system considering CCF. The MCs of a k-out-of-n system can be easily obtained by using the cut set X_j derived in Section 2.4. The partial order between two vectors $\boldsymbol{x} = (x_1, \ldots, x_n)$ and $\boldsymbol{y} = (y_1, \ldots, y_n)$ is defined and used in the algorithm.

$$
\boldsymbol{x} = \boldsymbol{y} : \text{if } x_i = y_i \text{ for } i = 1, 2, \ldots, n,
$$

$$
\boldsymbol{x} < \boldsymbol{y} : \text{if } x_i \leq y_i \text{ for } i = 1, 2, \ldots, n \text{ and } \boldsymbol{x} \neq \boldsymbol{y}.
$$

Step 0. For each $x \in X_j$, $j = n - k + 1, \ldots, n$ create an n-dimensional vector x' whose elements are $x_1, x_2, \ldots, x_n$ in x. X'_j denotes the set of x'. Prepare a list L.

Step 1. Include all $x' \in X'_{n-k+1}$ in L.

Step 2. For each y' in $X'_{n-k+2}, \ldots, X'_n$, if $x' < y'$ for at least one $x' \in L$, delete y', otherwise add y' to L.

Step 3. $x' \in L$ implies a prime implicant corresponding to an MC of the system.

The number of MCs for an identical prime implicant can be derived from the same coefficient in Eq.(14).

For example, the MCs of a 2-out-of-4 system are given as follows.

In Step 0, using the algorithm in Section 2.4,

$X'_3 = \{(3,0,0,0), (1,1,0,0), (0,0,1,0)\}$,

$X'_4 = \{(4,0,0,0), (2,1,0,0), (1,0,1,0), (0,0,0,1),$
$(0,2,0,0)\}$.

Step 1, $L = \{(3,0,0,0), (1,1,0,0), (0,0,1,0)\}$.

Step 2, for $j = 4$, $L = \{(3,0,0,0), (1,1,0,0), (0,0,1,0),$
$(0,0,0,1), (0,2,0,0)\}$.

Therefore, if we denote C_i as a CCBE involving i components and C_i^j as a cut set containing j C_is, $C_1^3, C_1 C_2, C_3, C_4$ and C_2^2 are the MCs of the system. The numbers of MCs for the corresponding implicants are given by the coefficients in Eq.(14) as 4, 12, 4, 1 and 3, respectively. Finally, the rare event approximation of the system failure probability is $4Q_1^3 + 12Q_1 Q_2 + 4Q_3 + Q_4 + 3Q_2^2$.

2.6   Numerical Examples

Example 1

We consider k-out-of-n systems with i.i.d. components. The total failure rate, λ_T, of a component is 0.01 or 0.0001. The proportion of CCF involving two components within λ is $\alpha_2 = 0.2$. That of m components is $\alpha_{m-1}/2$ for $m = 3, 4, \ldots, n$. The rest, $1 - \sum_{i=2}^n \alpha_i$, is α_1. The failure probabilities of the CCBEs are derived by using λ and α_i. Tables 1 and 2 show the failure probabilities of the 2-out-of-n system given by Eq.(26) and those obtained by the rare event approximation presented in Section 2.5, and their relative errors at $t=100$. Here, we use the probabilities analyzed by Markov analysis and calculated by the Runge-Kutta method as the exact system failure probabilities. Figure 2 shows the relative errors for $k = 1, 2, 3$

and $n = 5$ when $\lambda_T = 0.01$.

Table 1   Failure probabilities of 2-out-of-n systems ($\lambda_T=0.01$, $t=100$).

n	Markov	Eq.(26) (Error %)	Rare event approx. (Error %)
2	0.8347	0.7542 (-9.6)	1.1378 (36.3)
4	0.4389	0.4243 (-3.3)	0.6065 (38.2)
6	0.2012	0.2128 (5.8)	0.2944 (46.3)
8	0.0861	0.0947 (10.0)	0.1320 (53.4)
10	0.0351	0.0389 (10.8)	0.0553 (57.5)
15	0.0033	0.0034 (4.4)	0.0050 (54.4)
18	0.0009	0.0012 (30.4)	0.0018 (94.4)

Table 2   Failure probabilities of 2-out-of-n systems ($\lambda_T=0.0001$, $t=100$).

n	Markov	Eq.(26) (Error %)	Rare event approx. (Error %)
2	1.78×10^{-2}	1.78×10^{-2} (-0.1)	1.79×10^{-2} (0.4)
4	1.86×10^{-3}	1.88×10^{-3} (0.7)	1.88×10^{-3} (0.8)
6	4.28×10^{-4}	4.35×10^{-4} (1.5)	4.35×10^{-4} (1.6)
8	1.02×10^{-4}	1.05×10^{-4} (2.3)	1.05×10^{-4} (2.3)
10	2.49×10^{-5}	2.56×10^{-5} (3.1)	2.56×10^{-5} (3.1)
15	7.42×10^{-7}	7.79×10^{-7} (5.0)	7.79×10^{-7} (5.0)
18	9.09×10^{-8}	9.65×10^{-8} (6.2)	9.65×10^{-8} (6.2)

We can see significant errors in the rare event approximation in Table 1, regardless of the magnitude of the failure probability. From Table 2, we also see that the errors from the independence assumption dominate the whole approximation errors for the system with small failure probability.

Example 2

Next we consider a asymmetric system with three components. Of course, it is not so difficult to deal with more large systems, the explanations of a system model become more complicated. Let $\lambda_{1T} = \lambda_{2T} = 0.001$ and $\lambda_{3T} = 0.002$. Following the concrete representation in Section 2.4.1, we set $\alpha_{1,2}^{(2)} = 0.1$, $\alpha_{1,3}^{(2)} = 0.1$, $\alpha_{2,3}^{(2)} = 0.2$ and $\alpha_{1,2,3}^{(3)} = 0.05$, respectively. As a result, the rates of an independent failure of A_1, A_2 and A_3 ($\alpha_1^{(1)}, \alpha_2^{(1)}, \alpha_3^{(1)}$) are 0.75, 0.65 and 0.65, respectively. From Eqs.(8) and (9), failure rates and occurrence probabilities are calculated. Then, from a method shown in Section 2.3 and 2.4.1, the system failure probability is calculated. Table 3 shows the results. Note that these results contain errors originated from

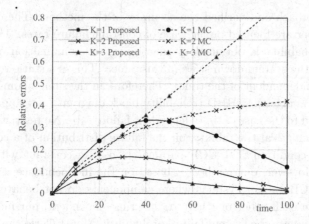

Fig. 2 Relative errors system failure probability of k-out-of-5 system.

the assumption of independence between CCBEs.

Table 3 Failure probabilities of k-out-of-3 systems.

t	$k=1$	$k=2$	$k=3$
0	0	0	0
10	0.0021	0.0132	0.0394
20	0.0044	0.0266	0.0775
30	0.0068	0.0404	0.1144
40	0.0094	0.0544	0.1501
50	0.0122	0.0687	0.1848
60	0.0152	0.0832	0.2184
70	0.0183	0.0979	0.2510
80	0.0217	0.1128	0.2826
90	0.0252	0.1279	0.3133
100	0.0288	0.1431	0.3431

2.7 Conclusion of Section 2

We dealt with common-cause failures in a k-out-of-n system and derived the system failure probability. The presented procedure follows the well-known implicit approach. We formulated the system failure probability for a general k-out-of-n system. The method was able to apply to systems with non-identical components. The implicit modeling includes some assumptions to model common-cause failures. We pointed out the errors included in this approach and verified the accuracy of the method. The discussion in this paper are focused on the case of constant failure rates. The system failure probability is obtained by identifying the combination of CCBEs leading to the system down state in this paper. This is a static representation (i.e., independent of the time). Therefore, in the same manner as FTA (fault tree analysis) or RBD (reliability block diagram), our approach can be extended to the case of time-dependent failure rate. No restriction, other than mathematical tractability, on the failure distribution of a component under the condition that CCF parameters α_k are constant with respect to time. However, our method is based on the independence assumption between CCBEs. For systems where components do not behave independently from each other or where α_k are time-dependent, our method will just approximate the system failure probability. Monte Carlo simulation or other modeling techniques for a dynamic system is more suitable in these cases. Regardless of whether constant failure rate or not, the assumption of independence between CCBEs is substantial in CCF analysis. Removing the assumption and providing a dynamic analysis for a system where the order of failures is taken into account are the future work.

3 System Failure Probability using Multivariate Exponential Distribution

3.1 *HMO Model*

In PRA, the system failure probability is traditionally obtained by Inclusion-Exclusion based method after obtaining the minimal cut sets in the system as shown in Section 2.2. However, this approach results to contain some estimation errors as shown in the previous section. Therefore, we introduce another method based on shock model and multivariate exponential distribution to estimate system failure probability of a system.

Marshall and Olkin considered the independent exponential shock model called Marshall-Olkin type shocks[Marchall and Olkin (1967); Vasely (1977)]. In the model, a system consisting of two components is subjected to shocks originating from three sources and occurring at random times. The shock from the first source destroys the first component, the shock from the second source destroys the second component and the shock from the third source destroys both components. They derived the joint survival function (bivariate exponential distribution) of the system, which has exponential marginals. They also extended the idea to a multivariate case. Several independent sources of shocks are considered for an n component system. The sources produce shocks that destroy only one specific component and shocks that destroy several components simultaneously. They derived the survival function as an MVE and some of its properties[Marchall and Olkin (1967)]. In recent years, numerous papers dealing with extensions of Marshall-Olkin distributions have appeared. However, the Marshall-Olkin model is not yet a commonly used mathematical model in the field of risk analysis, even though it has been considered to be a suitable model for CCF analysis in the field of statistics. One of the reasons for this is the difficulty of formulating the system reliability or unreliability for various system structures such as a k-out-of-n system using this model.

In this section, the homogeneous Marshall-Olkin (HMO) model and the MVE for the survival function are introduced. Let us consider a system with n components. Suppose that the system is subjected to shocks originating from $2^n - 1$ independent sources (CCBEs). Let I_i be a non-empty subset of the indices $1, 2, \ldots, n$. A shock from source i ($i = 1, 2, \ldots, 2^n - 1$) occurs at a random time U_i and simultaneously destroys all components belonging to I_i, i.e., it induces CCF with $|I_i|$ components. In the Marshall-Olkin model, each failure source is assumed to have an exponential distribution for its time of occurence;

$$P[U_i > t] = e^{-\lambda'_i t}, \tag{18}$$

where λ'_i is the occurrence rate associated with source i. The HMO model includes the assumption that the occurrence rate depends on the number of destroyed components, $|I_i|$. CCFs are most likely to occur in the homogeneous situation that identical components are used in the same environment or failures are chiefly caused by the same maintenance error. Thus, the distribution of U_i in the HMO model is [1]

$$P[U_i > t] = e^{-\lambda_{|I_i|} t}. \tag{19}$$

The random variable of the failure time of component j is denoted as X_j and satisfies

$$X_j = \min(U_i | \ j \in I_i).$$

---

[1] The occurrence rate λ in Eq.(19) is the same as λ' in Eq.(18). It is explicitly distinguished here from λ' in the homogeneous model because the meaning of the suffix is different from that of λ'. The suffix of λ' denotes the type of shock and that of λ denotes the number of destroyed components.

Then the joint survival function for an n-component system is

$$\bar{F}(t_1, t_2, \ldots, t_n)$$
$$= \exp\left[-\lambda_1 \sum_{i=1}^{n} t_i - \lambda_2 \sum_{i<j} \max(t_i, t_j) - \cdots - \lambda_n \max(t_1, t_2, \ldots, t_n)\right]. \quad (20)$$

Equation (20) is the joint survival function of HMO type shock model, where the number of destroyed CCF components depends on the magnitude of the shock. Furthermore, the probability $\bar{F}_n(t)$ that none of the component has failed at time t for an n-component system is

$$\bar{F}_n(t) = \exp\left[-\sum_{k=1}^{n}\binom{n}{k}\lambda_k t\right]. \quad (21)$$

From the definition of the marginal distribution,

$$F_n(t) = \sum_{i=0}^{n}(-1)^i\binom{n}{i}\bar{F}_i(t), \quad (22)$$

where $\bar{F}_0(t) = 1$.

Let us follow the above description by considering the case of $n = 3$. Seven types of shocks are assumed as follows; $I_1 = \{1\}, I_2 = \{2\}, I_3 = \{3\}, I_4 = \{1,2\}, I_5 = \{1,3\}, I_6 = \{2,3\}, I_7 = \{1,2,3\}$. Thus, $P[U_1 > t] = P[U_2 > t] = P[U_3 > t] = e^{-\lambda_1 t}$, $P[U_4 > t] = P[U_5 > t] = P[U_6 > t] = e^{-\lambda_2 t}$, $P[U_7 > t] = e^{-\lambda_3 t}$ and $X_1 = \min(U_1, U_4, U_5, U_7)$, $X_2 = \min(U_2, U_4, U_6, U_7)$, $X_3 = \min(U_3, U_5, U_6, U_7)$. Then,

$$\begin{aligned}
\bar{F}(t_1, t_2, t_3) &= P[X_1 > t_1, X_2 > t_2, X_3 > t_3]\\
&= P[\min(U_1, U_4, U_5, U_7) > t_1, \min(U_2, U_4, U_6, U_7) > t_2,\\
&\quad \min(U_3, U_5, U_6, U_7) > t_3]\\
&= P[U_1 > t_1, U_2 > t_2, U_3 > t_3, U_4 > \max(t_1, t_2), U_5 > \max(t_1, t_3),\\
&\quad U_6 > \max(t_2, t_3), U_7 > \max(t_1, t_2, t_3)]\\
&= \exp[-\lambda_1 t_1 - \lambda_1 t_2 - \lambda_1 t_3 - \lambda_2 \max(t_1, t_2) - \lambda_2 \max(t_1, t_3)\\
&\quad - \lambda_2 \max(t_2, t_3) - \lambda_3 \max(t_1, t_2, t_3)], \quad (23)
\end{aligned}$$

$$\bar{F}_3(t) = \exp[-3\lambda_1 t - 3\lambda_2 t - \lambda_3 t],$$
$$F_3(t) = 1 - 3\bar{F}_1(t) + 3\bar{F}_2(t) - \bar{F}_3(t).$$

3.2 Model Description

The system is a coherent k-out-of-n:G redundant system, i.e., it is composed of n identical but non-independent components and every component is relevant. The system functions if at least k out of n components are functioning. The system is subjected to random shocks following the HMO model described in the previous section.

3.3 Marginal Distributions of HMO Model

As an example, we consider the case of $n = 3$, whose survival function is given by Eq.(23). The two-dimensional marginal is

$$\bar{F}(t_1, t_2) = \bar{F}(t_1, t_2, 0)$$
$$= \exp\left[-\lambda_1 t_1 - \lambda_1 t_2 - \lambda_2 \max(t_1, t_2) - \lambda_2 \max(t_1, 0)\right.$$
$$\left. -\lambda_2 \max(t_2, 0) - \lambda_3 \max(t_1, t_2, 0)\right]$$
$$= \exp\left[-\lambda_1 t_1 - \lambda_1 t_2 - \lambda_2 \max(t_1, t_2) - \lambda_2 t_1 - \lambda_2 t_2 - \lambda_3 \max(t_1, t_2, 0)\right].$$

The two-dimensional marginal when $t_1 = t_2 = t$ is

$$\bar{F}_2(t) = \exp\left[-2\lambda_1 t - 3\lambda_2 t - \lambda_3 t\right] = \exp\left[-\sum_{k=1}^{3}\left\{\binom{3}{k} - \binom{1}{k}\right\}\lambda_k\, t\right],$$

where $\binom{i}{k} = 0$ for $k > i$. Then the one-dimensional marginal is

$$\bar{F}_1(t) = \exp\left[-\lambda_1 t - 2\lambda_2 t - \lambda_3 t\right] = \exp\left[-\sum_{k=1}^{3}\left\{\binom{3}{k} - \binom{2}{k}\right\}\lambda_k\, t\right].$$

A similar argument yields the $(n - j)$-dimensional marginal of Eq.(20). Consider $\bar{F}(t_1, t_2 \ldots, t_j, t_{j+1}, \ldots, t_n)$. The terms involving only $t_1, t_2, \ldots, t_j$ in the exponential portion of Eq.(20) are

$$-\lambda_1 \sum_{i=1}^{j} t_i - \lambda_2 \sum_{i_1 < i_2 \leq j} \max(t_{i_1}, t_{i_2}) - \lambda_3 \sum_{i_1 < i_2 < i_3 \leq j} \max(t_{i_1}, t_{i_2}, t_{i_3}) -$$
$$\cdots - \lambda_j \max(t_1, t_2, \ldots, t_j). \tag{24}$$

Setting $t_1 = t_2 = \ldots = t_j = t$, this can be written as $-\sum_{k=1}^{j} \lambda_k \binom{j}{k} t$. As the $(n - j)$-dimensional marginal is given by $\bar{F}(t_{j+1}, t_{j+2}, \ldots, t_n) = \bar{F}(0, \ldots, 0, t_{j+1}, t_{j+2}, \ldots, t_n)$, Eq.(24) becomes 0 and the other terms in Eq.(20) remain in the marginal. Setting $t_1 = t_2 = \ldots, t_{n-j} = t$, we obtain

$$\bar{F}_{n-j}(t) = \exp\left[-\sum_{k=1}^{n}\left\{\binom{n}{k} - \binom{j}{k}\right\}\lambda_k\, t\right]. \tag{25}$$

Therefore, all the marginal distributions of the MVE are also exponential distributions.

3.4 *Reliability of a k-out-of-n System*

Theorem 9.1. The reliability $R_{k/n}(t)$ of a k-out-of-n:G system at time t which is subjected to shocks following the HMO model is

$$R_{k/n}(t) = \sum_{i=k}^{n} \binom{n}{i} \sum_{j=0}^{n-i} (-1)^j \binom{n-i}{j} \bar{F}_{i+j}(t). \qquad (26)$$

Proof. The i-dimensional marginal $\bar{F}_i(t)$ is the probability that i arbitrary components function at time t regardless of the states of the other $n-i$ components. Therefore, $\bar{F}_i(t)$ is the probability that at least i components including i specific components function at time t. Then the probability $P_{i;n}(t)$ that only the i specific components function is

$$P_{i;n}(t) = \bar{F}_i(t) - \binom{n-i}{1}\bar{F}_{i+1}(t) + \binom{n-i}{2}\bar{F}_{i+2}(t) - \cdots$$

$$= \sum_{j=0}^{n-i}(-1)^j \binom{n-i}{j}\bar{F}_{i+j}(t).$$

The second term is the probability that at least $i+1$ specific components function, including the i previously mentioned components and one additional component. Because the second term includes the probability that at least $i+2$ components survive, the subsequent terms are required. From the exchangeability of marginals, Eq.(26) is derived. ∎

Corollary 9.1. If $k = n$, then the system has a series structure and the reliability is $\bar{F}_n(t)$, given by Eq.(21). If $k = 1$, then the system is a parallel system and the reliability is

$$R_{1/n}(t) = \sum_{i=1}^{n}(-1)^{i-1}\binom{n}{i}\bar{F}_i(t). \qquad (27)$$

Proof. This is obvious for $k = n$. Substituting 1 to k in Eq.(26) gives,

$$R_{1/n}(t) = \sum_{i=1}^{n}\sum_{j=0}^{n-i}(-1)^j \binom{n}{i}\binom{n-i}{j}\bar{F}_{i+j}(t)$$

$$= \sum_{u=1}^{n}\sum_{v=1}^{u}(-1)^{u-v}\binom{n}{v}\binom{n-v}{u-v}\bar{F}_u(t)$$

$$= \sum_{u=1}^{n}\binom{n}{u}\bar{F}_u(t)\sum_{v=1}^{u}(-1)^{u-v}\binom{u}{v}$$

$$= \sum_{u=1}^{n}(-1)^{u-1}\binom{n}{u}\bar{F}_u(t).$$

Here, in the second equation both summations are resummings, and in the last equation, we use

$$\sum_{v=1}^{u}(-1)^{u-v}\binom{u}{v} = (-1)^{u-1}. \quad \blacksquare$$

We can confirm Eq.(27) from Eq.(21), which gives the unreliability of an n-series system as follows:

$$R_{1/n}(t) = 1 - F_n(t) = 1 - \sum_{i=0}^{n}(-1)^i\binom{n}{i}\bar{F}_i(t)$$

$$= -\sum_{i=1}^{n}(-1)^i\binom{n}{i}\bar{F}_i(t) = \sum_{i=1}^{n}(-1)^{i-1}\binom{n}{i}\bar{F}_i(t).$$

Corollary 9.2. If $\lambda_2 = \lambda_3 = \ldots, \lambda_{n-1} = 0$, the reliability of a k-out-of-n:G system is

$$R_{k/n}(t) = \bar{G}_n(t)\sum_{i=k}^{n}\binom{n}{i}\{\bar{G}_1(t)\}^i\{G_1(t)\}^{n-i}, \tag{28}$$

where $G_1(t) = 1 - e^{-\lambda_1 t}$ is the occurrence time distribution of independent shocks, $G_n(t) = 1 - e^{-\lambda_n t}$ is that of a shock which destroys all components, and $\bar{G}_i(t) = 1 - G_i(t)$ for $i = 1, n$.

Proof. In this case, from Eqs.(21), (22) and (25),

$$\bar{F}_i(t) = \bar{G}_n(t)\{\bar{G}_1(t)\}^i, \ F_i(t) = \bar{G}_n(t)\{G_1(t)\}^i, \ i = 1, 2, \ldots, n.$$

Substituting $\bar{F}_i(t)$ in Eq.(26) gives,

$$R_{k/n}(t) = \bar{G}_n(t)\sum_{i=k}^{n}\binom{n}{i}\left\{\sum_{j=0}^{n-i}(-1)^j\binom{n-i}{j}\{\bar{G}_1(t)\}^{i+j}\right\}$$

$$= \bar{G}_n(t)\sum_{i=k}^{n}\binom{n}{i}\{\bar{G}_1(t)\}^i\left\{\sum_{j=0}^{n-i}(-1)^j\binom{n-i}{j}\{\bar{G}_1(t)\}^j\right\}. \tag{29}$$

Using the binomial theorem, Eq.(28) is obtained. $\blacksquare$

The model in Corollary 9.2 corresponds to the β-factor model in CCF analysis. Eq.(28) shows that the reliability is given by the product of two independent survival functions associated with the independent failure mode and CCF. Furthermore, the survival function of the independent failure mode is given by a binomial distribution. This is a reasonable result for this model. Eq.(29) is consistent with Theorem 9.1 in [Chae and Clark (1986)]. Therefore, our theorem generalizes the BO formulation.

In this section, we proposed a formula to provide the reliability of k-out-of-n system using MVE. It is an alternative method to take into account the influence of CCFs in PRA. If CCF failure rates are obtained, the reliability of a system is obtained by a closed form. Note that our model is different from the conventional CCF parametric models in that the possibility of repeated failures are accepted. However, since it is difficult to remove repeated failures completely in actual systems, the possibility of repeated failures overestimates reliability in conventional methods. Thus we can say that the proposed formula is useful for PSA with conventional failure assumption because it evaluates reliability keeping on the safe side.

3.5   *Markov Chain Representation*

Continuous time Markov analysis is a commonly used method in reliability analysis when all the event occurrences follow exponential distributions. The HMO model can be analyzed using a one-dimensional Markov chain because all the shocks occur independently and follow exponential occurrence time distributions. Let state i be the system state that i components fail in a k-out-of-n system, $i = 0, 1, \ldots, n$. The transition rate p_{ij} from state i to state j is given by

$$
p_{ij} = \begin{cases} \dbinom{n-i}{j-i} \displaystyle\sum_{l=0}^{i} \dbinom{i}{l} \lambda_{j-i+l}, & j > i, \\ \\ 0, & otherwise. \end{cases} \tag{30}
$$

In Eq.(30), $\binom{n-i}{j-i}$ is the number of combinations of choosing $j-i$ components from the remaining $n-i$ components, and the summation is the sum of the possible failure rates from each of the component combinations in state i. Note that the new $j - i$ components must fail in the transition from state i to state j and that repeated failures are allowed by the assumption of independence for shock occurrences. Denoting the probability of state i at time t as $P_i(t)$, the following differential equations are derived:

$$
\frac{dP_i(t)}{dt} = \sum_{j=0}^{i-1} p_{ji} P_j(t) - \sum_{j=i+1}^{n} p_{ij} P_i(t), \quad i = 0, 1, \ldots, n. \tag{31}
$$

With the initial probabilities $P_0(0) = 1$, $P_i(0) = 0$, for $i = 1, \ldots, n$, Eq.(31) can be solved numerically and the reliability of a k-out-of-n system is given by $R_{k/n}(t) = \sum_{i=0}^{n-k} P_i(t)$.

4 Conclusion

We dealt with common-cause failures in a k-out-of-n system and derived the system failure probability. The presented procedure follows the well-known implicit approach. We formulated the system failure probability/reliability for a general k-out-of-n system following the conventional inclusion-exclusion based method and MVE based method. We pointed out the errors included in inclusion-exclusion based method and verified the accuracy of the method. This errors essentially comes from the assumption of independence between CCBEs. For systems where components do not behave independently from each other, our method will just approximate the system failure probability.

On the other hand, in MVE based method, we relaxed the model assumption in Bayramoglu and Ozkut's earlier study by considering all combinations of components in a system as shocks and formulated the reliability. Our formulation was a generalized version of that in Bayramoglu and Ozkut's study and its accuracy was confirmed by Markov analysis. We also numerically compared the system reliability between inclusion-exclusion-based method and Bayramoglu and Ozkut's β-factor-based method. We hope that the result in this paper will increase the communication between PRA engineers and statisticians, who conventionally work in different fields of study.

Acknowledgments

This research was partially supported by JSPS KAKENHI Grant Numbers 25350490 and 16K01308. The authors thank the JSPS for their support.

References

Watson, J. A., and Edwards, G. T. (1979). *A Study of Common-Mode Failures, R-146, Safety and Reliability Directorate*, (United Kingdom Atomic Energy Authority).

U.S. Nuclear Regulatory Commission (1983). *PRA Procedures Guide*, NUREG/CR2300.

International Atomic Energy Agency (IAEA) (2011). *IAEA International Fact Finding Expert Mission of the Fukushima Dai-Ichi NPP Accident following the Great East Japan Earthquake and Tsunami*, http://www-pub.iaea.org/MTCD/meetings/PDFplus/2011/cn200/documentation/cn200_Final-Fukushima-Mission_Report.pdf.

U.S. Nuclear Regulatory Commission (1998). *Guidelines on Modeling Common-Cause Failures in Probabilistic Risk Assessment*, NUREG/CR5485.

Vesely, W.E.(1977). Estimating common-cause failure probabilities in reliability and risk analyses: Marshall-Olkin specializations, Nuclear Systems Reliability Engineering and Risk Assessment (J.B. Fussell & G.R. Burdick, Eds), (Society of Industrial and Applied Mathematics).

Dhillon, B.S. and Anude,O.C.(1994). Common-Cause Failures in Engineering Systems: A review, *Int'l J. Reliability, Quality and Safety Eng.*, **1**, pp.103–129.

Vaurio, J.K.(1994). The theory and quantification of commoncause shock events for redundant standby systems, *Reliability Eng. and System Safety*, **43**, 3, pp.289–305.

Chae, C. and Clark, G.M.(1986). System reliability in the presence of common-cause failures, *IEEE Trans. Reliability*, **R-35**, 1,pp.32–35.

U.S. Nuclear Regulatory Commission (1983). *PRA Procedures Guide*. NUREG/CR2300.

Yuge T., Yanagi S. (2015). *Estimating failure probability of a k-out-of-n system considering common-cause failures, Trans. on Fundam. Electron. Commun. Comput. Sci. (IEICE)*, E98-A, pp.2025-30.

Yuge T., Maruyama M. and Yanagi S. (2016). *Reliability of a k-out-of-n system with common-cause failures using multivariate exponential distribution. Procedia Computer Science*, 96, pp.968–976.

Marshall A.W., Olkin I.(1967). *A multivariate exponential distribution. J. Amer. Statist. Assoc.*, 62, pp.30–44.

Barlow R.E.and Proschan F. (1975). *Statistical theory of reliability and life testing*, *3rd ed.* Holt, Rinehart and Winston.

Bayramoglu I and Ozkut M.(2015). *The reliability of coherent systems subjected to Marshall-Olkin type shocks. IEEE Trans. on Reliability*, 64, pp.435–43.

Chapter 10

Comparison Between Parallel and Standby Redundant Systems

Won Young Yun[1], Toshio Nakagawa[2]

[1] *Department of Industrial Engineering,*
Pusan National University,

[2] *Department of Business Administration,*
Aichi Institute of Technology

1 Introduction

Redundancy of units is used to achieve required system reliability. A number of papers have treated the optimum redundancy problems. Barlow and Proschan (1965) obtained the optimal number of redundant units for the cases of maximizing system reliability and maximizing the expected system life in stochastic failure systems. Nakagawa (1984) studied the problem of determining the optimal number of redundant units which minimized the expected cost rate. Yun and Bai (1986) considered the same redundant optimization problem with common cause failures. Yun (1989) considered a redundancy optimization problem of standby systems. Kuo *et al.* (2001) summarized redundancy optimization problems. Recently, Chen *et al.* (2014) compared the two systems which had different cost structures.

In this paper, we compare the two typical redundant systems: parallel and standby systems. First, we consider simple parallel and standby systems and compare the mean times to system failures in two systems. Then, we compare the expected cost rates of the two systems. Theoretically, the standby system is more efficient than the parallel system and has long mean times to system failures and less expected cost rate. But, the switching device in the standby system may be not perfect in practice and the performance of the standby system depends on the success probability of the switching device. Additionally, dependence between redundant units in the systems is studied to compare the parallel and standby systems. Common cause failure and load sharing models are assumed and the mean times to system failures and the expected cost rates are compared in the two redundant systems. In numerical examples, we investigate the effect of model parameters to the optimal number of redundant units in parallel and standby systems. Finally, we consider preventive maintenance models of parallel and standby redundant systems.

1.1 *Notation*

$F(t), \overline{F}(t)$	:	distribution and survival functions of the failure time of one unit
$F_c(t), \overline{F}_c(t)$	:	distribution and survival function of common cause failure
μ	:	the mean life of one unit, $\int_0^\infty \overline{F}(t) \mathrm{d}t$
p	:	switching success probability $(0 < p < 1)$
c_p	:	fixed cost for replacement of a parallel system
c_s	:	fixed cost of replacement of a standby system
c	:	replacement cost of each unit
λ	:	constant failure rate of one unit
λ_c	:	constant failure rate of common cause failure

1.2 *Assumptions*

1. The system is used to failure and preventive replacement is not considered.
2. N $(N = 1, 2, \cdots)$ identical units are used to make the parallel and standby systems.
3. The failures of units are independent.
4. The switching device is imperfect and has the failure probability $(1-p)$.
5. Replacement times are negligible.

2 Cost Models

In this section, we consider simple parallel and standby systems and compare the mean times to system failure and the expected cost rates of the two systems.

2.1 Mean Times to System Failure and Expected Cost Rates

The mean life of the parallel system ($MTTF$) is

$$MTTF_p = \int_0^\infty [1 - F(t)^N]dt, \qquad (N = 1, 2, ...).$$

The mean life of the standby system is

$$MTTF_s = \mu[(1 + 2p + 3p^2 + ... + (N-1)p^{N-2})(1-p) + Np^{N-1}]$$

$$= \mu(1 + p + p^2 + ... + Np^{N-1}) = \mu\frac{1 - p^N}{1 - p}, \qquad (1)$$

which increases strictly with p from μ to $N\mu$ and increases strictly with N from μ to $\mu/(1-p)$.

For given N, we can find the value of p^* that gives the equal mean times of parallel and standby systems as follows.

$$\mu\frac{1 - p^N}{1 - p} = \int_0^\infty \left[1 - F(t)^N\right] dt. \qquad (2)$$

When $N = 1$, p^* is any value and we set that $p^* = 0$.

If $p > p^*$, $MTTF$ of the standby system is greater than $MTTF$ of the parallel system. Otherwise, the parallel system is better than the standby system.

Example 10.1. In particular, when $F(t) = 1 - e^{-\lambda t}$, Eq. (2) is simplified as follows;

$$\frac{1 - p^N}{1 - p} = \sum_{j=1}^N \frac{1}{j}. \qquad (3)$$

We derive the value of p^* which satisfies the Eq. (3). If we compare p^j with $1/(j+1)$, we can easily have $p \geq 1/2 \geq 1/N \geq p^{N-1}$ ($N = 2, 3, ...$). In particular, when $N = 2$, $p = 1/2$, and $p > 1/2 > 1/N > p^{N-1}$ ($N = 3, 4, ...$). Next, noting that

$$\frac{1 - p^N}{1 - p} = \sum_{j=0}^{N-1} \frac{1}{j+1}, \qquad \frac{1 - p^{N+1}}{1 - p} = \sum_{j=0}^N \frac{1}{j+1}.$$

we have

$$\frac{1 - (p_{N+1}^*)^{N+1}}{1 - p_{N+1}^*} = \frac{1 - (p_N^*)^N}{1 - p_N^*} + \frac{1}{N+1},$$

Table 1   Success probabilities of switching for equal MTTFs.

N	p^*	N	p^*
1	0	11	0.673
2	0.500	12	0.681
3	0.541	13	0.688
4	0.571	14	0.694
5	0.595	15	0.700
6	0.614	16	0.705
7	0.629	17	0.710
8	0.643	18	0.715
9	0.654	19	0.719
10	0.664	20	0.722
		∞	1.000

i.e.,

$$\sum_{j=0}^{N-1} [(p_{N+1}^*)^j - (p_N^*)^j] + (p_N^*)^j = \frac{1}{N+1}.$$

Noting that

$$(p_{N+1}^*)^j \le \frac{1}{N+1},$$

we easily know $p_{N+1}^* > p_N^*$ and p_N^* increases strictly with N ($N \ge 2$) from $1/2$ to 1. Table 1 shows the value of p^* that satisfies Eq. (3) for given N.

From Table 1, we can know that the success probability p^* increases in N and the standby system with many redundant units needs high success probability of the switching device to give longer $MTTF$ than the parallel system with same redundant units.

Now we consider the replacement at system failures and the expected cost rates of the standby and parallel system are given by

Standby case : $C_S(N, p) = \dfrac{1 - p}{\mu} \dfrac{c_s + c_N}{1 - p^N}.$ (4)

Parallel case : $C_P(N) = \dfrac{c_p + cN}{\int_0^\infty [1 - F(t)^N] dt}.$ (5)

Theorem 10.1. We consider a simple expected cost rate $C(N) = (c_1 + c_2 N)/S(N)$ where $S(N)$ is the expected duration of a cycle. If $S(N)$ is increasing in N and $S(N + 1) - S(N)$ is decreasing in N, the optimal number N minimizing the expected cost rate $C(N)$ exists and is unique.

Proof. The necessary condition of the optimal N minimizing $C(N)$ is:
From $C(N^* + 1) \geq C(N^*)$,
$$C(N^* + 1) - C(N^*)$$
$$= \frac{c_2 N[S(N^*) - S(N^* + 1)] + c_2 S(N^*) + c_1[S(N^*) - S(N^* + 1)]}{S(N^* + 1)S(N^*)} \geq 0,$$
and if $S(N^* + 1) - S(N^*) > 0$, then the inequality is
$$\frac{S(N^*)}{S(N^* + 1) - S(N^*)} - N^* \geq \frac{c_1}{c_2}.$$
Let $Q(N) = \frac{S(N)}{S(N+1) - S(N)} - N$, and then $Q(N^*) \geq \frac{c_1}{c_2}$. ∎

From the inequality $C(N^*) \leq C(N^* - 1)$, we obtain the inequality $Q(N^* - 1) < c_2/c_1$.

Here
$$Q(N^* + 1) - Q(N^*)$$
$$= S(N^* + 1) \left[\frac{1}{S(N^* + 2) - S(N^* + 1)} - \frac{1}{S(N^* + 1) - S(N^*)} \right] > 0.$$
Thus, $Q(N)$ is increasing in N and the value of N^* satisfying the necessary condition exits and is unique.

In order to find the optimal N^* minimizing Eq. (4), we should check the mean time to failure $MTTF_s(N)$. The mean time is an increasing function and
$$MTTF_s(N + 1) - MTTF_s(N) = (1 - p^{N+1}) - (1 - p^N) = p^N(1 - p).$$
Thus, $MTTF_s(N + 1) - MTTF_s(N)$ is decreasing in N. From Theorem 10.1, there exists a finite and unique optimal N for the standby system.

For the parallel system, there also exists a finite and unique solution that minimizes Eq. (5) because $\int_0^\infty [1 - F(t)^N] dt$ is an increasing function of N and $\int_0^\infty \overline{F}(t) F(t)^N dt$ is a decreasing function of N (Refer Chen et al. (2014)).

Example 10.2. In particular, when $F(t) = 1 - e^{-\lambda t}$, Table 2 shows the optimal redundant units N^* and the optimal expected cost rates for the parallel and standby systems with different fixed costs and success probability of switching device. In Table 2, the expected cost rates are $\mu C_S(N, p)$ and $\mu C_P(N)$.

The optimal redundant units increase in the fixed cost of replacement and the parallel system is better than the standby system in cases with low success probability of switching in the standby system. The last column shows the values of p^* that gives equal optimal values of expected cost rates in parallel and standby cases.

Table 2   Optimal redundant units and expected cost rates ($c = 1$, $c_p = c_s$)

c_s	Parallel case	Standby case p			p value $C_s(N^*, p) = C_p(N^*)$
		0.5	0.7	0.9	
1	1=2	1=2	2	4	0.5000
	(2.0000)	(2.0000)	(1.7647)	(1.4539)	
2	2	2	3	6	0.5000
	(2.6667)	(2.6667)	(2.2831)	(1.7074)	
4	3	2=3	4	8	0.5408
	(3.8182)	(4.0000)	(3.1583)	(2.1070)	
8	5	3	5	10	0.5788
	(5.6934)	(6.2857)	(4.6879)	(2.7636)	
16	8	4	6	13	0.6171
	(8.8305)	(10.6667)	(7.4800)	(3.8884)	

3   Cost Models with Common Cause Failures

In this section, we consider a dependence model between redundant units in parallel and standby systems which assumes common cause failures. Thus, all working units are failed by the common cause failure. Then, only one unit is operated in the standby system and the operating unit fails by internal failures and common cause failure, whichever occurs first. Thus, $MTTF$ of the standby system is

$$MTTF_s = \int_0^\infty \overline{F}(t)\overline{F}_c(t)\mathrm{d}t\frac{1 - p^N}{1 - p},$$

and $MTTF$ of the parallel system is

$$MTTF_p = \int_0^\infty [1 - F(t)^N]\overline{F}_c(t)\mathrm{d}t.$$

In particular, when $F(t) = 1 - e^{-\lambda t}$ and $F_c(t) = 1 - e^{-\lambda_c t}$, the mean times to failure of the parallel and standby systems are

$$MTTF_p = \sum_{j=1}^N \binom{N}{j}(-1)^{j+1}\frac{1}{\lambda_c + j\lambda} \quad \text{and} \quad MTTF_s = \frac{1}{\lambda_c + \lambda}\frac{1 - p^N}{1 - p}.$$

Thus, for given N, we can find the value of p^* that satisfies the below equation.

$$\frac{1}{\lambda_c + \lambda}\frac{1 - p^N}{1 - p} = \sum_{j=1}^N \binom{N}{j}(-1)^{j+1}\frac{1}{\lambda_c + j\lambda}. \tag{6}$$

If $p > p^*$, $MTTF$ of the standby system is greater than $MTTF$ of the parallel system with same number of units. Table 3 shows the values of

Table 3   Success probabilities of switching for equal $MTTFs$

N	λ_c/λ				
	0	0.05	0.1	0.2	0.5
1	0	0	0	0	0
2	0.500	0.488	0.476	0.455	0.400
3	0.541	0.528	0.517	0.494	0.437
4	0.571	0.558	0.546	0.524	0.465
5	0.595	0.582	0.570	0.547	0.486
6	0.614	0.601	0.589	0.565	0.502
7	0.629	0.617	0.604	0.580	0.516
8	0.643	0.630	0.618	0.593	0.527
9	0.654	0.641	0.628	0.604	0.536
10	0.664	0.651	0.638	0.613	0.544
11	0.673	0.660	0.647	0.621	0.551
12	0.681	0.667	0.654	0.628	0.557
13	0.688	0.674	0.661	0.635	0.562
14	0.694	0.681	0.667	0.641	0.567
15	0.700	0.686	0.673	0.646	0.571
16	0.715	0.691	0.678	0.650	0.575
17	0.710	0.696	0.682	0.655	0.578
18	0.715	0.700	0.686	0.659	0.581
19	0.719	0.704	0.690	0.663	0.584
20	0.722	0.708	0.694	0.666	0.586
∞	1.000	1.000	1.000	1.000	1.000

p that satisfies Eq. (6). Clearly, when $\lambda_c = 0$, p^* corresponds to that of Table 1.

From Table 3, we can know that the success probability decreases in λ_c, and increases in N and the standby system with many redundant units needs high success probability of the switching device to give longer $MTTF$ than the parallel system with same redundant units.

If we replace the failed systems by new ones, the expected cost rates of the standby and parallel systems are given

Standby case : $C_S(N,p) = (\lambda_c + \lambda)(1-p)\dfrac{c_s + cN}{1 - p^N}.$

Parallel case : $C_p(N) = \dfrac{c_p + cN}{\sum_{j=1}^{N} \binom{N}{j}(-1)^{j+1}\frac{1}{\lambda_c+j\lambda}}.$

The optimal redundant units of the standby system are equal to the optimal numbers of the simple standby system in Table 2. For the parallel system, we check $MTTF$ of the parallel system.

$$MTTF_p(N+1) - MTTF_p(N) = \int_0^\infty F(t)^N \overline{F}(t)\overline{F}_c(t)\mathrm{d}t$$

Table 4 Optimal redundant units and expected cost rates of the parallel and standby systems ($c = 1$, $c_p = c_s$)

c_s	$\lambda_c = 0.05, \lambda = 1$							
	Parallel case		*p* (standby system)					
			0.5		0.7		0.9	
1	1	(2.0010)	1=2	(2.1000)	2	(1.8529)	4	(1.5266)
2	2	(2.6682)	2	(2.8000)	3	(2.3973)	6	(1.7927)
4	3	(3.8206)	2=3	(4.2000)	4	(3.3162)	8	(2.2123)
8	5	(5.6976)	3	(6.6000)	5	(4.9223)	10	(2.9018)
16	8	(8.8377)	4	(11.2000)	6	(7.8540)	13	(4.0828)

c_s	$\lambda_c = 0.1, \lambda = 1$							
	Parallel case		*p* (standby system)					
			0.5		0.7		0.9	
1	1	(2.0020)	1=2	(2.2000)	2	(1.9412)	4	(1.5993)
2	2	(2.6698)	2	(2.9333)	3	(2.5114)	6	(1.8781)
4	3	(3.8231)	2=3	(4.4000)	4	(3.4741)	8	(2.3177)
8	5	(5.7018)	3	(6.9143)	5	(5.1567)	10	(3.0400)
16	7	(8.8846)	4	(11.7333)	6	(8.2280)	13	(4.2772)

c_s	$\lambda_c = 0.2, \lambda = 1$							
	Parallel case		*p* (standby system)					
			0.5		0.7		0.9	
1	1	(2.0040)	1=2	(2.4000)	2	(2.1176)	4	(1.7447)
2	2	(2.6729)	2	(3.2000)	3	(2.7397)	6	(2.0488)
4	3	(3.8280)	2=3	(4.8000)	4	(3.7900)	8	(2.5284)
8	4	(5.7759)	3	(7.5429)	5	(5.6255)	10	(3.3163)
16	7	(8.8987)	4	(12.8000)	6	(8.9760)	13	(4.6660)

c_s	$\lambda_c = 0.5, \lambda = 1$							
	Parallel case		*p* (standby system)					
			0.5		0.7		0.9	
1	1	(2.0100)	1=2	(3.0000)	2	(2.6471)	4	(2.1809)
2	2	(2.6822)	2	(4.0000)	3	(3.4247)	6	(2.5610)
4	2	(4.0233)	2=3	(6.0000)	4	(4.7375)	8	(3.1605)
8	4	(5.7999)	3	(9.4286)	5	(7.0318)	10	(4.1454)
16	5	(9.2644)	4	(16.0000)	6	(11.2200)	13	(5.8326)

decreases in N. Thus, the optimal redundant unit of the parallel system exists and its number is finite from Theorem 10.1. Table 4 shows the optimal N^* and the optimal values of the expected cost rates of two redundant systems.

From Table 4, we can know that the optimal redundant units increase in the fixed cost of replacement and the parallel system is better than the standby system in cases with low success probability of switching in the standby system. The parallel system is also better than the standby system in cases with high failure rates λ_c of common cause failures.

4 Load Sharing Models

In this section, we consider a load sharing model to compare the redundant systems. Additionally, we assume that the total load is constant over time and it is shared equally by the working components. To obtain the system reliability of redundant systems, the relationship between load size and failure distribution of units needed. In this paper, we assume the power rule relation [Nelson (1990)]; [Yun and Cha (2010b)] and the failure rate of working units is

$$\lambda_\ell = \rho_0 L^{\rho_1},$$

where L is the total load and ρ_0, ρ_1 are parameters of the relationship between failure rate and load. Since the working units share the total load equally, the load amount to each working unit when i units among N units fail,

$$\ell(i) = \frac{L}{N - i}, \qquad i = 0, 1, \ldots, N - 1.$$

Thus, when i units fail, the failure rate of each working unit is given

$$\lambda(i) = \rho_0 \left(\frac{L}{N - i} \right)^{\rho_1}.$$

Let $T(i, N)$ be the inter-arrival time interval between $i - 1^{th}$ and i^{th} failures in the parallel system with N. Then, the system failure time is

$$\sum_{i=1}^{N} T(i, N),$$

and $T(i, N)$ follows an exponential distribution. Thus, the mean time to the parallel system with N units is

$$MTTF_p = \sum_{i=1}^{N} E[T(i, N)] = \frac{\sum_{i=1}^{N} (N - i + 1)^{\rho_1 - 1}}{\rho_0 L^{\rho_1}}.$$

For the standby system, one operating unit covers whole load and the $MTTF$ is given simply and the mean time to the system failure is given

$$MTTF_s = \frac{1}{\rho_0 L^{\rho_1}} \frac{1 - p^N}{1 - p}.$$

Table 5   Success probabilities of switching for equal $MTTF_s$

N	ρ_1			
	0.3	0.5	0.7	0.9
1	0	0	0	0
2	0.616	0.707	0.812	0.933
3	0.653	0.739	0.835	0.942
4	0.680	0.762	0.851	0.948
5	0.702	0.780	0.863	0.953
6	0.719	0.794	0.873	0.957
7	0.733	0.806	0.882	0.960
8	0.746	0.816	0.889	0.962
9	0.756	0.825	0.894	0.965
10	0.766	0.833	0.900	0.966
11	0.774	0.840	0.904	0.968
12	0.781	0.846	0.908	0.970
13	0.788	0.851	0.912	0.971
14	0.794	0.856	0.915	0.972
15	0.799	0.860	0.918	0.973
16	0.804	0.865	0.923	0.974
17	0.809	0.868	0.923	0.975
18	0.813	0.872	0.926	0.976
19	0.817	0.875	0.928	0.977
20	0.821	0.878	0.930	0.977
∞	1.000	1.000	1.000	1.000

Thus, the success probability of switching is obtained from the following equation.

$$\frac{1-p^N}{1-p} = \sum_{i=1}^{N}(N-i+1)^{\rho_1-1}.$$

Thus, for given N, Table 5 shows the value of p^* that satisfies the above equation.

We can find the same trend for success probability of switching in Table 1. The expected cost rates of the standby and parallel systems are given

Standby case : $C_S(N,p) = (\rho_0 L^{\rho_1})(1-p)\dfrac{c_s + cN}{1-p^N}.$

Parallel case : $C_p(N) = (\rho_0 L^{\rho_1})\dfrac{c_p + cN}{\sum_{i=1}^{N}(N-i+1)^{\rho_1-1}}.$

For the standby system, the optimal number of redundant units exists and is finite obviously. For the parallel system, we let $S_p(N) = MTTF_p(N)$

Table 6 Optimal redundant units and expected cost rates of parallel and standby systems ($c = 1$, $c_p = c_s$)

c_s	Parallel							
	ρ_1							
	0.3		0.5		0.7		0.9	
1	2	(1.8569)	3	(1.7510)	4	(1.5668)	11	(1.2758)
2	3	(2.4050)	4	(2.1548)	7	(1.8181)	20	(1.3549)
4	5	(3.2350)	7	(2.7378)	12	(2.1430)	39	(1.4437)
8	8	(4.4985)	12	(3.5643)	22	(2.5583)	75	(1.5417)
16	14	(6.4418)	22	(4.7342)	42	(3.0835)	148	(1.6488)

c_s	Standby					
	p					
	0.5		0.7		0.9	
1	1=2	(2.0000)	2	(1.7647)	4	(1.4539)
2	2	(2.6667)	3	(2.2831)	6	(1.7074)
4	2=3	(4.0000)	4	(3.1583)	8	(2.1070)
8	3	(6.2857)	5	(4.6879)	10	(2.7636)
16	4	(10.6667)	6	(7.4800)	13	(3.8884)

and

$$S_p(N+1) - S_p(N) = \sum_{i=1}^{N+1}(N-i+2)^{\rho_1-1} - \sum_{i=1}^{N}(N-i+1)^{\rho_1-1}$$
$$= (N+1)^{\rho_1-1} > 0.$$

If $\rho_1 < 1$,

$$[S_p(N+2)-S_p(N+1)]-[S_p(N+1)-S_p(N)] = (N+2)^{\rho_1-1}-(N+1)^{\rho_1-1} < 0.$$

Thus, $MTTF_p(N+1) - MTTF_p(N)$ is decreasing in N. From Theorem 10.1, N^* is finite and unique.

If $\rho_1 \geq 1$, $C(n+1) < C(n)$, that is, the optimal number of redundant units is infinite. Table 6 shows the optimal redundant units and values of $\mu C_S(N,p)$ and $\mu C_P(N)$ for different parameters.

From Table 6, we can know that the optimal redundant units increase in the fixed cost of replacement. The optimal redundant units in the parallel system increase in the parameter ρ_1. The parallel system is better than the standby system in cases with low success probability of switching in the standby system.

5 Extended Models

In previous sections, we assume that we replace redundant systems at system failures and do not consider various actions in the operation phase.

Now we consider age-based preventive maintenance (PM) in redundant systems and obtain system MTTFs and expected cost rates of parallel and standby systems.

The redundant systems are replaced at time T preventively. If the system is failed before T, then the system is replaced correctively.

Firstly, we obtain the mean times to failures of redundant systems. If the system is replaced preventively at age T and there are unlimited spares, the mean life of redundant systems ($MTTF$) is given [Nakagawa (2005)]

$$MTTF_{pm} = \frac{1}{F_N(T)} \int_0^T \overline{F}_N(t) dt,$$

where $F_N(t)$ is the distribution function of redundant systems with N units. The distribution functions of parallel and standby systems are given as follows:

Parallel case : $F_N(t) = F(t)^N$.

Standby case : $F_N(t) = \sum_{i=1}^{N-1} p^{i-1}(1-p)F^{(i)}(t) + p^{N-1}F^{(N)}(t)$.

where $F^{(N)}(t)$ is the N-th convolution of $F(t)$.

Thus, the mean lives of parallel and standby systems are

Parallel case : $MTTF_{pm}(T) = \dfrac{\int_0^T [1 - F(t)^N] dt}{1 - F(T)^N}$.

Standby case :

$$MTTF_{sm}(T) = \frac{\int_0^T [1 - \sum_{i=1}^{N-1} p^{i-1}(1-p)F^{(i)}(t) + p^{N-1}F^{(N)}(t)] dt}{\sum_{i=1}^{N-1} p^{i-1}(1-p)F^{(i)}(T) + p^{N-1}F^{(N)}(T)}.$$

Now we obtain the expected cost rates of redundant systems under preventive maintenance. Let c_{pm} and c_{sm} be the fixed cost of preventive replacement of parallel and standby systems, respectively. The expected cost rates of redundant systems are

Standby case :

$$C_S(N,p,T) = \frac{(c_s - c_{sm})[\sum_{i=1}^{N-1} p^{i-1}(1-p)F^{(i)}(t) + p^{N-1}F^{(N)}(t)] + c_{sm} + cN}{\int_0^T [1 - \sum_{i=1}^{N-1} p^{i-1}(1-p)F^{(i)}(t) + p^{N-1}F^{(N)}(t)] dt}.$$

Parallel case : $\quad C_P(N, T) = \dfrac{c_{pm}[1 - F(T)^N] + c_p F(T)^N + cN}{\int_0^T [1 - F(t)^N]dt}.$

If the failure rate of components is constant, i.e., $F(t) = 1 - e^{-\lambda t}$, the distribution function of the redundant systems are given

Parallel case : $\quad F_N(t) = \left(1 - e^{-\lambda t}\right)^N.$

Standby case :

$$F_N(t) = \sum_{i=1}^{N-1} p^{i-1}(1 - p) \left[1 - \sum_{j=1}^{i-1} \frac{e^{-\lambda t}(\lambda t)^j}{j!}\right] + p^{N-1} \left[1 - \sum_{j=1}^{N-1} \frac{e^{-\lambda t}(\lambda t)^j}{j!}\right].$$

Thus, the mean lives and expected cost rates can be obtained easily. Finally, in the model with common cause failures and load sharing model, we can also consider preventive maintenance problems similarly.

6 Conclusion

In this paper, we consider parallel and standby systems with identical units to improve the system reliability. We assume that the switching device of the standby system is imperfect and has the failure probability. The mean times to system failures and the expected cost rates are obtained and compared. The efficiency of the standby system depends on the success probability of switching device. Additionally, common cause failure is included to compare the two redundant systems. From numerical examples, we can know that the standby system is better than the parallel system in cases that reliable switching device is used and the failure rate of common cause failures is low. For further studies, age and condition-based maintenances can be applied together. Warm standby models can be also studied to compare the two redundant systems [Yun and Cha (2010a)].

References

Barlow, R.E. and Proschan, F. (1965). *Mathematical Theory of Reliability* (Wiley, New York).

Chen, M., Wang, M., and Zhao, X. (2014). Which standby or parallel system is more useful in reliability theory, Proc of 6th APARM. p. 65–72.

Kuo, W., Prasad, V.R., Tillman, F.A., and Hwang, C.L. (2001). Optimal Reliability Design, Cambridge University Press.

Nakagawa, T. (1984). Optimal number of units for a parallel system, *Journal of Applied Probability*, **21**, pp. 431–436.

Nakagawa, T. (2005). *Maintenance Theory of Reliability*, (Springer, London).

Nakagawa, T. (2008), *Advanced Reliability Models and Maintenance Policies*, (Springer, London).

Nakagawa, T. and Zhao, X. (2015). A survey of replacement policies for parallel systems with newly proposed approaches, International Journal of Performability Engineering, **11**, pp. pp. 321–328.

Nelson, W. (1990). *Accelerated Testing*, (Wiley, New York).

Yun, W.Y. (1989). Optimal number of redundant units for a standby system, *Reliability Engineering and System Safety* **25**, pp. 365–369.

Yun, W.Y., and Bai, D.S. (1986). Optimal Numbers of Redundant Units for Parallel Systems with Common Mode Failures, *Reliability Engineering and System Safety* **16**, pp. 201–206.

Yun, W.Y. and Cha, J.H. (2010). Optimal design of a general warm standby system, *Reliability Engineering and System Safety* **95**, pp. 880–886.

Yun, W.Y. and Cha, J.H. (2010). A stochastic model for a general load-sharing system under overload condition, *Applied Stochastic Models in Business and Industry* **26**, pp. 624–638.

PART 3
Reliability Applications

Chapter 11

System Reliability of an Intermittent Production System

Ping-Chen Chang[1], Cheng-Fu Huang[2], Yi-Kuei Lin[3], and Po-Shiang Shih[3]

[1]*Department of Industrial Engineering and Management, National Quemoy University.*

[2]*Department of Business Administration, Feng Chia University.*

[3] *Department of Industrial Management, National Taiwan University of Science & Technology.*

1   Introduction

From the perspectives of both reliability analysis and operations management, production performance is dependent on the capacity of the whole production system. Meanwhile, the capacities of workstations affect the capacity that a production system can provide. Therefore, it is a crucial task to evaluate the system reliability, which is generally defined as probability of demand satisfaction, of a production system for comprehending whether it can provide sufficient capacity to satisfy customers' demand or not. For the sake of practical needs in manufacturing industry, this chapter is contributed to studying the system reliability of a production system.

Production systems can be classified into two types: continuous production system (CPS) and intermittent production system (IPS) [Schmitt et.al (2016)]; [Hendry et.al (1989)]; [Kim et.al (1993)]; [Stevenson et.al (2005)]; [Stevenson et.al (2015)]; [Jacobs et.al (2014)]; [Stevenson et.al (2015)]. In a CPS, high volumes of highly standardized items are produced for stocking and selling. The customers' orders are fulfilled from the inventory directly [Stevenson et.al (2015)]. On the other hand, items in the IPS are produced according to orders from customers. To satisfy their specified requirements, the various operations that are processed require frequent adjustments to the machines. This causes discontinuous operations in production, and thus the process is intermittent. In practice, intermittent production plays a critical role for low-volume, high-variety items [Stevenson et.al (2015)]. The demand of customers for greater product variety has led to the make-to-order system; thus, IPS has become increasingly common in production. In a changing market environment, IPS has the capability to respond quickly to customer demands. An important factor affecting the makespan is the number of normal machines in each workstation of an IPS. In real life, a number of normal machines in a workstation may present multiple levels due to the possibility of maintenance and failure. Therefore, the number of normal machines in each workstation is stochastic.

Several studies have been applying stochastic production network (SPN) to investigate the performance of a production system with stochastic capacity. Lin and Chang (2012) proposed a typical SPN model to consider a CPS with reliability evaluation. Thereafter, a great deal of research has examined SPN model and applied their findings to the CPS in several scenarios, such as single [Lin and Chang (2012)], parallel [Lin and Chang (2013, 2015)] and joint production lines [Lin and Chang (2013)]. Moreover, service level [Fiondella et.al (2015)], time threshold [Lin et.al (2016)], and quality improvement [Sun et.al (2015)] are well studied in CPS. However, studies on system reliability evaluation for the IPS is not that much as it is for the CPS; no SPN model is studied for an IPS so far. Therefore, a valuable issue emerges to study the system reliability of an IPS in the context of SPN model.

To evaluate the system reliability by applying SPN model, each arc can be regarded as a workstation with stochastic capacity (number of normal machines) and each node can be considered as a buffer or conveyor. However, since the previous studies [Lin and Chang (2012, 2013, 2015)];[Fiondella et.al (2015)];[Sun et.al (2015)];[Lin et.al (2016)] are studied for a CPS, they did not consider time constraint in model building and system reliability evaluation. This chapter considers the stochastic number of normal machines in an IPS by transforming the IPS into an SPN. System reliability, which is defined as the probability that an IPS can complete demand d within time constraint T, is utilized to measure the performance of the IPS. To calculate system reliability, an algorithm based on depth-first search (DFS) is proposed to search all the lower boundary points that satisfy both demand and time constraint. The lower boundary point represents the minimal number of normal machines needed at each workstation. Such lower boundary points are referred to as minimal machine vectors (MMVs). In terms of MMVs, the system reliability of an IPS can be derived by the recursive sum of disjoint products (RSDP) algorithm [Zuo et.al (2007)];[Bai et.al (2015)]. A practical example of a printed circuit board (PCB) production system is demonstrated to explain the procedure of deriving system reliability. A further analysis and discussion on the PCB example are addressed for managerial implications.

2 Model Building

The IPS is modeled as a SPN by an activity-on-arrow (AOA) diagram. Let $G(N, A, P, M, S)$ denote an IPS, where N represents the set of nodes (buffers), $A = \{a_i \mid i = 1, 2, \ldots, n\}$ is the set of arcs (workstations), $P = \{p_i \mid i = 1, 2, \ldots, n\}$ with p_i being the processing time of a_i, $S = \{s_i \mid i = 1, 2, \ldots, n\}$ with s_i being the number of items that can be processed simultaneously by a machine in a_i, and $M = \{m_i \mid i = 1, 2, \ldots, n\}$ with m_i being the maximal number of normal machines in a_i. A workstation a_i that consists of M_i identical machines performs $(M_i + 1)$ capacity levels. The level zero represents that all the machines in a workstation are malfunctioning; on the contrary, the level M_i represents that all the machines are operating normally. In this chapter, four assumptions are addressed as follows:

1) All nodes (buffers) are perfectly reliable. This implies that buffers are with infinite storages.
2) The numbers of normal machines in different arcs (workstations) are statistically independent.
3) The number of normal machines x_i in each arc (workstation) is an integer-valued random variable according to a probability distribution obtained from historical data.
4) The batch size b is delivered to a downstream workstation when the processing of all the items is completed by the current workstation.

Each workstation has to provide sufficient number of machines to satisfy demand d within time constraint T. Let $\tau(d, b, X)$ denote the makespan for demand d and batch size b under the machine vector X. Any machine vector $X = (x_1, x_2, \ldots, x_n)$ with $\tau(d, b, X) \leq T$ satisfies the demand d within time constraint T. Let Ω be the set of such vectors X, the system reliability, $R_{d,T}$, is formulated as:

$$R_{d,T} = \sum \Pr\{X \mid X \in \Omega\}, \tag{1}$$

where $\Pr\{X\} = \Pr\{x_1\} \times \Pr\{x_2\} \times \cdots \times \Pr\{x_n\}$ by Assumption II. When the network size is very large, evaluating system reliability by enumerating all X in Ω and then summing up their probabilities is an inefficient method. The MMV, $V = (v_1, v_2, \ldots, v_n)$, represents the minimal number of normal machines that each workstation should provide to satisfy d and T. If a vector Y is smaller than the MMV, then $\tau(d, b, X) > T$. With such MMVs, system reliability can be evaluated efficiently. Thus, any machine vector X is an MMV if and only if (i) $X \in \Omega$ and (ii) $\tau(d, b, Y) > T$ for any capacity vector Y with $Y < X$. Suppose there are totally q MMVs: $V_1, V_2, \ldots, V_q$, the system reliability can be modified as Eq. (2) in terms of MMVs.

$$R_{d,T} = \Pr\{X \mid X \geq V_j, j = 1, 2, \ldots, q\} = \Pr\left\{ \bigcup_{j=1,2,\ldots q} X \geq V_j \right\}. \tag{2}$$

There are several methods are applicable to compute $\Pr\{\bigcup_{j=1,2,\ldots q} X \geq V_j\}$, such as inclusion-exclusion principle [Hudson et.al (1985)];[Janan (1985)], disjoint-event method [Hudson et.al (1985)];[Yarlagadda et.al (1991)], state-space decomposition [Aven (1985)], and RSDP algorithm [Zuo et.al (2007)];[Bai et.al (2015)]. Jane et.al (2008) proved that the state-space decomposition method is more efficient for computation and storage than the inclusion-exclusion principle. Besides, the RSDP algorithm, which is based on the sum of disjoint products, has higher efficiency than the state-space decomposition method for large networks [Zuo et.al (2007)]. More recently, Bai et.al (2015) developed ordering heuristics to improve the efficiency of the RSDP algorithm. Hence, the RSDP algorithm with ordering heuristic is employed in this study to compute $\Pr\{\bigcup_{j=1,2,\ldots q} X \geq V_j\}$ for evaluation system reliability.

3   Completion Time Analysis

In order to see whether the demand can be completed within the given time constraint, this section analyzes the completion time of an ISP. First, the special case when the demand is less than or equal to the batch size b is studied. That is, the demand d is delivered to a downstream workstation in one batch because $d \leq b$. This special case is subsequently extended to the general case of a demand being processed by several batches when $d > b$. Therefore, cycle time is involved in the general case. Completion

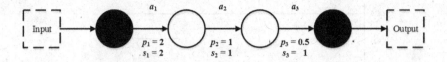

Fig. 1   Special case with three machines.

time and cycle time affect the generating of MMVs. The detailed analysis is introduced as follows.

3.1   *The Special Case*

The completion time for each workstation to process the demand d is measured according to the number of normal machines in the workstation. The completion time c_i for workstation a_i can be calculated from Eq. (3).

$$c_i = \left\lceil \frac{d}{x_i \times s_i} \right\rceil \times p_i. \tag{3}$$

The first term $\lceil d/(x_i \times s_i) \rceil$ is the number of repetitions to process d by a_i, where x is the smallest integer such that $\lceil x \rceil \geq x$. When an order is processed by several processes to complete the final items, the throughput time, denoted by $\xi(d, X)$ for demand d under the machine vector X, of the order is the summation of completion times for all the workstations. The makespan is equal to the throughput time in this special case, because the order is completed in one batch. The makespan cannot exceed the time constraint T as shown in Eq. (4).

$$\xi(d, X) = \sum_{i=1}^{n} c_i \leq T. \tag{4}$$

For instance, an IPS with three workstations $\{a_1, a_2, a_3\}$ associated with $P = \{2, 1, 0.5\}$ and $S = \{2, 1, 1\}$, shown as Fig. 1; the completion time c_i for each a_i is calculated as the following equations when $d = 5$.

$\boxed{i = 1}$ $c_1 = \lceil 5/(1 \times 2) \rceil = 6,$

$\boxed{i = 2}$ $c_2 = \lceil 5/(1 \times 1) \rceil \times 1 = 5,$

$\boxed{i = 3}$ $c_3 = \lceil 5/(1 \times 1) \rceil \times 0.5 = 2.5.$

Therefore, throughput time for $d = 5$ and $X = (1, 1, 1)$ is $\xi(d, X) = c_1 + c_2 + c_3 = 6 + 5 + 2.5 = 13.5$ as shown in Fig. 2.

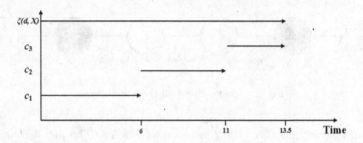

Fig. 2   Throughput time for special case.

It may be noted that only one batch is considered so far. The general case should be able to further deal with $d > b$, and thus the demand is processed in several batches.

3.2   *The General Case when Demand is Fulfilled by Batch Processing*

In the general case, the demand is completed in several batches. The completion time for the first batch is identical to throughput time, and then the IPS will output b items within the cycle time. The cycle time of an IPS is the maximum time among the completion times of all the workstations. The makespan $\tau(d, b, X)$ is formulated as Eq. (5).

$\tau(d, b, X) =$ throughput time + remaining batches $\times$ cycle time

$$= \sum_{i=1}^{n} \left\lceil \frac{b}{x_i \times s_i} \right\rceil \times p_i + \left(\left\lceil \frac{d}{b} \right\rceil - 1 \right) \times \max_{1 \leq i \leq n} \left(\left\lceil \frac{b}{x_i \times s_i} \right\rceil \times p_i \right). \quad (5)$$

Take another IPS with three workstations for instance; given $b = 5$, $P = \{2, 1, 0.5\}$ and $S = \{1, 1, 1\}$ as shown in Fig. 3. To satisfy an order with $d = 15$, three batches are necessary because batch size $b = 5$. The throughput time for the first batch under $X = (1, 1, 1)$ is $10 + 5 + 2.5 = 17.5$. Because c_1 is the cycle time (i.e. a_1 is the bottleneck), makespan for the second batch is (throughput time for the first batch $+ c_1$). Therefore, the makespan to complete the second batch under $X = (1, 1, 1)$ is $17.5 + 1 \times 10 = 27.5$. Similarly, the makespan for the third batch under $X = (1, 1, 1)$ $17.5 + 2 \times 10 = 37.5$, and so on (see Fig. 4).

The formulations of completion time and cycle time affect the generating of MMVs. Here, we conclude an important property for cycle time as the following remark.

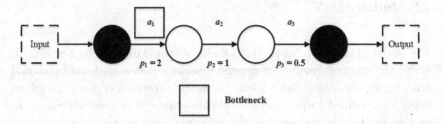

Fig. 3   Example for IPS.

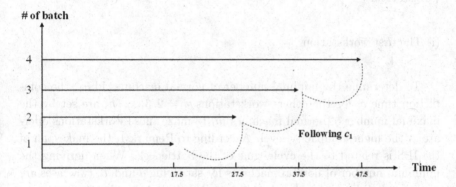

Fig. 4   Makespan analysis of IPS.

Remark 11.1. If the bottleneck in an IPS is a_w under the machine vector $X = (x_1, x_2, \ldots, x_n)$, the remaining batches will output following cycle time c_w.

4   Minimal Machine Vectors

To evaluate system reliability efficiently, the MMVs should be determined first. It is known that the completion time $\tau(d, b, X)$ of each MMV X cannot exceed T. To obtain all the MMVs, the initial MMV is derived first. In terms of the initial MMV, all the other MMV candidates can be generated by the DFS method.

4.1   *Initial MMV*

The initial MMV is an MMV that can be obtained directly by Eq. (5). To derive the minimal number of normal machines that a workstation should provide, all the other workstations (with the exception of the determined ones) are assumed to provide a maximal number of normal machines. In particular, the minimal number of normal machines for each workstation is derived according to the location (sequence in the IPS). Each workstation is either the first workstation, or an intermediate workstation, or the last workstation.

(i) The first workstation

To determine the minimal number of normal machines in a_1, the completion time c_i for the others workstations, $i = 2, 3, \ldots, n$, are set by the maximal number of normal machines m_i to make those workstations operate at the highest capacity level. According to Remark 1, the makespan of the IPS is related to the cycle time of the bottleneck. When deriving the minimum number of normal machines for satisfying d and T, two cases are considered: (a) a_1 is the bottleneck and (b) a_1 is not the bottleneck.

For case (a), the cycle time is equal to $\lceil b/(x_i \times s_i) \rceil \times p_1$. Under time constraint T, Eq. (5) is modified as Eq. (6).

$$\left\lceil \frac{b}{x_1 \times s_1} \right\rceil \times p_1 + \sum_{j=2}^{n} \left\lceil \frac{b}{m_j \times s_j} \right\rceil \times p_j + \left(\left\lceil \frac{d}{b} \right\rceil - 1 \right) \times \left\lceil \frac{b}{x_1 \times s_1} \right\rceil \times p_1 \leq T. \quad (6)$$

The number of normal machines must be an integer according to Assumption 3. Thus, we intend to find the smallest integer value of x_1 to satisfy d and T. Such a value is the minimal number of normal machines for a_1; it is denoted by v_1, and can be computed by Eq. (7).

$$v_1 = \left\lceil b / \left(\left\lceil \frac{T - \sum_{j=2}^{n} \left\lceil \frac{b}{m_j \times s_j} \right\rceil \times p_j}{p_1 \times \left\lceil \frac{d}{b} \right\rceil} \right\rceil \times s_1 \right) \right\rceil. \quad (7)$$

For case (b), where a_1 is not the bottleneck, the cycle time is equal to $\max_{2 \leq j \leq n} (c_j)$. Under time constraint T, Eq. (5) is revised as Eq. (8).

$$\left\lceil \frac{b}{x_1 \times s_1} \right\rceil \times p_1 + \sum_{j=2}^{n} \left\lceil \frac{b}{m_j \times s_j} \right\rceil \times p_j + \left(\left\lceil \frac{d}{b} \right\rceil - 1 \right) \times \max_{2 \leq j \leq n} (c_j) \leq T. \quad (8)$$

To derive v_1, Eq. (8) is modified as Eq. (9).

$$v_1 = \left\lceil b \middle/ \left(\left\lceil \frac{T - \sum_{j=2}^{n} \left\lceil \frac{b}{m_j \times s_j} \right\rceil \times p_j - (\lceil \frac{d}{b} \rceil - 1) \times \max_{2 \leq j \leq n} (c_j)}{p_1} \right\rceil \times s_1 \right) \right\rceil. \tag{9}$$

By combining Eqs. (7) and (9), Eq. (10) is obtained, in which the minimal number of normal machines v_1 is given as the maximum value obtained from Eqs. (7) and (9), because the required cycle time calls for more machines.

$$v_1 = \max \left(\begin{array}{c} \left\lceil b \middle/ \left(\left\lceil \frac{T - \sum_{j=2}^{n} \left\lceil \frac{b}{m_j \times s_j} \right\rceil \times p_j - (\lceil \frac{d}{b} \rceil - 1) \times \max_{2 \leq j \leq n} (c_j)}{p_1} \right\rceil \times s_1 \right) \right\rceil, \\ \left\lceil b \middle/ \left(\left\lceil \frac{T - \sum_{j=2}^{n} \left\lceil \frac{b}{m_j \times s_j} \right\rceil \times p_j}{p_1 \times \lceil \frac{d}{b} \rceil} \right\rceil \times s_1 \right) \right\rceil \end{array} \right). \tag{10}$$

(ii) Intermediate workstation

When v_1 is determined, the remaining time for the other workstations except a_1 is equal to T minus c_1. Similarly, once the values v_1 to v_i are determined, the remaining time for workstations a_{i+1} to a_n is T minus the completion time of previous workstations, that is, $T - \sum_{j=1}^{i-1} c_j$. Using $(T - \sum_{j=1}^{i-1} c_j)$ to substitute T, Eq. (10) is modified as Eq. (11), from which the minimal number v_i of normal machines for the second to the penultimate workstation can be computed.

$$v_i = \max \left(\begin{array}{c} \left\lceil b \middle/ \left(\left\lceil \frac{T - \sum_{j=1}^{i-1} \left\lceil \frac{b}{v_j \times s_j} \right\rceil \times p_j - \sum_{j=i+1}^{n} \left\lceil \frac{b}{m_j \times s_j} \right\rceil \times p_j - (\lceil \frac{d}{b} \rceil - 1) \times \max_{1 \leq j \leq n, j \neq i} (c_j)}{p_i} \right\rceil \times s_i \right) \right\rceil, \\ \left\lceil b \middle/ \left(\left\lceil \frac{T - \sum_{j=1}^{i-1} \left\lceil \frac{b}{v_j \times s_j} \right\rceil \times p_j - \sum_{j=i+1}^{n} \left\lceil \frac{b}{m_j \times s_j} \right\rceil \times p_j}{p_i \times \lceil \frac{d}{b} \rceil} \right\rceil \times s_i \right) \right\rceil \end{array} \right),$$

$$\text{for } i = 2, 3, \ldots, n - 1. \tag{11}$$

(iii) The last workstation

While deriving the minimal number of machines for a_n, the previous minimal machines $v_1, v_2, \ldots, v_{n-1}$ have been already determined. The remaining processing time for a_n is equal to the time constraint T minus the completion time of previous workstations $c_1, c_2, \ldots, c_{n-1}$, that is $(T - \sum_{j=1}^{n-1} c_j)$. Using $(T - \sum_{j=1}^{n-1} c_j)$ to substitute for T, Eq. (10) is revised as Eq. (12) to calculate v_n directly.

$$
v_n = \max \left(\begin{bmatrix} b / \left(\left\lfloor \dfrac{T - \sum\limits_{j=1}^{n-1} \left\lceil \frac{b}{v_j \times s_j} \right\rceil \times p_j - \left(\lceil \frac{d}{b} \rceil - 1 \right) \times \max\limits_{1 \leq j \leq n-1}(c_j)}{p_n} \right\rfloor \times s_n \right) \end{bmatrix}, \\ \begin{bmatrix} b / \left(\left\lfloor \dfrac{T - \sum\limits_{j=1}^{n-1} \left\lceil \frac{b}{v_j \times s_j} \right\rceil \times p_j}{p_n \times \lceil \frac{d}{b} \rceil} \right\rfloor \times s_n \right) \end{bmatrix} \right).
$$

$$(12)$$

Minimal number of normal machines v_i for each workstation is therefore derived using the above equations. The derived vector $V_1 = (v_1, v_2, \ldots v_n)$ is an MMV, and is set as the initial MMV. Based on the initial MMV, the other MMV candidates can be generated by the following important characteristic.

Remark 11.2. From the initial MMV, another MMV candidate can be generated, if one workstation can provide more machines than the current number of normal machines, while the other workstations may reduce the number of machines without exceeding the time constraint.

4.2 *Generated all MMV Candidates*

DFS is a tree-structured searching algorithm that starts at the root and explores as deep as possible along each branch before backtracking. It is a method to search for all possible solutions in a search tree. The top of the tree is defined as the root, which is level 0; then it goes down to the next level (i.e. level 1) which refers to the number of normal machines in a_1, and so on. Hence, there are n levels (level 0 is excluded) in the tree for an IPS with n workstations. Once searching is performed to the last level, an MMV candidate will be generated. Each parent node in level i can be expanded up to m_{i+1} child nodes. When the child node reaches m_{i+1}, then the algorithm goes back to level $i - 1$ to continue expanding until the number of machines in level 1 reaches m_1. By repeating the expanding process, all possible MMVs can be generated. However, this approach may take a long time because of the time spent in searching for unnecessary child nodes. Therefore, we propose an efficient DFS algorithm to avoid searching for unnecessary child nodes.

When the parent node is expanded to the child node in level i, the child node increases one extra machine $v_i + 1$; then, the algorithm finds the minimal number of normal machines in the remaining levels $i+1$ to n. In most cases, however, the time consumed in level i may not decrease by increasing only one machine. Thus, the number of normal machines in the remaining levels remains the same as at present. To reduce unnecessary expansion and make the expansion more efficient, the increased number of machines has to decrease the time consumed in level i. The following technique is proposed to determine the number of machines to be increased in a level. Let α be the index of the level that is expanded, and β be the number of times that a_α processes the batch; $\beta = b/(x_\alpha \times s_\alpha)$. After the expansion, β' must be smaller than the previous one. For instance, an order must process a workstation in level α, the batch $b = 20$, and $s_\alpha = 1$. The machine will expand from $v_\alpha = 5$, then the next child node can be generated as follows:

$$\boxed{v_\alpha = 5} \quad \beta = 20/\lceil(5 \times 1)\rceil = 4,$$

$$\boxed{v_\alpha = 6} \quad \beta' = 20/\lceil(6 \times 1)\rceil = 4, \quad \beta' = \beta$$

$$\boxed{v_\alpha = 7} \quad \beta' = 20/\lceil(7 \times 1)\rceil = 3, \quad \beta' < \beta$$

Thus, the next child node is set to $v_\alpha = 7$, and uses this node to find the number of machines for the remaining levels.

Remark 11.3. Let $\beta = b/\lceil(x_\alpha \times s_\alpha)\rceil$ be the number of times that a_α process the batch, and the β' after expanded must be smaller than previous one.

If the last level is expanded up to another child node $v_n + 1$, the machine vector $(v_1, v_2, \ldots, v_n + 1)$ must satisfy the order, and it is definitely larger than the machine vector $(v_1, v_2, \ldots, v_n)$. Thus, the last level cannot be expanded to another child node. When the penultimate level is expanded up to another child node $v_{n-1} + 1$, it means that there may be time remaining to process the last workstation, and the minimal number of normal machines in a_n may reduce. When the minimal number of normal machines does not reduce, the machine vector $(v_1, v_2, \ldots, v_{n-1} + 1, v_n)$ must be larger than the previous machine vector $(v_1, v_2, \ldots, v_{n-1}, v_n)$. Therefore, this machine vector cannot be an MMV candidate. For instance, there are already generated q MMV candidates, when the penultimate level is expanded to another child node v_n, v_n must be smaller than the number of normal machines in the last workstation of the previously generated MMV V_q, denoted by $V[q, n]$.

Finally, remove non-minimal ones from the MMV candidates, the MMVs $V_1, V_2, \ldots, V_q$, can be obtained. Subsequently, the system reliability can be calculated in terms of MMVs.

4.3　*Algorithm to Generate all MMVs*

An IPS with n workstations, processing time p_i, and maximal capacity M_i, which can be modeled as a network G with probability of number of normal machines. Then, given a demand d and time constraint T, all of minimal machine vectors are obtained by following algorithm.

Algorithm for system reliability.
Input: G, d, and T

Step 1. Compute the MMV candidates.

(1.0) Initialize $i = 1$, $\alpha = 1$, $q = 0$, $c_i = 0$ for $i = 1$ to n
　　　// i is an index to check which minimal machine is derived.
　　　// α is an index that that which level is expanded.
　　　// q is a number that how many candidates are generated.

(1.1) Compute minimal number of normal machines from a_1 to a_n.

$$
v_1 = \left(\left\lceil b / \left(\left\lfloor \frac{T - \sum_{j=2}^{n} \left\lceil \frac{b}{m_j \times s_j} \right\rceil \times p_j - \left(\lceil \frac{d}{b} \rceil - 1 \right) \times \max_{2 \le j \le n} (c_j)}{p_1} \right\rfloor \times s_1 \right) \right\rceil, \left\lceil b / \left(\left\lfloor \frac{T - \sum_{j=2}^{n} \left\lceil \frac{b}{m_j \times s_j} \right\rceil \times p_j}{p_1 \times \lceil \frac{d}{b} \rceil} \right\rfloor \times s_1 \right) \right\rceil \right)
\tag{13}
$$

$$
v_i = \max \left(\left\lceil b / \left(\left\lfloor \frac{T - \sum_{j=1}^{i-1} \left\lceil \frac{b}{v_j \times s_j} \right\rceil \times p_j - \sum_{j=i+1}^{n} \left\lceil \frac{b}{m_j \times s_j} \right\rceil \times p_j - \left(\lceil \frac{d}{b} \rceil - 1 \right) \times \max_{1 \le j \le n, j \ne i} (c_j)}{p_i} \right\rfloor \times s_i \right) \right\rceil, \left\lceil b / \left(\left\lfloor \frac{T - \sum_{j=1}^{i-1} \left\lceil \frac{b}{v_j \times s_j} \right\rceil \times pj - \sum_{j=i+1}^{n} \left\lceil \frac{b}{m_j \times s_j} \right\rceil \times p_j}{p_i \times \lceil \frac{d}{b} \rceil} \right\rfloor \times s_i \right) \right\rceil \right)
$$

$$
\text{for } i = 2, 3, \ldots, n-1,
\tag{14}
$$

$$v_n = \left(\left[b \Big/ \left(\left\lfloor \frac{T - \sum_{j=1}^{n-1} \left\lceil \frac{b}{v_j \times s_j} \right\rceil \times p_j - \left(\lceil \frac{d}{b} \rceil - 1 \right) \times \max\limits_{1 \le j \le n-1}(c_j)}{p_n} \right\rfloor \times s_n \right) \right], \left[b \Big/ \left(\left\lfloor \frac{T - \sum_{j=1}^{n-1} \left\lceil \frac{b}{v_j \times s_j} \right\rceil \times p_j}{p_n \times \lceil \frac{d}{b} \rceil} \right\rfloor \times s_n \right) \right] \right).$$

(15)

(1.2) Generate an MMV candidate in terms of following rule:

IF $\alpha \ne n - 1$, $q \leftarrow q + 1$ MMV, candidate $X_q = (x_1, x_2, \dots, x_n)$, and let $\alpha = n - 1$.

ELSE IF $v_n < V[q, n]$, $q \leftarrow q + 1$, MMV candidate $X_q = (x_1, x_2, \dots, x_n)$, and let $\alpha = n - 1$.

(1.3) Check whether search αth workstation machine up to maximal machine.

IF $v_\alpha = m_\alpha$ or $v_n = 1$, go to step 1.4.

ELSE Let $\beta = \lceil d/(x_i \times b_i) \rceil$, $v_\alpha \leftarrow v_\alpha + 1$ until $\lceil d/(x_i \times b_i) \rceil > \beta$, let $i = \alpha + 1$ and go to step 1.1.

(1.4) Update α to check other workstation.

IF $\alpha = 1$, go to step 2.

ELSE Let $\alpha \leftarrow \alpha - 1$ and go to step 1.3.

Step 2. Suppose the result of step 1 is: $V_1, V_2, \dots, V_q$. Remove those non-minimal ones in $\{V_1, V_2, \dots, V_q\}$ to obtain all MMVs for d and T as follows:

(2.0) $I = \varnothing$ (I is a stack which stores index of each non-MMV)

(2.1) For $i = 1$ to q and $i \notin I$

(2.2) For $j = i + 1$ to q and $j \notin I$.

(2.3) If $V_i \le V_j$, $I = I \cup \{j\}$. Elseif $V_i > V_j$ $I = I \cup \{i\}$ and go to 2.6

(2.4) $j \leftarrow j + 1$

(2.5) V_i is an MMV

(2.6) $i \leftarrow i + 1$

Step 3. Suppose $V_1, V_2, \dots, V_q$ are all MMVs. System reliability can be evaluated as $R_{d,T} = \Pr \left\{ \bigcup_{j=1,2,\dots q} X \ge V_j \right\}$.

Output: System reliability $R_{d,T}$

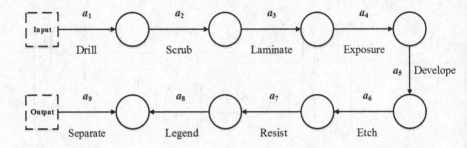

Fig. 5 PCB production system

5 Illustrative Example

A PCB production system with nine workstations ($n = 9$) is shown in the form of an AOA diagram in Fig. 5. For single-sided board manufacturing, the input raw material is a board with a thin layer of copper foil. For different product types, the production processes and sequences may be different. Normally, the regular production process for a PCB starts with the automated drilling machines (a_1) by which holes are drilled through the board for mounting electronic components on it. Subsequently, the scrubbing machines (a_2) are used for cleaning the board. After scrubbing, the laminators (a_3) laminate the board with a dry film, and the exposure machines (a_4) let the photoresist film get hardened; then, the photoresist film developing machines (a_5) show the line pattern on the board. By chemical etching (a_6) and resist stripping (a_7), the copper that is not a part of the circuit pattern is removed. After the resist stripping process, the legend printing machines (a_8) print the required logos or letters on the board. Finally, the separators (a_9) cut the board to the specific size.

Such a production system is modeled as an SFN. Each arc performs $m_i + 1$ possible levels and has its own processing time. For example, the drilling workstation consists of four identical machines; this means that this workstation has five levels $\{0, 1, 2, 3, 4\}$. The lowest level zero refers to all the machines are malfunctioning, whereas the highest level refers to all the machines are operating properly.

For the condition that PCB production system has to satisfy demand $d = 370$ within the time constraint $T = 480$ (minutes), the system reliability can be obtained by following steps:

Step 1: Compute the MMV candidates.

Table 1 Data of workstations.

a_i	p_i	s_i	x_i	Prob.	a_i	p_i	s_i	x_i	Prob.
			0	0.0001				0	0.0001
			1	0.0002				1	0.0005
a_1	15.48	5	2	0.0088	a_6	2	1	2	0.0135
			3	0.1415				3	0.1714
			4	0.8493				4	0.8145
								0	0.0001
a_1	0.25	0	0	0.01	a_7	1.87	1	1	0.0012
			1	0.99				2	0.0576
								3	0.9604
			0	0.0001				0	0.0004
a_3	0.7	1	1	0.0198	a_8	1	1	1	0.0392
			2	0.9801				2	0.9604
			0	0.0001					
			1	0.0004					
a_4	3	1	2	0.0135	a_9	2	2	0	0.0025
			3	0.1715				1	0.0950
			4	0.8145				2	0.9205
			0	0.0001					
a_5	1.22	1	1	0.0046					
			2	0.1106					
			3	0.8847					

(1.0) $i = 1$, $\alpha = 1$, $q = 0$, $c_i = 0$

(1.1) Compute minimal number of normal machines form a_1.

$\boxed{i = 1}$

$$v_1 = \max \left(\begin{bmatrix} 20/ \left(\left\lceil \left| \frac{480 - 5 - 7 - \ldots - 18 \times 13.09}{15.48} \right| \times 5 \right) \right\rceil \end{bmatrix}, \\ \begin{bmatrix} 20/ \left(\left\lceil \left| \frac{480 - 5 - 7 - \ldots - 10}{15.48 \times 19} \right| \times 5 \right) \right\rceil \end{bmatrix} \right) = 4,$$

$\boxed{i = 2}$

$$v_2 = \max \left(\begin{bmatrix} 20/ \left(\left\lceil \left| \frac{480 - 15.48 - 7 - \ldots - 18 \times 15.48}{0.25} \right| \times 1 \right) \right\rceil \end{bmatrix}, \\ \begin{bmatrix} 20/ \left(\left\lceil \left| \frac{480 - 15.48 - 7 - \ldots - 10}{0.25 \times 19} \right| \times 1 \right) \right\rceil \end{bmatrix} \right) = 1,$$

$\vdots$

$\boxed{i = 10}$

$$v_{10} = \max\left(\left\lceil 20 / \left(\left\lfloor \frac{480 - 15.48 - 5 - \ldots - 18 \times 15.48}{2} \right\rfloor \times 2\right)\right\rceil, \left\lceil 20 / \left(\left\lfloor \frac{480 - 15.48 - 5 - \ldots - 10}{2 \times 19} \right\rfloor \times 2\right)\right\rceil\right) = 2.$$

(1.3) $\alpha \neq 8$, $q \leftarrow 1$, MMV candidate $V_1 = (4, 1, 1, 4, 2, 2, 3, 2, 2)$, and let $\alpha \leftarrow 8$.

(1.4a) check whether the number of normal machines in a_8 is maximal. $v_8 = m_8$, and let $\alpha \leftarrow 7$, then check v_7.

(1.4b) check whether the number of normal machines in a_7 is maximal. $v_7 = m_7$, and let $\alpha \leftarrow 6$, then check v_6.

(1.4b) check whether the number of normal machines in a_6 is maximal. $v_6 < m_6$, and $\beta = \lceil 20/(2 \times 1) \rceil = 10$, $v_3 \leftarrow 3$, $\beta' = \lceil 20/(3 \times 1) \rceil = 7$, $\beta' < \beta$, then $i \leftarrow 7$, and go back to step (1.1) to compute MMV.

(1.1a) compute the minimal number of normal machines form a_7.

$$\boxed{i = 7}$$

$$v_7 = \max\left(\left\lceil 20 / \left(\left\lfloor \frac{480 - 15.48 - 5 - \ldots - 18 \times 13.09}{15.48} \right\rfloor \times 5\right)\right\rceil, \left\lceil 20 / \left(\left\lfloor \frac{480 - 15.48 - 5 - \ldots - 10}{15.48 \times 19} \right\rfloor \times 5\right)\right\rceil\right) = 3,$$

$$\vdots$$

$$\boxed{i = 9}$$

$$v_9 = \max\left(\left\lceil 20 / \left(\left\lfloor \frac{480 - 15.48 - 5 - \ldots - 18 \times 15.48}{2} \right\rfloor \times 2\right)\right\rceil, \left\lceil 20 / \left(\left\lfloor \frac{480 - 15.48 - 5 - \ldots - 10}{2 \times 19} \right\rfloor \times 2\right)\right\rceil\right) = 2.$$

(1.3) $\alpha \neq 9$, $q \leftarrow 1$, MMV candidate $V_2 = (4, 1, 1, 4, 2, 3, 2, 2, 2)$, and let $\alpha \leftarrow 9$.

$$\vdots$$

After calculating in step 1, 36 MMV candidates are generated, showed in table 2, using those candidates can find out the MMV in Step 2.

Step 2: Remove those non-minimal ones in $\{V_1, V_2, \ldots, V_{36}\}$ to obtain all MMV, the result is provided in Table 3 and the partial of the search

Table 2   MMV candidates.

$V_1 = (4, 1, 1, 4, 2, 2, 3, 2, 2)$	$V_{19} = (4, 1, 2, 4, 2, 2, 3, 1, 2)$
$V_2 = (4, 1, 1, 4, 2, 3, 2, 2, 2)$	$V_{20} = (4, 1, 2, 4, 2, 2, 3, 2, 1)$
$V_3 = (4, 1, 1, 4, 2, 3, 3, 1, 2)$	$V_{21} = (4, 1, 2, 4, 2, 3, 2, 1, 2)$
$V_4 = (4, 1, 1, 4, 2, 3, 3, 2, 1)$	$V_{22} = (4, 1, 2, 4, 2, 3, 2, 2, 1)$
$V_5 = (4, 1, 1, 4, 2, 4, 2, 2, 2)$	$V_{23} = (4, 1, 2, 4, 2, 3, 3, 1, 2)$
$V_6 = (4, 1, 1, 4, 2, 4, 3, 1, 2)$	$V_{24} = (4, 1, 2, 4, 2, 3, 3, 2, 1)$
$V_7 = (4, 1, 1, 4, 2, 4, 3, 2, 1)$	$V_{25} = (4, 1, 2, 4, 2, 4, 2, 1, 2)$
$V_8 = (4, 1, 1, 4, 3, 2, 2, 2, 2)$	$V_{26} = (4, 1, 2, 4, 2, 4, 2, 2, 1)$
$V_9 = (4, 1, 1, 4, 3, 2, 3, 2, 2)$	$V_{27} = (4, 1, 2, 4, 2, 4, 3, 1, 1)$
$V_{10} = (4, 1, 1, 4, 3, 3, 2, 2, 2)$	$V_{28} = (4, 1, 2, 4, 3, 2, 2, 1, 2)$
$V_{11} = (4, 1, 1, 4, 3, 3, 3, 1, 2)$	$V_{29} = (4, 1, 2, 4, 3, 2, 2, 2, 1)$
$V_{12} = (4, 1, 1, 4, 3, 3, 3, 2, 1)$	$V_{30} = (4, 1, 2, 4, 3, 2, 3, 1, 2)$
$V_{13} = (4, 1, 1, 4, 3, 4, 2, 1, 2)$	$V_{31} = (4, 1, 2, 4, 3, 2, 3, 2, 1)$
$V_{14} = (4, 1, 1, 4, 3, 4, 2, 2, 1)$	$V_{32} = (4, 1, 2, 4, 3, 3, 2, 1, 2)$
$V_{15} = (4, 1, 1, 4, 3, 4, 3, 1, 2)$	$V_{33} = (4, 1, 2, 4, 3, 3, 2, 2, 1)$
$V_{16} = (4, 1, 1, 4, 3, 4, 3, 2, 1)$	$V_{34} = (4, 1, 2, 4, 3, 3, 3, 1, 1)$
$V_{17} = (4, 1, 2, 3, 3, 4, 3, 2, 2)$	$V_{35} = (4, 1, 2, 4, 3, 4, 2, 1, 1)$
$V_{18} = (4, 1, 2, 4, 2, 2, 2, 2, 2)$	$V_{36} = (4, 1, 2, 4, 3, 4, 3, 1, 1)$

Table 3   MMVs.

$V_1 = (4, 1, 1, 4, 2, 2, 3, 2, 2)$	$V_{19} = (4, 1, 2, 4, 2, 2, 3, 1, 2)$
$V_2 = (4, 1, 1, 4, 2, 3, 2, 2, 2)$	$V_{20} = (4, 1, 2, 4, 2, 2, 3, 2, 1)$
$V_3 = (4, 1, 1, 4, 2, 3, 3, 1, 2)$	$V_{21} = (4, 1, 2, 4, 2, 3, 2, 1, 2)$
$V_4 = (4, 1, 1, 4, 2, 3, 3, 2, 1)$	$V_{22} = (4, 1, 2, 4, 2, 3, 2, 2, 1)$
$V_8 = (4, 1, 1, 4, 3, 2, 2, 2, 2)$	$V_{27} = (4, 1, 2, 4, 2, 4, 3, 1, 1)$
$V_{13} = (4, 1, 1, 4, 3, 4, 2, 1, 2)$	$V_{28} = (4, 1, 2, 4, 3, 2, 2, 1, 2)$
$V_{14} = (4, 1, 1, 4, 3, 4, 2, 2, 1)$	$V_{29} = (4, 1, 2, 4, 3, 2, 2, 2, 1)$
$V_{17} = (4, 1, 2, 3, 3, 4, 3, 2, 2)$	$V_{34} = (4, 1, 2, 4, 3, 3, 3, 1, 1)$
$V_{18} = (4, 1, 2, 4, 2, 2, 2, 2, 2)$	$V_{35} = (4, 1, 2, 4, 3, 4, 2, 1, 1)$

tree is shown in Fig. 6. Finally, we have 18 MMVs after comparison.

Step 3: System reliability can be evaluated as

$R_{370,480} = \Pr\{\bigcup_{j=1,2,\ldots 18} X \geq V_j\}$, the system reliability $R_{370,480}$ is 0.7611 after calculating.

In this case, the system reliability $R_{370,480}$ is 0.7611, which means that the production manager has 76.11% confidence in completing the order within the time constraint. If the manager wants to know how much quantity can be completed with the production system in a working day (480 min), then the parameter analysis can be used to find the appropriate demand that can be fulfilled.

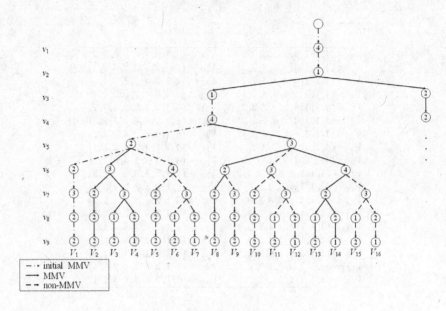

Fig. 6 Search tree of the example.

Table 4 Results of experiments for $d = 200$ to 400.

d	# of MMV candidates	# of MMVs	System reliability	CPU time (sec.)
200	266	23	0.9853	0.0179
220	224	23	0.9842	0.0270
240	218	63	0.9840	0.0603
260	155	8	0.8355	0.0063
280	144	72	0.8249	0.0037
300	84	21	0.8249	0.0097
320	50	2	0.8236	0.0029
340	49	7	0.8211	0.0044
360	59	25	0.8209	0.0105
380	36	18	0.7611	0.0042
400	16	1	0.5817	0.0013

For $T = 480$, we analyze the system reliability for demand in the range $d = 200$ to 400 in increments of 20. The summary of the experimental results are provided in Table 4. The system reliability does not increase significantly when $d < 240$, while it decreases significantly when $d > 380$. Hence, producing items for $d = 240$ in 480 min is suggested to achieve reasonable system reliability. Another appropriate level that is suggested is to produce items for $d = 360$ within the same time constraint, because the system reliability decreases drastically when the demand is greater than 360. The proposed algorithm is programmed with MATLAB programming language and executed on a personal computer level with Core^{TM} i7 - 4770 3.4GHz and 8G RAM. The experimental results show that the average time for execution is 0.0135s. Thus, with the proposed algorithm, system reliability can be achieved in a reasonable time, and decisions can be made to avoid delay in production.

6 Discussion and Conclusion

The stochastic production network (SPN) is widely applied to investigate the performance of a production system with stochastic capacity. The intermittent production system (IPS) is a common production mode and the number of normal machines in each workstation of an IPS would affect the makespan. This chapter utilizes an SPN model to construct an IPS as well as considers stochastic number of normal machines and batch processing. Considering the demand, cycle and completion times, the concept of minimal machine vectors (MMV) is proposed to represent the minimal number of normal machines that each workstation should provide to satisfy demand and time constraint. Then an algorithm is proposed to generate all MMVs. In particular, a DFS approach is integrated into the algorithm to avoid implicit enumeration when searching MMVs. This DFS-based algorithm provides a systematic methodology to search all MMVs. Taking the illustrative example for instance, the enumeration approach generates $4 \times 1 \times 2 \times 4 \times 3 \times 4 \times 3 \times 2 \times 2 = 4608$ candidates to search all the MMVs, while the proposed algorithm generates only 36 candidates to obtain all the MMVs. By using the generated MMVs, system reliability is calculated more efficiently.

System reliability can be considered as a Key Performance Indicators (KPI) to indicate the probability that the IPS satisfies demand d within time constraint T. In other words, using system reliability, the production manager can comprehend whether the customer demand can be met or not. In addition, using parameter analysis, the production manager can investigate the trend of system reliability under different demand levels. Thus, the production manager can decline an order that is beyond the production capacity in a working day. The production manager may adopt system reliability as a capability indicator to guarantee the performance of the IPS and to ensure that customers' requirements are satisfied. In addition, decision makers can decide that an order should be accepted or not according to system reliability.

References

Aven, T., (1985). Reliability evaluation of multistate systems with multistate components, *IEEE Transactions on Reliability*, R-34, pp. 473–479.

Bai, G., Zuo, M. J. and Tian, Z. (2015). Ordering heuristics for reliability evaluation of multistate networks, *IEEE Transactions on Reliability*, 64, pp. 1015–1023.

Fiondella, L., Lin, Y. K. and Chang, P. C. (2015). System performance and reliability modeling of a stochastic-flow production network: a confidence-based approach, *IEEE Transactions on Systems, Man, and Cybernetics: Systems*, 45, pp. 1437–1447.

Hendry, L. C. and Kingsman, B. G. (1989). Production planning systems and their applicability to make-to-order companies, *European Journal of Operational Research*, 40, pp. 1–15.

Hudson, J. C. and Kapur, K. C. (1985). Reliability bounds for multistate systems with multistate components, *Operations Research*, 33, 153–160.

Jacobs, F. R. and Chase, R. B. (2014) *Operations and Supply Chain Management*, (McGraw-Hill Inc., NY, USA).

Janan, X. (1985). On multistate system analysis, *IEEE Transactions on Reliability*, 34, pp. 329–337.

Jane, C. C., and Laih, Y. W. (2008). A practical algorithm for computing multistate two-terminal reliability, *IEEE Transactions on Reliability*, 57, pp. 295–302.

Kim, Y. and Lee, J. (1993). Manufacturing strategy and production systems: an integrated framework, *Journal of Operations Management*, 11, pp. 3–15.

Lin, Y. K. and Chang, P. C. (2012). System reliability of a manufacturing network with reworking action and different failure rates, *International Journal of Production Research*, 50, pp. 6930–6944.

Lin, Y. K. and Chang, P. C. (2013). A novel reliability evaluation technique for stochastic flow manufacturing networks with multiple production lines, *IEEE Transactions on Reliability*, 61, pp. 92–104.

Lin, Y. K. and Chang, P. C. (2015). A novel model for a manufacturing system with joint production lines in terms of prior-set, *International Journal of Systems Science*, 46, pp. 340–354.

Lin, Y. K., Huang, D. H. and Yeng, L. C. L. (2016). Reliability evaluation of a hybrid flow-shop with stochastic capacity within a time constraint, *IEEE Transactions on Reliability*, 65, pp. 867–877.

Schmitt, T. G., Klastorin, T. and Shtub, A. (1985). Production classification system: concepts, models and strategies, *International Journal of Production Research*, 23, pp. 563–578.

Stevenson, M., Hendry, L. C. and Kingsman, B. G. (2005). A review of production planning and control: the applicability of key concepts to the make-to-order industry, *International Journal of Production Research*, 43, pp. 869–898.

Stevenson, W. J. (2015) *Operations Management*,12th Ed. (McGraw-Hill Inc., NY, USA).

Sun, S. W., Chang, P. C. and Lin, Y. K. (2015). Confidence-based reliability evaluation of multistate production network with process improvement, *International Journal of Reliability, Quality and Safety Engineering*, 22, 1550028.

Yarlagadda, R. A. O. and Hershey, J. (1991). Fast algorithm for computing the reliability of a communication network, *International Journal of Electronics*, 70, pp. 549–564.

Zuo, M. J., Tian, Z. and Huang, H.Z. (2007). An efficient method for reliability evaluation of multistate networks given all minimal path vectors, *IIE Transactions*, 39, pp. 811–817.

Chapter 12

Cumulative Backup Policies for Database Systems

Xufeng Zhao [1], Syouji Nakamura[2], Cunhua Qian[3]
and Shey-Huei Sheu[4]

[1] *Department of Mechanical and Industrial Engineering,*
Qatar University,

[2] *Department of Life Management,*
Kinjo Gakuin University,

[3] *School of Economics and Management,*
Nanjing Tech University,

[4] *Department of Statistics and Informatics Science,*
Providence University

1 Introduction

A database management system (DBMS) can be set to implement a hierarchy of daily, weekly and monthly backups, including mix and match modes between full backup and incremental backups [Mcdowall (2001)]. The backup processes themselves will consume systems resources and have the least amount of interference with normal operations of database [Ricart et al. (2005)], so that how to lower the time costs of data backups and failure recoveries has become a primary point of concern [Qian et al. (2002); Nakamura et al. (2003)].

The incremental backup includes differential and cumulative backup modes, and both have advantages and disadvantages [Fong and Manley (2007); Microsoft (2012)]: Differential backup exports only the data files updated since the last backup (a full or differential backup). It is much smaller and quicker than full backups, and the data restoration after breakdown needs the last full backup plus all the differential backups until the point-in-time of breakdown. Cumulative backup exports all data files updated since the last full backup. The advantage to this mode is quicker recovery time, requiring only a full backup and the last cumulative backup to restore the entire updated data. Obviously, full backup is necessary for both differential and cumulative backups as renewal actions. However, a full backup exports all the data files updated since the last full backup and require long periods of backup and recovery.

In this chapter, the cumulative backup scheme is observed. We consider a database system that is running for 24/7 and has several random busy states of updating data. In this case, it would be wasteful to pause the running system for cumulative backups when it is busy with applications. Using the random maintenance theory in reliability [Nakagawa (2014)] and renewal theory [Osaki (1992)], we suppose that cumulative backups are scheduled in random ways for the random busy states of updates and full backups are made at decision variables of time T, update N and data volume K. Their expected backup and recovery cost rates are obtained and optimum solutions of full backup times are found to minimize them. In addition, three backup policies are compared analytically and numerically.

However, we don't know the exact times when updates occur, and we also cannot know the exact volume of data for this update, but it can be assumed as a random variable. We give the above assumptions as the costs of backup and recovery depend on the total exported/imported data. Random updates with random volumes of updated data forms a compound stochastic process, which has similar formulation of shock and damage process in reliability [Nakagawa (2007)], so that the technique of cumulative damage models can be used for modeling.

2 Backup and Recovery

We suppose in a database system that:

- Data updates randomly at a renewal process according to an identical distribution $F(t)$ with a density function $f(t) \equiv \mathrm{d}F(t)/\mathrm{d}t$ and finite mean $1/\lambda \equiv \int_0^\infty \overline{F}(t)\mathrm{d}t$, where $\overline{\Phi}(t) \equiv 1 - \Phi(t)$ for any function $\Phi(t)$.
- A volume W_j $(j = 1, 2, \cdots)$ of updated data due to the jth update has an identical distribution $G(x) \equiv \Pr\{W_j \leq x\}$ with finite mean

$1/\omega \equiv \int_0^\infty \overline{G}(x)\mathrm{d}x.$

- Database failure occurs randomly with a general distribution $D(t)$ that has a density function $d(t) \equiv \mathrm{d}D(t)/\mathrm{d}t$ and finite mean $1/\mu \equiv \int_0^\infty \overline{D}(t)\mathrm{d}t$. The failure rate $r(t) \equiv d(t)/\overline{D}(t)$ is supposed to be increasing with t strictly to $r(\infty)$ that might be infinity.
- A full backup should be made correctively after database failure as a renewal point for the whole backup plans.

We next introduce the following costs for backup and recovery schemes:

- c_F is a constant cost of full backup.
- $c_K + c_0 x$ is the cost for cumulative backup when a total volume x of data has been updated.
- $c_R + c_0 x$ is the recovery cost after failure when a total volume x of data has been updated.

We denote for $j = 1, 2, \cdots$ that

$$M_j(K) \equiv \int_0^K (c_K + c_0 x)\mathrm{d}G^{(j)}(x),$$

$$N_j(K) \equiv \int_0^K (c_R + c_0 x)\mathrm{d}G^{(j)}(x).$$

Then, $\sum_{i=1}^j M_i(K)$ is the expected cost of j cumulative backups, and $N_j(K)$ is the recovery cost when the jth cumulative backup is implemented. In particular, we denote

$$M_j \equiv \lim_{K \to \infty} M_j(K) = c_K + \frac{jc_0}{\omega},$$

$$N_j \equiv \lim_{K \to \infty} N_j(K) = c_R + \frac{jc_0}{\omega}.$$

3 Optimum Backup Policies

In order to protect the security of data and prevent the enormous recovery cost due to failure, we obtain three expected cost rates for backup schemes and obtain their optimum full backup policies when it is scheduled preventively at planned time T, update number N and data volume K.

3.1 *Optimum T^**

Suppose that a full backup is scheduled preventively at time T $(0 < T \le \infty)$. Then, the probability that a full backup is implemented at time T is

$$\overline{D}(T) \sum_{j=0}^{\infty} [F^{(j)}(T) - F^{(j+1)}(T)] = \overline{D}(T),$$

and the probability that it is implemented at failure is

$$\sum_{j=0}^{\infty} \int_0^T [F^{(j)}(t) - F^{(j+1)}(t)]dD(t) = D(T),$$

where $F^{(j)}(t)$ $(j = 1, 2, \cdots)$ is the j-fold convolution of $F(t)$ and $F^{(0)}(t) \equiv 1$ for any $t \ge 0$.

The mean time to full backup is

$$T\overline{D}(T) + \int_0^T t dD(t) = \int_0^T \overline{D}(t)dt, \qquad (1)$$

and the expected cost until full backup is

$$\tilde{C}(T) = \overline{D}(T) \sum_{j=0}^{\infty} \left(c_F + \sum_{i=1}^{j} M_i \right) [F^{(j)}(T) - F^{(j+1)}(T)]$$

$$+ \sum_{j=0}^{\infty} \left(c_F + \sum_{i=1}^{j} M_i + N_j \right) \int_0^T [F^{(j)}(t) - F^{(j+1)}(t)]dD(t)$$

$$= c_F + c_R D(T) + \left(c_K + \frac{c_0}{\omega} \right) \int_0^T \overline{D}(t)dM_F(t)$$

$$+ \frac{c_0}{\omega} \left[-\overline{D}(T)M_F(T) + \sum_{j=1}^{\infty} j \int_0^T \overline{D}(t)dF^{(j)}(t) \right], \qquad (2)$$

where $M_F(t) \equiv \sum_{j=1}^{\infty} F^{(j)}(t)$.

Therefore, the expected cost rate is

$$C(T) = \frac{c_F + c_R D(T) + (c_K + c_0/\omega) \int_0^T \overline{D}(t)dM_F(t)}{\int_0^T \overline{D}(t)dt}.$$

$$\frac{+(c_0/\omega)[-\overline{D}(T)M_F(T) + \sum_{j=1}^{\infty} j \int_0^T \overline{D}(t)dF^{(j)}(t)]}{\int_0^T \overline{D}(t)dt}. \qquad (3)$$

We find optimum T^* to minimize $C(T)$ when $r(t)$ increases with t. Differentiating $C(T)$ with respect to T and setting it equal to zero,

$$c_R \int_0^T \overline{D}(t)[r(T) - r(t)]dt + c_K \int_0^T \overline{D}(t)[m_F(T) - m_F(t)]dt$$

$$+ \frac{c_0}{\omega} \left\{ \int_0^T \overline{D}(t)[r(T)M_F(T) - r(t)M_F(t)]dt \right.$$

$$\left. + \sum_{j=1}^{\infty} j \int_0^T \overline{D}(t)[f^{(j)}(T) - f^{(j)}(t)]dt \right\} = c_F, \qquad (4)$$

where $f^{(j)}(t) \equiv dF^{(j)}(t)/dt$ and $m_F(t) \equiv dM_F(t)/dt$.

In particular, when $F(t) = 1 - e^{-\lambda t}$, (4) is

$$c_R \int_0^T \overline{D}(t)[r(T) - r(t)]dt$$

$$+ \frac{\lambda c_0}{\omega} \left\{ \int_0^T \overline{D}(t)[Tr(T) - tr(t)]dt + \int_0^T \overline{D}(t)(\lambda T - \lambda t)dt \right\} = c_F, \quad (5)$$

whose left-hand side increase strictly with T to ∞. Therefore, there exists a finite and unique T^* $(0 < T^* < \infty)$ which satisfies (5).

In addition, when $D(t) = 1 - e^{-\mu t}$, (5) is

$$\frac{\lambda}{\mu}\left(1 + \frac{\lambda}{\mu}\right)(\mu T - 1 + e^{-\mu T}) = \frac{c_F}{c_0/\omega}, \qquad (6)$$

and the resulting cost rate is

$$\frac{C(T^*)}{\lambda} = \frac{c_0}{\omega}\left(1 + \frac{\mu}{\lambda}\right)\lambda T^* + \frac{\mu}{\lambda}c_R + c_K + \frac{c_0}{\omega}. \qquad (7)$$

Table 1 presents optimum λT^* in (6) and its cost rate $C(T^*)/\lambda$ in (7) when $c_0 = 1.0$, $c_K = 1.0, c_R = 1.0$ and $\omega = 1.0$. It is of interest that the expected number of updates λT^*, i.e., cumulative backups, until full backup decreases with the mean value of failure time $1/\mu$ and increases with the cost of full backup.

3.2 Optimum N^*

Suppose that a full backup is scheduled preventively at a number N ($N = 1, 2, \cdots$) of updates, i.e., at a number N of cumulative backups. Then, the probability that a full backup is implemented at update N is

$$\int_0^{\infty} \overline{D}(t)dF^{(N)}(t) = \int_0^{\infty} F^{(N)}(t)dD(t),$$

Table 1 Optimum λT^* and its cost rate $C(T^*)/\lambda$ when $c_0 = 1.0$, $c_K = 1.0$, $c_R = 1.0$ and $\omega = 1.0$.

μ/λ	$c_F = 5.0$		$c_F = 10.0$	
	λT^*	$C(T^*)/\lambda$	λT^*	$C(T^*)/\lambda$
0.01	3.163	5.205	4.483	6.538
0.02	3.164	5.247	4.494	6.604
0.03	3.165	5.290	4.506	6.671
0.04	3.166	5.333	4.517	6.738
0.05	3.167	5.376	4.529	6.806
0.06	3.169	5.419	4.541	6.873
0.07	3.170	5.462	4.553	6.942
0.08	3.171	5.505	4.565	7.010
0.09	3.173	5.549	4.577	7.079
0.10	3.174	5.592	4.590	7.149

and the probability that it is implemented at failure is

$$\int_0^\infty [1 - F^{(N)}(t)]\mathrm{d}D(t) = \int_0^\infty D(t)\mathrm{d}F^{(N)}(t).$$

The mean time to full backup is

$$\int_0^\infty t\overline{D}(t)\mathrm{d}F^{(N)}(t) + \int_0^\infty t[1 - F^{(N)}(t)]\mathrm{d}D(t) = \int_0^\infty \overline{D}(t)[1 - F^{(N)}(t)]\mathrm{d}t,$$
(8)

and the expected cost until full backup is

$$\tilde{C}(N) = \left(c_F + \sum_{i=1}^N M_i\right)\int_0^\infty F^{(N)}(t)\mathrm{d}D(t)$$

$$+ \sum_{j=0}^{N-1}\left(c_F + \sum_{i=1}^j M_i + N_j\right)\int_0^\infty [F^{(j)}(t) - F^{(j+1)}(t)]\mathrm{d}D(t)$$

$$= c_F + \sum_{j=1}^N \left(c_K + \frac{jc_0}{\omega}\right)\int_0^\infty F^{(j)}(t)\mathrm{d}D(t)$$

$$+ \sum_{j=0}^{N-1}\left(c_R + \frac{jc_0}{\omega}\right)\int_0^\infty [F^{(j)}(t) - F^{(j+1)}(t)]\mathrm{d}D(t).$$
(9)

Therefore, the expected cost rate is

$$C(N) = \frac{c_F + \sum_{j=1}^N (c_K + jc_0/\omega)\int_0^\infty F^{(j)}(t)\mathrm{d}D(t) + \sum_{j=0}^{N-1}(c_R + jc_0/\omega)\int_0^\infty [F^{(j)}(t) - F^{(j+1)}(t)]\mathrm{d}D(t)}{\int_0^\infty \overline{D}(t)[1 - F^{(N)}(t)]\mathrm{d}t}.$$
(10)

We find optimum N^* to minimize $C(N)$. Forming the inequality $C(N+1) - C(N) \geq 0$,

$$Q(N) \int_0^\infty \overline{D}(t)[1 - F^{(N)}(t)]dt - \sum_{j=1}^N \left(c_K + \frac{jc_0}{\omega}\right) \int_0^\infty F^{(j)}(t)dD(t)$$

$$- \sum_{j=0}^{N-1} \left(c_R + \frac{jc_0}{\omega}\right) \int_0^\infty [F^{(j)}(t) - F^{(j+1)}(t)]dD(t) \geq c_F, \qquad (11)$$

where

$$Q(N) \equiv \frac{[c_K + (N+1)c_0/\omega]\int_0^\infty F^{(N+1)}(t)dD(t)}{\int_0^\infty \overline{D}(t)[F^{(N)}(t) - F^{(N+1)}(t)]dt}.$$

Let $L(N)$ denote the left-hand side of (11). If $Q(N)$ increases strictly with N to $Q(\infty)$, and

$$L(\infty) \equiv \frac{Q(\infty)}{\mu} - \sum_{j=1}^\infty \left(c_K + \frac{jc_0}{\omega}\right) \int_0^\infty F^{(j)}(t)dD(t)$$

$$- c_R - \frac{c_0}{\omega} \int_0^\infty M_F(t)dD(t) > c_F,$$

then there exists a unique and minimum N^* $(1 \leq N^* < \infty)$ which satisfies (11).

In particular, when $D(t) = 1 - e^{-\mu t}$,

$$\frac{Q(N)}{\mu} = \left[c_K + \frac{(N+1)c_0}{\omega}\right] \frac{F^*(\mu)}{1 - F^*(\mu)} + c_R + \frac{Nc_0}{\omega},$$

which increases strictly with N to ∞. Thus, optimum N^* satisfies

$$\frac{1}{1 - F^*(\mu)} \sum_{j=1}^N \{1 - [F^*(\mu)]^j\} \geq \frac{c_F}{c_0/\omega}, \qquad (12)$$

whose left-hand side increases with N from 1 to ∞.

When $F(t) = 1 - e^{-\lambda t}$, (11) is

$$\left(c_R + \frac{Nc_0}{\omega}\right) \left\{Q(N) \int_0^\infty \overline{D}(t)[1 - F^{(N)}(t)]dt - \int_0^\infty [1 - F^{(N)}(t)]dD(t)\right\}$$

$$+ \frac{c_0}{\omega} \sum_{j=0}^{N-1} (N - j) \int_0^\infty F^{(j)}(t)dD(t) \geq c_F, \qquad (13)$$

which increases strictly with N to ∞, where

$$Q(N) = \frac{\int_0^\infty (\lambda t)^N e^{-\lambda t} dD(t)}{\int_0^\infty (\lambda t)^N e^{-\lambda t} \overline{D}(t) dt}.$$

In addition, when $D(t) = 1 - e^{-\mu t}$, $Q(N) = \mu$ and (13) is

$$\sum_{j=0}^{N-1} (N - j) \left(\frac{\lambda}{\lambda + \mu} \right)^j \geq \frac{c_F}{c_0/\omega}, \tag{14}$$

which agrees with (12) when $F^*(\mu) = \lambda/(\lambda + \mu)$.

Table 2   Optimum N^* and its cost rate $C(N^*)/\lambda$ when $c_0 = 1.0$, $c_K = 1.0, c_R = 1.0$ and $\omega = 1.0$.

μ/λ	$c_F = 5.0$		$c_F = 10.0$	
	N^*	$C(N^*)/\lambda$	N^*	$C(N^*)/\lambda$
0.01	3	4.687	5	6.030
0.02	3	4.707	5	6.060
0.03	3	4.726	5	6.091
0.04	3	4.746	5	6.121
0.05	3	4.766	5	6.152
0.06	3	4.786	5	6.183
0.07	3	4.806	5	6.214
0.08	3	4.825	5	6.246
0.09	3	4.845	5	6.277
0.10	3	4.864	5	6.308

Table 2 presents optimum N^* in (14) and its cost rate $C(N^*)/\lambda$ in (10) when $c_0 = 1.0$, $c_K = 1.0, c_R = 1.0$ and $\omega = 1.0$. Comparing with Table 1, $C(N^*) < C(T^*)$, i.e., full backup scheduled at update N is more economical than that at time T.

3.3   *Optimum K^**

Suppose that a full backup is scheduled preventively at a volume K ($0 < K \leq \infty$) of updated data. Then, the probability that a full backup is implemented at volume K is

$$\sum_{j=0}^{\infty} [G^{(j)}(K) - G^{(j+1)}(K)] \int_0^\infty \overline{D}(t) dF^{(j+1)}(t),$$

and the probability that it is implemented at failure is

$$\sum_{j=0}^{\infty} G^{(j)}(K) \int_0^{\infty} [F^{(j)}(t) - F^{(j+1)}(t)] \mathrm{d}D(t).$$

The mean time to full backup is

$$\sum_{j=0}^{\infty} [G^{(j)}(K) - G^{(j+1)}(K)] \int_0^{\infty} t\overline{D}(t)\mathrm{d}F^{(j+1)}(t)$$

$$+ \sum_{j=0}^{\infty} G^{(j)}(K) \int_0^{\infty} t[F^{(j)}(t) - F^{(j+1)}(t)]\mathrm{d}D(t)$$

$$= \sum_{j=0}^{\infty} G^{(j)}(K) \int_0^{\infty} [F^{(j)}(t) - F^{(j+1)}(t)]\overline{D}(t)\mathrm{d}t, \tag{15}$$

and the expected number of cumulative backups until full backup is

$$\sum_{j=0}^{\infty} j[G^{(j)}(K) - G^{(j+1)}(K)] \int_0^{\infty} \overline{D}(t)\mathrm{d}F^{(j+1)}(t)$$

$$+ \sum_{j=0}^{\infty} jG^{(j)}(K) \int_0^{\infty} [F^{(j)}(t) - F^{(j+1)}(t)]\mathrm{d}D(t)$$

$$= \sum_{j=1}^{\infty} G^{(j)}(K) \int_0^{\infty} \overline{D}(t)\mathrm{d}F^{(j)}(t). \tag{16}$$

Note that if the full backup is implemented at the $(j+1)$th update of volume K, then the cost of the $(j+1)$th cumulative backup is

$$\sum_{j=0}^{\infty} \int_0^K \left\{ \int_{K-x}^{\infty} [c_K + c_0(x+y)]\mathrm{d}G(y) \right\} \mathrm{d}G^{(j)}(x) \int_0^{\infty} \overline{D}(t)\mathrm{d}F^{(j+1)}(t).$$
$$\tag{17}$$

Thus, the total cost of cumulative backups until full backup is

$$\widetilde{C}(K) = c_F + \sum_{j=1}^{\infty} M_j(K) \int_0^{\infty} \overline{D}(t)\mathrm{d}F^{(j)}(t)$$

$$+ \sum_{j=0}^{\infty} \int_0^K \left\{ \int_{K-x}^{\infty} [c_K + c_0(x+y)]\mathrm{d}G(y) \right\} \mathrm{d}G^{(j)}(x)$$

$$\int_0^{\infty} \overline{D}(t)\mathrm{d}F^{(j+1)}(t) + \sum_{j=0}^{\infty} N_j(K) \int_0^{\infty} [F^{(j)}(t) - F^{(j+1)}(t)]\mathrm{d}D(t)$$

$$=c_F + \sum_{j=0}^{\infty} \int_0^K (c_K + c_0 x)dG^{(j)}(x) \int_0^{\infty} \overline{D}(t)dF^{(j+1)}(t)$$

$$+ \frac{c_0}{\omega} \sum_{j=0}^{\infty} G^{(j)}(K) \int_0^{\infty} \overline{D}(t)dF^{(j+1)}(t)$$

$$+ \sum_{j=0}^{\infty} \int_0^K (c_R + c_0 x)dG^{(j)}(x) \int_0^{\infty} [F^{(j)}(t) - F^{(j+1)}(t)]dD(t). \qquad (18)$$

Therefore, the expected cost rate is

$$C(K) = \frac{\begin{array}{l} c_F + \sum_{j=0}^{\infty} \int_0^K (c_K + c_0 x)dG^{(j)}(x) \int_0^{\infty} \overline{D}(t)dF^{(j+1)}(t) \\ + (c_0/\omega) \sum_{j=0}^{\infty} G^{(j)}(K) \int_0^{\infty} \overline{D}(t)dF^{(j+1)}(t) \\ + \sum_{j=0}^{\infty} \int_0^K (c_R + c_0 x)dG^{(j)}(x) \int_0^{\infty} [F^{(j)}(t) - F^{(j+1)}(t)]dD(t) \end{array}}{\sum_{j=0}^{\infty} G^{(j)}(K) \int_0^{\infty} [F^{(j)}(t) - F^{(j+1)}(t)]\overline{D}(t)dt}.$$
$$(19)$$

When $F(t) = 1 - e^{-\lambda t}$ and $D(t) = 1 - e^{-\mu t}$,

$$\frac{C(K)}{\lambda} = \frac{c_F + c_0 \sum_{j=0}^{\infty} [\lambda/(\lambda+\mu)]^j \int_0^K x dG^{(j)}(x)}{\sum_{j=0}^{\infty} [\lambda/(\lambda+\mu)]^{j+1} G^{(j)}(K)} + \frac{\mu}{\lambda} c_R + c_K + \frac{c_0}{\omega}. \qquad (20)$$

We find optimum K^* to minimize $C(K)$. Differentiating $C(K)$ with respect to K and setting it equal to zero,

$$\sum_{j=0}^{\infty} \left(\frac{\lambda}{\lambda+\mu} \right)^j \int_0^K (K - x)dG^{(j)}(x) = \frac{c_F}{c_0}, \qquad (21)$$

whose left-hand side increases with K from 0 to ∞. Therefore, there exist a finite and unique K^* $(0 < K^* < \infty)$ which satisfies (21), and the resulting cost rate is

$$\frac{C(K^*)}{\lambda} = c_0 \left(1 + \frac{\mu}{\lambda} \right) K^* + \frac{\mu}{\lambda} c_R + c_K + \frac{c_0}{\omega}. \qquad (22)$$

Table 3 presents optimum ωK^* in (21) and its cost rate $C(K^*)/\lambda$ in (22) when $c_0 = 1.0$, $c_K = 1.0$, $c_R = 1.0$ and $\omega = 1.0$. Comparing with Table 2, $C(K^*) < C(N^*)$, i.e., full backup scheduled at volume K is more economical than that at update N.

Table 3 Optimum ωK^* and its cost rate $C(K^*)/\lambda$ when $c_0 = 1.0$, $c_K = 1.0$, $c_R = 1.0$ and $\omega = 1.0$.

μ/λ	$c_F = 5.0$		$c_F = 10.0$	
	ωK^*	$C(K^*)/\lambda$	ωK^*	$C(K^*)/\lambda$
0.01	2.331	4.364	3.613	5.660
0.02	2.345	4.412	3.644	5.737
0.03	2.359	4.460	3.674	5.815
0.04	2.373	4.508	3.705	5.893
0.05	2.387	4.556	3.735	5.972
0.06	2.401	4.605	3.765	6.051
0.07	2.414	4.653	3.795	6.131
0.08	2.428	4.702	3.825	6.211
0.09	2.441	4.751	3.854	6.271
0.10	2.454	4.800	3.884	6.302

4 Comparisons of Optimum Policies

In order to compare the backup models with respective decision variables T, N and K, we propose the following integrated models, and comparisons are conducted from the optimizations of these models.

4.1 *Comparison of T and N*

Suppose that a full backup is scheduled preventively at time T $(0 < T \leq \infty)$ or at a number N $(N = 1, 2, \cdots)$ of updates, whichever occurs first. Then, the expected cost rate is

$$C(T, N) = \frac{c_F + \sum_{j=1}^{N}(c_K + jc_0/\omega)\int_0^T \overline{D}(t)\mathrm{d}F^{(j)}(t) + \sum_{j=0}^{N-1}(c_R + jc_0/\omega)\int_0^T [F^{(j)}(t) - F^{(j+1)}(t)]\mathrm{d}D(t)}{\int_0^T \overline{D}(t)[1 - F^{(N)}(t)]\mathrm{d}t}. \tag{23}$$

Obviously, $\lim_{N \to \infty} C(T, N) = C(T)$ in (3) and $\lim_{T \to \infty} C(T, N) = C(N)$ in (10).

When $F(t) = 1 - e^{-\lambda t}$ and $D(t) = 1 - e^{-\mu t}$, (23) is

$$\frac{C(T, N)}{\lambda} = \frac{c_F + \sum_{j=1}^{N}(c_K + jc_0/\omega)[\lambda/(\lambda + \mu)]^j F_p^{(j)}(T) + \sum_{j=0}^{N-1}(c_R + jc_0/\omega)[\mu/(\lambda + \mu)][\lambda/(\lambda + \mu)]^j F_p^{(j+1)}(T)}{\sum_{j=0}^{N-1}[\lambda/(\lambda + \mu)]^{j+1} F_p^{(j+1)}(T)},$$

i.e.,

$$\frac{C(T,N)}{\lambda} = \frac{c_F + (c_0/\omega)\sum_{j=0}^{N-1} j[\lambda/(\lambda+\mu)]^j F_p^{(j+1)}(T)}{\sum_{j=0}^{N-1}[\lambda/(\lambda+\mu)]^{j+1} F_p^{(j+1)}(T)} + \frac{\mu}{\lambda}c_R + c_K + \frac{c_0}{\omega},$$

(24)

where

$$F_p^{(j)}(T) = \sum_{i=j}^{\infty} \frac{[(\lambda+\mu)T]^i}{i!} e^{-(\lambda+\mu)T} \quad (j = 0,1,2,\cdots).$$

We find optimum T_F^* and N_F^* to minimize $C(T,N)$ in (24). Forming the inequality $C(T, N+1) - C(T,N) \geq 0$,

$$\sum_{j=0}^{N-1}(N-j)\left(\frac{\lambda}{\lambda+\mu}\right)^j F_p^{(j+1)}(T) \geq \frac{c_F}{c_0/\omega},$$

(25)

whose left-hand side increases strictly with N to ∞. Thus, there exists a unique and minimum N_F^* ($1 \leq N_F^* < \infty$) which satisfies (25). Note that the left-hand side of (25) increases strictly with T to that of (14), then N_F^* decreases with T to N^* given in (14).

Next, differentiating (24) with respect to T and setting it equal to zero,

$$\frac{\sum_{j=0}^{N-1} j[(\lambda T)^j/j!]}{\sum_{j=0}^{N-1}[(\lambda T)^j/j!]} \sum_{j=0}^{N-1}\left(\frac{\lambda}{\lambda+\mu}\right)^j F_p^{(j+1)}(T) - \sum_{j=0}^{N-1} j\left(\frac{\lambda}{\lambda+\mu}\right)^j F_p^{(j+1)}(T)$$
$$= \frac{c_F}{c_0/\omega}.$$

(26)

Substituting (25) for (26),

$$\frac{\sum_{j=0}^{N-1} j[(\lambda T)^j/j!]}{\sum_{j=0}^{N-1}[(\lambda T)^j/j!]} \leq N,$$

which always holds for any N, that is, optimum policy to minimize $C(T,N)$ is $(T_F^* = \infty, N_F^* = N^*)$, where N^* is given in (14). That means full backup policy scheduled at update N is better than that at time T, which also agrees with the comparison of Table 1 and Table 2.

Furthermore, note that

$$\frac{\sum_{j=0}^{N-1} j[(\lambda T)^j/j!]}{\sum_{j=0}^{N-1}[(\lambda T)^j/j!]} \quad (N \geq 2)$$

(27)

increases strictly with T from 0 to $N - 1$, then the left-hand side of (26) increases strictly with T from 0 to

$$\sum_{j=0}^{N-1} (N - 1 - j) \left(\frac{\lambda}{\lambda + \mu}\right)^j < \sum_{j=0}^{N-1} (N - j) \left(\frac{\lambda}{\lambda + \mu}\right)^j,$$

which agrees with that of (14), then we obtain

- If given $N \leq N^*$, then $T_F^* = \infty$.
- If given $N > N^*$, then there exists a finite and unique T_F^* $(0 < T_F^* < \infty)$ which satisfies (26), and the resulting cost rate is

$$\frac{C(T_F^*, N)}{\lambda} = \frac{c_0}{\omega} \left(1 + \frac{\mu}{\lambda}\right) \frac{\sum_{j=0}^{N-1} j[(\lambda T_F^*)^j / j!]}{\sum_{j=0}^{N-1}[(\lambda T_F^*)^j / j!]} + \frac{\mu}{\lambda} c_R + c_K + \frac{c_0}{\omega}. \quad (28)$$

In addition, (27) increases strictly with N to λT, the left-hand side of (26) increases with N to

$$\frac{\lambda}{\mu} \left(1 + \frac{\lambda}{\mu}\right) (\mu T - 1 + e^{-\mu T}),$$

which agrees with (6). Thus, T_F^* decreases strictly with N to T^* given in (6).

Tables 4 and 5 present optimum N_F^* for given λT and λT_F^* for given N, when $c_0 = 1.0$, $c_K = 1.0$, $c_R = 1.0$, $c_F = 5.0$ and $\omega = 1.0$.

Table 4   Optimum N_F^* for given λT when $c_0 = 1.0$, $c_K = 1.0$, $c_R = 1.0$, $c_F = 5.0$ and $\omega = 1.0$.

μ/λ	$\lambda T = 1.0$ N_F^*	$\lambda T = 2.0$ N_F^*	$\lambda T = 5.0$ N_F^*
0.01	6	4	3
0.02	6	4	3
0.03	6	4	3
0.04	6	4	3
0.05	6	4	3
0.06	6	4	3
0.07	6	4	3
0.08	6	4	3
0.09	6	4	3
0.10	6	4	3

Table 5　Optimum λT_F^* for given N when $c_0 = 1.0$, $c_K = 1.0$, $c_R = 1.0$, $c_F = 5.0$ and $\omega = 1.0$.

μ/λ	$N = 1$	$N = 5$	$N = 10$
	λT_F^*	λT_F^*	λT_F^*
0.01	∞	4.731	3.174
0.02	∞	4.745	3.175
0.03	∞	4.759	3.176
0.04	∞	4.774	3.177
0.05	∞	4.788	3.178
0.06	∞	4.803	3.180
0.07	∞	4.819	3.181
0.08	∞	4.835	3.183
0.09	∞	4.851	3.184
0.10	∞	4.867	3.186

4.2　*Comparison of T and K*

Suppose that a full backup is scheduled preventively at time T $(0 < T \leq \infty)$ or at a volume K $(0 < K \leq \infty)$ of updated data, whichever occurs first. Then, the expected cost rate is

$$
C(T, K) = \frac{
\begin{aligned}
&c_F + \sum_{j=0}^{\infty} \int_0^K (c_K + c_0 x) dG^{(j)}(x) \int_0^T \overline{D}(t) dF^{(j)}(t) \\
&+ (c_0/\omega) \sum_{j=0}^{\infty} G^{(j)}(K) \int_0^T \overline{D}(t) dF^{(j+1)}(t) \\
&+ \sum_{j=0}^{\infty} \int_0^K (c_R + c_0 x) dG^{(j)}(x) \int_0^T [F^{(j)}(t) - F^{(j+1)}(t)] dD(t)
\end{aligned}
}{
\sum_{j=0}^{\infty} G^{(j)}(K) \int_0^T [F^{(j)}(t) - F^{(j+1)}(t)] \overline{D}(t) dt
}.
$$

(29)

Obviously, $\lim_{K \to \infty} C(T, K) = C(T)$ in (3) and $\lim_{T \to \infty} C(T, K) = C(K)$ in (19).

When $F(t) = 1 - e^{-\lambda t}$ and $D(t) = 1 - e^{-\mu t}$, (29) is

$$
\frac{C(T, K)}{\lambda} = \frac{c_F + c_0 \sum_{j=0}^{\infty} \int_0^K x dG^{(j)}(x) [\lambda/(\lambda + \mu)]^j F_p^{(j+1)}(T)}{\sum_{j=0}^{\infty} G^{(j)}(K) [\lambda/(\lambda + \mu)]^{j+1} F_p^{(j+1)}(T)}
$$
$$
+ \frac{\mu}{\lambda} c_R + c_K + \frac{c_0}{\omega}.
$$

(30)

We find optimum T_F^* and K_F^* to minimize $C(T, K)$ in (30). Differentiating $C(T, K)$ with respect to K and setting it equal to zero,

$$
\sum_{j=0}^{\infty} \int_0^K (K - x) dG^{(j)}(x) \left(\frac{\lambda}{\lambda + \mu}\right)^j F_p^{(j+1)}(T) = \frac{c_F}{c_0},
$$

(31)

whose left-hand side increases strictly with K from 0 to ∞. Thus, there exists a finite and unique K^* $(0 < K^* < \infty)$ which satisfies (31), and the resulting cost rate is

$$\frac{C(T, K_F^*)}{\lambda} = c_0 \left(1 + \frac{\mu}{\lambda}\right) K_F^* + \frac{\mu}{\lambda} c_R + c_K + \frac{c_0}{\omega}. \tag{32}$$

Note that the left-hand side of (31) increases strictly with T to that of (21), then K_F^* decreases with T to K^* given in (21).

Next, differentiating $C(T, K)$ with respect to T and setting it equal to zero,

$$\frac{\sum_{j=0}^{\infty} \int_0^K x \mathrm{d}G^{(j)}(x)[(\lambda T)^j / j!]}{\sum_{j=0}^{\infty} G^{(j)}(K)[(\lambda T)^j / j!]} \sum_{j=0}^{\infty} G^{(j)}(K) \left(\frac{\lambda}{\lambda + \mu}\right)^j F_p^{(j+1)}(T)$$

$$- \sum_{j=0}^{\infty} \int_0^K x \mathrm{d}G^{(j)}(x) \left(\frac{\lambda}{\lambda + \mu}\right)^j F_p^{(j+1)}(T) = \frac{c_F}{c_0}. \tag{33}$$

Substituting (31) for (33),

$$\frac{\sum_{j=0}^{\infty} \int_0^K x \mathrm{d}G^{(j)}(x)[(\lambda T)^j / j!]}{\sum_{j=0}^{\infty} G^{(j)}(K)[(\lambda T)^j / j!]} = K,$$

which does not hold for any K, that is, optimum policy to minimize $C(T, K)$ is $(T_F^* = \infty, K_F^* = K^*)$, where K^* is given in (21). That means full backup policy scheduled at volume K is better than that at time T, which also agrees with the comparison of Table 1 and Table 3.

Furthermore, note that if $\int_0^K x \mathrm{d}G^{(j)}(x)/G^{(j)}(K)$ increases strictly with j to K, then the left-hand side of (33) increases strictly with T to

$$\sum_{j=0}^{\infty} \left(\frac{\lambda}{\lambda + \mu}\right)^j \int_0^K (K - x) \mathrm{d}G^{(j)}(x),$$

which agrees with that of (21), then we obtain

- If given $K \leq K^*$, then $T_F^* = \infty$.
- If given $K > K^*$, then there exists a finite and unique T_F^* $(0 < T_F^* < \infty)$ which satisfies (33), and the resulting cost rate is

$$\frac{C(T_F^*, K)}{\lambda} = c_0 \left(1 + \frac{\mu}{\lambda}\right) \frac{\sum_{j=0}^{\infty} \int_0^K x \mathrm{d}G^{(j)}(x)[(\lambda T_F^*)^j / j!]}{\sum_{j=0}^{\infty} G^{(j)}(K)[(\lambda T_F^*)^j / j!]}$$

$$+ \frac{\mu}{\lambda} c_R + c_K + \frac{c_0}{\omega}. \tag{34}$$

Tables 6 and 7 present optimum ωK_F^* for given λT and λT_F^* for given ωK, when $c_0 = 1.0$, $c_K = 1.0$, $c_R = 1.0$, $c_F = 5.0$ and $\omega = 1.0$.

Table 6   Optimum ωK_F^* for given λT when $c_0 = 1.0$, $c_K = 1.0$, $c_R = 1.0$, $c_F = 5.0$ and $\omega = 1.0$.

μ/λ	$\lambda T = 1.0$	$\lambda T = 2.0$	$\lambda T = 5.0$
	ωK_F^*	ωK_F^*	ωK_F^*
0.01	5.467	3.366	2.447
0.02	5.442	3.363	2.457
0.03	5.417	3.361	2.467
0.04	5.393	3.359	2.478
0.05	5.369	3.356	2.488
0.06	5.347	3.354	2.498
0.07	5.324	3.352	2.509
0.08	5.302	3.351	2.519
0.09	5.280	3.349	2.529
0.10	5.259	3.348	2.540

Table 7   Optimum λT_F^* for given ωK when $c_0 = 1.0$, $c_K = 1.0$, $c_R = 1.0$, $c_F = 5.0$ and $\omega = 1.0$.

μ/λ	$\omega K = 1.0$	$\omega K = 5.0$	$\omega K = 10.0$
	λT_F^*	λT_F^*	λT_F^*
0.01	∞	4.909	3.299
0.02	∞	4.925	3.301
0.03	∞	4.941	3.303
0.04	∞	4.957	3.304
0.05	∞	4.973	3.306
0.06	∞	4.990	3.308
0.07	∞	5.007	3.310
0.08	∞	5.025	3.312
0.09	∞	5.042	3.314
0.10	∞	5.060	3.316

4.3   *Comparison of N and K*

Suppose that a full backup is scheduled preventively at a number N ($N = 1, 2, \cdots$) of updates or at a volume K ($0 < K \leq \infty$) of updated data, whichever occurs first. Then, the expected cost rate is

$$C(N,K) = \frac{\begin{array}{l} c_F + \sum_{j=0}^{N-1} \int_0^K (c_K + c_0 x) dG^{(j)}(x) \int_0^\infty \overline{D}(t) dF^{(j+1)}(t) \\ + (c_0/\omega) \sum_{j=0}^{N-1} G^{(j)}(K) \int_0^\infty \overline{D}(t) dF^{(j+1)}(t) \\ + \sum_{j=0}^{N-1} \int_0^K (c_R + c_0 x) dG^{(j)}(x) \int_0^\infty [F^{(j)}(t) - F^{(j+1)}(t)] dD(t) \end{array}}{\sum_{j=0}^{N-1} G^{(j)}(K) \int_0^\infty [F^{(j)}(t) - F^{(j+1)}(t)] \overline{D}(t) dt}.$$

(35)

Obviously, $\lim_{K \to \infty} C(N,K) = C(N)$ in (10) and $\lim_{N \to \infty} C(N,K) = C(K)$ in (20).

When $F(t) = 1 - e^{-\lambda t}$ and $D(t) = 1 - e^{-\mu t}$, (35) is

$$\frac{C(N,K)}{\lambda} = \frac{\begin{array}{l} c_F + \sum_{j=0}^{N-1} \int_0^K (c_K + c_0 x) dG^{(j)}(x)[\lambda/(\lambda+\mu)]^{j+1} \\ + (c_0/\omega) \sum_{j=0}^{N-1} G^{(j)}(K)[\lambda/(\lambda+\mu)]^{j+1} \\ + \sum_{j=0}^{N-1} \int_0^K (c_R + c_0 x) dG^{(j)}(x)[\mu/(\lambda+\mu)][\lambda/(\lambda+\mu)]^j \end{array}}{\sum_{j=0}^{N-1} G^{(j)}(K)[\lambda/(\lambda+\mu)]^{j+1}},$$

i.e.,

$$\frac{C(N,K)}{\lambda} = \frac{c_F + c_0 \sum_{j=0}^{N-1} \int_0^K x dG^{(j)}(x)[\lambda/(\lambda+\mu)]^j}{\sum_{j=0}^{N-1} G^{(j)}(K)[\lambda/(\lambda+\mu)]^{j+1}} + \frac{\mu}{\lambda} c_R + c_K + \frac{c_0}{\omega}.$$

(36)

We find optimum N_F^* and K_F^* to minimize $C(N,K)$ in (36). Differentiating $C(N,K)$ with respect to K and setting it equal to zero,

$$\sum_{j=0}^{N-1} \left(\frac{\lambda}{\lambda+\mu} \right)^j \int_0^K (K-x) dG^{(j)}(x) = \frac{c_F}{c_0},$$

(37)

whose left-hand side increases strictly with K from 0 to ∞. Thus, there exists a finite and unique K_F^* $(0 < K_F^* < \infty)$ which satisfies (37), and the resulting cost rate is

$$\frac{C(N,K_F^*)}{\lambda} = c_0 K_F^* \left(1 + \frac{\mu}{\lambda} \right) + \frac{\mu}{\lambda} c_R + c_K + \frac{c_0}{\omega}.$$

(38)

Note that the left-hand side of (38) increases strictly with N to that of (21), then K_F^* decreases with N to K^* given in (21).

Next, forming the inequality $C(N+1,K) - C(N,K) \geq 0$,

$$\frac{\int_0^K x \mathrm{d}G^{(N)}(x)}{G^{(N)}(K)} \sum_{j=0}^{N-1} G^{(j)}(K) \left(\frac{\lambda}{\lambda+\mu}\right)^j - \sum_{j=0}^{N-1} \int_0^K x \mathrm{d}G^{(j)}(x) \left(\frac{\lambda}{\lambda+\mu}\right)^j$$

$$\geq \frac{c_F}{c_0}. \tag{39}$$

Substituting (37) for (39),

$$\frac{\int_0^K x \mathrm{d}G^{(N)}(x)}{G^{(N)}(K)} \geq K,$$

which does not hold for any K, that is, optimum policy to minimize $C(N,K)$ is $(N_F^* = \infty, K_F^* = K^*)$, where K^* is given in (21). That means full backup policy scheduled at volume K is better than that at update N, which also agrees with the comparison of Tables 2 and 3.

Furthermore, note that if $\int_0^K x \mathrm{d}G^{(N)}(x)/G^{(N)}(K)$ increases strictly with N to K, then the left-hand side of (39) increases strictly with N to that of (21), then we obtain

- If given $K \leq K^*$, then $N_F^* = \infty$.
- If given $K > K^*$, then there exists a unique and minimum N_F^* $(0 < N_F^* < \infty)$ which satisfies (39).

Tables 8 and 9 present optimum ωK_F^* for given N and N_F^* for given ωK, when $c_0 = 1.0$, $c_K = 1.0$, $c_R = 1.0$, $c_F = 5.0$ and $\omega = 1.0$.

Table 8   Optimum ωK_F^* for given N when $c_0 = 1.0$, $c_K = 1.0$, $c_R = 1.0$, $c_F = 5.0$ and $\omega = 1.0$.

μ/λ	$N = 1$	$N = 2$	$N = 5$
	ωK_F^*	ωK_F^*	ωK_F^*
0.01	5.000	2.985	2.350
0.02	5.000	2.995	2.364
0.03	5.000	3.005	2.378
0.04	5.000	3.015	2.391
0.05	5.000	3.025	2.405
0.06	5.000	3.035	2.419
0.07	5.000	3.045	2.432
0.08	5.000	3.054	2.445
0.09	5.000	3.064	2.458
0.10	5.000	3.073	2.471

Table 9   Optimum N_F^* for given ωK when $c_0 = 1.0$, $c_K = 1.0$, $c_R = 1.0$, $c_F = 5.0$ and $\omega = 1.0$.

μ/λ	$\omega K = 1.0$	$\omega K = 5.0$	$\omega K = 10.0$
	N_F^*	N_F^*	N_F^*
0.01	∞	4	3
0.02	∞	4	3
0.03	∞	4	3
0.04	∞	4	3
0.05	∞	4	3
0.06	∞	4	3
0.07	∞	4	3
0.08	∞	4	3
0.09	∞	4	3
0.10	∞	4	3

5   Conclusions

This chapter has discussed three cumulative backup models to obtain their optimum full backup times, i.e., cumulative backups are scheduled at updates in random ways and full backups are made at decision variables of planned time T, update number N and data volume K. General assumptions of data backup and failure recovery have been given firstly in Section 2. It has been found in Section 3, from numerical examples in Tables 1-3, that full backup scheduled at volume K is the more economical than those at time T and update N, while full backup at T is the most costly policy the among three policies. In Section 4, the above numerical results have been proved in analytical ways. Not only that, we have also found optimum full backup times for respective given policies analytically and numerically in Section 4.

References

Mcdowall, R.D. (2001). Computer (In) security-2: computer system backup and recovery. The Quality Assurance Journal, **5** pp.149–155.

Ricart, G., Epstein, M., Laube, S. (2005). Data backup. US Patent 6,892,221.

Qian, C., Nakamura, S., Nakagawa, T. (2002). Optimal backup policies for a database system with incremental backup. Electronics and Communications in Japan Part 3, **85**, pp.1–9.

Nakamura, S., Qian, C., Fukumoto, S., Nakagawa, T. (2003). Optimal backup policy for a database system with incremental and full backup. Mathematical and computer modelling, **11**, pp.1373–1379.

Fong, Y., Manley, S. (2007). Efficient true image recovery of data from full, differential, and incremental backups. US Patent 7,251,749.

Microsoft Support, Description of full, incremental, and differential backups. Retrieved 21, August, 2012.

Nakagawa, T. (2014). Random Maintenance Policies, Springer.

Osaki, S. (1992) Applied Stochastic System Modeling, Springer.

Nakagawa, T. (2007) Shock and Damage Models in Reliability Theory, Springer.

Chapter 13

Reliability Analysis of Distributed Communication Processing for a Cloud System with Secondary Data Center

Mitsutaka Kimura

Department of International Culture Studies,
Gifu City Woman's College

1 Introduction

Cloud system has been used in infrastructures of many industries. In order to reduce response time to clients, a distributed communication processing for a cloud system has been proposed [Weiss (2007); Okuno, et al. (2010); Yamada, et al. (2010)]. The system consists of some intelligent nodes and a data center. The intelligent nodes provide application service near clients. Therefore they enable clients to provide short response time to their requests for service[Okuno, et al. (2010); Yamada, et al. (2010)]. The data center manages all of the client data and application software. In the previous research, a message scheme between intelligent nodes and clients has been proposed in order to reduce response time experienced by clients [Tsutsumi and Okuno (2011)]. It is also important to consider policies to make regular backups of client data from all of intelligent node to a data center. This is called replication. We considered the replication policy which is best for the system. That is, we derived the expected cost and discussed an optimal replication interval to minimize it[Kimura et al. (2015)]. Next, we derived the cost effectiveness and discussed an optimal number of intelligent nodes to minimize it [Kimura et al. (2015)]. This chapter considers two policies to reduce the interruption time caused by replication. That is, we consider two reliability models of distributed communication processing for a cloud system with a primary data center and a secondary data center. The primary data center is located near intelligent nodes. Therefore it enables intelligent nodes to provide short replication time. The secondary data center is located in a remote place. Therefore it enables clients to protect clients data from a disaster.

In Section 2, we consider a server system consists of a monitor, a primary data center, a secondary data center and n intelligent nodes. All of intelligent nodes transmit the database content to the primary data center in operation after the server in the intelligent node updates the data by requesting from client at k times. The primary data center transmits the database content to the secondary data center at a constant time. We consider replication scheme to reduce the loss costs of replication interruption. We formulate the stochastic model of distributed communication processing for a cloud system with a secondary data center, and derive the expected numbers of the replication, of updating the client data at intelligent nodes and of waiting replication from n intelligent nodes to the primary data center. Further, we calculate the expected cost and discuss an optimal replication interval to minimize it [Kimura et al. (2016)].

It is important to consider the actions to facilitate adaptation to transmit the database content from all of intelligent nodes to the primary data center. In Section 3, we consider an extended stochastic model of distributed communication processing for a cloud system with a secondary data center, in which intelligent nodes waits replication until the primary data center gets into the state of an idle activity. That is, after the server in the intelligent node updates the data by requesting from client at k times, the monitor repeatedly confirms the state of a primary data center and waits until the primary data center gets into the state of an idle activity and orders to execute replication. We assume a server system model is identical to Section 2 and derive the expected numbers of the replication, of updating the client data at intelligent nodes and of waiting replication from n intelligent nodes to the primary data center. Further, we derive the expected cost and discuss an optimal replication interval to minimize it.

2 Model 1

This section formulates the stochastic model of distributed communication processing for a cloud system with a secondary data center. We show that there exists an optimal replication interval k^* to minimize the expected cost including the operation cost between a primary data center and a secondary data center. The $n(n = 1, 2, \cdots)$ intelligent nodes provide the application service when a client requests the application. In this chapter, we consider how to make regular backups of client data from n intelligent nodes to primary data center. The intelligent nodes transmit the database content to the primary data center in operation after the server in the intelligent node updates the data by requesting from client at $k(k = 1, 2, \cdots)$ times. If the primary data center is transmitting the database content to the secondary data center, it waits the completion of the transmission at a constant time. Thereafter, the intelligent nodes transmit the database content to the primary data center. We derive the expected numbers of the replication, of updating the client data at intelligent nodes and of waiting replication from n intelligent nodes to the primary data center. Further, we calculate the expected cost and discuss an optimal replication interval to minimize it. Finally, numerical examples are given.

2.1 Reliability Quantities

We assume a cloud system consists of a monitor, a primary data center , a secondary data center and n intelligent nodes as shown in Figure 1:

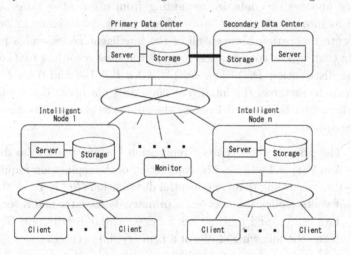

Fig. 1 Outline of a server system.

A primary data center, a secondary data center and n intelligent nodes consist of identical server and storage, and each intelligent node can serve as backup when another intelligent node breaks down. Both the primary data center and the secondary data center manage all of the data and application data for client. The monitor orders each intelligent node to serve the request of each client. The server in the intelligent node provides the application when a client requests the application. The monitor orders n intelligent nodes to transmit all of client data to a primary data center after the server in the intelligent node updates the data by requesting of client at times k, and furthermore, orders the primary data center to transmit all of client data to the secondary data center. When one of n intelligent nodes breaks down by some failures such as a disaster or crush failure, the client service is migrated from the intelligent node to another one.

We formulate the stochastic model as follows:

(1) A client requests the use of application, and its time has a general distribution $A(t)$. The monitor orders the intelligent node to meet the request for the client. The server in the intelligent node updates the storage database when a client requests the data update. The completion of the data update requires the time according to a general distribution $B(t)$.

(2) The monitor orders all of the intelligent nodes to transmit all of client data to the data center in operation after the server in the intelligent node updates the data by requesting from client at k times. Then, the monitor confirms the state of a primary data center in order to execute replication between all of the intelligent nodes and a primary data center. The confirmation requires the time according to a constant time distribution $D(t)$. i.e., $D(t) \equiv 1$ for $t \geq 1/d$ and 0 for $t < 1/d$. Then, the server in the intelligent node does not break down while the confirmation is executed because the confirmation provides the fastest access time.

(i) The primary data center's replication has an exponential distribution $V(t) = 1 - e^{-vt}$. The completion of the replication requires the time according to an exponential distribution $G(t) = 1 - e^{-gt}$. Then it waits replication between a primary data center and a secondary data center, and its time has an exponential distribution $G(t)$. We define the following states of a primary data center:

State 0: Primary data center is in an idle activity.
State 1: Primary data center executes replication.

The states of a primary data center defined above form a two-state Markov process [Osaki (1992)]. Thus, we have the following probabilities under the initial condition that $P_{00}(0) = 1, P_{10}(0) = 1$:

$$P_{00}(t) = \frac{g}{v+g} + \frac{v}{v+g}e^{-(v+g)t}, \quad P_{01}(t) = 1 - P_{00}(t),$$

$$P_{10}(t) = \frac{g}{v+g} - \frac{g}{v+g}e^{-(v+g)t}, \quad P_{11}(t) = 1 - P_{10}(t),$$

where $P_{ij}(t)$ are probabilities that the primary data center is in State $i(i = 0)$ at time 0 and State $j(j = 0, 1)$ at time $t(> 0)$.

(ii) The completion of a intelligent node's replication requires the time according to a general distribution $W(t)$, i.e., the replication time of $i(i = 1, 2, \cdots, n)$ intelligent nodes has a general distribution $W^{(i)}(t)$, where $\Phi^{(i)}(t)$ is the i-fold convolution of $\Phi(t)$ and $\Phi^{(i)}(t) \equiv \Phi^{(i-1)}(t) * \Phi(t), \Phi^{(0)}(t) \equiv 1$.

(iii) If the server in the intelligent node breaks down while the replication is executed, the monitor immediately orders to migrate the client service from the intelligent node to another intelligent node.

(iv) The monitor, a primary data center and a secondary data center do not break down.

(3) When one of n intelligent nodes breaks down by failures such as a disaster and crash failure and so on, the client service is migrated from the intelligent node to another intelligent node. The intelligent node breaks down according to an exponential distribution $F(t) = 1 - e^{-\lambda t}$.

Under the above assumptions, we define the following states of the server system:

State 2: System begins to operate or restart by $n(n = 1, 2, \cdots)$ intelligent nodes.

State 3: When the server in the intelligent node updates the data at $k(k = 1, 2, \cdots)$ times, the monitor start to confirm the state of a primary data center.

State R: n intelligent node's replication begins.

State R_W: System waits a primary data center's replication.

State F: One of $n(n = 1, 2, \cdots)$ intelligent nodes breaks down.

The system states defined above form a Markov renewal process [Nakagawa (2011)], where F is an absorbing state. A transition diagram between system states is shown in Figure 2.

Let $\Phi^*(s)$ be the Laplace-Stieltjes (LS) transform of any function $\Phi(t)$. The LS transforms of transition probabilities $Q_{i,j}(t)(i = 2, 3, R, R_W; j = 2, 3, R, R_W, F)$ are given by the following equations :

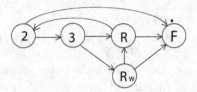

Fig. 2   Transition diagram between a server system states.

$$Q_{2,3}^*(s) = \int_0^\infty e^{-st}\overline{F}(t)dH^{(k)}(t), Q_{2,F}^*(s) = \int_0^\infty e^{-st}[1 - H^{(k)}(t)]dF(t),$$

$$Q_{3,R}^*(s) = P_{00}(1/d)e^{-s/d}, \qquad Q_{3,R_W}^*(s) = P_{01}(1/d)e^{-s/d},$$

$$Q_{R,2}^*(s) = \int_0^\infty e^{-st}\overline{F}(t)dW^{(n)}(t), Q_{R,F}^*(s) = \int_0^\infty e^{-st}[1 - W^{(n)}(t)]dF(t),$$

$$Q_{R_W,R}^*(s) = \int_0^\infty e^{-st}\overline{F}(t)dG(t), \quad Q_{R_W,F}^*(s) = \int_0^\infty e^{-st}\overline{G}(t)dF(t),$$

where $H(t) \equiv A(t) * B(t)$ and $\overline{\Phi}(t) \equiv 1 - \Phi(t)$.

We derive the expected number M_R of replications from State 2 to State F. The expected number $M_{2,R}(t)$ in $[0,t]$ is given by following equation:

$$M_{2,R}(t) = Q_{2,3}(t) * [Q_{3,R}(t) + Q_{3,R_W}(t) * Q_{R_W,R}(t)] * Q_{R,2}(t) * [1 + M_{2,R}(t)]. \tag{1}$$

The LS transform $M_{2,R}^*(s)$ is

$$M_{2,R}^*(s) = \frac{Q_{2,3}^*(s)[Q_{3,R}^*(s) + Q_{3,R_W}^*(s)Q_{R_W,R}^*(s)]Q_{R,2}^*(s)}{1 - Q_{2,3}^*(s)[Q_{3,R}^*(s) + Q_{3,R_W}^*(s)Q_{R_W,R}^*(s)]Q_{R,2}^*(s)}. \tag{2}$$

Hence, the expected number M_R to State F is

$$M_R \equiv \lim_{s \to 0}[M_{2,R}^*(s)] = \frac{1 - X_1(k,n)}{X_1(k,n)}, \tag{3}$$

where

$$X_1(k,n) \equiv 1 - \int_0^\infty \overline{F}(t)dH^{(k)}(t)\left[P_{00}(1/d) + P_{01}(1/d)\int_0^\infty \overline{F}(t)dG(t)\right]$$

$$\times \int_0^\infty \overline{F}(t)dW^{(n)}(t) = 1 - Z_1(n)[H^*(\lambda)]^k,$$

$$Z_1(n) = \frac{g + \lambda P_{00}(1/d)}{\lambda + g}[W^*(\lambda)]^n.$$

Similarly, the expected number of updating the client data in intelligent nodes before State F, denoted by M_A, is derived as follows: The expected number $M_A(t)$ in $[0, t]$ is given by following equation:

$$
M_A(t) = \sum_{i=1}^{k} \int_0^t (i-1) H^{(i-1)}(t) * \overline{H}(t) dF(t) + k \left[\int_0^t \overline{F}(t) dH^{(k)}(t) \right]
$$
$$
*[\{Q_{3,R}(t) + Q_{3,R_W}(t) * Q_{R_W,R}(t)\} * Q_{R,F}(t)
$$
$$
+ Q_{3,R_W}(t) * Q_{R_W,F}(t)]
$$
$$
+ Q_{2,3}(t) * [Q_{3,R}(t) + Q_{3,R_W}(t) * Q_{R_W,R}(t)] * Q_{R,2}(t) * M_A(t),
$$

and its LS transform is

$$
M_A^*(s) = \frac{\begin{array}{c} \sum_{i=1}^{k} \int_0^\infty e^{-st} H^{(i)}(t) dF(t) - k \int_0^\infty e^{-st} H^{(k)}(t) dF(t) \\ + k \int_0^\infty e^{-st} \overline{F}(t) dH^{(k)}(t) \\ \times \left[\begin{array}{c} \{P_{00}(1/d)e^{-s/d} + P_{01}(1/d)e^{-s/d} \int_0^\infty e^{-st}\overline{F}(t)dG(t)\} \\ \times \int_0^\infty e^{-st}[1 - W^{(n)}](t)dF(t) \\ + P_{01}(1/d)e^{-s/d}\int_0^\infty e^{-st}\overline{G}(t)dF(t) \end{array} \right] \end{array}}{\begin{array}{c} 1 - \int_0^\infty e^{-st}\overline{F}(t)dH^{(k)}(t) \\ \times \left[P_{00}(1/d)e^{-s/d} + P_{01}(1/d)e^{-s/d}\int_0^\infty e^{-st}\overline{F}(t)dG(t) \right] \\ \times \int_0^\infty e^{-st}\overline{F}(t)dW^{(n)}(t) \end{array}}. \quad (4)
$$

Hence, the expected number M_A before State F is

$$
M_A \equiv \lim_{s \to 0} [M_A^*(s)] = \frac{Y_1(k,n)}{X_1(k,n)}, \quad (5)
$$

where

$$
Y_1(k,n) \equiv \sum_{i=1}^{k} \left[\int_0^\infty \overline{F}(t) dH^{(i)}(t) - 1 + X_1(k,n) \right]
$$
$$
= \sum_{i=1}^{k} \left\{ [H^*(\lambda)]^i - Z_1(n)[H^*(\lambda)]^k \right\}.
$$

Similarly, the expected number of waiting n intelligent node's replication before State F, denoted by M_{R_W}, is derived as follows: The expected numbers $M_{2,R_W}(t)$ in $[0, t]$ is given by following equation:

$$
M_{2,R_W}(t) = Q_{2,3}(t) * Q_{3,R_W}(t) + Q_{2,3}(t) * [Q_{3,R_W}(t) * Q_{R_W,R}(t) + Q_{3,R}(t)]
$$
$$
* Q_{R,2}(t) * M_{2,R_W}(t),
$$

and its LS transform is

$$M_{2,R_W}^*(s) = \frac{Q_{2,3}^*(s)Q_{3,R_W}^*(s)}{1 - Q_{2,3}^*(s)[Q_{3,R}^*(s) + Q_{3,R_W}^*(s)Q_{R_W,R}^*(s)]Q_{R,2}^*(s)}. \tag{6}$$

Hence, the expected number M_{R_W} before State F is

$$M_{R_W} = \frac{P_{01}(1/d)\int_0^\infty \overline{F}(t)dH^{(k)}(t)}{X_1(k,n)} = \frac{P_{01}(1/d)[H^*(\lambda)]^k}{X_1(k,n)}. \tag{7}$$

2.2   Optimal Policy

We propose an optimal policy to reduce the loss costs of replication interruption. That is, we calculate the expected cost to State F and derive an optimal replication interval k^* to minimize it. Let c_A be the cost for an updated data at the intelligent node, c_R be the cost of a replication and c_W be the loss cost of a replication interruption. We define the expected cost $C_1(k,n)$ as follows:

$$\begin{aligned} C_1(k,n) &\equiv c_R M_R + c_A M_A + c_W M_{R_W} \\ &= \frac{c_R + c_A Y_1(k,n) + C_W}{X_1(k,n)} - c_R - C_W, \end{aligned} \tag{8}$$

where $C_W \equiv [c_W P_{01}(1/d)]/Z_1(n)$. We seek an optimal replication interval $k^*(1 \le k^* \le \infty)$ which minimizes $C_1(k,n)$ in (8) for given n. From $C_1(k+1,n) - C_1(k,n) \ge 0$,

$$\frac{Y_1(k+1,n) - Y_1(k,n)}{X_1(k+1,n) - X_1(k,n)}X_1(k,n) - Y_1(k,n) \ge \frac{c_R + C_W}{c_A}. \tag{9}$$

Denoting the left-hand side of (9) by $L_1(k,n)$,

$$\begin{aligned} L_1(k,n) - L_1(k-1,n) = \\ \left[\frac{Y_1(k+1,n) - Y_1(k,n)}{X_1(k+1,n) - X_1(k,n)} - \frac{Y_1(k,n) - Y_1(k-1,n)}{X_1(k,n) - X_1(k-1,n)}\right]X_1(k,n). \end{aligned}$$

If $[Y_1(k+1,n) - Y_1(k,n)]/[X_1(k+1,n) - X_1(k,n)]$ increases strictly with k, then there exists a finite and unique minimum $k^*(1 \le k^* \le \infty)$ which satisfies (9). In this case,

$$\frac{Y_1(k+1,n) - Y_1(k,n)}{X_1(k+1,n) - X_1(k,n)} = \frac{H^*(\lambda)}{1 - H^*(\lambda)}\frac{1 - Z_1(n)}{Z_1(n)} + k,$$

there exists a finite and unique minimum $k^*(1 \leq k^* < \infty)$ which satisfies (9).

Example 13.1.

We compute numerically an optimal replication interval k^* which minimizes $C_1(k, n)$ in (8) when $A(t) \equiv 1 - e^{-\alpha t}, B(t) \equiv 1 - e^{-\beta t}$ and $W(t) \equiv 1 - e^{-wt}$, i.e.,

$$D^*(\lambda) = \frac{\alpha\beta}{(\lambda+\alpha)(\lambda+\beta)}, \qquad W^*(\lambda) = \frac{w}{\lambda+w}.$$

Suppose that the mean time $1/d$ required for the confirmation of the state of the primary data center. It is assumed that the time required for the completion of the data update is $d/\beta = 2$, the number of intelligent nodes is $n = 2$, the mean generation interval of request the use of application is $d/\alpha = 2 \sim 6$, the mean generation interval of an intelligent node down is $d/\lambda = 1000, 5000$, the mean time required for the replication between all of intelligent nodes and a primary data center is $d/w = 10, 30$, the mean generation interval of replication between a primary data center and a secondary data center is $d/v = 50, 200$, the mean time required for the replication between a primary data center and a secondary data center is $d/g = 10, 100$. Further, we introduce the following costs : The cost rate for an updated data in the intelligent node to the cost for replication is $c_R/c_A = 5$ and the cost rate for an replication interruption is $c_W/c_A = 1, 4$. Table 1 gives the optimal replication interval k^* which minimizes the expected cost $C_1(k, n)/c_A$.

For example, when $c_A = 1, c_R = 5, c_W = 4$ and $d/\beta = 2, d/v = 50, d/g = 100, d/\alpha = 2, d/w = 10, d/\lambda = 1000$, the optimal replication interval is $k^* = 46$. This indicates that k^* increase with d/λ and c_W/c_A. The other hand, k^* decrease with d/α and d/g. i.e., we should execute replication at short intervals.

3 Model 2

This section considers an extended stochastic model of distributed communication processing for a cloud system with a secondary data center, in which the monitor keeps the state of a primary data center under constant scrutiny. That is, in order to execute replication between all of the intelligent nodes and the primary data center , the monitor conforms the state of a primary data center after the server in the intelligent node updates the data by requesting from client at k times. Then, the monitor repeatedly

Table 1   Optimal replication interval k^* to minimize $C_1(k,n)/c_A$ when $d/\beta = 2$ and $n = 2$.

c_W/c_A	d/v	d/g	d/w	d/λ					
				1000			5000		
				d/α					
				2	4	6	2	4	6
1	50	10	10	47	39	35	109	90	78
			30	35	32	29	98	83	73
		100	10	46	39	34	108	89	78
			30	34	31	29	97	82	73
	200	10	10	47	39	35	108	90	78
			30	35	32	29	98	83	73
		100	10	46	39	35	108	90	78
			30	35	31	29	97	82	73
4	50	10	10	47	39	35	109	90	79
			30	35	32	29	98	83	74
		100	10	46	39	35	109	90	79
			30	35	32	29	98	83	73
	200	10	10	47	39	35	109	90	78
			30	35	32	29	98	83	73
		100	10	47	39	35	109	90	78
			30	35	32	29	98	83	73

confirms the state of a primary data center and waits until the primary data center gets into the state of an idle activity and orders to execute replication. We assume the same cloud system model as Section 2, and derive the expected numbers of replications, updating the client data in intelligent nodes and of waiting replication from n intelligent nodes to the primary data center. Further, we derive the expected cost and discuss an optimal replication interval k^* to minimize it.

3.1   *Reliability Quantities*

A cloud computing system consists of a monitor, n intelligent nodes a primary data center and a secondary data center [Okuno, et al. (2010); Kimura et al. (2015)]. The server in the intelligent node provides the application and updates the client data by requesting of client. The monitor confirms the state of a primary data center after the server in the intelligent node has updated the client data at times k. If the primary data center is executing the replication with a secondary data center, it waits at a constant time. Thereafter, the monitor confirms the state again. It executes the same process until the primary data center gets into the state of an idle activity, and orders n intelligent nodes to execute the replication to the primary data center. Then, we formulate the stochastic model in the same manner as Section 2. The waiting time of the replication has an exponential distribution $G_1(t)$ for the first time with mean $1/g_1$ and has an exponential distribution $G_2(t)$ more than first time with mean $1/g_2(1/g_2 \le 1/g_1)$. We define the following states of a cloud system. States 2, 3, R and F are denoted in Model 1, and State R_W is divided into two states:

State W_1: System waits a primary data center's replication for the first
time.

State W_2: System waits a primary data center's replication more than the
first time.

A transition diagram between system states is shown in Figure 3.

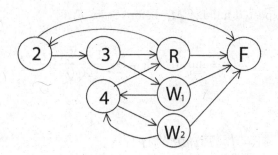

Fig. 3   Transition diagram between a server system states.

Let $\Phi^*(s)$ be the Laplace-Stieltjes (LS) transform of any function $\Phi(t)$. The LS transforms of transition probabilities $Q_{i,j}(t)(i = 2, 3, R, W_1, W_2; j = 2, 3, R, W_1, W_2, F)$ are given by the following equations:

$$Q_{2,3}^*(s) = \int_0^\infty e^{-st}\overline{F}(t)dH^{(k)}(t), \quad Q_{2,F}^*(s) = \int_0^\infty e^{-st}[1 - H^{(k)}(t)]dF(t),$$

$$Q_{3,R}^*(s) = P_{00}(1/d)e^{-s/d}, \quad Q_{3,W_1}^*(s) = P_{01}(1/d)e^{-s/d},$$

$$Q_{4,R}^*(s) = P_{10}(1/d)e^{-s/d}, \quad Q_{4,W_2}^*(s) = P_{11}(1/d)e^{-s/d}$$

$$Q_{R,2}^*(s) = \int_0^\infty e^{-st}\overline{F}(t)dW^{(n)}(t), \quad Q_{R,F}^*(s) = \int_0^\infty e^{-st}[1 - W^{(n)}(t)]dF(t),$$

$$Q_{W_i,4}^*(s) = \int_0^\infty e^{-st}\overline{F}(t)dG_i(t), \quad Q_{W_i,F}^*(s) = \int_0^\infty e^{-st}\overline{G_i}(t)dF(t)(i = 1, 2).$$

The expected number $M_{2,R}(t)$ of replications before State F in $[0,t]$ is given by the following equation:

$$
\begin{aligned}
M_{2,R}(t) = {} & Q_{2,3}(t) * [Q_{3,R}(t) + Q_{3,W_1}(t) * Q_{W_1,4}(t) \\
& * \{1 + M_{4,W_2}(t) * Q_{W_2,4}(t)\} * Q_{4,R}(t)] \\
& * Q_{R,2}(t) * [1 + M_{2,R}(t)], \\
M_{4,W_2}(t) = {} & Q_{4,W_2}(t) * [1 + Q_{W_2,4}(t) * M_{4,W_2}(t)],
\end{aligned}
$$

and its LS transform is

$$
M_{2,R}^*(s) = \frac{Q_{2,3}^*(s) \left[Q_{3,R}^*(s) + \frac{Q_{3,W_1}^*(s)Q_{W_1,4}^*(s)Q_{4,R}^*(s)}{1 - Q_{4,W_2}^*(s)Q_{W_2,4}^*(s)} \right] Q_{R,2}^*(s)}{1 - Q_{2,3}^*(s) \left[Q_{3,R}^*(s) + \frac{Q_{3,W_1}^*(s)Q_{W_1,4}^*(s)Q_{4,R}^*(s)}{1 - Q_{4,W_2}^*(s)Q_{W_2,4}^*(s)} \right] Q_{R,2}^*(s)}. \tag{10}
$$

Hence, the expected number M_R before State F_1 is

$$
M_R \equiv \lim_{s \to 0}[M_R^*(s)] = \sum_{i=1}^{n} \frac{1 - X_2(k,i)}{X_2(k,i)}, \tag{11}
$$

where

$$
\begin{aligned}
X_2(k,n) = {} & 1 - \int_0^\infty \overline{F}(t) dH^{(k)}(t) \\
& \times \left[P_{00}(1/d) + \frac{P_{01}(1/d)P_{10}(1/d)\int_0^\infty \overline{F}(t)dG_1(t)}{1 - P_{11}(1/d)\int_0^\infty \overline{F}(t)dG_2(t)} \right] \int_0^\infty \overline{F}(t)dW^{(n)}(t), \\
= {} & 1 - Z_2[W^*(\lambda)]^n[H^*(\lambda)]^k, \\
Z_2 \equiv {} & P_{00}(1/d) + \frac{P_{01}(1/d)P_{10}(1/d)\int_0^\infty \overline{F}(t)dG_1(t)}{1 - P_{11}(1/d)\int_0^\infty \overline{F}(t)dG_2(t)} \\
= {} & P_{00}(1/d) + \frac{g_1}{\lambda + g_1} \frac{(\lambda + g_2)P_{01}(1/d)P_{10}(1/d)}{\lambda + g_2 P_{10}(1/d)}.
\end{aligned}
$$

Similarly, the expected number of updating the client data in intelligent nodes before State F, denoted by M_A, is derived as follows: The expected number $M_A(t)$ in $[0,t]$ is given by following equation:

$$M_A(t) = \sum_{i=1}^{k} \int_0^t (i-1) H^{(i-1)}(t) * \overline{H}(t) dF(t) + k \left[\int_0^t \overline{F}(t) dH^{(k)}(t) \right]$$

$$* \begin{bmatrix} Q_{3,W_1}(t) * \{ Q_{W_1,F}(t) + Q_{W_1,4}(t) * M_{4,W_2}(t) * Q_{W_2,F}(t) \} \\ + [Q_{3,R}(t) + Q_{3,W_1}(t) * Q_{W_1,4}(t) \\ * \{ 1 + M_{4,W_2}(t) * Q_{W_2,4}(t) \} * Q_{4,R}(t)] * Q_{R,F}(t) \end{bmatrix}$$

$$+ Q_{2,3}(t) * [Q_{3,R}(t) + Q_{3,W_1}(t) * Q_{W_1,4}(t)$$

$$* \{ 1 + M_{4,W_2}(t) * Q_{W_2,4}(t) \} * Q_{4,R}(t)]$$

$$* Q_{R,2}(t) * M_A(t), \tag{12}$$

and its LS transform is

$$M_A^*(s) = \cfrac{\begin{matrix} \sum_{i=1}^{k} \int_0^\infty e^{-st} H^{(i)}(t) dF(t) - k \int_0^\infty e^{-st} H^{(k)}(t) dF(t) \\ + k \int_0^\infty e^{-st} \overline{F}(t) dH^{(k)}(t) \\ \times \begin{bmatrix} P_{01}(1/d) e^{-s/d} \begin{bmatrix} \int_0^\infty e^{-st} \overline{G_1}(t) dF(t) \\ + \frac{P_{11}(1/d) e^{-s/d} \int_0^\infty e^{-st} \overline{F}(t) dG_1(t)}{1 - P_{11}(1/d) e^{-s/d} \int_0^\infty e^{-st} \overline{F}(t) dG_2(t)} \\ \times \int_0^\infty e^{-st} \overline{G_2}(t) dF(t) \end{bmatrix} \\ + \begin{bmatrix} P_{00}(1/d) e^{-s/d} \\ + \frac{P_{01}(1/d) P_{10}(1/d) (e^{-s/d})^2 \int_0^\infty e^{-st} \overline{F}(t) dG_1(t)}{1 - P_{11}(1/d) e^{-s/d} \int_0^\infty e^{-st} \overline{F}(t) dG_2(t)} \\ \times \int_0^\infty e^{-st} [1 - W^{(n)}(t)] dF(t) \end{bmatrix} \end{bmatrix} \end{matrix}}{\begin{matrix} 1 - \int_0^\infty e^{-st} \overline{F}(t) dH^{(k)}(t) \\ \times \left[P_{00}(1/d) e^{-s/d} + \frac{P_{01}(1/d) P_{10}(1/d) (e^{-s/d})^2 \int_0^\infty e^{-st} \overline{F}(t) dG_1(t)}{1 - P_{11}(1/d) e^{-s/d} \int_0^\infty e^{-st} \overline{F}(t) dG_2(t)} \right] \\ \times \int_0^\infty e^{-st} \overline{F}(t) dW^{(n)}(t) \end{matrix}}.$$

$$\tag{13}$$

Hence, the expected number M_A before State F is

$$M_A \equiv \lim_{s \to 0} [M_A^*(s)] = \frac{Y_2(k,n)}{X_2(k,n)}, \tag{14}$$

where

$$Y_2(k,n) \equiv \sum_{i=1}^{k} \left[\int_0^\infty \overline{F}(t) dH^{(i)}(t) - 1 + X_2(k,n) \right],$$

$$= \sum_{i=1}^{k} \{ [H^*(\lambda)]^i - Z_2 [W^*(\lambda)]^n [H^*(\lambda)]^k \}.$$

Similarly, the expected number of waiting n intelligent node's replication before State F, denoted by M_W, is derived as follows: The expected numbers $M_{2,W_1}(t)$ and $M_{2,W_2}(t)$ in $[0,t]$ is given by following equation:

$$
\begin{aligned}
M_{2,W_1}(t) = {} & Q_{2,3}(t) * Q_{3,W_1}(t) + Q_{2,3}(t) * [Q_{3,R}(t) + Q_{3,W_1}(t) * Q_{W_1,4}(t) \\
& * \{1 + M_{4,W_2}(t) * Q_{W_2,4}(t)\} * Q_{4,R}(t)] * Q_{R,2}(t) * M_{2,W_1}(t),
\end{aligned}
$$

$$
\begin{aligned}
M_{2,W_2}(t) = {} & Q_{2,3}(t) * Q_{3,W_1}(t) * Q_{W_1,4}(t) * M_{4,W_2}(t) + Q_{2,3}(t) \\
& *[Q_{3,R}(t) + Q_{3,W_1}(t) * Q_{W_1,4}(t) * \{1 + M_{4,W_2}(t) * Q_{W_2,4}(t)\} \\
& *Q_{4,R}(t)] * Q_{R,2}(t) * M_{2,W_2}(t),
\end{aligned}
$$

and their LS transforms are

$$
M_{2,W_1}^*(s) = \frac{Q_{2,3}^*(s)Q_{3,W_1}^*(s)}{1 - Q_{2,3}^*(s)\left[Q_{3,R}^*(s) + \frac{Q_{3,W_1}^*(s)Q_{W_1,4}^*(s)Q_{4,R}^*(s)}{1-Q_{4,W_2}^*(s)Q_{W_2,4}^*(s)}\right]Q_{R,2}^*(s)},
$$

$$
M_{2,W_2}^*(s) = \frac{\frac{Q_{2,3}^*(s)Q_{3,W_1}^*(s)Q_{W_1,4}^*(s)Q_{4,W_2}^*(s)}{1-Q_{4,W_2}^*(s)Q_{W_2,4}^*(s)}}{1 - Q_{2,3}^*(s)\left[Q_{3,R}^*(s) + \frac{Q_{3,W_1}^*(s)Q_{W_1,4}^*(s)Q_{4,R}^*(s)}{1-Q_{4,W_2}^*(s)Q_{W_2,4}^*(s)}\right]Q_{R,2}^*(s)}.
$$

Hence, the expected number M_W before State F is

$$
\begin{aligned}
M_W &\equiv \lim_{s \to 0}[M_{2,W_1}^*(s) + M_{2,W_2}^*(s)] = \frac{Z_3 P_{01}(1/d) \int_0^\infty \overline{F}(t)dH^{(k)}(t)}{X_2(k,n)} \\
&= \frac{Z_3 P_{01}(1/d)[H^*(\lambda)]^k}{X_2(k,n)},
\end{aligned}
\tag{15}
$$

where

$$
Z_3 \equiv 1 + \frac{P_{11}(1/d) \int_0^\infty \overline{F}(t)dG_1(t)}{1 - P_{11}(1/d) \int_0^\infty \overline{F}(t)dG_2(t)} = 1 + \frac{g_1}{\lambda + g_1} \frac{(\lambda + g_2)P_{11}(1/d)}{\lambda + g_2 P_{10}(1/d)}.
$$

3.2 Optimal Policy

We propose an optimal policy to reduce the waste of waiting the replication in the same manner as Section 2. That is, we calculate the expected cost and derive an optimal replication interval k^* to minimize it. We define the expected cost $C_2(k,n)$ as follows:

$$C_2(k,n) \equiv c_R M_R + c_A M_A + c_W M_W,$$

$$= \frac{c_R + c_A Y_2(k,n) + c_W \dfrac{Z_3 P_{01}(1/d)}{Z_2 \int_0^\infty \overline{F}(t)dW^{(n)}(t)}}{X_2(k,n)}$$

$$- c_R - c_W \frac{Z_3 P_{01}(1/d)}{Z_2 \int_0^\infty \overline{F}(t)dW^{(n)}(t)}. \tag{16}$$

We seek an optimal replication interval $k^*(1 \leq k^* \leq \infty)$ which minimizes $C_2(k,n)$ in (16) for given n. From $C_2(k+1,n) - C_2(k,n) \geq 0$,

$$\frac{Y_2(k+1,n) - Y_2(k,n)}{X_2(k+1,n) - X_2(k,n)} X_2(k,n) - Y_2(k,n) \geq \frac{c_R + c_W \dfrac{Z_3 P_{01}(1/d)}{Z_2 \int_0^\infty \overline{F}(t)dW^{(n)}(t)}}{c_A}. \tag{17}$$

Denoting the left-hand side of (17) by $L_2(k,n)$,

$$L_2(k,n) - L_2(k-1,n) =$$
$$\left[\frac{Y_2(k+1,n) - Y_2(k,n)}{X_2(k+1,n) - X_2(k,n)} - \frac{Y_2(k,n) - Y_2(k-1,n)}{X_2(k,n) - X_2(k-1,n)} \right] X_2(k,n).$$

If $[Y_2(k+1,n) - Y_2(k,n)]/[X_2(k+1,n) - X_2(k,n)]$ increases strictly with k, then there exists a finite and unique minimum $k^*(1 \leq k^* \leq \infty)$ which satisfies (17). In this case, because

$$\frac{Y_2(k+1,n) - Y_2(k,n)}{X_2(k+1,n) - X_2(k,n)} = \frac{H^*(\lambda)}{1 - H^*(\lambda)} \frac{1 - Z_2[W^*(\lambda)]^n}{Z_2[W^*(\lambda)]^n} + k,$$

there exists a finite and unique minimum $k^*(1 \leq k^* < \infty)$ which satisfies (17).

Example 13.2.

We compute numerically an optimal replication interval k^* which minimizes $C_2(k,n)$ in (16) when $A(t) \equiv 1 - e^{-\alpha t}, B(t) \equiv 1 - e^{-\beta t}$ and $W(t) \equiv 1 - e^{-wt}$. Suppose that the mean time $1/d$ required for the confirmation of the state of the primary data center. It is assumed that the time required for the completion of the data update is $d/\beta = 2$, the number of intelligent nodes is $n = 2$, the mean generation interval of request the use of application is $d/\alpha = 2 \sim 6$, the mean generation interval of an intelligent node down is $d/\lambda = 1000, 5000$, the mean time required for the replication between all of intelligent nodes and a primary data center is $d/w = 10$, the mean generation interval of replication between a primary data center and a secondary data center is $d/v = 10, 50$, the mean time required for the replication between a primary data center and a secondary data center is $d/g_1 = 10, 20$, the mean time of waiting the replication is $d/g_2 = 5, 10$. Further, we introduce the following costs : The cost rate for an updated data in the intelligent node to the cost for replication is $c_R/c_A = 5$ and the cost rate for an replication interruption is $c_W/c_A = 1, 4$. Table 2 gives the optimal replication interval k^* which minimizes the expected cost $C_2(k, n)/c_A$.

Table 2   Optimal replication interval k^* to minimize $C_2(k, n)/c_A$ when $d/\beta = 2$, $d/w = 10$ and $n = 2$.

c_w/c_A	d/v	d/g_1	d/g_2	d/λ					
				1000			5000		
				d/α					
				2	4	6	2	4	6
1	10	10	5	50	42	38	118	98	85
			10	49	42	37	117	97	85
		20	5	53	45	40	126	105	92
			10	50	43	38	124	103	90
	50	10	5	47	40	35	110	91	80
			10	47	40	35	110	91	80
		20	5	48	40	36	112	93	81
			10	47	40	35	112	93	81
4	10	10	5	63	53	47	146	121	106
			10	62	52	46	145	120	105
		20	5	75	63	56	176	146	127
			10	71	61	54	172	143	125
	50	10	5	50	42	37	117	97	84
			10	50	42	37	117	96	84
		20	5	53	45	40	125	103	90
			10	52	44	39	124	103	90

For example, when $c_R/c_A = 5, c_W/c_A = 4$ and $d/\beta = 2, d/v = 50, d/g_1 = 20, d/g_2 = 10, d/\alpha = 2, d/w = 10, d/\lambda = 1000$, the optimal replication interval is $k^* = 52$. This indicates that k^* increase with d/λ and c_W/c_A. The other hand, k^* decrease with d/α, d/g_1 and d/g_2. i.e., we should execute replication at short intervals.

By comparison with Table 1, optimal k^* is larger than then k^* in Table 1. That is, when the waiting time of the replication between the primary data center and the secondary data center is large, we should execute replication at long intervals.

4 Conclúsions

This chapter has analytically studied the two stochastic models of distributed communication processing for a cloud system with a secondary data center in Section 2 and an extended model in Section 3. Further, we have derived the reliability measures by using the theory of Markov renewal processes, and have discussed the optimal policy which minimizes the expected cost. From numerical examples, we have shown that the optimal replication interval decreases as the waiting time of the replication between the primary data center and the secondary data center increases. That is, we should execute replication at long intervals when the waiting time of the replication between the primary data center and the secondary data center is large. If these parameters would be statistically estimated from actual systems, we could determine the best policy.

References

Weiss, A. (2007). *Computing in the clouds, netWorker*, **11**, pp. 16–25 .

Okuno, M., Ito, D., Miyamoto, H., Aoki, H., Tsushima, Y and Yazaki, T. (2010). *A study on distributed information and communication processing architecture for next generation cloud system, The Technical Report of The Institute of Electronics, Information and Communication Engineers*, **109**, 448, NS2009-204, pp. 241–246.

Tsutsumi, S. and Okuno, M. (2011). *A Messaging Scheme for Wide-Area Distributed Applications, The Technical Report of The Institute of Electronics, Information and Communication Engineers*, **110**, 448, NS2010-258, pp. 533–538.

Yamada, S., Marukawa, J., Ishii, D., Okamoto, S. and Yamanaka, N. (2010). *A Study of Parallel Transmission Technique with GMPLS in Intelligent Cloud Network, The Technical Report of The Institute of Electronics, Information and Communication Engineers*, **109**, 455, PN2009-95, pp. 51–56.

Kimura, M., Imaizumi, M. and Nakagawa, T. (2015). *Replication Policy of Real-Time Distributed System for Cloud Computing, International Journal of Reliability, Quality and Safety Engineering*, **22**, 05, 1550024-1-1550024-15, (15pages), DOI:10.1142/S0218539315500242.

Kimura, M., Imaizumi, M. and Nakagawa, T. (2016). *Reliability Modelling of Distributed Communication Processing for a Cloud System with Secondary Data Center, Proceeding of Advanced Reliability and Maintenance Modeling VII (Seoul, Korea)*, pp. 211–218.

Osaki, S., (1992). *Applied Stochastic System Modeling*, Springer-Verlag, Berlin.

Nakagawa, T., (2011). *Stochastic Processes with Applications to Reliability Theory*, Springer, London.

Chapter 14

Reliability Consideration of a System in Cloud Computing Environment

Mitsuhiro Imaizumi

School of Contemporary Management,
Aichi Gakusen University

1 Introduction

As the Internet technology has developed, cloud computing which is a kind of Internet-based computing has been widely spread. Recently, huge amounts of data have been generated and have been stored in the server of cloud computing environment. These data are collected and are analyzed and their results are utilized in many areas of business [Tanimoto et al. (2013), Naruse and Nakagawa (2012)].

In terms of processing of huge amounts of data, the scheme to execute the processing of data effectively is required. To realize the processing of huge amounts of data effectively, a distributed processing system has been widely used in cloud computing environment instead of a traditional relational database management system. The distributed processing system has scalability.

On the other hand, the demand for improvement of the reliability of a cloud computing system has also increased. In many companies, the cloud computing system has been set up in remote locations. The companies can share huge amounts of data and utilize them among their business facilities by configuring a cloud computing system [Armbrust et al. (2009)].

In terms of operating cloud system in remote locations, there exist some problems when the failure of cloud system occurs. In such cases, workers need to go to the remote locations and maintain the system. It takes time and entails a lot of costs. In order to cope with this problem, several schemes have been proposed [Banzai et al (2009);ENISA (2009)]. The system which has redundant devices is one of them [Vishwanath et al (2009)].

In this chapter, we pay attention to systems in cloud computing environment, and treat two stochastic models. Using the theory of Markov renewal processes [Osaki (1992)], we derive the reliability measures. Although the simulation about the policy for the cloud computing system has already been introduced [Shibamura et al (2010)], there are few formalized stochastic models. Compared to simulation models, we can derive the measures such as the mean processing times directly, and show the existence of optimal value concretely by using analytical models.

In Section 2, we formulate stochastic models for a distributed processing system in cloud computing environment. The distributed processing system executes the processing of a data and returns its result in response to the request of the client. A data is replicated and is divided into n small data respectively. Replicated n small data are executed with consistency. The mean time until the processing of a data is successful and the expected cost are derived. Moreover, optimal policies which minimize them are discussed.

In Section 3, we consider the optimal management policy for a redundant cloud system in remote locations. The cloud system consists of a large number of diverse devices. The failure of servers is mainly caused by the failure of hard disk and errors in memory. The past failure statistics of hard disk drives in a cloud environment were examined in [Hiwatashi and Iwamura (2012)]. Measurements of memory errors in a large fleet of servers were analyzed in [Schroeder et al (2009)]. On the other hand, maintenance theory of redundant systems were summarized [Nakagawa (2005), Nakagawa (2008)]. We apply this theory to a complicated cloud system, and formulate stochastic models of it. We derive the steady-state availability of the system and discuss optimal policies which maximize it.

2 Reliability Analysis of a Distributed Processing System

2.1 *Model*

We pay attention to a distributed processing system in cloud computing environment. The distributed processing system consists of many servers and makes up large amounts of storage.

2.1.1 *Model* 1.1

(1) The distributed processing system executes the processing of a data and returns its result in response to the request of the client. A data is replicated and is divided into n small data respectively by the distributed processing system. Replicated n small data are executed sequentially. The processing times of small data have an exponential distributions $A(t) = 1 - e^{-\frac{n}{a}t}$ with finite a/n.

(2) When the processing of each small data terminates, the processing results are compared by the distributed processing system. The comparison time has a general distribution $B(t)$ with finite mean b.

(3) If the comparison of processing results of small data does not agree, then it is executed again after a delay which obeys a general distribution $G(t)$ with finite mean μ.

(4) If the comparison of results agrees, then the processing of next small data is executed. After the processing of n small data has completed, all processing results of a data are compared. The comparison time has a general distribution $U(t)$ with finite mean u. The probability that its comparison agrees is $p(0 < p \le 1)$. If its comparison agrees, then the processing result of a data is correct. On the other hand, If its comparison does not agree, then the processing result of a data is not correct. In this case, the processing of a data executes again from the beginning after a delay which obeys a general distribution $W(t)$ with finite mean w.

(5) Errors in the execution of the processing of small data occur independently according to an exponential distribution $F(t) = 1 - e^{-\lambda t}$. Errors are detected by the distributed processing system when the processing of each small data terminates. Undetected errors are detected finally by comparing all results of a data. If errors occur, the results do not agree. Aside from disagreement due to errors, we assume that the comparison of processing results of small data does not agree independently with probability $1 - q_n$.

(6) When all processing of n small data are completed, and the comparison of processing result of a data agrees, the processing of a data is completed successfully.

Under above assumption, we define the following state of the system:

State 0: Processing of a data starts.
State i: Processing of the i-th small data completed $(i = 1, 2, \cdots, n)$.

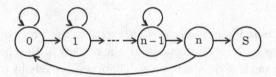

Fig. 1   Transition diagram between system states.

State S: Processing of a data completed successfully.

The system states defined above form a Markov renewal process where State S is an absorbing state. Transition diagram between system states is shown Fig. 1.

Let $Q_{i,j}(t)(i = 0, 1, \cdots, n; j = 0, 1, \cdots, n, S)$ be one-step transition probabilities of a Markov renewal process. Then, by the similar method of [Yasui et al. (2002)], we have the following equation:

$$Q_{i,i}(t) = \left[\int_0^t (1 - e^{-2\lambda u}) dA(u)\right] * B(t) * G(t)$$

$$+ (1 - q_n)\left[\int_0^t e^{-2\lambda u} dA(u)\right] * B(t) * G(t), \tag{1}$$

$$Q_{i,i+1}(t) = q_n\left[\int_0^t e^{-2\lambda u} dA(u)\right] * B(t), \tag{2}$$

$$Q_{n,0}(t) = (1 - p)U(t) * W(t), \tag{3}$$

$$Q_{n,S}(t) = pU(t), \tag{4}$$

where the asterisk mark denotes Stieltjes convolution; i.e., $\Phi_1(t) * \Phi_2(t) \equiv \int_0^t \Phi_2(t - u) d\Phi_1(t)$.

First, we derive the mean processing time $\ell_1(n)$ until the processing of a data is completed successfully. Let $H_{0,S}(t)$ be the first-passage distribution from State 0 to State S. Then, we have

$$H_{0,S}(t) = \left[\sum_{j=1}^\infty Q_{0,0}^{(j-1)}(t) * Q_{0,1}(t)\right] * \left[\sum_{j=1}^\infty Q_{1,1}^{(j-1)}(t) * Q_{1,2}(t)\right] * \cdots$$

$$* \left[\sum_{j=1}^\infty Q_{n-1,n-1}^{(j-1)}(t) * Q_{n-1,n}(t)\right] * [Q_{n,S}(t) + Q_{n,0}(t) * H_{0,S}(t)],$$

$$\tag{5}$$

where $\Phi^{(i)}(t)$ denotes the i-fold Stieltjes convolution of a distribution $\Phi(t)$, i.e., $\Phi^{(i)}(t) \equiv \Phi^{(i-1)}(t) * \Phi(t)$, $\Phi^{(0)}(t) \equiv 1$.

Let $\phi(s)$ be the Laplace-Stieltjes (LS) transform of any function $\Phi(t)$, i.e., $\phi(s) \equiv \int_0^\infty e^{-st} d\Phi(t)$ for $Re(s) > 0$. Taking the LS transforms of (5) and arranging them,

$$h_{0,S}(s) = \frac{\left[\dfrac{q_{0,1}(s)}{1 - q_{0,0}(s)}\right]^n q_{n,S}(s)}{1 - \left[\dfrac{q_{0,1}(s)}{1 - q_{0,0}(s)}\right]^n q_{n,0}(s)}. \tag{6}$$

Thus, the mean time $\ell_1(n)$ is given by the following equation.

$$\ell_1(n) \equiv \int_0^\infty t \, dH_{0,S}(t) = \lim_{s \to 0} \frac{-d[h_{0,S}(s)]}{ds}$$

$$= \frac{1}{p}\left\{\frac{1}{q_n}\left[(2\lambda a + n)\left(\frac{a}{n} + b\right) + 2\lambda a\mu + (1 - q_n)n\mu\right] + u + (1 - p)w\right\}. \tag{7}$$

2.1.2 *Model* 1.2

We modify Model 1.1.

If the K-th comparison of processing results of small data does not agree, once the processing is interrupted, and restarts again from the beginning after a delay which obeys a general distribution $V(t)$ with finite mean v. In terms of Model 1.2, we assume that $q_n = 1$.

Under above assumption, we define the following state of the system:

State 0: Processing of a data starts.
State i : Processing of the i-th small data completed $(i = 1, 2, \cdots, n)$.
State F: Processing of a data is interrupted.
State S: Processing of a data completed successfully.

The system states defined above form a Markov renewal process. Transition diagram between system states is shown Fig. 2.

Transition probabilities are given by the following equations.

$$Q_{i,i}(t) = \left[\int_0^t (1 - e^{-2\lambda t}) dA(t)\right] * B(t) * G(t), \tag{8}$$

$$Q_{i,i+1}(t) = \left[\sum_{j=1}^K Q_{i,i}^{(j-1)}(t)\right] * \left[\int_0^t e^{-2\lambda t} dA(t)\right] * B(t), \tag{9}$$

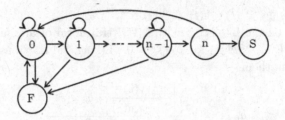

Fig. 2 Transition diagram between system states.

$$Q_{i,F}(t) = Q_{i,i}^{(K)}(t), \tag{10}$$
$$Q_{n,0}(t) = (1-p)U(t) * W(t), \tag{11}$$
$$Q_{n,S}(t) = pU(t), \tag{12}$$
$$Q_{F,0}(t) = V(t). \tag{13}$$

Next, we derive the mean processing time $\ell_2(n)$ until the processing of a data is completed successfully. Let $H_{0,i}(t)(i = S, n, F)$ be the first-passage distribution from State 0 to State i. Then, we have

$$H_{0,S}(t) = H_{0,n}(t) * [Q_{n,S}(t) + Q_{n,0}(t) * H_{0,S}(t)], \tag{14}$$

$$H_{0,n}(t) = \sum_{j=1}^{\infty} [H_{0,F}(t) * Q_{F,0}(t)]^{(j-1)}$$
$$* [Q_{0,1}(t) * Q_{1,2}(t) * \cdots * Q_{n-1,n}(t)], \tag{15}$$

$$H_{0,F}(t) = Q_{0,F}(t) + Q_{0,1}(t) * Q_{1,F}(t) + Q_{0,1}(t) * Q_{1.2}(t) * Q_{2,F}(t)$$
$$+ \cdots + Q_{0,1}(t) * Q_{1.2}(t) * \cdots * Q_{n-2,n-1}(t) * Q_{n-1,F}(t). \tag{16}$$

By the similar analysis of Model 1.1, the mean time $\ell_2(n)$ is given by the following equation,

$$\ell_2(n) \equiv \int_0^{\infty} t \, dH_{0,S}(t)$$
$$= \frac{X(n) + v + \sum_{i=1}^{n-1} \left[1 - \left(\frac{2\lambda a}{2\lambda a + n} \right)^k \right]^{i-1} X(n)}{p \left[1 - \left(\frac{2\lambda a}{2\lambda a + n} \right)^k \right]^n}$$
$$+ \frac{1}{p} [u + (1-p)w - v], \tag{17}$$

where

$$X(n) \equiv \left[1 - \left(\frac{2\lambda a}{2\lambda a + n}\right)^k\right]\left[\frac{(2\lambda a + n)(\frac{a}{n} + b) + 2\lambda a \mu}{n}\right].$$

Moreover, we derive the expected processing number M_{Pn} of small data until the processing of n small data complete without interruption. Let $M_{Pn}(t)$ be the expected processing number until the processing of n small data complete in an interval $(0, t]$. Then, we have

$$M_{Pn}(t) = \left[\sum_{j=1}^{K}(j-1)Q_{0,0}^{(j-1)}(t)\right] * \left[\sum_{j=1}^{K}Q_{1,1}^{(j-1)}(t)\right] * \cdots$$

$$* \left[\sum_{j=1}^{K}Q_{n-1,n-1}^{(j-1)}(t)\right] * \left[\int_0^t e^{-2\lambda t}dA(t)\right]^{(n)} * B(t)^{(n)}$$

$$+ \left[\sum_{j=1}^{K}Q_{0,0}^{(j-1)}(t)\right] * \left[\sum_{j=1}^{K}(j-1)Q_{1,1}^{(j-1)}(t)\right] * \cdots$$

$$* \left[\sum_{j=1}^{K}Q_{n-1,n-1}^{(j-1)}(t)\right] * \left[\int_0^t e^{-2\lambda t}dA(t)\right]^{(n)} * B(t)^{(n)}$$

$$* \cdots$$

$$+ \left[\sum_{j=1}^{K}Q_{0,0}^{(j-1)}(t)\right] * \left[\sum_{j=1}^{K}Q_{1,1}^{(j-1)}(t)\right] * \cdots$$

$$* \left[\sum_{j=1}^{K}(j-1)Q_{n-1,n-1}^{(j-1)}(t)\right] * \left[\int_0^t e^{-2\lambda t}dA(t)\right]^{(n)} * B(t)^{(n)} + n.$$

$$(18)$$

Thus, the expected processing number is given by

$$M_{Pn} = \lim_{t\to\infty} M_{Pn}(t)$$

$$= \lim_{s\to 0} n \left[\sum_{j=1}^{K}(j-1)q_{0,0}(s)^{j-1}\right]\left[\sum_{j=1}^{K}q_{0,0}(s)^{j-1}\right]^{n-1}$$

$$\times [a(s+2\lambda)b(s)]^n + n.$$

$$= n \left[\frac{2\lambda a}{2\lambda a + n} - K \left(\frac{2\lambda a}{2\lambda a + n} \right)^K + (K-1) \left(\frac{2\lambda a}{2\lambda a + n} \right)^{K+1} \right]$$

$$\times \left[1 - \left(\frac{2\lambda a}{2\lambda a + n} \right)^K \right]^{n-1} \frac{n}{2\lambda a + n} + n. \tag{19}$$

Further, we derive the expected interruption number M_{Fn} until the processing of n small data complete. Let $M_{Fn}(t)$ be the expected interruption number until the processing of n small data complete in an interval $(0, t]$. Then, we have

$$M_{Fn}(t) = \sum_{j=1}^{\infty} (j-1)[H_{0,F}(t) * Q_{F,0}(t)]^{(j-1)}$$

$$* Q_{0,1}(t) * Q_{1,2}(t) * \cdots * Q_{n-1,n}(t). \tag{20}$$

Thus, the expected interruption number is given by

$$M_{Fn} = \lim_{t \to \infty} M_{Fn}(t)$$

$$= \lim_{s \to 0} \sum_{j=1}^{\infty} (j-1)[h_{0,F}(s)q_{F,0}(s)]^{j-1} q_{0,1}(s)q_{1,2}(s) \times \cdots \times q_{n-1,n}(s)$$

$$= \frac{1 - \left[1 - \left(\frac{2\lambda a}{2\lambda a+n} \right)^K \right]^n}{\left[1 - \left(\frac{2\lambda a}{2\lambda a+n} \right)^K \right]^2}.$$

2.2 Optimal Policy

2.2.1 Policy 1.1

We discuss an optimal policy which minimizes the mean time until the processing of a data is completed successfully. We seek an optimal division number n_1^* which minimizes $\ell_1(n)$. From the inequality $\ell_1(n+1) - \ell_1(n) \geq 0$, we have

$$q_n Y(n+1) - q_{n+1} Y(n) + (1 + 2\lambda a\mu)(q_n - q_{n+1}) \geq 0, \tag{21}$$

where

$$Y(n) \equiv (2\lambda a + n) \left(\frac{a}{n} + b \right).$$

We consider the special case where $q_n = q$. In this case, (21) is

$$n(n+1) \geq \frac{2\lambda a^2}{b + (1-q)\mu}. \tag{22}$$

Denoting the left side of (22) by $L(n)$,

$$L(1) = 2,$$
$$L(\infty) = \infty,$$
$$L(n) - L(n-1) > 0.$$

Hence, $L(n)$ is strictly increasing in n from $L(1)$ to ∞.

Therefore, we have the following optimal policy:

(i) If $(1/\lambda) < a^2/[b+(1-q)\mu]$, then there exists a finite and unique $n_1^*(> 1)$ which satisfies (22).
(ii) If $(1/\lambda) \geq a^2/[b + (1-q)\mu]$, then $n_1^* = 1$.

2.2.2 Policy 1.2

In terms of Model 1.2, we obtain the expected cost and discuss an optimal policy which minimizes it. Let c_1 be the cost for processing of small data and c_2 be the cost for an interruption. Then, we define the expected cost $C(n)$ until the processing of n small data complete as

$$
\begin{aligned}
C(n) &\equiv c_1 M_{Pn} + c_2 M_{Fn} \\
&= c_1 \left\{ n \left\{ \frac{2\lambda a}{2\lambda a + n} - K \left[\frac{2\lambda a}{2\lambda a + n} \right]^K + (K-1) \left[\frac{2\lambda a}{2\lambda a + n} \right]^{K+1} \right\} \right. \\
&\quad \left. \times \left\{ 1 - \left[\frac{2\lambda a}{2\lambda a + n} \right]^K \right\}^{n-1} \frac{n}{2\lambda a + n} + n \right\} \\
&\quad + c_2 \frac{1 - \left\{ 1 - \left[\frac{2\lambda a}{2\lambda a + n} \right]^K \right\}^n}{\left\{ 1 - \left[\frac{2\lambda a}{2\lambda a + n} \right]^K \right\}^2},
\end{aligned}
\tag{23}
$$

where

$$C(1) = c_1 \left\{ \left[\frac{2\lambda a}{2\lambda a + 1} - K \left(\frac{2\lambda a}{2\lambda a + 1} \right)^K + (K-1) \left(\frac{2\lambda a}{2\lambda a + 1} \right)^{K+1} \right] \right.$$

$$\left. \times \frac{1}{2\lambda a + 1} + 1 \right\} + c_2 \frac{1 - \left\{ 1 - \left[\frac{2\lambda a}{2\lambda a + 1} \right]^K \right\}^n}{\left\{ 1 - \left[\frac{2\lambda a}{2\lambda a + 1} \right]^K \right\}^2},$$

$$C(\infty) = \infty.$$

We seek an optimal number n_2^* which minimizes $C(n)$. From the inequality $C(n+1) - C(n) \geq 0$, we have

$$\frac{M_{P(n+1)} - M_{Pn}}{M_{Fn} - M_{F(n+1)}} \geq \frac{c_2}{c_1}. \tag{24}$$

Denoting the left side of (24) by $L(n)$,

$$L(1) = \frac{M_{P2} - M_{P1}}{M_{F1} - M_{F2}}. \tag{25}$$

Hence, when $[M_{P(n+1)} - M_{Pn}][M_{F(n-1)} - M_{Fn}] > [M_{Fn} - M_{F(n+1)}][M_{Pn} - M_{P(n-1)}]$ then $L(n)$ is strictly increasing in n from $L(1)$.

Thus, we have the following optimal policy:

(i) If $L(1) < c_2/c_1$, then there exists a finite and unique $n_2^*(> 1)$ which satisfies (24).

(ii) If $L(1) \geq c_2/c_1$, then $n_2^* = 1$.

2.3   Numerical Examples

We compute numerically the mean time $\ell_1(n)$, the optimal division number n_1^* which minimizes $\ell_1(n)$ and the optimal number n_2^* which minimizes $C(n)$. Suppose that the comparison time b of processing results of small data is a unit time of the system in order to investigate the relative tendency of performance measures. It is assumed that the mean processing time when a data is not divided is $a/b = 100 \sim 400$, the mean time to error occurrence is $(1/\lambda)/b = 5000 \sim 25000$, the mean time until the processing of each small data is executed again is $\mu/b = 1$, the mean comparison time of processing results of a data is $u/b = 1$, the mean time until the processing of a data is executed again is $w/b = 1$, the probability that the comparison of processing results of small data agrees is $q_n = q = 0.8 \sim 1.0$ and the probability that the comparison of processing results of a data agrees is

$p = 0.8 \sim 1.0$. Further, the cost c_1 for processing of small data is a unit of cost, the cost rate of an interruption is $c_2/c_1 = 1000 \sim 4000$.

Table 1 gives the optimal number n_1^* which minimizes $\ell_1(n)$ when $q = 1$. For example, when $a/b = 300$ and $(1/\lambda)/b = 10000$, the optimal number is $n_1^* = 4$. This indicates that n_1^* decreases with $(1/\lambda)/b$, however, increases with a/b. In particular, when $(1/\lambda)/b$ is large and a/b is small, $n_1^* = 1$. In this case, we should not divide a data.

Table 1   Optimal number n_1^* to minimizes $\ell_1(n)$.

a/b	(1/λ)/b				
	5000	10000	15000	20000	25000
100	2	2	1	1	1
200	4	3	2	2	2
300	6	4	4	3	3
400	8	6	5	4	4

Table 2 gives the mean time $\ell_1(n_1^*)$ when a data is divided into n_1^* small data and $(1/\lambda)/b = 5000$. This indicates that $\ell_1(n_1^*)$ decreases with p and

Table 2   Mean time $\ell_1(n_1^*)$.

a/b	p	q		
		0.8	0.9	1.0
100	0.8	172	150	132
	0.9	152	133	117
	1.0	137	120	105
200	0.8	334	294	262
	0.9	297	262	233
	1.0	267	235	209
300	0.8	497	439	392
	0.9	442	390	348
	1.0	397	351	313
400	0.8	660	583	522
	0.9	586	519	464
	1.0	527	467	417

q. When p and q are small, $\ell_1(n_1^*)$ becomes large compared to the mean processing time a/b when a data is not divided.

Table 3 gives the optimal number n_2^* which minimizes $C(n)$ when $(1/\lambda)/b = 5000$. This indicates that n_2^* decreases with K, however, in-

Table 3 Optimal number n_2^* to minimizes $C(n)$.

a/b	K							
	2				3			
	c_2/c_1							
	1000	2000	3000	4000	1000	2000	3000	4000
100	1	2	2	2	1	1	1	1
200	2	3	4	5	1	1	1	3
300	4	5	6	7	1	2	2	2
400	5	7	8	10	2	2	3	3

creases with c_2/c_1 and a/b. In particular, when c_2/c_1 and a/b are small, $n_2^* = 1$.

3   Reliability Analysis of a Redundant Cloud System

3.1   *Model*

We pay attention to a redundant cloud system. The cloud system has active devices and standby devices.

(1) The cloud system has K_1 containers which consist of M_1 active contain-ers and N_1 standby containers. When the failure of an active container has occurred, it switches over to one of standby containers. The standby container does not fail. When the failure of $(N_1 + 1)$ active containers has occurred, the cloud system goes to faulty state.

(2) The container has K_2 racks which consist of M_2 active racks and N_2 standby racks. When the failure of an active rack has occurred, it switches over to one of standby racks. The standby rack does not fail. When the failure of $(N_2 + 1)$ active racks has occurred, the container goes to faulty state.

(3) The rack has K_3 servers which consist of M_3 active servers and N_3 standby servers. When the failure of an active server has occurred, it switches over to one of standby servers. The standby server does not fail. If the failure of $(N_3 + 1)$ active servers has occurred, the rack goes to faulty state.

(4) The failure of an active server occurs according to a general distribution $F(t)$ with finite mean $1/\lambda$.

(5) The cloud system is inspected and maintained at time T. After the maintenance, the system returns to an initial state. We define the dis-

tribution of $A(t)$ as follows:

$$A(t) \equiv \begin{cases} 1 : t \geq T, \\ 0 : t < T. \end{cases}$$

The inspection and maintenance need the time according to a general distribution $G_R(t)$ with finite mean $1/\mu_R$. When the failure of server has occurred, the inspection and maintenance need the time according to a general distribution $G_E(t)$ with finite mean $1/\mu_E$. When the failure of $(N_3 + 1)$ server has occurred, and the rack goes to faulty state, it undergoes the maintenance right away. Its maintenance needs the time according to a general distribution $G_F(t)$ with finite mean $1/\mu_F$ $(1/\mu_R < 1/\mu_F,\ 1/\mu_E < 1/\mu_F)$.

(6) When the failure of rack has occurred, the inspection and maintenance need the time according to a general distribution $G_E(t)$ with finite mean $1/\mu_E$. When the failure of (N_2+1) rack has occurred, and the container goes to faulty state, it undergoes the maintenance right away. Its maintenance needs the time according to a general distribution $G_F(t)$ with finite mean $1/\mu_F$.

(7) When the failure of container has occurred, the inspection and maintenance need the time according to a general distribution $G_E(t)$ with finite mean $1/\mu_E$. When the failure of $(N_1 + 1)$ container has occurred, and the system goes to faulty state, it undergoes the maintenance right away. Its maintenance needs the time according to a general distribution $G_F(t)$ with finite mean $1/\mu_F$.

Fig. 3 draws the outline of a cloud system.

3.1.1 *Model* 2.1

First, we consider the simple case that the system has two active servers and one standby server. That is, we consider the case that $K_1 = 1$ ($M_1 = 1, N_1 = 0$), $K_2 = 1$ ($M_2 = 1, N_2 = 0$), $K_3 = 3$ ($M_3 = 2, N_3 = 1$).

We define the following states of the system:

State 0: The system begins to operate as an initial condition.

State R: The maintenance of a system begins at time T when all active servers do not fail.

State E: The maintenance of a system begins at time T when the failure of one active server has occurred.

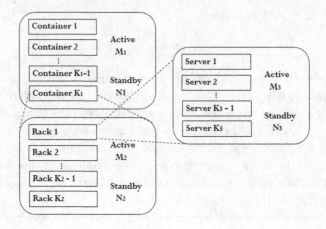

Fig. 3   Outline of a cloud system.

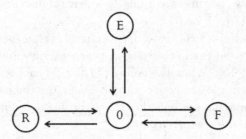

Fig. 4   Transition diagram between system states.

State F: The failure of two active servers has occurred, and the system goes to faulty state.

The states defined above form a Markov renewal process. Transition diagram between system states is shown Fig. 4.

Let $Q_{ij}(t)(i, j = 0, R, E, F)$ be one-step transition probabilities of a Markov renewal process. Then, we have

$$Q_{0,R}(t) = \int_0^t \overline{F}(u)^2 dA(u), \tag{26}$$

$$Q_{0,E}(t) = 2 \int_0^t [F(u) - F^{(2)}(u)]\overline{F}(u)dA(u), \tag{27}$$

$$Q_{0,F}(t) = 2 \int_0^t \overline{A}(u)\overline{F}(u)dF^{(2)}(u)$$

$$+2 \int_0^t \overline{A}(u)[F(u) - F^{(2)}(u)]dF(u), \tag{28}$$

$$Q_{z,0}(t) = G_z(t) \quad (z = R, E, F). \tag{29}$$

When $F(t) = 1 - e^{-\lambda t}$,

$$Q_{0,R}(t) = \int_0^t e^{-2\lambda u}dA(u),$$

$$Q_{0,E}(t) = 2 \int_0^t \lambda u e^{-2\lambda u}dA(u),$$

$$Q_{0,F}(t) = 4 \int_0^t \overline{A}(u)\lambda^2 u e^{-2\lambda u}du.$$

We derive the steady-state availability of the system. When the system is in State 0 at time 0, the transition probability $P_{0,0}(t)$ that it is in State 0 at time t is given by

$$P_{0,0}(t) = Q_{0,R}(t) * Q_{R,0}(t) * P_{0,0}(t) + Q_{0,E}(t) * Q_{E,0}(t) * P_{0,0}(t)$$
$$+Q_{0,F}(t) * Q_{F,0}(t) * P_{0,0}(t)$$
$$+1 - Q_{0,R}(t) - Q_{0,E}(t) - Q_{0,F}(t). \tag{30}$$

Taking the LS transforms of (30) and arranging them,

$$p_{0,0}(s) = \frac{1 - q_{0,R}(s) - q_{0,E}(s) - q_{0,F}(s)}{1 - q_{0,R}(s)q_{R,0}(s) - q_{0,E}(s)q_{E,0}(s) - q_{0,F}(s)q_{F,0}(s)}.$$

Thus, the steady-state availability $P(T)$ of the system is given by

$$P(T) \equiv \lim_{t \to \infty} P_{0,0}(t) = \lim_{s \to 0} p_{0,0}(s) = \frac{X(T)}{Y(T)}, \tag{31}$$

where

$$X(T) \equiv -q'_{0,R}(0) - q'_{0,E}(0) - q'_{0,F}(0)$$
$$= T\{\overline{F}(T)^2 + 2[F(T) - F^{(2)}(T)]\overline{F}(T)\}$$
$$+2 \int_0^T t\overline{F}(t)dF^{(2)}(t) + 2 \int_0^T t[F(t) - F^{(2)}(t)]dF(t)$$
$$> 0,$$

$$Y(T) \equiv X(T) + \overline{F}(T)^2 \left(\frac{1}{\mu_R}\right) + 2\overline{F}(T)[F(T) - F^{(2)}(T)] \left(\frac{1}{\mu_E}\right)$$

$$+ [2\overline{F}(T)F^{(2)}(T) + F(T)^2] \left(\frac{1}{\mu_F}\right),$$

where $\psi'(s)$ is the differential function of $\psi(s)$. For example, $-q'_{0,R}(0)$ is the mean transition time from State 0 to State R.

3.1.2 *Model 2.2*

Next, we consider the case that the system has two active racks and one standby server. Each server has two active servers and one standby server. That is, we consider the case that $K_1 = 1$ ($M_1 = 1, N_1 = 0$), $K_2 = 3$ ($M_2 = 2, N_2 = 1$), $K_3 = 3$ ($M_3 = 2, N_3 = 1$).

We define the following states of the system:

State 0: The system begins to operate as an initial condition.

State R: The maintenance of a system begins at time T when all active racks do not fail.

State E: The maintenance of a system begins at time T when the failure of one active rack has occurred.

State F: The failure of two active racks has occurred, and the system goes to faulty state.

One-step transition probabilities is given by the following equations:

$$Q_{0,R}(t) = \int_0^t \overline{D}(u)^2 dA(u), \tag{32}$$

$$Q_{0,E}(t) = 2 \int_0^t [D(u) - D^{(2)}(u)]\overline{D}(u)dA(u), \tag{33}$$

$$Q_{0,F}(t) = 2 \int_0^t \overline{A}(u)\overline{D}(u)dD^{(2)}(u)$$

$$+ 2 \int_0^t \overline{A}(u)[D(u) - D^{(2)}(u)]dD(u), \tag{34}$$

$$Q_{z,0}(t) = G_z(t) \quad (z = R, E, F), \tag{35}$$

where

$$D(t) \equiv 2 \int_0^t \overline{F}(u)dF^{(2)}(u) + 2 \int_0^t [F(u) - F^{(2)}(u)]dF(u). \tag{36}$$

When $F(t) = 1 - e^{-\lambda t}$,

$$D(t) = 1 - e^{-2\lambda t} - 2\lambda t e^{-2\lambda t},$$

$$Q_{0,R}(t) = \int_0^t (e^{-2\lambda u} + 2\lambda u e^{-2\lambda u})^2 dA(u),$$

$$Q_{0,E}(t) = 4 \int_0^t \left(1 + \frac{8}{3}\lambda u + \frac{4}{3}\lambda^2 u^2\right) \lambda^2 u^2 e^{-4\lambda u} dA(u),$$

$$Q_{0,F}(t) = \frac{64}{3} \int_0^t \overline{A}(u)(1 + \lambda u)\lambda^4 u^3 e^{-4\lambda u} du.$$

3.2 Optimal Policy

We consider an optimal T^* which maximizes $P(T)$ in (31) when $1/\mu_R = 1/\mu_E$. Differentiating $P(T)$ with respect to T and setting it equal to zero, we have

$$X(T)\frac{B'(T)}{X'(T)} - B(T) = \frac{\mu_F}{\mu_R - \mu_F}, \qquad (37)$$

where

$$X'(T) = \overline{F}(T)^2 + 2\overline{F}(T)[F(T) - F^{(2)}(T)],$$
$$B(T) \equiv q_{0F}(0)$$
$$= 2\overline{F}(T)F^{(2)}(T) + F(T)^2,$$
$$B'(T) = 2F'(T)[F(T) - F^{(2)}(T)] + 2\overline{F}(T)[F^{(2)}(T)]'.$$

Denoting the left-hand side of (37) by $L(T)$, we have

$$L(0) = 0,$$
$$L'(T) = X(T)\frac{B''(T)X'(T) - B'(T)X''(T)}{X'(T)^2}.$$

Since $X(T) > 0$, $L(T)$ is strictly increasing in T from 0 when $B''(T)X'(T) > B'(T)X''(T)$. Thus, we have the following optimal policy:

(i) If $\mu_F/(\mu_R - \mu_F) < L(\infty)$, there exists a finite and unique T^* which satisfies (37).
(ii) If $\mu_F/(\mu_R - \mu_F) \geq L(\infty)$, $T^* = \infty$.

Especially, in terms of Model 2.1, we seek an optimal T_1^* which maximizes $P(T)$ when $F(t) = 1 - e^{-\lambda t}$. In this case, equation (37) becomes

$$\frac{4\lambda T(1 - e^{-2\lambda T} - \lambda T e^{-2\lambda T})}{1 + 2\lambda T} - (1 - e^{-2\lambda T} - 2\lambda T e^{-2\lambda T}) = \frac{\mu_F}{\mu_R - \mu_F}. \qquad (38)$$

Table 4   Optimal T_1^* to maximize the steady-state availability in Model 2.1.

$1/\lambda$	$(1/\mu_F)/(1/\mu_R)$				
	2	5	10	15	20
1000	466	300	213	175	152
2000	932	599	426	349	303
3000	1398	899	639	523	454

Denoting the left-hand side of (38) by $\tilde{L}_1(T)$, we have

$$\tilde{L}_1(0) = 0,$$
$$\tilde{L}_1(\infty) = 1,$$
$$\tilde{L}_1'(T) = X(T)\left(\frac{2\lambda}{1 + 2\lambda T}\right)^2 > 0.$$

Hence, $\tilde{L}_1(T)$ is strictly increasing in T from 0 to 1. Thus, if $1 > \mu_F/(\mu_R - \mu_F)$, i.e., $\mu_R/\mu_F > 2$, then there exists a finite and unique T_1^* which satisfies (38).

3.3   *Numerical Example*

We compute numerically the optimal T_1^* which maximize the steady-state availability $P(T)$. Suppose that the mean maintenance time $1/\mu_R$ when the system is inspected at time T is a unit time of the system in order to investigate the relative tendency of performance measure. It is assumed that the mean maintenance time $1/\mu_F$ when the system goes to faulty state is $2 \sim 20$ and the mean time $1/\lambda$ until the failure of an active server occurs is $1000 \sim 3000$.

Table 4 gives the optimal T_1^* which maximizes the steady-state availability. For example, when $1/\lambda = 2000$ and $(1/\mu_F)/(1/\mu_R) = 10$, the optimal $T_1^* = 426$. This indicates that T_1^* decreases with $(1/\mu_F)/(1/\mu_R)$, however increases with $1/\lambda$. When $1/\mu_F$ is large, T_1^* has to be small to prevent system failure.

4   Conclusion

Recently, cloud computing has been widely used. In terms of a cloud computing system, the schemes with high-speed processing and high reliability are required. From this point of view, we have formulated stochastic models for systems in cloud computing environment. Using the theory of Markov renewal processes, we have obtained the reliability measures. Finally, to understand the results easily, we have given numerical examples of each model and have evaluated them for various standard parameters. If some parameters are estimated from actual data, we could select the best policy.

First we have formulated stochastic models for a distributed processing system in cloud computing environment and have derived the mean time until the processing of a data is successful and the expected cost. Further, we have discussed optimal policies which minimize them. From numerical examples, we have shown the optimal division number which minimizes the mean processing time decreases with the mean time to error occurrence, however, increases the size of a data.

Second, we have formulated stochastic models for a redundant cloud system. The cloud system consists of containers, racks and servers where each device has active and standby devices. Under the assumption that the cloud system becomes failure when the failure of some devices has occurred, we have derived the steady-state probability. Further, we have discussed optimal policies which maximize it. From numerical examples, we have shown that the optimal time which maximizes the steady-state availability decreases with the mean maintenance time when the system goes to faulty state, however, increases with the mean time until the failure of an active server occurs.

It would be very important to evaluate and improve the reliability of a cloud computing system. The results derived in this paper would be applied in practical fields by making some suitable modifications and extensions. Further studies for such subject would be expected.

References

Tanimoto, S., Seki, Y., Iwashita, M., Sato, H. and Kanai, A., (2013). *Risk Assessment of Big Data Service, Trans. IEICE of Japan*, J96-A pp.189–194.

Naruse, K. and Nakagawa, T., (2012). *Optimal Checking Times for Series Database Systems, Advanced reliability and maintenance modeling V*, pp.366–373.

Armbrust, M., et al., (2009). *Above the Clouds: A Berkeley View of Cloud Computing, Technical Report No. UCV/EECS-2009-28*, University of California at Berkeley.

Banzai, T., Koizumi, H., Kanbayashi, R. and Sato, M. (2009). *Design of a Cloud Computing System for Program Testing Environments, IPSJ SIG Technical Report*, pp.1–8.

Vishwanath, K. V., Greenberg, A. and Reed, D. A., (2009). *Modular Data Centers: How to Design Them?*, LSAP '09.

European Network and Information Security Agency, (2009). *Cloud Computing: Benefits, Risks and Recommendations for Information Security.*

Osaki, S. (1992). *Applied Stochastic System Modeling*, Springer-Verlag, Berlin.

Shibamura, H., Susukita, R., Hirao, T., Yoshida, M., Kando, T., Miwa, H., Miyoshi, I., Inoue, K. and Murakami, K., (2010). *OpenNSIM Interconnect Simulation Service via a Cloud Environment*, IPSJ SIG Technical Report.

Hiwatashi, J. and Iwamura, S., (2012). *Method of Handling Hard Disk Drive Failures in Cloud Computing Environment*, NTT Technical Review, Vol.10, No.9.

Schroeder, B., Pinheiro, E., and Weber, W.-D., (2009). *DRAM Errors in the Wild: A Large-Scale Field Study*, SIGMETRICS/Performance '09.

Nakagawa, T. (2005). it Maintenance Theory of Reliability, Springer-Verlag, London.

Nakagawa, T. (2008). *Advanced Maintenance Models and Maintenance Policies*, Springer-Verlag, London.

Yasui, K., Nakagawa, T. and Sandoh, H., (2002). *Reliability models in data communication systems, in Stochastic Models in Reliability and Maintenance*, ed. S. Osaki, Springer-Verlag, Berlin, pp.281–301.

PART 4
Maintenance Policies

Two-Dimensional Maintenance with Repair Time Threshold and Generalized Age Replacement Policy

Minjae Park[1], Ki Mun Jung[2] and Dong Ho Park[3]

[1] College of Business Administration,
Hongik University,

[2] Department of Informational Statistics,
Kyungsung University,

[3] Industry Academic Cooperation Foundation,
Hallym University

1 Introduction

One of the well-known basic types of maintenance policies is the classical age replacement policy (ARP), which was suggested [Barlow and Hunter (1960)], under which a preventive replacement (PR) is put in place when the product reaches a pre-determined age τ without failure and a failure replacement (FR) is put in place if the product fails before reaching the PR age τ. The ARP has been extensively studied and extended by many authors since it was introduced in the literature. For example, Barlow and Proschan discussed the maintenance cost under the ARP and derived the optimum replacement age over an infinite time span [Barlow and Proschan (1996)]. Sheu and Chien considered a generalized ARP of a system with a random lead-time subject to shocks, which can occur according to the non-homogeneous Poisson process (NHPP) [Sheu and Chien (2004)]. In particular, Yeh, Chen and Chen (YCC) considered the ARP for non-repairable products under a renewable free replacement warranty (FRW) and determined the optimal PR age by minimizing the long-run expected cost rate from the perspective of the customer [Yeh et.al. (2005)]. YCC also compared the ARP under a renewable FRW with or without the warranty by investigating the effects of the renewable FRW on the optimal ARP [Yeh et.al. (2005)]. Later, many researchers proposed several extended versions of the ARP maintenance models based on YCC's model by considering various types of warranty policies and other factors [Chien (2008, 2010); Chien and Chen (2007)].

Although most of the warranties considered in the literature so far are based on one factor of the product failure time only, there exist two dimensional warranties which are dependent on two factors at the time of the product failures. One of such two-dimensional warranties considers the age and usage of the product as two factors affecting the warranty policy and have been introduced [Chukova et.al. (2007)] and among many others [Iskandar et.al. (2005)]. However, there are certain situations where the information on the actual usage of the product is quite difficult to obtain at the time of the product failures. To complement such a drawback, Park, Jung and Park recently proposed the minimal repair-replacement maintenance of a product and incorporate such maintenance concept into developing a new warranty policy[Park et.al. (2013)]. Two-dimensional maintenance action, which was suggested [Park et.al. (2016)], considered both the failure time and its corresponding repair time as two factors affecting the maintenance action where either minimal repair or replacement is conducted when the product failures occur. To determine whether the failed product would be minimally repaired or replaced by a new product, a repair time threshold is introduced as a criterion for such a maintenance action. The warranty adapting such a maintenance action is referred to as a minimal repair-replacement warranty (MRRW) in article.

Two-dimensional maintenance process under the renewable MRRW works as follows. At the sale of the product, the manufacturer offers a renewable warranty with a fixed length of warranty period. When the product failure occurs during the warranty period, it is initially minimally repaired. If the repair is completed within the repair time threshold, the failed product is restored to an "as bad as old" state with the same intensity function and is returned back to the operation. However, if the repair takes more than the repair time threshold, then the failed product is replaced with a new product and the warranty is renewed. Note that if the repair time threshold is taken to be equal to zero and infinity, the MRRW is reduced to replacement warranty and minimal-repair warranty, respectively.

In this chapter, a warranted cost model is developed based on the renewable MRRW and the generalized ARP is newly defined adapting the two-dimensional maintenance with the repair time threshold. In Section 1.2, a renewable MRRW is described in details and the life cycle of the product is defined for the maintenance model, under which both failure time and repair time are considered simultaneously at the time of the product failure. Assuming certain cost structures, the expected cost rate during the life cycle of the product is derived under the MRRW as well. In Section1.3, the ARP is generalized to the case where two-dimensional maintenance is adapted on each failure of the product and the optimal preventive replacement age is determined minimizing the expected cost rate during the life cycle of the repairable product. Throughout this chapter, the repairable product is assumed to deteriorate monotonically as it ages.

2 Cost Model under Repair-replacement Warranty Policy

In this section, the MRRW model is described in details and a mathematical formula to evaluate the expected cost rate (ECR) is derived under the renewable MRRW, assuming certain cost structures. Under this model, the manufacturer determines the repair time threshold in advance, which specifies the time limit for the repair service, for the repairable product. In this section, both free MRRW and pro-rata MRRW are considered from the user's perspective. Under the free MRRW (FMRRW) policy, both minimal repair and replacement are performed free of charge to the user during the warranty period and under the pro-rata MRRW (PMRRW) policy, the user is responsible for the pro-rated replacement cost which is proportional to the length of use at the time of the product failure. The minimal repair cost is charged to the manufacturer even under the PMRRW during the warranty period. However, should the warranty period expires, the user must pay the entire maintenance costs incurred due to the product failure or mal-functioning. Under the renewable warranty policy, the warranty would be renewed automatically anew for the replaced product and the same warranty terms will be in effective again. Although the non-renewable warranty policy with a fixed warranty period could be other type of warranty policy to be considered, only the renewable warranty is studied in this chapter.

In the following, a renewable MRRW policy is described using the product failure time and its corresponding repair time as two factors recorded at the time of the product failure. Then the mathematical formulas to eval-

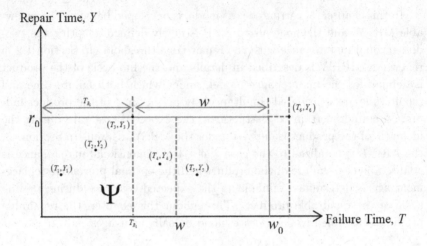

Fig. 1   Renewable minimal repair-replacement model.

uate the ECR are derived by consideration of several cost structures which determines the maintenance cost for minimal repair and replacement of the failed product either during the warranty period or following the warranty period from the user's point of view.

2.1   *Repair-replacement Warranty Model*

For $j = 1, 2, \ldots, T_{R_j}$ $(< w)$ denotes the inter-replacement time interval elapsed between $j - 1^{\text{th}}$ replacement and the jth replacement of the product during the warranty period. If $T_{R_1} < w$, then under the renewable FMRRW policy, the replacement service will be granted free of charge to the user, and the manufacturer will be responsible for the replacement of the failed product. Starting from T_{R_1}, the replaced new product will have the same renewable warranty with the length of period of w again as shown in Fig. 1.1. Let W_0 denote the length of warranty cycle which is defined as the time interval starting from the point of sale and ending at the expiration time of warranty. It is clear that for a non-renewable warranty, a warranty cycle coincides with a warranty period w.

However, for a renewable policy, W_0 is a r.v. depending on the total number of replacements that occur during the life cycle of the product, the inter-arrival times between two successive replacements during the warranty period and the length of initial warranty period. Let $N_T = N_\Psi + N_R$ be the total number of product failures during the warranty period, where N_Ψ and N_R are the number of minimal repairs and the number of replacements, respectively. Then, W_0 can be expressed as

$$W_0 = T_{R_1} + T_{R_2} + \cdots + T_{R_{N_R}} + w. \tag{1}$$

Fig. 1 depicts the case in which, if the first replacement occurs at time T_{R_1} and the second replacement does not occur until the warranty expires, then it is clear that $w_0 = T_{R_1} + w$, where w_0 is the realization of W_0. In Fig. 1 T_j and Y_j, $j = 1, 2, \ldots$ denote the time at which the jth failure occurs and the length of its corresponding repair time, respectively. The space Ψ denotes a warranty region which is censored by both the warranty period and the repair time threshold.

2.2 Length of Life Cycle

In this subsection, the expected length of life cycle of the product is formulated in the situations where the renewable MRRW policy is applied during the warranty period. Under the renewable MRRW, the manufacturer provides two kinds of warranty services on each product failure during the warranty period, the minimal repair initially and the replacement service if the repair work can't be completed within the repair time limit. In consideration of both repair and replacement services by the manufacturer during the warranty period and the maintenance work by the user during the maintenance period, the expected length of life cycle is to be derived. Let T be a *r.v.* representing the failure time of the product having $f(x)$ and $F(x)$ as its pdf and cdf, respectively. Let $T_1, T_2, \ldots$ denote the failure times of the product and let $Y_1, Y_2, \ldots$ denote the lengths of repair times which are assumed to be *i.i.d.* having $g(y)$ and $G(y)$ as its pdf and cdf, respectively. Note that the product is replaced N_R times during the warranty period under the renewable MRRW policy.

Although other product failures occur N_Ψ times within the warranty period, these failures are minimally repaired and thus do not affect the length of life cycle. Let δ denotes the fixed length of maintenance period after the warranty expires. Then, the length of life cycle can be expressed as

$$L(w, \delta) = W_0 + \delta = \sum_{j=1}^{N_R} T_{R_j} + (w + \delta),$$

where W_0 denotes the length of warranty cycle, given in Eq. (1). Let r_0 denote the pre-specified repair time threshold. It follows that given $N_R = n$, the expected length of life cycle can be represented as

$$E\big(L(w,\delta)|N_R = n\big) = \sum_{j=1}^{n} E\big(T_j|T_j \le w, Y_j \ge r_0, N_R = n\big) + (w + \delta)$$

$$= n \cdot \frac{\int_0^w t \cdot f(t)\mathrm{d}t}{F(w)\overline{G}(r_0)} + (w + \delta). \tag{2}$$

If r_0 approaches zero, then Eq. (2) becomes Eq. (3) below which coincides with the formula for the length of life cycle obtained in the Sahin and Polatoglu's replacement model [Sahin and Polatoglu (1996)].

$$E\big(L(w,\delta)|N_R = n\big) = n \cdot \frac{\int_0^w t \cdot f(t)\mathrm{d}t}{F(w)} + (w + \delta). \tag{3}$$

The replacement service is provided by the manufacturer only when the product fails during the warranty period and the repair service exceeds the pre-specified repair time limit. Thus, the number of product replacements during the warranty period has the following geometric distribution.

$$P(N_R = n) = \big\{\overline{F}(w) + F(w) \cdot G(r_0)\big\} \cdot \big\{F(w) \cdot \overline{G}(r_0)\big\}^n, \qquad n = 0, 1, 2, \ldots. \tag{4}$$

By taking the expectation for the conditional expectation of Eq. (2) with respect to N_R, the following expected length of life cycle is obtained under the renewable MRRW model.

$$E\big(L(w,\delta)\big) = E\big(E\big(L(w,\delta)|N_R = n\big)\big)$$

$$= \frac{\int_0^w t \cdot f(t)\mathrm{d}t}{\big\{1 - F(w) \cdot \overline{G}(r_0)\big\}} + (w + \delta). \tag{5}$$

The life span of a product is considered terminated when the product is replaced by a new one at the user's expense at the end of maintenance period. Under the maintenance model considered in this section, the length of maintenance period is assumed to be fixed at δ following the expiration of the renewing warranty term. Although there exist several maintenance models following the expiration of warranty period, including periodic maintenance models, Sahin and Polatoglu consider the situation where the product is replaced by a new one after a fixed length of maintenance period is elapsed [Sahin and Polatoglu (1996)].

2.3 Expected Maintenance Cost

In this section, the expectation for total maintenance cost incurred during the life cycle of the product is considered and thereby the expected cost rate per unit time is derived during the life cycle of the product. Let C_r, C_m and C_f denote the r.v.'s representing total replacement cost during the warranty period, total minimal repair cost and total failure cost during the life cycle of the product, for which the user is responsible, respectively. Further, let c_r be the fixed unit cost of replacement. Then, in order to maintain the product during its life cycle, the user would be charged the total amount of cost equaling $C_r + C_m + C_f + c_r$, where the last term c_r needs to be added because the system is replaced at the user's expense at the end of maintenance period. In this study, both FMRRW and PMRRW are considered based on two factors of failure time and repair time.

Under the renewing FMRRW, both minimal repair and replacement are performed at no charge to the user during the warranty period and thus, $P(C_r = 0) = 1$. However, under the renewing PMRRW, the user is responsible for the pro-rated replacement cost during the warranty period and thus, the user's replacement cost can be expressed as a function of T_{R_j}'s as follows:

$$C_r = \sum_{j=1}^{N_R} c_r \frac{T_{R_j}}{w}. \tag{6}$$

During the maintenance period, the minimal repair service only is conducted on each failure and no repair time limit is set. As a result, the failure intensity is assumed to follow the NHPP with the intensity rate of $\lambda(t)$. Let N_δ denote the number of failures during the maintenance period following the expiration of warranty. Then, the pdf of N_δ is given by

$$P(N_\delta = n_\delta) = \frac{e^{-\int_w^{w+\delta} \lambda(t)dt} \left[\int_w^{w+\delta} \lambda(t)dt\right]^{n_\delta}}{n_\delta!}, \tag{7}$$

and

$$E(N_\delta) = \int_w^{w+\delta} \lambda(t)dt. \tag{8}$$

Let c_m and c_{fm} denote the unit cost of minimal repair and the unit failure cost, respectively. Upon each product failure during the maintenance period, only the minimal repair is conducted. Therefore, if the product failure occurs N_δ times during the maintenance period, the total minimal repair cost can be evaluated as

$$C_m = c_m \cdot N_\delta. \tag{9}$$

Since the failure cost incurs during the maintenance period due to the stoppage of operation and it is evaluated proportionally to the number of minimal repairs conducted, the total failure cost during the maintenance period is obtained as follows.

$$C_f = c_{fm} \cdot N_\delta. \tag{10}$$

By adding the costs (6), (9) and (10), the total maintenance cost incurred during the life cycle of the product, which would be charged to the user under the renewing PMRRW, can be expressed as

$$C(w, \delta) = \sum_{j=1}^{N_R} c_r \frac{T_{R_j}}{w} + N_\delta \cdot (c_m + c_{fm}) + c_r. \tag{11}$$

Given $N_R = n$, it can be shown that the total conditional expected cost can be expressed as

$$E\big(C(w,\delta)|N_R = n\big) = \frac{c_r}{w} \sum_{j=1}^{n} E(T_j | T_j \le w, Y_j \ge r_0)$$
$$+ E(N_\delta) \cdot (c_m + c_{fm}) + c_r$$
$$= n \frac{c_r}{w} \frac{\int_0^w t \cdot f(t) \mathrm{d}t}{F(w) \cdot \overline{G}(r_0)} + (c_m + c_{fm}) \cdot \int_w^{w+\delta} \lambda(t) \mathrm{d}t + c_r. \tag{12}$$

By taking the expectation on $E(C(w, \delta)|N_R = n)$ of Eq. (12) with respect to N_R, the expected total maintenance cost under the renewable PMRR is obtained as

$$EC(w, \delta) = E\big(E(C(w, \delta)|N_R = n)\big)$$
$$= \frac{c_r}{w} \frac{\int_0^w t \cdot f(t) \mathrm{d}t}{1 - F(w) \cdot \overline{G}(r_0)} + (c_m + c_{fm}) \cdot \int_w^{w+\delta} \lambda(t) \mathrm{d}t + c_r. \tag{13}$$

If the first term of the second equation of Eq. (13) is excluded, it becomes the formula for the expected total maintenance cost under the renewing FMRRW. The expression, given in Eq. (13), is the total expected cost for which the user is responsible to maintain the product during the life cycle until the product is replaced by a new one at the expense of the user. The replacement cost at the end of maintenance period is included in the total expected cost. Dividing $E(C(w, \delta))$ of Eq. (13) by the expected length of life cycle, $E(L(w, \delta))$, given in Eq. (15), the expected cost rate per unit time is obtained during the life cycle of the product under the renewing PMRRW as

$$ECR(w,\delta) = \frac{\frac{c_r}{c_w} \cdot \int_0^w t \cdot f(t)\mathrm{d}t + \overline{F}(w) \cdot (c_m + c_{fm}) \cdot \int_w^{w+\delta} \lambda(t)\mathrm{d}t + \overline{F}(w) + c_r}{\int_0^w t \cdot f(t)\mathrm{d}t + \overline{F}(w) \cdot (w+\delta)}.$$
(14)

If r_0 approaches zero, then Eq. (14) becomes Eq. (15) below which is the same as the one given in Sahin and Polatoglu's replacement model [Sahin and Polatoglu (1996)].

$$ECR(w,\delta) = \frac{\frac{c_r}{c_w} \cdot \int_0^w t \cdot f(t)\mathrm{d}t / \{1 - F(w) \cdot \overline{G}(r_0)\} + (c_m + c_{fm}) \cdot \int_w^{w+\delta} \lambda(t)\mathrm{d}t + c_r}{\int_0^w t \cdot f(t)\mathrm{d}t / \{1 - F(w) \cdot \overline{G}(r_0)\} + (w+\delta)}.$$
(15)

Under the renewable warranty policy, the age of the product is always equal to w when the warranty is expired, regardless whether it is FMRRW or PMRRW. Thus, from the user's perspective, the expected cost rate during the maintenance period can be formulated as

$$ECR(\delta) = \frac{(c_m + c_{fm}) \int_w^{w+\delta} \lambda(t)\mathrm{d}t + c_r}{\delta},$$
(16)

under both renewable FMRRW and PMRRW policies. Note that the maintenance period is assumed to have a fixed length of δ.

3 Generalized Age Replacement Policy with Minimal Repair-replacement Warranty

In this section, the ARP which was suggested by Barlow and Hunter is generalized to the situation where two-dimensional maintenance actions can be taken upon the product failures [Barlow and Hunter (1960)]. Such an age replacement policy is referred to as a MRRW-ARP in this section. Under the MRRW-ARP, the product is replaced either at the pre-determined PR age or at the FR time of the product, whichever occurs first. The FR is conducted if a failure occurs before reaching the PR age and the failed product cannot be minimally repaired within the repair time threshold. On the other hand, the PR is put in place if either the product reaches the PR age without failures, or all the failures before reaching the PR age can be minimally repaired within the repair time threshold. The life cycle of a product is defined as the inter-replacement time between two successive replacements of the product from the customer's perspective.

The first attempt to incorporate the concept of warranty policy into the ARP was made by Yeh, Chen and Chen (YCC) for non-repairable products under renewing free replacement warranty [Yeh et.al. (2005)]. To obtain the optimal PR age under the ARP, YCC considered both situations where the PR is conducted within the warranty period and the PR is conducted following the warranty period [Yeh et.al. (2005)]. Although in most situations the PR would be planned after the warranty expires from the customer's perspective, there exist certain situations where the customer prefers to replace the product preventively even before the expiration of the warranty rather than wait until the warranty expires. For instance, if the failure cost is extremely high compared to the minimal repair cost, the customer may want the PR action to reduce the failure cost even before the warranty expires because the failure cost is usually borne by the customer with or without the warranty. However, it is reasonable to assume that the PR is planned in general after the warranty expires.

In this section, the two-dimensional maintenance proposed by Park, Jung and Park (PJP) is adapted to define a new MRRW-ARP, which is a generalization of the ARP with respect to the maintenance action when the product failure occurs [Park et.al. (2013)]. Under the MRRW-ARP, the failed product is either minimally repaired or replaced based on the length of repair time, while under the existing ARP, the failed product is immediately replaced by a new one each time a failure occurs. However, the product is preventively replaced at the PR age if the replacement does not occur until reaching the PR age under both policies. Note that under the MRRW-ARP, the product reaches the PR age only when either no failures occur at all or all the failures can be repaired within the repair time threshold and thus no replacement occurs before the PR age.

A renewable free MRRW is incorporated into the MRRW-ARP and several cost models evaluating the maintenance cost of the product is developed and the optimal PR age is determined to minimize the expected cost rate during the life cycle of the product. Under the renewable free MRRW-ARP warranty, it is assumed that both the replacement cost and minimal repair cost are borne by the manufacturer during the warranty period. However, the failure cost which is incurred due to the failure of the product is assumed to be charged to the customer with or without the warranty. The penalty for late delivery, monetary loss due to no operation of the manufacturing process, or other expenses not covered by the warranty even during the warranty period, etc., could be considered as the failure cost. Based on such cost structures, the expected cost rate during the life cycle of the product is evaluated from the perspective of the customer in this section. Similar approaches had been adapted to incorporate the existing ARP and to obtain the optimal PR age in YCC when a free renewable warranty is assumed [Yeh et.al. (2005)].

Let ω denote the length of warranty period when the MRRW-ARP is provided for a repairable product. Under the renewable MRRW-ARP, the life cycle of a product starts with a new purchase of the product and ends either at the PR age, denoted by τ, or at the time of the product's failure if its corresponding repair time exceeds the threshold r, whichever comes first. The product reaches the PR age in cases that either no failures occur during the warranty period or all the failures preceding the PR age are only minimally repaired. Note that the number of minimal repairs carried out during the life cycle of the product is random.

To formulate the warranty cost models under the MRRW-ARP in conjunction with the renewing free warranty from the customer's perspective, it is needed to set a certain cost structure that can be applied during the life cycle of the product. Three possible costs of minimal repair cost, replacement cost and failure cost are assumed to incur when the product fails or the product reaches the PR age. Since the PR is a planned replacement with the product still operating, only the replacement cost is incurred with no failure cost. However, if the failure occurs during the life cycle of the product, the failure cost incurs regardless of whether the failed product is minimally repaired or is replaced. When the replacement occurs due to the product's failure, it is referred to as a failure replacement (FR).

When the failure occurs before reaching the PR age τ and its repair exceeds the repair time threshold, an FR is performed with a failure cost $c_F > 0$ and a replacement cost $c_P > 0$. However, if the repair can be completed within the threshold, only the minimal repair is conducted with the failure cost and the minimal repair cost $c_M > 0$. If the product reaches the PR age τ without experiencing the replacement, then a PR is conducted at the expense of the customer. For the cost structure applicable in this section, it is assumed that under the renewable free MRRW-ARP, both replacement cost and minimal repair cost are charged to the manufacturer during the warranty period.

However, the failure cost is borne by the customer even during the warranty period. Table 1 summarizes the cost structures from both the manufacturer's and the customer's perspectives under the MRRW-ARP during the warranty period. In this section, a cost model is established under the renewable free MRRW-ARP from the customer's perspective to evaluate the expected cost rate during the life cycle of the product. For studying the warranted MRRW-ARP, the cost model is established for two

Table 1   Cost structure upon failure within renewing warranty period

	Customer pays	Manufacturer pays
Minimal repair	c_F	c_M
Failure replacement	c_F	c_P
Preventive replacement	c_P	N/A

cases separately, when $\tau < \omega$ and $\tau \geq \omega$. For completeness of the discussion, the cost model which was developed in PJP under the unwarranted MRRW-ARP is briefly described [Park et.al. (2016)].

3.1   Cost Model for Unwarranted MRRW-ARP

PJP considers an unwarranted MRRW-ARP, under which the product is replaced at the PR age τ [Park et.al. (2016)], or upon the product's failure if the time required for the repair exceeds the repair time threshold r, whichever comes first. Let T be the failure time of the product. Then for an unwarranted case, the length of life cycle which is denoted by $T_0(\tau)$ can be described as

$$T_0(\tau) = \begin{cases} T & T \leq \tau, Y > r \\ \tau & T > \tau \text{ or all products that fail preceding } \tau \text{ are minimally} \\ & \text{repaired} \end{cases}$$

Let $e(\tau)$ represent the expected length of time elapsed until the occurrence of the first replacement before reaching the PR age τ. It can then be shown that

$$e(\tau) = E[T_0(\tau)|T_0(\tau) \leq \tau] = \frac{\int_0^\tau [\overline{F}(t)]^{\overline{G}(r)} dt}{1 - [\overline{F}(\tau)]^{\overline{G}(r)}}.$$

If $N_r(a, b)$ denotes the number of minimal repairs with the repair time threshold r in the interval (a, b), then PJP's model shows that [Park et.al. (2016)]

$$ECR_0(\tau) = \frac{k_1[1 - [\overline{F}(\tau)]^{\overline{G}(r)}] + k_2[\overline{F}(\tau)]^{\overline{G}(r)}}{\int_0^\tau [\overline{F}(t)]^{\overline{G}(r)} dt},$$

where $k_1 = (c_F + c_M) \cdot E[N_r(0, T_0^*(\tau))] + c_F + c_P$, $k_2 = (c_F + c_M) \cdot E[N_r(0, \tau)] +$

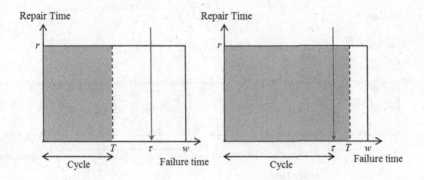

Fig. 2 Two possible situations under which the replacement can take place: $T_1(\tau) < \tau < \omega$ and $T_1(\tau) = \tau$.

c_P, and

$$E[N_r(0,\tau)] = \left[\int_0^\tau \nu(u)\mathrm{d}u\right]G(r)[\overline{F}(\tau)]^{\overline{G}(r)},$$

$$E[N_r(0,T_0{}^*(\tau))] \approx \left[\int_0^{e(\tau)} \nu(u)\mathrm{d}u\right]G(r)[\overline{F}(e(\tau))]^{\overline{G}(r)}. \qquad (17)$$

Here, $T_0{}^*(\tau)$ denotes the length of life cycle of the product when it is less than τ. For more detailed discussions regarding the cost model for unwarranted MRRW-ARP, see PJP [Park et.al. (2016)].

3.2 *Cost Model when PR Occurs within Warranty Period*

The total warranty cost incurred during the life cycle of the product depends on the total number of failures within the warranty period and whether or not such failures can be repaired within the repair time threshold. Let $T_1(\tau)$ denote the length of life cycle of the product in the case where the PR occurs before the renewing MRRW-ARP warranty expires. Then, $\tau < \omega$ in this case and $T_1(\tau)$ can be expressed as

$$T_1(\tau) = \begin{cases} T & T \le \tau < \omega \text{ and } Y > r \\ \tau & \tau < T < \omega \text{ or all products that fail preceding } \tau \text{ are minimally} \\ & \text{repaired} \end{cases}$$

Because the replacement occurs within the warranty period, the customer is responsible only for each failure cost. Thus, the total cost incurred

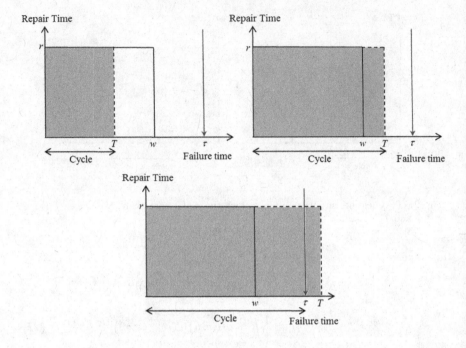

Fig. 3   Three possible replacements when $\tau \geq \omega$.

during the life cycle of the product from the customer's perspective, denoted by $C_1(\tau)$, can be evaluated as

$$C_1(\tau) = \begin{cases} c_F \cdot N_r(0, T_1(\tau)) + c_F & T_1(\tau) < \tau < \omega \\ c_F \cdot N_r(0, \tau) + c_P & T_1(\tau) = \tau < \omega \end{cases}. \tag{18}$$

Because the expected length of life cycle is exactly the same as that of the unwarranted case, except that the PR age occurs within the warranty period, it is considered that $E[T_1(\tau)] = E[T_0(\tau)]$ and $E[N_r(0, T_1{}^*(\tau))] = E[N_r(0, T_0{}^*(\tau))]$. Here, $T_1{}^*(\tau)$ is the length of the life cycle when $T_1(\tau) < \tau$. Thus, by using 18, the expected cost rate can be evaluated as

$$ECR_1(\tau) = \frac{k_3 \cdot (1 - \overline{F}(\tau)^{\overline{G}(r)}) + k_4 \cdot \overline{F}(\tau)^{\overline{G}(r)}}{\int_0^\tau [\overline{F}(t)]^{\overline{G}(r)} \, \mathrm{d}t} \tag{19}$$

3.3 Cost Model when PR is Applied after Warranty Expires

In the next, a situation is considered where the PR age τ is set after the renewable MRRW-ARP warranty expires. Let $T_2(\tau)$ denote the length of life cycle of the product when $\tau \geq \omega$. In this case, there are three possible situations under which the replacement can take place: $T_2(\tau) \leq \omega \leq \tau$, $\omega < T_2(\tau) < \tau$, and $T_2(\tau) = \tau$. Fig. 3 illustrates the life cycle of the product when the PR occurs after the renewable MRRW-ARP warranty expires. Under the MRRW-ARP with $\tau \geq \omega$, the life cycle of the product can be expressed as

$$T_2(\tau) = \begin{cases} T & T \geq \omega \text{ and } Y > r \\ T & \omega < T < \tau \text{ and } Y > r \\ \tau & T \geq \tau \text{ or all products that fail preceding } \tau \text{ are minimally} \\ & \text{repaired} \end{cases}$$

The total cost incurred during the life cycle of the product from the customer's perspective when $\tau \geq \omega$, denoted by $C_2(\tau)$, can be evaluated by

$$C_2(\tau) = \begin{cases} c_F \cdot N_r(0, T_2(\tau)) + c_F & T_2(\tau) < \omega \\ c_F \cdot N_r(0, \omega) + (c_F + c_M) \cdot N_r(\omega, T_2(\tau)) + c_F + c_P & \omega \geq T_2(\tau) < \tau \\ c_F \cdot N_r(0, \omega) + (c_F + c_M) \cdot N_r(\omega, \tau) + c_P & T_2(\tau) = \tau \end{cases}.$$

$$(20)$$

Again, because the expected length of life cycle can be evaluated in the same manner as that of the unwarranted case, except the fact that the PR age falls after the expiration of the warranty, it is considered that $E[T_2(\tau)] = E[T_0(\tau)]$ and $E[N_r(0, T_2^*(\tau))] = E[N_r(0, T_2^{**}(\tau))] = E[N_r(0, T_0^*(\tau))]$, where $T_2^*(\tau)$ and $T_2^{**}(\tau)$ are the lengths of the life cycle when $T_2(\tau) < \omega$ and $\leq T_2(\tau) < \tau$, respectively. Thus, by using (20), the expected cost rate can be evaluated as

$$ECR_2(\tau) = \frac{k_5(1 - \overline{F}(\omega)^{\overline{G}(r)}) + k_6(\overline{F}(\omega)^{\overline{G}(r)} - \overline{F}(\tau)^{\overline{G}(r)}) + k_7(\overline{F}(\tau)^{\overline{G}(r)})}{\int_0^\tau [\overline{F}(t)]^{\overline{G}(r)} dt},$$

$$(21)$$

where

$$k_5 = c_F \cdot E[N_r(0, T_2^*(\tau))] + c_F,$$

$$k_6 = c_F \cdot E[N_r(0, \omega)] + (c_F + c_M) \cdot E[N_r(\omega, T_2^{**}(\tau))] + c_F + c_P,$$

$$\tilde{k}_7 = c_F \cdot E[N_r(0, \omega)] + (c_F + c_M) \cdot E[N_r(\omega, \tau)] + c_P,$$

$$E[N_r(0, \omega)] = \left[\int_0^w \nu(u) du \right] G(r) [\overline{F}(w)]^{\overline{G}(r)},$$

$$E[N_r(\omega, \tau)] = \left[\int_w^\tau \nu(u) du \right] G(r) [\overline{F}(\tau)]^{\overline{G}(r)},$$

and

$$E[N_r(\omega, T_2^{**}(\tau))] = E[N_r 0, T_2^{**}(\tau))] - E[N_r(0, w)].$$

4   Conclusion

The main purpose of this chapter is to incorporate the concept of MRRW into the long-standing age replacement policy suggested by Barlow and Hunter (1960) and is to determine the optimal preventive replacement (PR) age by minimizing the expected cost rate during the productfs life cycle. In this study, we formulate the warranty cost model from the customerfs perspective during the life cycle of the repairable product and determine the optimal PR age under the renewable free MRRW-ARP. As the objective criterion for the optimality, we adapt the expected cost rate during the productfs life cycle. For the cost structure, the minimal repair cost and replacement cost are borne by the manufacturer during the warranty period and the failure cost is charged to the customer, regardless of whether the product is with warranty or without warranty. In this chapter, a new maintenance model, MRRW-ARP, which incorporates the concept of repair time threshold into the original age replacement model is suggested and the optimal preventive replacement age is derived based on the MRRW-ARP. While PJP (2016b) extends Barlow and Hunterfs (1960) age replacement model by consideration of two factors of failure time and repair time and examines its basic properties with no warranty implemented, this chapter deals with the MRRW policy in conjunction with PJPfs (2016b) model to propose an optimal preventive replacement age. Both of these studies were carried out from the customerfs perspective. It would be an interesting future study to examine MRRW-ARP from the manufacturerfs point of view. In this case, the manufacturer is responsible only during the warranty period and thus the formulation of the warranty cost model will be entirely different from the ones derived in this chapter.

References

Barlow, R.E. and Hunter, L. (1960). Optimum preventive maintenance policies, *Operations Research*, 8, pp. 90–100.

Barlow, R.E. and Proschan, F. (1996). *Mathematical Theory of Reliability vol. 17*, Siam.

Sheu, S. and Chien, Y. (2004). Optimal age-replacement policy of a system subject to shocks with random lead-time, *European Journal of Operational Research*, 159, pp. 132–144.

Yeh, R., Chen, G. and Chen, M. (2005). Optimal age-replacement policy for nonrepairable products under renewing free-replacement warranty, *IEEE Transactions on Reliability.* 54, pp. 92–97.

Chien, Y.-H. (2008). Optimal age-replacement policy under an imperfect renewing free-replacement warranty, *IEEE Transactions on Reliability*, 57, pp. 125–133.

Chien, Y.-H. (2010). Optimal age for preventive replacement under a combined fully renewable free replacement with a pro-rata warranty, *International Journal of Production Economics*, 124, pp. 198–205.

Chien, Y.-H. and Chen, J.-A. (2007). Optimal age-replacement policy for repairable products under renewing free-replacement warranty, *International Journal of Systems Science*, 38, pp. 759–769.

Sahin, I. and Polatoglu, H. (1996). Maintenance strategies following the expiration of warranty, *IEEE transactions on reliability*, 45, pp. 220–228.

Chukova, S., Hayakawa, Y. and Johnston, M. (2007). Optimal two-dimensional warranty repair strategy, *Proceedings of the Institution of Mechanical Engineers, Part O: Journal of Risk and Reliability*, 221, pp. 265–273.

Iskandar, B., Murthy, D. and Jack, N. (2005). A new repair-replace strategy for items sold with a two-dimensional warranty, *Computers and Operations Research*, 32, pp. 669–682.

Park, M., Jung, K. M. and Park, D. H. (2013). Optimal post-warranty policy with repair time threshold for minimal repair, *Reliability Engineering and System Safety*, 111, pp. 147–153.

Park, M., Jung, K. M. and Park, D. H. (2016). A generalized age replacement policy for systems under renewing repair-replacement warranty, *IEEE Transactions on Reliability*, 65, pp. 604–612.

Rigdon, S. E. and Basu, A. P. (1998). The power law process: a model for the reliability of repairable systems, *Journal of Quality Technology*, 21, pp. 251–260.

Rardin, R. (1998). Optimization in operations research, *Prentice Hall*.

Chapter 16

General Inspection Models with Renewal Points

Mingchih Chen[1], Xufeng Zhao[2] and Toshio Nakagawa[3]

[1] *Graduate Institute of Business Administration,*
Fu Jen Catholic University,

[2] *Department of Mechanical and Industrial Engineering,*
Qatar University,

[3] *Department of Business Administration,*
Aichi Institute of Technology

1   Introduction

Most systems have to be checked at suitable times to detect their failures, which are called inspection policies in reliability theory. Optimal times of inspection intervals to minimize the total expected costs until failure detection were derived [Barlow and Proscham (1965)] and various inspection models and their computations were summarized [Nakagawa (2005)]. When the systems are operating for successive working cycles, it has been proposed that making maintenances, e.g., inspection, maintenance and replacement, in a strict periodic fashion is impossible or impractical in practice [Nakagawa (2014)]. For such systems, random inspection policies in which they are conducted at random times or at the completion of working times were modeled in theory and their applications in detecting faults for computer systems were discussed [Nakagawa et al. (2010); Nakagawa et al. (2011); Zhao et al. (2014); Chen et al. (2014)].

Recently, when the failure time follows an exponential distribution, the policies of inspection first and last were modeled to fit for the successive running operations, using the new approaches of whichever occurs first and last [Zhao and Nakagawa (2015)], and their optimal policies were obtained and compared analytically. Furthermore, combining periodic and random policies, inspection overtime in which systems are checked at the first completion of working cycle over a planned time T was proposed and comparisons among inspection first, last and overtime were discussed [Zhao and Nakagawa (2015)].

It would be of interest to formulate the general inspection models, combing the constant and random policies to satisfy the commonly planned and randomly needed inspection times. This chapter firstly considers a random inspection policy in which the unit is checked at random times forming a renewal process [Nakagawa (2011)]. By formulating the inter-arrival distributions of inspection times in renewal theory [Osaki (1992)], the policies of inspection first, inspection last, and inspection overtime are investigated. The general models of inspection first and last with constant inspection time T and n variables of inspection times intervals are formulated.

Furthermore, inspection models with three variables T, Y_1 and Y_2 are investigated, of which a new inspection model called inspection middle is proposed. We derive the expected cost rates and optimal policies to minimize them when the distribution of failure time is exponential. Finally, we summarize the comparison results among inspection first, last and middle.

2 Random Inspection Models

It is assumed that an operating unit has a failure distribution $F(t)$ with finite mean $1/\lambda \equiv \int_0^\infty \overline{F}(t)dt < \infty$, where $\overline{\Phi}(t) \equiv 1 - \Phi(t)$ for any function $\Phi(t)$. The unit is checked at random times $S_j \equiv Y_1 + Y_2 + \cdots + Y_j$ ($j = 1, 2, \cdots$), where $S_0 \equiv Y_0 \equiv 0$, and random variables Y_j are independent with each other and have an identical distribution $G(t) \equiv \Pr\{Y_j \leq t\}$ with finite mean $1/\theta \equiv \int_0^\infty \overline{G}(t)dt$ ($0 < \theta < \infty$).

Denoting $G^{(j)}(t) \equiv \Pr\{S_j \leq t\}$ ($j = 1, 2, \cdots$) as the j-fold Stieltjes convolution of $G(t)$ with itself, where $G^{(0)}(t) \equiv 1$ for $t \geq 0$, and $M(t) \equiv \sum_{j=1}^\infty G^{(j)}(t)$, which represents the expected number of random inspections conducted during $(0, t]$, so that random inspection times S_j form a renewal process with a renewal function $M(t)$.

Let c_R be the cost for each inspection and c_D be the down time cost per unit of time for the interval elapsed from failure to its detection at the forthcoming inspection. Then, the total expected cost until failure detection is [Nakagawa (2005)]

$$C_R(G) =$$

$$\sum_{j=0}^{\infty} \int_0^{\infty} \left(\int_0^t \left\{ \int_{t-x}^{\infty} [(j+1)c_R + c_D(x+y-t)] dG(y) \right\} dG^{(j)}(x) \right) dF(t)$$

$$= \left(c_R + \frac{c_D}{\theta} \right) \left[1 + \int_0^{\infty} \overline{F}(t) dM(t) \right] - \frac{c_D}{\lambda}. \tag{1}$$

When $F(t) = 1 - e^{-\lambda t}$, noting that

$$\int_0^{\infty} e^{-\lambda t} dM(t) = \frac{G^*(\lambda)}{1 - G^*(\lambda)},$$

where $\Phi^*(\lambda) \equiv \int_0^{\infty} e^{-\lambda t} d\Phi(t)$ for $\lambda > 0$ and any function $\Phi(t)$, (1) becomes

$$C_R(G) = \frac{c_R + c_D/\theta}{1 - G^*(\lambda)} - \frac{c_D}{\lambda}. \tag{2}$$

2.1 *Inspection First, Last and Overtime*

We consider the following policies of inspection first, inspection last and inspection overtime:

(1) Inspection First

Suppose that the unit is checked at times T or Y_j, whichever occurs first. Then, by setting $Z_j \equiv \min\{T, Y_j\}$ $(j = 1, 2, \cdots)$, Z_j has a distribution

$$G_F(t) \equiv \Pr\{Z_j \le t\} = \begin{cases} G(t) & t < T, \\ 1 & t \ge T, \end{cases}$$

and has a mean time

$$\frac{1}{\theta_F} \equiv E\{Z_j\} = \int_0^{\infty} \overline{G}_F(t) dt = \int_0^T \overline{G}(t) dt.$$

Thus, from (1), the expected cost is

$$C_R(G_F) = \left(c_R + \frac{c_D}{\theta_F} \right) \left[1 + \int_0^{\infty} \overline{F}(t) dM_F(t) \right] - \frac{c_D}{\lambda}, \tag{3}$$

where $M_F(t) \equiv \sum_{j=1}^{\infty} G_F^{(j)}(t)$.

When $F(t) = 1 - e^{-\lambda t}$, noting that

$$G_F^*(\lambda) = \int_0^{\infty} e^{-\lambda t} dG_F(t) = e^{-\lambda T} + \int_0^T G(t) \lambda e^{-\lambda t} dt,$$

we have

$$M_F^*(\lambda) + 1 = \frac{1}{\int_0^T \overline{G}(t)\lambda e^{-\lambda t}dt}.$$

Thus, (3) becomes

$$C_F(T) = \frac{c_R + c_D \int_0^T \overline{G}(t)dt}{\int_0^T \overline{G}(t)\lambda e^{-\lambda t}dt} - \frac{c_D}{\lambda}. \tag{4}$$

(2) Inspection Last

Suppose that the unit is checked at times T or Y_j, whichever occurs last. Then, by setting $\widetilde{Z}_j \equiv \max\{T, Y_j\}$ ($j = 1, 2, \cdots$), $\widetilde{Z}_j$ has a distribution

$$G_L(t) \equiv \Pr\{\widetilde{Z}_j \le t\} = \begin{cases} 0 & t < T, \\ G(t) & t \ge T, \end{cases}$$

and has a mean time

$$\frac{1}{\theta_L} \equiv E\{\widetilde{Z}_j\} = \int_0^\infty \overline{G}_L(t)dt = T + \int_T^\infty \overline{G}(t)dt.$$

Thus, from (1), the expected cost is

$$C_R(G_L) = \left(c_R + \frac{c_D}{\theta_L}\right)\left[1 + \int_0^\infty \overline{F}(t)dM_L(t)\right] - \frac{c_D}{\lambda}, \tag{5}$$

where $M_L(t) \equiv \sum_{j=1}^\infty G_L^{(j)}(t)$.

When $F(t) = 1 - e^{-\lambda t}$, noting that

$$G_L^*(\lambda) = \int_0^\infty e^{-\lambda t}dG_L(t) = \int_T^\infty G(t)\lambda e^{-\lambda t}dt,$$

we have

$$M_L^*(\lambda) + 1 = \frac{1}{1 - \int_T^\infty G(t)\lambda e^{-\lambda t}dt}.$$

Thus, (5) becomes

$$C_L(T) = \frac{c_R + c_D[T + \int_T^\infty \overline{G}(t)dt]}{1 - \int_T^\infty G(t)\lambda e^{-\lambda t}dt} - \frac{c_D}{\lambda}. \tag{6}$$

Clearly, $C_L(0) = C_F(\infty) = C_R(G)$ in (2).

(3) Inspection Overtime

Suppose that the unit is checked at the first completion of some Y_j over time T. Then $\widehat{Z}_j \equiv Y_1 + Y_2 + \cdots + Y_j$ has a distribution

$$G_O(t) \equiv \Pr\{\widehat{Z}_j \leq t\} = \begin{cases} 0 & t < T, \\ \sum_{i=0}^{\infty} \int_0^T [G(t-u) - G(T-u)]dG^{(i)}(u) & t \geq T, \end{cases}$$

and has a mean time

$$\frac{1}{\theta_O} \equiv E\{\widehat{Z}_j\} = T + \sum_{i=0}^{\infty} \int_T^{\infty} \left[\int_0^T \overline{G}(t-u)dG^{(i)}(u) \right] dt.$$

Thus, from (1), the expected cost is

$$C_R(G_O) = \left(c_R + \frac{c_D}{\theta} \right) \left[1 + \int_0^{\infty} \overline{F}(t)dM_O(t) \right] - \frac{c_D}{\lambda}, \tag{7}$$

where $M_O(t) \equiv \sum_{j=1}^{\infty} G_O^{(j)}(t)$.

When $F(t) = 1 - e^{-\lambda t}$ and $G(t) = 1 - e^{-\theta t}$,

$$G_O^*(\lambda) = \sum_{i=0}^{\infty} \int_T^{\infty} \left\{ \int_0^T [e^{-\theta(T-u)} - e^{-\theta(t-u)}]dG^{(i)}(u) \right\} \lambda e^{-\lambda t} dt$$

$$= \frac{\theta}{\theta + \lambda} e^{-\lambda T},$$

and

$$\frac{1}{\theta_O} = T + \sum_{i=0}^{\infty} \int_T^{\infty} \left[\int_0^T \theta e^{-\theta(t-u)}dG^{(i)}(u) \right] dt = T + \frac{1}{\theta}.$$

Thus, (7) becomes

$$C_O(T) = \frac{c_R + c_D(T + 1/\theta)}{1 - [\theta/(\theta + \lambda)]e^{-\lambda T}} - \frac{c_D}{\lambda}. \tag{8}$$

2.2 Optimum Policies

We find optimum inspection times T_F^*, T_L^* and T_O^* to minimize $C_F(T)$, $C_L(T)$ and $C_O(T)$, respectively, when $F(t) = 1 - e^{-\lambda t}$ and $G(t) = 1 - e^{-\theta t}$.

From (4), the expected cost of inspection first is

$$C_F(T) = \frac{c_R + (c_D/\theta)(1 - e^{-\theta T})}{[\lambda/(\theta + \lambda)][1 - e^{-(\theta+\lambda)T}]} - \frac{c_D}{\lambda}. \tag{9}$$

In particular, when $\theta \to 0$, i.e., the unit is inspected only at time T,

$$C(T) = \frac{c_R + c_D T}{1 - e^{-\lambda T}} - \frac{c_D}{\lambda}, \tag{10}$$

which agrees with the expected cost of periodic inspection. Optimum T^* to minimize $C(T)$ satisfies

$$\frac{1}{\lambda}(e^{\lambda T} - 1) - T = \frac{c_R}{c_D}, \tag{11}$$

and the resulting cost is

$$C(T^*) = \frac{c_D}{\lambda}(e^{\lambda T^*} - 1). \tag{12}$$

Differentiating $C_F(T)$ with respect to T and setting it equal to zero,

$$\frac{1}{\theta + \lambda}(e^{\lambda T} - 1) - \frac{\lambda}{\theta(\theta + \lambda)}(1 - e^{-\theta T}) = \frac{c_R}{c_D}, \tag{13}$$

whose left-hand side increases strictly with T from 0 to ∞. Thus, there exists a finite and unique T_F^* $(0 < T_F^* < \infty)$ which satisfies (13), and the resulting cost is

$$C_F(T_F^*) = \frac{c_D}{\lambda}(e^{\lambda T_F^*} - 1). \tag{14}$$

In addition, the left-hand side of (13) increases strictly with $1/\theta$ from 0 to that of (11), and so that, T_F^* decreases strictly with $1/\theta$ to T^* and $T_F^* > T^*$.

From (6), the expected cost of inspection last is

$$C_L(T) = \frac{c_R + (c_D/\theta)(\theta T + e^{-\theta T})}{1 - e^{-\lambda T} + [\lambda/(\theta + \lambda)]e^{-(\theta + \lambda)T}} - \frac{c_D}{\lambda}. \tag{15}$$

Differentiating $C_L(T)$ with respect to T and setting it equal to zero,

$$\frac{1}{\lambda}[e^{\lambda T} - (1 + \lambda T)] - \frac{\lambda}{\theta(\theta + \lambda)}e^{-\theta T} = \frac{c_R}{c_D}, \tag{16}$$

whose left-hand side increases strictly with T from $-\lambda/[\theta(\theta + \lambda)]$ to ∞. Thus, there exists a finite and unique T_L^* $(0 < T_L^* < \infty)$ which satisfies (16), and the resulting cost is

$$C_L(T_L^*) = \frac{c_D}{\lambda}(e^{\lambda T_L^*} - 1). \tag{17}$$

In addition, the left-hand side of (16) decreases with $1/\theta$ from that of (11), and so that, T_L^* increases strictly with $1/\theta$ from T^* and $T_L^* > T^*$.

Finally, differentiating $C_O(T)$ with respect to T and setting it equal to zero,

$$\left(\frac{1}{\lambda} + \frac{1}{\theta}\right)(e^{\lambda T} - 1) - T = \frac{c_R}{c_D}, \tag{18}$$

whose left-hand side increases strictly with T from 0 to ∞. Thus, there exists a finite and unique T_O^* $(0 < T_O^* < \infty)$ which satisfies (18), and the resulting cost is

$$C_O(T_O^*) = \frac{c_D}{\lambda}\left[\left(1 + \frac{\lambda}{\theta}\right)e^{\lambda T_O^*} - 1\right]. \tag{19}$$

In addition, the left-hand side of (18) increases strictly with $1/\theta$ from that of (11), and so that, T_O^* decreases strictly with $1/\theta$ from T^* and $T_O^* < T^*$.

On the other hand, comparing the left-hand sides of (11) and (18),

$$\frac{1}{\lambda}(e^{\lambda T} - 1) - T < \left(\frac{1}{\lambda} + \frac{1}{\theta}\right)(e^{\lambda T} - 1) - T$$
$$< \frac{1}{\lambda}[e^{\lambda(T+1/\theta)} - 1] - \left(T + \frac{1}{\theta}\right), \tag{20}$$

which follows that $T_O^* < T^* < T_O^* + 1/\theta$. Thus, from (12) and (19), $C(T^*) < C_O(T_O^*)$, i.e., periodic inspection is better than inspection overtime.

Similarly, comparing the left-hand sides of (13) and (18),

$$\frac{\theta + \lambda}{\lambda}(e^{\lambda T} - 1) - \theta T - \frac{\theta}{\theta + \lambda}(e^{\lambda T} - 1) + \frac{\lambda}{\theta + \lambda}(1 - e^{-\theta T})$$
$$> \frac{\lambda^2 T}{\theta + \lambda} + \frac{\lambda}{\theta + \lambda}(1 - e^{-\theta T}) > 0, \tag{21}$$

which follows that $T_O^* < T_F^*$, and comparing the left-hand sides of (16) and (18), $T_O^* < T_L^*$.

Next, comparing the left-hand sides of (13) and (16),

$$L_{LF}(T) \equiv \frac{\theta}{\lambda}[e^{\lambda T} - (1 + \lambda T)] - \frac{\lambda}{\theta + \lambda}e^{-\theta T}$$
$$- \frac{\theta}{\theta + \lambda}(e^{\lambda T} - 1) + \frac{\lambda}{\theta + \lambda}(1 - e^{-\theta T}), \tag{22}$$

which increases strictly with T from $-\lambda/(\theta + \lambda)$ to ∞. Thus, there exists a finite and unique T_{LF} $(0 < T_{LF} < \infty)$ which satisfies $L_{LF}(T) = 0$. Thus, from (13), if

$$L_F(T_{LF}) = \frac{1}{\theta + \lambda}(e^{\lambda T_{LF}} - 1) - \frac{\lambda}{\theta(\theta + \lambda)}(1 - e^{-\theta T_{LF}}) \geq \frac{c_R}{c_D},$$

then $T_F^* \leq T_L^*$, and from (14) and (17), $C_F(T_F^*) \leq C_L(T_L^*)$, i.e., inspection first is better than inspection last. Conversely, if $L_{LF}(T_{LF}) < c_R/c_D$, then $T_L^* < T_F^*$, and $C_F(T_F^*) > C_L(T_L^*)$, i.e., inspection last is better than inspection first.

Table 1 presents optimum T_F^* in (13), T_L^* in (16), T_O^* in (18) and T^* in (11) and $L_F(T_{LF})$ for $1/\theta$ and c_R/c_D when $F(t) = 1 - e^{-t}$. As shown above, T_F^* decreases with $1/\theta$ to T^* and T_L^* increases with $1/\theta$ from T^* and $T_L^* < T^* < T_F^*$, and $T_O^* < T^* < T_O^* + 1/\theta$. Furthermore, when $1/\theta = 0.5$, $T_F^* < T_L^*$ for $L_F(T_{LF}) = 0.140 > c_R/c_D$, and inspection first is better than inspection last. Conversely, $T_L^* < T_F^*$ for $c_R/c_D > 0.140$, and inspection last is better than inspection first.

Table 1   Optimum T_F^*, T_L^*, T_O^*, T^* and $L_F(T_{LF})$ when $F(t) = 1 - e^{-t}$.

c_R/c_D	$1/\theta = 0.1$			$1/\theta = 0.5$			
	T_F^*	T_L^*	T_O^*	T_F^*	T_L^*	T_O^*	T^*
0.01	0.176	0.151	0.071	0.145	0.389	0.019	0.138
0.02	0.273	0.199	0.119	0.206	0.405	0.038	0.194
0.05	0.500	0.302	0.218	0.331	0.449	0.088	0.300
0.10	0.788	0.416	0.330	0.474	0.516	0.160	0.416
0.20	1.194	0.572	0.483	0.679	0.630	0.275	0.572
0.50	1.887	0.858	0.766	1.079	0.878	0.518	0.858
1.00	2.493	1.146	1.053	1.499	1.154	0.783	1.146
2.00	3.140	1.505	1.411	2.014	1.508	1.126	1.505
5.00	4.027	2.091	1.996	2.803	2.091	1.698	2.091
10.00	4.710	2.611	2.516	3.450	2.611	2.213	2.611
$L_F(T_{LF})$	0.006			0.140			

3   General Inspection Models

We extend inspection first and last to the general models with constant inspection time T and n random variables of inspection times and obtain their optimum policies analytically.

Suppose that the unit is inspected at time T or at random times $Y_{1j}, Y_{2j}, \cdots, Y_{nj}$ $(j = 1, 2, \cdots)$, whichever occurs first, where Y_{ij} $(i = 1, 2, \cdots, n)$ have an identical distribution $G_i(t) \equiv \Pr\{Y_{ij} \leq t\}$ with finite mean $1/\theta_i$ $(0 < \theta_i < \infty)$ for $j = 1, 2, \cdots$. Then, by setting $Z_{jn} \equiv \min\{T, Y_{1j}, \cdots, Y_{nj}\}$ $(j = 1, 2, \cdots)$, Z_{jn} has a distribution

$$G_{Fn}(t) \equiv \Pr\{Z_{jn} \leq t\} = \begin{cases} 1 - \prod_{i=1}^n \overline{G}_i(t) & t < T, \\ 1 & t \geq T, \end{cases}$$

and has a mean time

$$\frac{1}{\theta_{Fn}} \equiv E\{Z_{jn}\} = \int_0^\infty \overline{G}_{Fn}(t)\mathrm{d}t = \int_0^T \left[\prod_{i=1}^n \overline{G}_i(t)\right]\mathrm{d}t.$$

Thus, from (3), the expected cost is

$$C_R(G_{Fn}) = \left(c_R + \frac{c_D}{\theta_F}\right)\left[1 + \int_0^\infty \overline{F}(t)\mathrm{d}M_{Fn}(t)\right] - \frac{c_D}{\lambda}, \qquad (23)$$

where $M_{Fn}(t) \equiv \sum_{j=1}^\infty G_{Fn}^{(j)}(t)$.

When $F(t) = 1 - \mathrm{e}^{-\lambda t}$, noting that

$$G_{Fn}^*(\lambda) = \int_0^\infty \mathrm{e}^{-\lambda t}\mathrm{d}G_{Fn}(t) = 1 - \int_0^T \left[\prod_{i=1}^n \overline{G}_i(t)\lambda\mathrm{e}^{-\lambda t}\right]\mathrm{d}t,$$

we have

$$1 + M_{Fn}^*(\lambda) = \frac{1}{\int_0^T [\prod_{i=1}^n \overline{G}_i(t)\lambda\mathrm{e}^{-\lambda t}]\mathrm{d}t}.$$

Thus, (23) becomes

$$C_{Fn}(T) = \frac{c_R + c_D \int_0^T [\prod_{i=1}^n \overline{G}_i(t)]\mathrm{d}t}{\int_0^T [\prod_{i=1}^n \overline{G}_i(t)\lambda\mathrm{e}^{-\lambda t}]\mathrm{d}t} - \frac{c_D}{\lambda}. \qquad (24)$$

Optimum T_{Fn}^* to minimize $C_{Fn}(T)$ satisfies

$$\int_0^T \left[\prod_{i=1}^n \overline{G}_i(t)\right][\mathrm{e}^{\lambda(T-t)} - 1]\mathrm{d}t = \frac{c_R}{c_D}, \qquad (25)$$

and the resulting cost is

$$C_{Fn}(T_{Fn}^*) = \frac{c_D}{\lambda}(\mathrm{e}^{\lambda T_{Fn}^*} - 1). \qquad (26)$$

Similarly, when the unit is inspected at time T or at random times $Y_{1j}, Y_{2j}, \cdots, Y_{nj}$ ($j = 1, 2, \cdots$), whichever occurs last. Then, by setting $\widetilde{Z}_{jn} \equiv \max\{T, Y_{1j}, \cdots, Y_{nj}\}$ ($j = 1, 2, \cdots$), $\widetilde{Z}_{jn}$ has a distribution

$$G_{Ln}(t) \equiv \Pr\{\widetilde{Z}_{jn} \le t\} = \begin{cases} 0 & t < T, \\ \prod_{i=1}^n G_i(t) & t \ge T, \end{cases}$$

and has a distribution

$$\frac{1}{\theta_{Ln}} \equiv E\{\widetilde{Z}_{jn}\} = \int_0^\infty \overline{G}_{Ln}(t)\mathrm{d}t = T + \int_T^\infty \left[1 - \prod_{i=1}^n G_i(t)\right]\mathrm{d}t.$$

Thus, from (5), the expected cost is

$$C_R(G_{Ln}) \equiv \left(c_R + \frac{c_D}{\theta_{Ln}}\right)\left[1 + \int_0^\infty \overline{F}(t)\,\mathrm{d}M_{Ln}(t)\right] - \frac{c_D}{\lambda}. \qquad (27)$$

When $F(t) = 1 - e^{-\lambda t}$, noting that

$$G_{Ln}^*(\lambda) = \int_0^\infty e^{-\lambda t}\,\mathrm{d}G_{Ln}(t) = \int_T^\infty \left[\prod_{i=1}^n G_i(t)\right]\lambda e^{-\lambda t}\mathrm{d}t,$$

we have

$$M_{Ln}(\lambda) + 1 = \frac{1}{1 - \int_T^\infty [\prod_{i=1}^n G_i(t)]\lambda e^{-\lambda t}\mathrm{d}t}.$$

Thus, (27) becomes

$$C_{Ln}(T) = \frac{c_R + c_D\{T + \int_T^\infty [1 - \prod_{i=1}^n G_i(t)]\mathrm{d}t\}}{1 - \int_T^\infty [\prod_{i=1}^n G_i(t)\lambda e^{-\lambda t}]\mathrm{d}t} - \frac{c_D}{\lambda}. \qquad (28)$$

Optimum T_{Ln}^* to minimize $C_{Ln}(T)$ satisfies

$$\frac{e^{\lambda T} - (1 + \lambda T)}{\lambda} - \int_T^\infty \left[1 - \prod_{i=1}^n G_i(t)\right][1 - e^{-\lambda(t-T)}]\mathrm{d}t = \frac{c_R}{c_D}, \qquad (29)$$

and the resulting cost is

$$C_{Ln}(T_{Ln}^*) = \frac{c_D}{\lambda}(e^{\lambda T_{Ln}^*} - 1). \qquad (30)$$

Furthermore, when c_T is inspection cost at time T and c_i ($i = 1, 2, \cdots, n$) are respective inspection costs at times Y_{ij}, the expected cost in (24) is

$$C_{Fn}(T) = \frac{\begin{array}{c}c_T[\prod_{i=1}^n \overline{G}_i(T)] + c_D \int_0^T [\prod_{i=1}^n \overline{G}_i(t)]\mathrm{d}t \\ + \sum_{i=1}^n c_i \int_0^T [\prod_{j=1,j\neq i}^n \overline{G}_j(t)]\mathrm{d}G_i(t)\end{array}}{\int_0^T [\prod_{i=1}^n \overline{G}_i(t)\lambda e^{-\lambda t}]\mathrm{d}t} - \frac{c_D}{\lambda}, \qquad (31)$$

and (28) is

$$C_{Ln}(T) = \frac{\begin{array}{c}c_T[\prod_{i=1}^n G_i(T)] + c_D\{T + \int_0^T [1 - \prod_{i=1}^n G_i(t)]\mathrm{d}t\} \\ + \sum_{i=1}^n c_i \int_T^\infty [\prod_{j=1,j\neq i}^n \overline{G}_j(t)]\mathrm{d}G_i(t)\end{array}}{1 - \int_T^\infty [\prod_{i=1}^n G_i(t)\lambda e^{-\lambda t}]\mathrm{d}t} - \frac{c_D}{\lambda}. \qquad (32)$$

Table 2 optimum T_{Fn}^* in (25) and T_{Ln}^* in (29) when $F(t) = 1 - e^{-t}$ and $G_i(t) = 1 - e^{-\theta_i t}$ ($i = 1, 2, \cdots, n$), where $1/\theta_i = 0.01, 0.02, 0.05, 0.1, 0.2, 0.5, 1.0, 2.0, 5.0, 10.0$. This indicates that when

$n = 5$, $T^*_{Fn} > T^*_{Ln}$ for all n, and when $n = 10$, $T^*_{Fn} < T^*_{Ln}$ for $c_R/c_D \leq 0.5$ and $T^*_{Fn} > T^*_{Ln}$ for $c_R/c_D \geq 0.10$. This means that if c_R/c_D and n are large, inspection last is better than inspection first.

Table 2   Optimum T^*_{Fn} and T^*_{Ln} when $F(t) = 1 - e^{-t}$ and $G_i(t) = 1 - e^{-\theta_i t}$ ($i = 1, 2, \cdots, n$).

c_R/c_D	$n = 5$		$n = 10$	
	T^*_{Fn}	T^*_{Ln}	T^*_{Fn}	T^*_{Ln}
0.01	1.051	0.151	1.064	2.479
0.02	1.548	0.201	1.563	2.480
0.05	2.319	0.303	2.336	2.483
0.10	2.952	0.417	2.970	2.487
0.20	3.607	0.573	3.625	2.495
0.50	4.488	0.858	4.506	2.520
1.00	5.159	1.146	5.176	2.560
2.00	5.830	1.505	5.846	2.635
5.00	6.717	2.091	6.732	2.831
10.00	7.387	2.611	7.401	3.091

4   Inspection with Three Variables

We consider inspection models with variables T and Y_i ($i = 1, 2$) when $F(t) = 1 - e^{-\lambda t}$, where Y_i have general distributions $\Pr\{Y_i \leq t\} = G_i(t)$ with mean times $1/\theta_i$ ($i = 1, 2$).

4.1   *Inspection First*

Suppose that the unit is checked at times T, Y_1 or Y_2, whichever occurs first. Then, from (24), the expected cost is

$$C_F(T) = \frac{c_R + c_D \int_0^T \overline{G}_1(t)\overline{G}_2(t)dt}{\int_0^T \overline{G}_1(t)\overline{G}_2(t)\lambda e^{-\lambda t}dt} - \frac{c_D}{\lambda}. \tag{33}$$

Optimum T^*_F satisfies

$$\int_0^T \overline{G}_1(t)\overline{G}_2(t)[e^{\lambda(T-t)} - 1]dt = \frac{c_R}{c_D}, \tag{34}$$

and the resulting cost is

$$\lambda C_F(T^*_F) = c_D(e^{\lambda T^*_F} - 1). \tag{35}$$

4.2 Inspection Last

Suppose that the unit is checked at times T, Y_1 or Y_2, whichever occurs last. Then, from (28), the expected cost is

$$C_L(T) = \frac{c_R + c_D\{T + \int_T^\infty [1 - G_1(t)G_2(t)]dt\}}{1 - \int_T^\infty G_1(t)G_2(t)\lambda e^{-\lambda t}dt} - \frac{c_D}{\lambda}. \tag{36}$$

Optimum T_L^* satisfies

$$\frac{e^{\lambda T} - (1 + \lambda T)}{\lambda} - \int_T^\infty [1 - G_1(t)G_2(t)][1 - e^{-\lambda(t-T)}]dt = \frac{c_R}{c_D}, \tag{37}$$

and the resulting cost is

$$\lambda C_L(T_L^*) = c_D(e^{\lambda T_L^*} - 1). \tag{38}$$

4.3 Inspection Middle

Suppose that the unit is checked at times T, Y_1 or Y_2, whichever occurs middle. Then, the probability that the unit is checked at time T without failure is

$$\overline{F}(T)[G_1(T)\overline{G}_2(T) + \overline{G}_1(T)G_2(T)],$$

the probability that the unit is checked at time Y_1 without failure is

$$\int_0^T \overline{F}(t)G_2(t)dG_1(t) + \int_T^\infty \overline{F}(t)\overline{G}_2(t)dG_1(t),$$

the probability that the unit is checked at time Y_2 without failure is

$$\int_0^T \overline{F}(t)G_1(t)dG_2(t) + \int_T^\infty \overline{F}(t)\overline{G}_1(t)dG_2(t).$$

The probability that the failure is detected at time T is

$$F(T)[G_1(T)\overline{G}_2(T) + \overline{G}_1(T)G_2(T)],$$

and the mean time from failure to its detection at T is

$$[G_1(T)\overline{G}_2(T) + \overline{G}_1(T)G_2(T)] \int_0^T (T - u)dF(u). \tag{39}$$

The probability that the failure is detected at time Y_1 is

$$\int_0^T F(t)G_2(t)dG_1(t) + \int_T^\infty F(t)\overline{G}_2(t)dG_1(t),$$

and the mean time from failure to its detection at Y_1 is

$$\int_0^T G_2(t)\left[\int_0^t (t-u)\mathrm{d}F(u)\right]\mathrm{d}G_1(t) + \int_T^\infty \overline{G}_2(t)\left[\int_0^t (t-u)\mathrm{d}F(u)\right]\mathrm{d}G_1(t).$$
(40)

The probability that the failure is detected at time Y_2 is

$$\int_0^T F(t)G_1(t)\mathrm{d}G_2(t) + \int_T^\infty F(t)\overline{G}_1(t)\mathrm{d}G_2(t),$$

and the mean time from failure to its detection at Y_2 is

$$\int_0^T G_1(t)\left[\int_0^t (t-u)\mathrm{d}F(u)\right]\mathrm{d}G_2(t) + \int_T^\infty \overline{G}_1(t)\left[\int_0^t (t-u)\mathrm{d}F(u)\right]\mathrm{d}G_2(t).$$
(41)

Thus, from (39), (40) and (41), the mean time from failure to its detection is

$$[G_1(T)\overline{G}_2(T) + \overline{G}_1(T)G_2(T)]\int_0^T (T-u)\mathrm{d}F(u)$$

$$+ \int_0^T G_2(t)\left[\int_0^t (t-u)\mathrm{d}F(u)\right]\mathrm{d}G_1(t)$$

$$+ \int_T^\infty \overline{G}_2(t)\left[\int_0^t (t-u)\mathrm{d}F(u)\right]\mathrm{d}G_1(t) + \int_0^T G_1(t)\left[\int_0^t (t-u)\mathrm{d}F(u)\right]\mathrm{d}G_2(t)$$

$$+ \int_T^\infty \overline{G}_1(t)\left[\int_0^t (t-u)\mathrm{d}F(u)\right]\mathrm{d}G_2(t)$$

$$= \int_0^T [1 - G_1(t)G_2(t)]F(t)\mathrm{d}t + \int_T^\infty \overline{G}_1(t)\overline{G}_2(t)F(t)\mathrm{d}t.$$
(42)

The expected number of inspections until failure detection is

$$M(T) =$$

$$1 + \left\{1 - \int_0^T [1 - G_1(t)G_2(t)]\mathrm{d}F(t) + \int_T^\infty \overline{G}_1(t)\overline{G}_2(t)\mathrm{d}F(t)\right\}M(T),$$

i.e.,

$$M(T) = \frac{1}{\int_0^T [1 - G_1(t)G_2(t)]\mathrm{d}F(t) + \int_T^\infty \overline{G}_1(t)\overline{G}_2(t)\mathrm{d}F(t)}.$$
(43)

Therefore, the total expected cost is

$$
\begin{aligned}
C_M(T) &= \frac{c_R + c_D\{\int_0^T [1 - G_1(t)G_2(t)]F(t)\mathrm{d}t + \int_T^\infty \overline{G}_1(t)\overline{G}_2(t)F(t)\mathrm{d}t\}}{\int_0^T [1 - G_1(t)G_2(t)]\mathrm{d}F(t) + \int_T^\infty \overline{G}_1(t)\overline{G}_2(t)\mathrm{d}F(t)} \\
&= \frac{c_R + c_D\{\int_0^T [1 - G_1(t)G_2(t)]\mathrm{d}t + \int_T^\infty \overline{G}_1(t)\overline{G}_2(t)\mathrm{d}t\}}{\int_0^T [1 - G_1(t)G_2(t)]\lambda e^{-\lambda t}\mathrm{d}t + \int_T^\infty \overline{G}_1(t)\overline{G}_2(t)\lambda e^{-\lambda t}\mathrm{d}t} - \frac{c_D}{\lambda}.
\end{aligned}
\tag{44}
$$

Clearly,

$$
\lim_{T \to 0} C_M(T) = \lim_{T \to \infty} C_F(T), \quad \lim_{T \to \infty} C_M(T) = \lim_{T \to 0} C_L(T).
$$

Differentiating $C_M(T)$ with respect to T and setting it equal to zero,

$$
\int_0^T [1 - G_1(t)G_2(t)][e^{\lambda(T-t)} - 1]\mathrm{d}t
$$

$$
- \int_T^\infty \overline{G}_1(t)\overline{G}_2(t)[1 - e^{-\lambda(t-T)}]\mathrm{d}t = \frac{c_R}{c_D},
\tag{45}
$$

whose left-hand side increases strictly with T from

$$
- \int_0^\infty \overline{G}_1(t)\overline{G}_2(t)[1 - e^{-\lambda(t-T)}]\mathrm{d}t
$$

to ∞. Thus, there exists a finite and unique T_M^* ($0 < T_M^* < \infty$) which satisfies (45), and the resulting cost is

$$
\lambda C_M(T_M^*) = c_D(e^{\lambda T_M^*} - 1).
\tag{46}
$$

Furthermore, when the unit is checked at $\max\{Y_1, Y_2\}$ before time T, at time T for the cases of $\{Y_1 < T < Y_2\}$ and $\{Y_2 < T < Y_1\}$, or at $\min\{Y_1, Y_2\}$ after time T, the model also agrees with inspection middle in (44), i.e., the approaches of whichever occurs first and last are included within inspection middle.

4.4   *Comparisons*

(1) Inspection First and Middle

Note from (35) and (46) that if $T_M^* < T_F^*$, inspection middle is better than replacement first. We compare the models of inspection first and middle as follows: Let $L_F(T)$ be the left-hand side of (34) and $L_M(T)$ be the left-hand side of (45), and

$$L_{MF}(T) \equiv L_M(T) - L_F(T)$$

$$= \int_0^T [1 - G_1(t)G_2(t)][e^{\lambda(T-t)} - 1]dt - \int_T^\infty \overline{G}_1(t)\overline{G}_2(t)[1 - e^{-\lambda(t-T)}]dt$$

$$- \int_0^T \overline{G}_1(t)\overline{G}_2(t)[e^{\lambda(T-t)} - 1]dt$$

$$= \int_0^T [G_1(t)\overline{G}_2(t) + \overline{G}_1(t)G_2(t)][e^{\lambda(T-t)} - 1]dt$$

$$- \int_T^\infty \overline{G}_1(t)\overline{G}_2(t)[1 - e^{-\lambda(t-T)}]dt, \tag{47}$$

which increases strictly with T from

$$L_{MF}(0) = - \int_0^\infty \overline{G}_1(t)\overline{G}_2(t)(1 - e^{-\lambda t})dt < 0 \tag{48}$$

to ∞. Thus, there exists a finite and unique T_{MF} $(0 < T_{MF} < \infty)$ which satisfies $L_{MF}(T) = 0$.

Therefore, the comparison results are given as:

(i) If $L_M(T_{MF}) \geq c_R/c_D$, then $T_F^* \leq T_M^*$, i.e., inspection first is better than inspection middle.

(ii) If $L_M(T_{MF}) < c_R/c_D$, then $T_F^* > T_M^*$, i.e., inspection middle is better than inspection first.

This indicates that if c_R/c_D becomes larger, we should conduct inspection middle. In other words, if inspection cost c_R is smaller or the downtime cost c_D is larger, the unit should be inspected as earlier as possible, and vice versa.

(2) Inspection Last and Middle

We next compare the models of inspection last and middle as follows: Let $L_L(T)$ be the left-hand side of (37), and

$$L_{LM}(T) \equiv L_L(T) - L_M(T)$$

$$= \int_0^T [e^{\lambda(T-t)} - 1]dt - \int_T^\infty [1 - G_1(t)G_2(t)][1 - e^{-\lambda(t-T)}]dt$$

$$- \int_0^T [1 - G_1(t)G_2(t)][e^{\lambda(T-t)} - 1]dt$$

$$+ \int_T^\infty \overline{G}_1(t)\overline{G}_2(t)[1 - e^{-\lambda(t-T)}]dt$$

$$= \int_0^T G_1(t)G_2(t)[e^{\lambda(T-t)} - 1]dt$$

$$- \int_T^\infty [G_1(t)\overline{G}_2(t) + \overline{G}_1(t)G_2(t)][1 - e^{-\lambda(t-T)}]dt, \tag{49}$$

which increases strictly with T from

$$L_{LM}(0) = - \int_0^\infty [G_1(t)\overline{G}_2(t) + \overline{G}_1(t)G_2(t)](1 - e^{-\lambda t})dt < 0$$

to ∞. Thus, there exists a finite and unique T_{LM} $(0 < T_{LM} < \infty)$ which satisfies $L_{LM}(T) = 0$.

Therefore, the comparison results are given as:

(i) If $L_M(T_{LM}) \geq c_R/c_D$, then $T_M^* \leq T_L^*$, i.e., inspection middle is better than inspection last.
(ii) If $L_M(T_{LM}) < c_R/c_D$, then $T_M^* > T_L^*$, i.e., inspection last is better than inspection middle.

Finally, we summarize the following comparisons of inspection first, last and middle:

(i) If $L_M(T_{MF}) \geq c_R/c_D$ and $L_M(T_{LM}) \geq c_R/c_D$, then $C_F(T_F^*) < C_M(T_M^*) < C_L(T_L^*)$.
(ii) If $L_M(T_{MF}) < c_R/c_D < L_M(T_{LM})$ and $L_F(T_{LF}) \geq c_R/c_D$, then $C_M(T_M^*) < C_F(T_F^*) < C_L(T_L^*)$.
(iii) If $L_M(T_{LM}) < c_R/c_D < L_M(T_{MF})$ and $L_F(T_{LF}) < c_R/c_D$, then $C_M(T_M^*) < C_L(T_L^*) < C_F(T_F^*)$.
(iv) If $L_M(T_{MF}) < c_R/c_D$ and $L_M(T_{LM}) \leq c_R/c_D$, then $C_L(T_L^*) < C_M(T_M^*) < C_F(T_F^*)$.

This means that as c_R/c_D becomes larger, the ranking of inspections moves to inspection first, middle and last, and replacement middle is not the worst policy among the three policies.

Table 3   Optimum T_F^*, T_L^*, T_M^*, $L_M(T_{MF})$ and $L_M(T_{LM})$ when $F(t) = 1 - e^{-t}$ and $G_i(\theta) = 1 - e^{-\theta_i t}$ $(i = 1, 2)$.

c_R/c_D	$1/\theta_1 = 0.1, 1/\theta_2 = 0.5$			$1/\theta_1 = 0.5, 1/\theta_2 = 1.0$		
	T_F^*	T_L^*	T_M^*	T_F^*	T_L^*	T_M^*
0.01	0.186	0.336	0.141	0.148	0.642	0.226
0.02	0.293	0.355	0.200	0.213	0.650	0.258
0.05	0.550	0.408	0.321	0.348	0.675	0.338
0.10	0.869	0.485	0.460	0.507	0.715	0.442
0.20	1.304	0.610	0.660	0.741	0.789	0.598
0.50	2.026	0.871	1.054	1.201	0.974	0.907
1.00	2.645	1.151	1.468	1.674	1.207	1.237
2.00	3.299	1.507	1.979	2.234	1.532	1.659
5.00	4.191	2.091	2.765	3.060	2.098	2.350
10.00	4.875	2.611	3.410	3.722	2.613	2.950
$L_M(T_{MF})$	0.000			0.043		
$L_M(T_{LM})$	0.129			0.803		

(3) Numerical Examples

Table 3 presents optimum T_F^* in (34), T_L^* in (37) and T_M^* in (45) when $F(t) = 1 - e^{-t}$ and $G_i(\theta) = 1 - e^{-\theta_i t}$ $(i = 1, 2)$ for $1/\theta_1 = 0.1, 1/\theta_2 = 0.5$ and $1/\theta_1 = 0.5, 1/\theta_2 = 1.0$. As shown above, $T_M^* < T_F^*$ or $T_M^* < T_L^*$. Furthermore, when $1/\theta_1 = 0.5$ and $1/\theta_2 = 1.0$, $T_F^* < T_M^* < T_L^*$ for $c_R/c_D < 0.043$, $T_M^* < T_F^* < T_L^*$ for $0.043 < c_R/c_D < 0.803$, and $T_L^* < T_M^* < T_F^*$ for $c_R/c_D > 0.803$. This means that inspection middle is better than inspection first or last as c_R/c_D is large.

5   Conclusions

In order to formulate general inspection models with constant inspection time T and random inspection times Y_j $(j = 1, 2, \cdots, n)$, we have firstly obtained the distributions of random inspection times and their mean times to inspection for inspection first, last and overtime. Next, we have extended inspection first and last to the general models with constant inspection time T and n variables Y_{ij} $(i = 1, 2, \cdots, n)$ of inspection times intervals. Finally, when inspections are conducted at three variable times T, Y_1 and Y_2, inspection first, last and middle are discussed analytically and compared with each other. It has been indicated that inspection middle includes the approaches of whichever occurs first and last. It has also been shown that inspection first, last, overtime, and middle can be compared in analytical ways to find which model can be conducted in an economical way.

References

Barlow, R. E. and Proschan, F. (1965). Mathematical Theory of Reliability (Wiley, New York).

Chen, M., Zhao, X., and Nakagawa, T. (2014). Periodic and random inspections for a computer system. In: Nakamura, S. Qian, C. H. and Chen, M. (eds.) Reliability Modeling with Applications (World Scientific, Singapore), pp.249-267.

Nakagawa, T. (2005). Mathematical Theory of Reliability (Springer, London).

Nakagawa, T., Mizitani, S., and Chen, M. (2010). A summary of periodic and random inspection policies. Reliability Engineering & System Safety, **95**, pp.906-911.

Nakagawa, T., Zhao, X., and Yum, W.Y. (2011). Optimal age replacement and inspection policies with random failure and replacement times. International Journal of Reliability Safely Engineering, **18**, pp.1-12.

Nakagawa, T. (2011). Stochastic Processes with Applications to Reliability Theory (Springer, London).

Nakagawa, T. (2014). Random Maintenance Policies (Springer, London).

Osaki, S. (1992) Applied Stochastic System Modeling (Springer, Berlin)

Zhao, X., Chen, M. and Nakagawa, T. (2014). Optimal time and random inspection policies for computer systems. Applied Mathematical Information Science, **82**, pp.413-417.

Zhao, X. and Nakagawa, T. (2015). Optimal periodic and random inspection first, last, and overtime policies. International Journal of System Science, **46**, pp.1648-1660.

Chapter 17

A Summary of Replacement Policies for Continuous Damage Models

Kodo Ito[1], Syouji Nakamura[2] and Nakagawa Toshio[3]

[1] *Faculty of Symbiotic Systems Science,*
Fukushima University,

[2] *Department of Life Management,*
Kinjo Gakuin University,

[3] *Department of Business Administration,*
Aichi Institute of Technology

1 Introduction

Reliability is one of fundamental measures of products and maintenance is indispensable to hold the products in high reliable. Various kinds of maintenance policies are represented and they assumed that states of products have only two states *i.e.*, "normal" and "fail". In case of real products, there exist some states from perfect normal state to perfect fail one, and the practical maintenance of high reliable products can be possible when such states monitoring is considered in establishing maintenance policies. For example, airframes are suffering serious environmental stresses continuously, which may grow cracks on airframes. Because airframes adopt a damage tolerant design, aircraft with innumerable small-scale cracks can operate normally. By adopting suitable maintenance policies, these cracks could be renovated before they would grow up to a catastrophic level.

331

Shocks occur due to time and each shock causes a damage to a product. When shocks occur at a renewal process, the total damage due to each shock is additional, and the product fails according to Palmgrem-Miner rule when cumulative damage exceeds a threshold level [Schijve, J. (2004)]. This is called the cumulative damage model and forms a cumulative processes [Nakagawa, T. (2011)]. Several kinds of damage models were discussed, their maintenance policies were analyzed, and optimal policies were studied analytically [Nakagawa, T. (2007)].

This paper considers continuous damage models where the total damage increases linearly with time t and the unit fails when the total damage exceeds a failure level K [Ito, K. and Nakagawa, T. (2008)]. To prevent failure, the unit is replaced preventively at time $T (0 < T \leq \infty)$. Then, when the total damage increases normally and exponentially, the expected cost rates are obtained, using an age replacement policy [Nakagawa, T. (2005)]. Next, when the unit works for a job with random working times, replacement first, last and overtime [Nakagawa, T. (2014)] for continuous damage models are proposed and their expected cost rates are obtained. Furthermore, applying these models to inspection policies, the total expected costs units failure detection are obtained. Optimal policies which minimize the expected costs are computed numerically.

2   Continuous Damage Model

Suppose that $Z(t)$ represents the total damage at time, and usually increases continuously time from $Z(0) = 0$. Then, we define that $Z(t) \equiv A_t t + B_t$ for $A_t \geq 0$. It is assumed that the unit fails when $Z(t)$ has exceeded a failure level $K > 0$. Then, the reliability at time t is

$$R(t) = \Pr\{Z(t) \leq K\} = \Pr\{A_t t + B_t \leq K\}.$$

(a) When $A_t \equiv \omega$ (constant), $K = k$ (constant) and B_t is distributed normally with mean 0 and variance $\sigma^2 t$,

$$R(t) = \Pr\{B_t \leq k - \omega t\} = \Phi\left(\frac{k - \omega t}{\sigma\sqrt{t}}\right),$$

where $\Phi(x)$ is the standard normal distribution with mean 0 and variance 1, *i.e.*, $\Phi(x) \equiv (1/\sqrt{2\pi}) \int_{-\infty}^{x} \exp(-u^2/2) du$.

(b) When $B_t \equiv 0$, $K = k$ and A_t is distributed normally with mean ω and variance σ^2/t,

$$R(t) = \Pr\left\{A_t \le \frac{k}{t}\right\} = \Phi\left(\frac{k - \omega t}{\sigma\sqrt{t}}\right),$$

which agrees with (a).

(c) When $A_t \equiv \omega$, $B_t \equiv 0$ and K is distributed normally with mean k and variance σ^2,

$$R(t) = \Pr\{\omega t \le K\} = \Phi\left(\frac{k - \omega t}{\sigma}\right).$$

When K is distributed normally with mean k and variance $\sigma^2 t$, $R(t)$ agrees with (a) and (b).

(d) Replacing $\alpha \equiv \sigma/\sqrt{\omega k}$ and $\beta \equiv k/\omega$ in (a) or (b),

$$R(t) = \Phi\left[\frac{1}{\alpha}\left(\sqrt{\frac{\beta}{t}} - \sqrt{\frac{t}{\beta}}\right)\right],$$

which is called Birnbaum-Saunders distribution [Nakagawa, T. (2007)]. This is widely applied to fatigue failure for material strength subject to stresses [Nakagawa, T. (2007)].

(e) When B_t is a standard Brown motion,

$$Z(t) = \omega t + \sigma B_t,$$

with positive drift ω and variance σ^2 forms the Wiener process or Brownian motion process [Nakagawa, T. (2007)].

3 Age Replacement Policies

When the unit fails when the total damage has exceeded a failure level K for constant K, it is replaced at time T $(0 < T \le \infty)$. Then, the expected cost rate is [Nakagawa, T. (2005)]

$$C(T) = \frac{c_F - (c_F - c_T)R(T)}{\int_0^T R(t)dt}. \tag{1}$$

where $c_T = $ replacement cost at time T and $c_F = $ replacement cost at failure with $c_F > c_T$, and optimal T^* satisfies

$$h(T)\int_0^T R(t)dt + R(T) = \frac{c_F}{c_T - c_T}, \tag{2}$$

where $h(t) \equiv -dR(t)/dt/R(t)$. Using (a)-(e), we consider several replacement policies for a continuous damage model.

Table 1 Optimal T_1^* and $C(T_1^*)$ when $\omega = \sigma^2 = 1$.

$\frac{c_F}{c_T}$	K = 5		K = 10		K = 15		K = 20	
	T_1^*	$\frac{C(T_1^*)}{c_T}$	T_1^*	$\frac{C(T_1^*)}{c_T}$	T_1^*	$\frac{C(T_1^*)}{c_T}$	T_1^*	$\frac{C(T_1^*)}{c_T}$
5	2.5	0.483	6.0	0.198	9.2	0.119	13.1	0.084
10	2.0	0.559	5.1	0.219	8.7	0.130	12.0	0.090
20	1.8	0.626	4.6	0.237	7.8	0.139	11.3	0.095
50	1.6	0.704	4.1	0.260	7.1	0.149	10.6	0.102

3.1 Policy 1

Suppose that $A_t \equiv \omega$ (constant) and B_t is distributed normally with 0 and variance $\sigma^2 t$. Then, from (a),

$$R(t) = \Phi\left(\frac{K - \omega t}{\sigma\sqrt{t}}\right).$$

Similarly, when A_t is distribution normally with mean 0 and variance σ^2/t and $B_t \equiv 0$,

$$R(t) = \Phi\left(\frac{K - \omega t}{\sigma\sqrt{t}}\right). \tag{3}$$

Both cases are equal and the expected cost rate is given in (1). Thus, when $\omega = 1$ and $\sigma^2 = 1$, optimal T_1^* satisfies [Nakagawa, T. (2011)]

$$\frac{(K/T + 1)\phi(K/\sqrt{T} - \sqrt{T})}{2\sqrt{T}\Phi(K/\sqrt{T} - \sqrt{T})} \int_0^T \Phi\left(\frac{K}{\sqrt{t}} - \sqrt{t}\right) dt$$

$$+\Phi\left(\frac{K}{\sqrt{T}} - \sqrt{T}\right) = \frac{c_F}{c_F - c_T}. \tag{4}$$

where $\phi(x) \equiv (1/\sqrt{2\pi})\exp(-x^2/2)$, Table 1 presents optimal T_1^* and expected cost rate $C(T_1^*)$ when $\omega = \sigma^2 = 1$. Optimal T_1^* decreases with c_F/c_T and increases with K. For example, when K is twice, T_1^* becomes twice a little longer.

3.2 Policy 2

Suppose in (e) that $Z(t) = \omega t + B_t$, where B_t has an exponential distribution $[1 - \exp(-x/\sigma\sqrt{t})]$. That is, the total damage usually increases linearly with time t, however, it undegoes positively some change according to an exponential distribution. Then,

$$R(t) = \Pr\{B_t \leq x - \omega t\} = 1 - \exp\left(-\frac{x - \omega t}{\sigma\sqrt{t}}\right). \tag{5}$$

Table 2   Optimal T_2^* and $C(T_2^*)$ when $\omega = \sigma^2 = 1$.

$\frac{c_F}{c_T}$	$K = 5$		$K = 10$		$K = 15$		$K = 20$	
	T_2^*	$\frac{C(T_2^*)}{c_T}$	T_2^*	$\frac{C(T_2^*)}{c_T}$	T_2^*	$\frac{C(T_2^*)}{c_T}$	T_2^*	$\frac{C(T_2^*)}{c_T}$
5	2.2	0.762	4.8	0.292	7.8	0.170	10.9	0.116
10	1.6	1.103	3.8	0.365	6.4	0.205	9.2	0.137
20	1.1	1.336	3.1	0.446	5.3	0.242	7.8	0.159
50	0.8	1.813	2.3	0.568	4.3	0.298	6.5	0.192

Thus, the expected cost rate is [Nakagawa, T. (2011)], from (1),

$$C(T) = \frac{c_K - (c_K - c_T)\{1 - \exp[-(K - \omega T)/\sigma\sqrt{T}]\}}{\int_0^T \{1 - \exp[-(K - \omega t)/\sigma\sqrt{t}]\}dt}, \tag{6}$$

and optimal T^* satisfies

$$\frac{\left(\frac{K}{T} + \omega\right) \exp\left(-\frac{K - \omega T}{\sigma\sqrt{T}}\right)}{2\sigma\sqrt{T}\left[1 - \exp\left(-\frac{K - \omega T}{\sigma\sqrt{T}}\right)\right]} \int_0^T \left[1 - \exp\left(-\frac{K - \omega t}{\sigma\sqrt{t}}\right)\right] dt$$

$$- \exp\left(-\frac{K - \omega T}{\sigma\sqrt{T}}\right) = \frac{c_T}{c_F - c_T}. \tag{7}$$

Table 2 presents optimal T_2^* and expected cost rate $C(T_2^*)/c_T$ when $\omega = \sigma^2 = 1$. Table 2 shows the similar tendencies to Table 1 and optimal values of T_2^* are smaller than those of T_1^*.

3.3   Policy 3

Suppose that the replacement is planned at periodic times jT ($j = 1, 2, \cdots$) for a fixted $T > 0$. When the unit is replaced at time NT or at failure, whichever occurs first, the expected cost rate is [Nakagawa, T. (2007)]

$$C(N) = \frac{c_F - (c_F - c_T)R(NT)}{\int_0^{NT} R(t)dt} \qquad (N = 1, 2, \cdots), \tag{8}$$

and optimal N^* satisfies

$$\frac{R(NT) - R[(N + 1)T]}{\int_{NT}^{(N+1)T} R(t)dt} \int_0^{NT} R(t)dt + R(NT) \geq \frac{c_F}{c_F - c_T}. \tag{9}$$

When A_i is distributed normaly with mean 0 and variance σ^2/t and $B_t \equiv 0$, $R(t)$ is given in (3), and the expected cost rate and optimal N_1^* are derived from (8) and (9), respectively.

When $Z(t) = \omega t + B_t$ where B_t has an exponential distribution [1 −

Table 3   Optimal N_1^* and $C(N_1^*)$ when $\omega = \sigma^2 = 1$.

$\frac{c_F}{c_T}$	K = 5		K = 10		K = 15		K = 20	
	N_1^*	$\frac{C(N_1^*)}{c_T}$	N_1^*	$\frac{C(N_1^*)}{c_T}$	N_1^*	$\frac{C(N_1^*)}{c_T}$	N_1^*	$\frac{C(N_1^*)}{c_T}$
5	3	0.566	7	0.185	11	0.104	16	0.072
10	2	0.749	6	0.203	10	0.111	15	0.074
20	2	1.006	5	0.231	10	0.118	14	0.078
50	2	1.778	5	0.273	9	0.128	13	0.082

Table 4   Optimal N_2^* and $C(N_2^*)$ when $\omega = \sigma^2 = 1$.

$\frac{c_F}{c_T}$	K = 5		K = 10		K = 15		K = 20	
	N_2^*	$\frac{C(N_2^*)}{c_T}$	N_2^*	$\frac{C(N_2^*)}{c_T}$	N_2^*	$\frac{C(N_2^*)}{c_T}$	N_2^*	$\frac{C(N_2^*)}{c_T}$
5	3	0.525	7	0.174	11	0.099	16	0.068
10	2	0.726	6	0.195	10	0.107	15	0.071
20	2	0.975	5	0.226	10	0.113	14	0.075
50	2	1.723	5	0.266	9	0.125	14	0.080

$\exp(-x/\sigma\sqrt{t})$], $R(t)$ is given (5), and the expected cost rate and optimal N_2^* are derived from (8) and (9), respectively.

Table 3 presents optimal N_1^* and expected cost rate $C(N_1^*)/c_T$ and Table 4 presents optimal N_2^* and expected cost rate $C(N_2^*)/c_T$ when $\omega = \sigma^2 = 1$. Both Table 3 and 4 show the similar tendencies to Tables 1 and 2, respectively. These indicate that $T_1^* \leq N_1^*$ and $T_2^* \leq N_2^*$, and $C(N_1^*)$ and $C(N_2^*)$ are greater than $C(T_1^*)$ and $C(T_2^*)$, respectively.

4   Replacement First, Last and Overtime

The unit with continuous damage defined in Sect.2 works for a job with random time Y according to a distribution $G(t) \equiv P_r\{Y \leq t\}$ with finite mean $1/\theta$. Then, we consider the following replacemment first, replacement last, and replacement overtime:

4.1   *Replacement First*

Suppose that the unit is replaced at time T $(0 < T \leq \infty)$, at time Y, or at failure, whichever occurs first. Then, the expected cost rate is [Nakagawa, T. (2014)]

$$C_F(T) = \frac{c_F - (c_F - c_T)R(T)\overline{G}(T) - (c_F - c_R)\int_0^T R(t)dG(t)}{\int_0^T R(t)\overline{G}(t)dt}, \quad (10)$$

and when $c_T = c_R$, optimal T_F^* satisfies

$$\int_0^T R(t)\overline{G}(t)[h(T) - h(t)]dt = \frac{c_F}{c_F - c_T}, \quad (11)$$

where $h(t) \equiv -dR(t)/dt/R(t)$.

When $R(t)$ is given in (3) and $\omega = \sigma^2 = 1$,

$$h(t) = \frac{(K/t + 1)\phi(K/\sqrt{t} - \sqrt{t})}{2\sqrt{t}\phi(K/\sqrt{t} - \sqrt{t})}. \quad (12)$$

Thus, substituting $R(t)$ and $h(t)$ for (11), optimal T_F^* is computed numerically. When $R(t)$ is given in (5),

$$h(t) = \frac{K/t + w}{2\sigma\sqrt{t}\{\exp[(K - wt)/(\sigma\sqrt{t}) - 1]\}}. \quad (13)$$

4.2   Replacement Last

Suppose that the unit is replaced before failure at time T $(0 < T \leq \infty)$ or at time Y, whichever occurn last. Then, the expected cost rate is [5,p.32],

$$C_L(T) = \frac{c_F - (c_F - c_T)R(T)G(T) - (c_F - c_R)\int_T^\infty R(t)dG(t)}{\int_0^T \overline{F}(t)dt + \int_T^\infty R(t)\overline{G}(t)dt}, \quad (14)$$

and when $c_T = c_R$, optimal T_L^* satisfies

$$h(T)\left[\int_0^T R(t)dt + \int_T^\infty R(t)\overline{G}(t)dt\right] + R(T)G(T)$$

$$+ \int_T^\infty R(t)dG(t) = \frac{c_F}{c_F - c_T}. \quad (15)$$

Thus, substituting $R(t)$ and $h(t)$ derived in (1) for (15), optimal T_L^* are computed numerically.

4.3   Replacement Overtime

Suppose that the unit is replaced before failure at the first completion of working times Y_j over time T. Then, when $G(t) = 1 - \exp(-\theta t)$, the expected cost rate is [Nakagawa, T. (2014)]

$$C_O(T) = \frac{c_F - (c_F - c_O) \int_T^\infty R(t)\theta e^{-\theta(t-T)}dt}{\int_0^T R(t)dt + \int_T^\infty R(t)e^{-\theta(t-T)}dt},$$ (16)

and optimal T_O^* satisfies

$$Q(T;\theta) \int_0^T R(t)dt + R(T) = \frac{c_O}{c_F - c_O},$$ (17)

where

$$Q(T;\theta) \equiv -\frac{\int_T^\infty e^{-\theta t}dR(t)}{\int_T^\infty e^{-\theta t}R(t)dt} = \frac{e^{-\theta T}R(T)}{\int_T^\infty e^{-\theta t}R(t)dt} - \theta.$$

When $R(t)$ is given, optimal T_O^* are computed numerically.

4.4   Replacement with Nth Working Time

When the unit is replaced before failure at time T or at a planned number N ($N = 1, 2, \cdots$) of working times, whichever occurs first, the expected cost rate is [5,p.43]

$C_F(T, N)$

$$= \frac{c_F - (c_F - c_T)R(T)\left[1 - G^{(N)}(T)\right] - (c_F - c_N)\int_0^T R(t)dG^{(N)}(t)}{\int_0^T R(t)[1 - G^{(N)}(t)]dt},$$ (18)

where c_T = replacement cost at time T, c_N = replacement cost at work N and c_F = replacement cost at failure with $c_F > c_T$ and $c_F > c_N$.

When the unit is replaced before failure at time T or at work N, whichever occurs last, the expected cost rate is [Nakagawa, T. (2014)]

$C_L(T, N)$

$$= \frac{c_F - (c_F - c_T)R(T)G^{(N)}(T) - (c_F - c_N)\int_0^T R(t)dG^{(N)}(t)}{\int_0^T R(t)dt + \int_T^\infty R(t)[1 - G^{(N)}(t)]dt}.$$ (19)

In particular, when the unit is replaced only at work N ($N = 1, 2, \cdots$), the expected cost rate is

$$C(N) \equiv \lim_{T\to\infty} C_F(T, N) = \lim_{T\to 0} C_L(T, N)$$

$$= \frac{c_F - (c_F - c_N)\int_0^\infty R(t)dG^{(N)}(t)}{\int_0^\infty R(t)[1 - G^{(N)}(t)]dt},$$ (20)

Table 5   Optimal N_3^* and $C(N_3^*)$ when $\omega = \sigma^2 = 1$ and $G(t) = 1 - \exp(-t)$.

$\frac{c_F}{c_N}$	$K = 5$		$K = 10$		$K = 15$		$K = 20$	
	N_3^*	$\frac{C(N_3^*)}{c_N}$	N_3^*	$\frac{C(N_3^*)}{c_N}$	N_3^*	$\frac{C(N_3^*)}{c_N}$	N_3^*	$\frac{C(N_3^*)}{c_N}$
5	1	0.124	2	0.104	4	0.099	4	0.099
10	1	0.136	2	0.107	3	0.101	3	0.100
20	1	0.159	1	0.110	2	0.104	3	0.103
50	1	0.230	1	0.118	2	0.106	2	0.106

Table 6   Optimal N_4^* and $C(N_4^*)$ when $\omega = \sigma^2 = 1$ and $G(t) = 1 - \exp(-t)$.

$\frac{c_F}{c_N}$	$K = 5$		$K = 10$		$K = 15$		$K = 20$	
	N_4^*	$\frac{C(N_4^*)}{c_N}$	N_4^*	$\frac{C(N_4^*)}{c_N}$	N_4^*	$\frac{C(N_4^*)}{c_N}$	N_4^*	$\frac{C(N_4^*)}{c_N}$
5	1	0.182	2	0.136	4	0.122	5	0.114
10	1	0.229	2	0.148	3	0.126	4	0.117
20	1	0.321	1	0.156	2	0.132	4	0.120
50	1	0.599	1	0.174	2	0.140	3	0.125

and optimal N^* satisfies

$$Q_N \int_0^\infty [1 - G^{(N)}(t)]R(t)\mathrm{d}t + \int_0^\infty G^{(N)}(t)\mathrm{d}R(t) \geq \frac{c_F}{c_F - c_N}, \qquad (21)$$

where

$$Q_N \equiv \frac{\int_0^\infty [G^{(N)}(t) - G^{(N+1)}(t)]\mathrm{d}R(t)}{\int_0^\infty [G^{(N)}(t) - G^{(N+1)}(t)]R(t)\mathrm{d}t}.$$

When $R(t)$ is given in (3), then expected cost rate is obtained in (20) and optimal N_3^* are derived from (21). Similarly, when $R(t)$ is given in (5), the expected cost rate and optimal N_4^* are derived from (20) and (21), respectively.

Tables 5 and 6 present optimal N_3^* and N_4^*, and the expected cost rates $C(N_3^*)$ and $C(N_4^*)$ when $\omega = \sigma^2 = 1$ and $G(t) = 1 - \exp(-t)$, respectively. These indicate that $N_4^* \geq N_3^*$ and $C(N_4^*) \geq C(N_3^*)$, as shown in Tables 3 and 4.

4.5   Inspection Policies

The unit is checked at successive time T_j $(j = 1, 2, \cdots)$ where $T_0 = 0$ for a continuous damage model. Then, the expected cost until replacement is

[Nakagawa, T. (2005)]

$$C(T_1, T_2, \cdots) = \sum_{j=0}^{\infty} [c_I + c_D(T_{j+1} - T_j)] R(T_j) - c_D \int_0^{\infty} R(t) dt, \quad (22)$$

where c_I = cost of each check and c_D = cost per unit of time for the elapsed between failure and its detection. Optimal inspection schedule is [Nakagawa, T. (2005)]

$$T_{j+1} - T_j = -\frac{R(T_{j-1}) - R(T_j)}{R'(T_j)} - \frac{c_I}{c_D} \quad (j = 1, 2, \cdots). \quad (23)$$

In particular, when the checking times are periodic, $i.e.$, $T_j \equiv jT$ ($j = 1, 2, \cdots$) for fixed T (> 0), the total expected cost is

$$C(T) = (c_I + c_D T) \sum_{j=0}^{\infty} R(jT) - c_D \int_0^{\infty} R(t) dt, \quad (24)$$

and optimal T^* satisfies

$$\frac{\sum_{j=0}^{\infty} R(jT)}{\sum_{j=0}^{\infty} jR'(jT)} + T + \frac{c_I}{c_D} = 0. \quad (25)$$

Next, suppose that the unit operates for a finite interval $[0, S]$ and is checked at periodic times jT ($j = 1, 2, \cdots, N$) where $S \equiv NT$. Then, the total expected cost unit failure detection is [Schijve, J. (2004)]

$$C(T; S) = \left(c_I + \frac{c_D S}{N}\right) \sum_{j=0}^{N-1} R\left(\frac{jS}{N}\right) - c_D \int_0^S R(t) dt \quad (N = 1, 2, \cdots).$$

$$(26)$$

Thus, computing $C(N)$ for given S and $N = 1, 2, \cdots$, and comparing them, we obtain N^* and $T^* = S/N$. When the unit is checked at time T_j ($j = 1, 2, \cdots, N$) where $T_N = S$, the expected cost is, from (26),

$$C(\mathbf{T}; S) = \sum_{j=0}^{N-1} [c_I + c_D(T_{j+1} - T_j)] R(T_j) - c_D \int_0^S R(t) dt, \quad (27)$$

where $\mathbf{T} = T_1, T_2, \cdots, T_N$. Differentiating $C(\mathbf{T}; S)$ with T_j and setting it equal to zero,

$$T_{j+1} - T_j = -\frac{R(T_{j-1}) - R(T_j)}{R'(T_j)} - \frac{c_I}{c_D} \quad (j = 1, 2, \cdots, N-1). \quad (28)$$

For example, when $N = 3$, the checking times T_1 and T_2 satisfy

$$S - T_2 = -\frac{R(T_1) - R(T_2)}{R'(T_1)} - \frac{c_I}{c_D},$$

$$T_2 - T_1 = -\frac{1 - R(T_1)}{R'(T_1)} - \frac{c_I}{c_D}.$$

and the expected cost is

$$\frac{C(T_1, T_2; S)}{c_D} = \frac{c_I}{c_D} + T_1 + \left(\frac{c_I}{c_D} + T_2 - T_1\right) R(T_1)$$

$$+ \left(\frac{c_I}{c_D} + T_3 - T_2\right) R(T_2),$$

where $T_3 = S$.

From the above discussions, we compute T_j $(j = 1, 2, \cdots, N - 1)$ which satisfies (28), and substituting them for (27), we obtain the expected cost $C(\mathbf{T}; S)$. Next, comparing $C(\mathbf{T}; S)$ for all $N \geq 1$, we can get optimal N^* and times T_j^* $(j = 1, 2, \cdots, N^*)$.

When $R(t) = 1 - \exp[-(x - \omega t)/\sigma\sqrt{t}]$ in (5), the expected cost for periodic inspection is, from (26),

$$\widetilde{C}(T; S) = C(T; S) + c_D \int_0^S R(t)\mathrm{d}t$$

$$= \left(c_I + \frac{c_D S}{N}\right) \sum_{j=0}^{N-1} \left[1 - \exp\left(-\frac{KN - j\omega S}{\sigma\sqrt{jNS}}\right)\right], \qquad (29)$$

where when $j = 0$, $\exp[-(KN - j\omega s)/(\sigma\sqrt{jNS})] \equiv 0$. Optimal T_j^* satisfy

$$T_{j+1} - T_j = 2\sigma\sqrt{T_j} \frac{\exp\left(-\frac{K - \omega T_j}{\sigma\sqrt{T_j}}\right) - \exp\left(-\frac{K - \omega T_{j-1}}{\sigma\sqrt{T_{j-1}}}\right)}{\left(\frac{K}{T_j} + \omega\right) \exp\left(-\frac{K - w T_j}{\sigma\sqrt{T_j}}\right)} - \frac{c_I}{c_D}$$

$$(j = 1, 2, \cdots, N - 1), \qquad (30)$$

and the expected cost is

$$\widetilde{C}(\mathbf{T}; S) = \sum_{j=0}^{N-1} \left\{c_I + c_D(T_{j+1} - T_j)\left[1 - \exp\left(-\frac{K - w T_j}{\sigma\sqrt{T_j}}\right)\right]\right\}, \qquad (31)$$

Tables 7 and 8 present optimal $T_1, T_2, \cdots, T_N$ and the expected cost $\widetilde{C}(\mathbf{T}, S)/c_D$ for $c_I/c_D = 0.2$ and $c_I/c_D = 0.1$, respectively, when $\omega = \sigma^2 = 1$ and $K = S = 20$. These indicate that the expected costs become minimum when N is 4 and 7 for $c_I/c_D = 0.2$ and $c_I/c_D = 0.1$, respectively.

Table 7   Optimal $T_1, T_2, \cdots, T_N$ and $\widetilde{C}(\mathbf{T}, S)/c_D$ when $R(t) = 1 - \exp[-(K - t)/\sqrt{t}]$, $K = S = 20$ and $c_I/c_D = 0.2$.

N	1	2	3	4	5	6	7	8
T_1	20.00	16.52	14.83	13.84	13.21	12.83	12.61	12.52
T_2		20.00	17.91	16.68	15.91	15.43	15.16	15.05
T_3			20.00	18.60	17.72	17.17	16.86	16.73
T_4				20.00	19.03	18.43	18.09	17.95
T_5					20.00	19.35	18.99	18.84
T_6						20.00	19.61	19.45
T_7							20.00	19.83
T_8								20.00
$\frac{\widetilde{C}(T,S)}{c_D}$	20.200	18.922	18.520	18.394	18.395	18.470	18.595	18.762

Table 8   Optimal $T_1, T_2, \cdots, T_N$ and $\widetilde{C}(\mathbf{T}, S)/c_D$ when $R(t) = 1 - \exp[-(K - t)/\sqrt{t}]$, $K = S = 20$ and $c_I/c_D = 0.1$.

N	1	2	3	4	5	6	7	8
T_1	20.00	16.44	14.65	13.54	12.78	12.24	11.85	11.57
T_2		20.00	17.79	16.41	15.47	14.80	14.31	13.96
T_3			20.00	18.43	17.35	16.59	16.03	15.63
T_4				20.00	18.82	17.98	17.37	16.93
T_5					20.00	19.09	18.43	17.96
T_6						20.00	19.30	18.79
T_7							20.00	19.47
T_8								20.00
$\frac{\widetilde{C}(T,S)}{c_D}$	20.100	18.720	18.215	17.982	17.872	17.828	17.826	17.852

For example, when $c_I/c_D = 0.2$ and $S = 20$, $N^* = 4$ and the unit should be checked at 13.84, 16.68, 18.60 for an operating interval $[0, 20]$.

5   Conclusions

We have considered a continuous damage model in which reliability functions are given in a normal distribution and an exponential distribution. Using such functions, the expected cost rates of age replacement, and of replacement first, last and overtime when the unit operates for a job with random working times are obtained. Furthermore, applying this method to an inspection policy, it is shown how to compute optimal checking times. This paper computes easily optimal optimal policies numerically, and gives their several examples and discuss about numerical results.

Acknowledgments

This work is supported by the Ministry of Education, Culture, Sports, Science in Japan (No. 15K03562)D

References

Schijve, J. (2004). *Fatigue of Structures and Materials*, Kluwer Academic Publishers, Dordrecht.

Nakagawa, T. (2007). *Shock and Damage Models in Reliability Theory*, Springer Verlag, London.

Nakagawa, T. (2005). *Maintenance Theory of Reliability*, Springer Verlag, London.

Nakagawa, T. (2011). *Stochastic Processes with Applications to Reliability Theory*, Springer Verlag, London.

Nakagawa, T. (2014). *Random Maintenance Policies*, Springer Verlag, London.

Ito, K. and Nakagawa, T. (2008). *Comparison of Three Cumulative Damage Models*, In S.H. Shen and T.Dohi (eds) *Advanced Reliability Modeling III*, McGraw-Hill, Taipei, pp.332–338.

Barlow, R.E. and Proschen, F. (1965). *Mathematical Theory of Reliability*, Wiley, New York.

Chapter 18

Extended Policies of Replacement First, Last, Overtime

Satoshi Mizutani[1] and Toshio Nakagawa[2]

[1]*Department of Media Informations,*
Aichi University of Technology,

[2]*Faculty of Management,*
Aichi Institute of Technology

1 Introduction

There have been many studies of maintenance and replacement policies using reliability theory [Barlow (1965); Osaki (1992); Nakagawa (2005)]. The published books [Osaki (ed); Pham (ed); Nakagawa (2005, 2008)] collected many maintenance and replacement models and their optimal policies. In this chapter, we show some extended optimal maintenance and replacement policies in which a unit such as equipment of plant is replaced before its failure to avoid the loss cost. Specifically, we treat following models: (1) Replacement first, (2) Replacement last, (3) Replacement overtime, and minimal repair models for above each models. We attempt to explain systemaically the models.

Maintenance models with random job cycle time were studied [Chen et.al. (2010b); Nakagawa (2008)]. Recently, Nakagawa and Zhao considered about replacement first and replacement last models [Nakagawa et.al. (2011); Zhao and Nakagawa (2013)]. Replacement first means that a unit is replaced at completion time of job cycles or preventive maintenance time whichever occur first. On the other hand, replacement last means that a unit is replaced at the event times whichever occur last. Under certain conditions, replacement last is better than replacement last [Zhao and Nakagawa (2013)]. Overtime maintenance model means that a unit is replaced at the first completion of job cycles over a planned time to avoid interruption of work [Nakagawa and Zhao (2015); Zhao and Nakagawa (2013); Zhao et.al. (2014)]. When failure rate of a unit remains undisturbed by any repair of failures, the repair is called minimal repair [Nakagawa (2005)]. i.e., the unit after each minimal repair has the same failure rate as before failure.

In this chapter, Section 2 introduces common assumptions for each models. Section 3 shows a model of age replacement first in which a unit is replaced at Nth job cycle ($N = 1, 2, \ldots$) or at time T ($T \geq 0$), whichever occurs first. We obtain the expected cost rates $C_{AF}(T, N)$, $C_A(T) \equiv \lim_{N \to \infty} C_{AF}(T, N)$, and $C_A(N) \equiv \lim_{T \to \infty} C_{AF}(T, N)$. Then, we discuss about optimal T_A^* which minimizes $C_A(T)$, optimal N_A^* which minimizes $C_A(N)$, and optimal T_{AF}^* and N_{AF}^* for $C_{AF}(T, N)$. Section 4 shows a model of age replacement last in which a unit is replaced at Nth job cycle or at time T, whichever occurs last. We obtain the expected cost rates $C_{AL}(T, N)$, and discuss about optimal T_{AL}^* and N_{AL}^*. Section 5 shows a model of age replacement overtime in which a unit is replaced at the first completion of job cycles over time T. We obtain the expected cost rate $C_{AO}(T)$ and discuss about optimal T_{AO}^*. Section 6 shows a model of replacement first with minimal repair. We obtain the expected cost rates $C_{PF}(T, N)$, $C_P(T) \equiv \lim_{N \to \infty} C_{PF}(T, N)$, and $C_P(N) \equiv \lim_{T \to \infty} C_{PF}(T, N)$. Then, we discuss about optimal T_P^*, N_P^*, T_{PF}^*, and N_{PF}^*. Section 7 shows a model of replacement last with minimal repair. We obtain the expected cost rate $C_{PL}(T, N)$, and discuss about optimal T_{PL}^* and N_{PL}^*. Section 8 shows a model of replacement overtime with minimal repair. We obtain the expected cost rate $C_{PO}(T, N)$ and discuss about T_{PO}^* and N_{PO}^*. We give numerical examples for some models.

2 Common Assumptions

We consider following common assumptions for each models:

1) The system is constituted of a unit. The unit has a failure time distribution $F(t)$ with finite mean $1/\mu$, and the probability density function is $f(t) \equiv F'(t)$, i.e., $F(t) = \int_0^t f(u)du$. The failure rate is $h(t) \equiv f(t)/\overline{F}(t)$, which monotonically increases with t from $h(0)$ to $h(\infty)$, where $\overline{\Phi}(t) \equiv 1 - \Phi(t)$.

2) The unit repeats the job with time distribution $G(t)$, and the probability density function is $g(t) \equiv G'(t)$. The rate of job cycle is $r(t) \equiv g(t)/\overline{G}(t)$, which decreases with t. $G^{(j)}(t)$ $(j = 1, 2, \dots)$ is the j-fold Stieltjes convolution of $G(t)$, and $G^{(0)}(t) \equiv 1$ for all $t \geq 0$, i.e., $G^{(j)}(t) \equiv \int_0^\infty G^{(j-1)}(t-u)dG(u)$.

3) A cost c_T is a replacement cost at time T, c_N is a replacement cost at completion of job cycle.

4) c_0 denote loss cost per unit of time from failure to replacement or minimal repair cost, by the context.

3   Age Replacement First

Suppose that the unit is replaced at completion time of Nth job cycle or at time T, whichever occurs first. Note that even if the unit has failed at Nth job cycle or at time T. Then, we can not use the unit until the replacement. Therefore, we introduce the loss cost per unit of time which incurs from failure to replacement, i.e., c_0 is the loss cost per unit of time. We do not consider occurrence of other failures for the failed unit.

Then, the probability that the unit is replaced at time T is

$$1 - G^{(N)}(T),$$

and the probability that it is replaced at Nth job cycle is

$$G^{(N)}(T).$$

The mean time to replacement is

$$T[1 - G^{(N)}(T)] + \int_0^T t\,dG^{(N)}(t) = \int_0^T [1 - G^{(N)}(t)]dt, \qquad (1)$$

and the mean time between failure and replacement is

$$[1 - G^{(N)}(T)]\int_0^T (T-t)dF(t) + \int_0^T \left[\int_0^T (t-u)dF(u)\right]dG^{(N)}(t)$$

$$= \int_0^T F(t)[1 - G^{(N)}(t)]dt. \qquad (2)$$

The expected cost rate is

$$C_{AF}(T, N) = \frac{c_N + (c_T - c_N)[1 - G^{(N)}(T)] + c_0 \int_0^T F(t)[1 - G^{(N)}(t)]dt}{\int_0^T [1 - G^{(N)}(t)]dt}. \qquad (3)$$

In particular, when the unit is replacement only at time T, the expected cost rate is

$$C_A(T) \equiv \lim_{N \to \infty} C_{AF}(T, N) = \frac{c_T + c_0 \int_0^T F(t)dt}{T},$$ (4)

which agrees with (5.9) in [Nakagawa (2005), p. 120] which is expected cost of block replacement which has no replacement at the failure.

When the unit is replaced only at Nth job cycle, the expected cost rate is

$$C_A(N) \equiv \lim_{T \to \infty} C_{AF}(T, N) = \frac{c_N + c_0 \int_0^T F(t)[1 - G^{(N)}(t)]dt}{N/\theta}.$$ (5)

3.1 *Optimal Policies*

We derive optimal policies which minimize the expected cost rates.

(1) Optimal T_A^*

We find optimal T_A^* to minimize $C_A(T)$. Differentiating $C_A(T)$ with respect to T and setting it equal to zero,

$$\int_0^T [F(T) - F(t)]dt = \frac{c_N}{c_0},$$ (6)

and the resulting cost rate is

$$C_A(T_A^*) = c_0 F(T_A^*).$$ (7)

From (6), if $1/\lambda \equiv \int_0^\infty \overline{F}(t)dt > c_N/c_0$, then a finite T_A^* $(0 < T_A^* < \infty)$ exists.

(2) Optimal N_A^*

We find optimal N_A^* to minimize $C_A(N)$. Forming the inequality $C_A(N + 1) - C_A(N) \geq 0$,

$$N \int_0^\infty F(t)[G^{(N)}(t) - G^{(N+1)}(t)]dt - \int_0^\infty F(t)[1 - G^{(N)}(t)]dt \geq \frac{c_N}{c_0}.$$ (8)

Letting $L_1(N)$ be the left-hand side of (8),

$$L_1(N + 1) - L_1(N) = (N + 1) \left\{ \int_0^\infty F(t)[G^{(N+1)}(t) - G^{(N+2)}(t)]dt \right.$$
$$\left. - \int_0^\infty F(t)[G^{(N)}(t) - G^{(N+1)}(t)]dt \right\}.$$

Thus, if $\int_0^\infty F(t)[G^{(j)}(t) - G^{(j+1)}(t)]dt$ increases strictly with j and $L_1(\infty) > c_N/c_0$, then there exists a finite and unique minimum N_A^* ($1 \le N_A^* < \infty$) which satisfies (8).

In particular, when $F(t) = 1 - e^{-\lambda t}$, (8) is rewritten as

$$\frac{1 - G^*(\lambda)}{\lambda} \sum_{j=0}^{N-1} [G^*(\lambda)^j - G^*(\lambda)^N] \ge \frac{c_N}{c_0}, \tag{9}$$

where $G^*(\lambda)$ is a Laplace-Stieltjes transform of $G(t)$, i.e., $G^*(\lambda) \equiv \int_0^\infty e^{-\lambda t} G(t)dt$. Left-hand side of (9) increases strictly with N from $[1 - G^*(\lambda)]^2/\lambda$ to $1/\lambda$. Thus, if $1/\lambda > c_N/c_0$, then there exists a finite unique minimum N_A^* which satisfies (9).

When $G(t) = 1 - e^{-\theta t}$, i.e., $G^{(j)}(t) = \sum_{i=j}^\infty [(\theta t)^i/i!]e^{-\theta t}$, (8) is

$$\frac{1}{\theta} \sum_{j=0}^{N-1} \int_0^\infty G^{(j+1)}(t)dF(t) - \frac{N}{\theta} \int_0^\infty G^{(N+1)}(t)dF(t)$$

$$= \frac{1}{\theta} \sum_{j=0}^{N-1} \int_0^\infty [G^{(j+1)}(t) - G^{(N+1)}(t)]dF(t) \ge \frac{c_N}{c_0}, \tag{10}$$

whose left-hand side increases strictly with N to $1/\lambda$. Thus, if $1/\lambda > c_N/c_0$, then there exists a finite and unique minimum N_A^* which satisfies (10).

(3) Optimal T_{AF}^* and N_{AF}^*

We find optimal T_{AF}^* and N_{AF}^* when $c_T = c_N$ and $1/\lambda > c_N/c_0$. Differentiating $C_{AF}(T, N)$ in (3) with respect to T and setting it equal to zero,

$$\int_0^T [F(T) - F(t)][1 - G^{(N)}(t)]dt = \frac{c_N}{c_0}, \tag{11}$$

whose left-hand side increases strictly with T to $\int_0^\infty \overline{F}(t)[1 - G^{(N)}(t)]dt$. Thus, if $\int_0^\infty \overline{F}(t)[1 - G^{(N)}(t)]dt > c_N/c_0$, then there exists a finite and unique T_{AF}^* ($0 < T_{AF}^* < \infty$) which satisfies (11), and the resulting cost rate is

$$C_{AF}(T_{AF}^*, N) = c_0 F(T_{AF}^*). \tag{12}$$

In addition, because the left-hand side of (11) increases strictly with N to that of (6), T_{AF}^* decreases strictly with N to T_A^* given in (6).

Table 1 optimal (t_a^*, n_a^*) when $1/\theta = 10.0$.

c_N/c_0	$1/\lambda$		
	100	150	200
2	(21.5, 2)	(25.9, 3)	(29.7, 3)
5	(35.5, 4)	(42.5, 4)	(48.4, 5)
10	(53.2, 6)	(62.8, 7)	(71.1, 7)
20	(82.4, 9)	(95.2, 10)	(106.4, 11)
30	(109.7, 12)	(123.7, 13)	(136.7, 14)
40	(137.6, 14)	(151.0, 16)	(164.9, 17)
50	(167.8, 18)	(178.3, 18)	(192.3, 20)

Next, forming the inequality $C_{AF}(T, N+1) - C_{AF}(T, N) \geq 0$,

$$\frac{\int_0^T F(t)[G^{(N)}(t) - G^{(N+1)}(t)]dt}{\int_0^T [G^{(N)}(t) - G^{(N+1)}(t)]dt} \int_0^T [1 - G^{(N)}(t)]dt$$

$$- \int_0^T F(t)[1 - G^{(N)}(t)]dt \geq \frac{c_N}{c_0}. \tag{13}$$

Substituting (11) for (13),

$$\frac{\int_0^T F(t)[G^{(N)}(t) - G^{(N+1)}(t)]dt}{\int_0^T [G^{(N)}(t) - G^{(N+1)}(t)]dt} \geq F(T),$$

which does not hold for any T, and $N_{AF}^* = \infty$. Thus, the optimal policy to minimize $C_{AF}(T, N)$ is $T_{AF}^* = T_A^*$ and $N_{AF}^* = \infty$.

3.2 Numerical Examples

We give numerical examples when the failure time has an exponential distribution $F(t) = 1 - \exp(-\lambda t)$ and the completion of a job cycles has an exponential distribution $G(t) = 1 - \exp(-\theta t)$. In table 1, we show optimal T_A^* which satisfies (6) and and N_A^* which satisfies (10) when $1/\theta = 10.0$.

We can see that T_A^* and N_A^* increases with c_N/c_0. This indicate that it is not necessary to replace the unit early when the loss cost per unit of time from failure to replacement is much smaller than the preventive replacement costs. Futher, we can see that T_A^* and N_A^* increases with $1/\lambda$. This indicate that we should replace the unit early to avoid the loss cost per unit of time when the mean time to failure is small.

4 Age Replacement Last

Suppose that the unit is replaced at Nth job cycle or at time T, whichever occurs last. c_0 is the loss cost per unit of time from failure to replacement.

Then, the probability that the unit is replaced at time T is $G^{(N)}(T)$, and the probability that it is replaced at Nth job cycle is $1 - G^{(N)}(T)$. The mean time to replacement is

$$TG^{(N)}(T) + \int_T^\infty t\,dG^{(N)}(t) = T + \int_T^\infty [1 - G^{(N)}(t)]dt, \qquad (14)$$

and the mean time between failure and replacement is

$$G^{(N)}(T) \int_0^T (T-t)dF(t) + \int_T^\infty \left[\int_0^t (t-u)dF(u) \right] dG^{(N)}(t)$$

$$= \int_0^T F(t)dt + \int_T^\infty F(t)[1 - G^{(N)}(t)]dt. \qquad (15)$$

The expected cost rate is

$$C_{AL}(T,N) = \frac{ \begin{array}{c} c_T + (c_N - c_T)[1 - G^{(N)}(T)] \\ + c_0\{\int_0^T F(t)dt + \int_T^\infty F(t)[1 - G^{(N)}(t)]dt\} \end{array} }{ T + \int_T^\infty [1 - G^{(N)}(t)]dt }. \qquad (16)$$

Clearly,

$$\lim_{N\to 0} C_{AL}(T,N) = \lim_{N\to\infty} C_{AF}(T,N) = C_A(T)$$

in (4), and

$$\lim_{T\to 0} C_{AL}(T,N) = \lim_{T\to\infty} C_{AF}(T,N) = C_A(N)$$

in (5).

4.1 *Optimal Policies*

We find optimal T_{AL}^* and N_{AL}^* to minimize $C_{AL}(T,N)$ when $c_N = c_T$ and $1/\lambda > c_N/c_0$. Differentiating $C_{AL}(T,N)$ with respect to T and setting it equal to zero,

$$\int_0^T [F(T) - F(t)]dt - \int_T^\infty [F(t) - F(T)][1 - G^{(N)}(t)]dt = \frac{c_N}{c_0}, \qquad (17)$$

whose left-hand side increases strictly with T to $1/\lambda$. Thus, there exists a finite and unique T_{AF}^* $(0 < T_{AL}^* < \infty)$ which satisfies (17), and the resulting cost rate is

$$C_{AL}(T_{AL}^*) = c_0 F(T_{AL}^*).$$

Next, forming $C_{AL}(T, N+1) - C_{AL}(T, N) \geq 0$,

$$\frac{\int_T^\infty F(t)[G^{(N)}(t) - G^{(N+1)}(t)]\mathrm{d}t}{\int_T^\infty [G^{(N)}(t) - G^{(N+1)}(t)]\mathrm{d}t} \left\{ T + \int_T^\infty [1 - G^{(N)}(t)]\mathrm{d}t \right\}$$

$$- \int_0^T F(t)\mathrm{d}t - \int_T^\infty F(t)[1 - G^{(N)}(t)]\mathrm{d}t \geq \frac{c_N}{c_0}. \qquad (18)$$

Substituting (17) for (18),

$$\frac{\int_T^\infty F(t)[G^{(N)}(t) - G^{(N+1)}(t)]\mathrm{d}t}{\int_T^\infty [G^{(N)}(t) - G^{(N+1)}(t)]\mathrm{d}t} \geq F(T),$$

which always hold for any N, and $N_{AL}^* = 0$. Thus, the optimal policy to minimize $C_{AL}(T, N)$ is $T_{AL}^* = T_A^*$ and $N_{AL}^* = 0$.

5 Age Replacement Overtime

Suppose that the unit is replaced at the first completion of job cycles over time T ($0 \leq T < \infty$). c_0 is the loss cost per unit of time from failure to replacement.

Then, the mean time to replacement is

$$\sum_{j=0}^\infty \int_0^T \left[\int_T^\infty u\mathrm{d}G(u - t) \right] \mathrm{d}G^{(j)}(t)$$

$$= T + \sum_{j=0}^\infty \int_0^T \left[\int_T^\infty \overline{G}(u - t)\mathrm{d}u \right] \mathrm{d}G^{(j)}(t), \qquad (19)$$

and the mean time between failure and replacement is

$$\sum_{j=0}^\infty \int_0^T \left\{ \int_T^\infty \left[\int_0^u (u - x)\mathrm{d}F(x) \right] \mathrm{d}G(u - t) \right\} \mathrm{d}G^{(j)}(t)$$

$$= \sum_{j=0}^\infty \int_0^T \left\{ \int_T^\infty \left[\int_0^u F(x)\mathrm{d}x \right] \mathrm{d}G(u - t) \right\} \mathrm{d}G^{(j)}(t). \qquad (20)$$

Therefore, the expected cost rate is

$$C_{AO}(T) = \frac{c_N + c_0 \sum_{j=0}^\infty \int_0^T \left\{ \int_T^\infty \left[\int_0^u F(x)\mathrm{d}x \right] \mathrm{d}G(u - t) \right\} \mathrm{d}G^{(j)}(t)}{T + \sum_{j=0}^\infty \int_0^T \left[\int_T^\infty \overline{G}(u - t)\mathrm{d}u \right] \mathrm{d}G^{(j)}(t)}. \qquad (21)$$

5.1   *Optimal Polices*

We find optimal T_{AO}^* to minimize $C_{AO}(T)$. Differentiating $C_{AO}(T)$ with respect to T and setting it equal to zero,

$$\theta \int_0^\infty \left[\int_T^{T+t} F(x)dx \right] dG(t) \left\{ T + \sum_{j=0}^\infty \int_0^T \left[\int_T^\infty \overline{G}(u-t)du \right] dG^{(j)}(t) \right\}$$

$$- \sum_{j=0}^\infty \left\{ \int_T^\infty \left[\int_0^u F(x)dx \right] dG(u-t) \right\} dG^{(j)}(t) = \frac{c_N}{c_0}, \tag{22}$$

whose left-hand side increases strictly with T to $1/\lambda$, because

$$\int_T^\infty \left[\int_0^u \overline{F}(x)dx \right] dG(u-t) = \int_0^T \overline{F}(x)dx + \int_T^\infty \overline{F}(t)\overline{G}(u-t)dt.$$

Thus, if $1/\lambda > c_N/c_0$, then there exists a finite and unique T_{AO}^* ($0 < T_{AO}^* < \infty$) which satisfies (22), and the resulting cost rate is

$$C_{AO}(T_{AO}^*) = c_0\theta \int_0^\infty \left[\int_{T_{AO}^*}^{T_{AO}^*+t} F(x)dx \right] dG(t).$$

In particular, when $G(t) = 1 - e^{-\theta t}$, the expected cost rate (21) is

$$C_{AO}(T) = \frac{c_N + c_0[\int_0^T F(t)dt + \int_T^\infty F(t)e^{-\theta(t-T)}dt]}{T + 1/\theta}, \tag{23}$$

and (22) is

$$\theta T \int_T^\infty F(t)e^{-\theta(t-T)}dt - \int_0^T \overline{F}(t)dt = \frac{c_N}{c_0}, \tag{24}$$

whose left-hand side increases strictly with T from 0 to $1/\lambda$. Thus, if $1/\lambda > c_N/c_0$, then there exists a finite and unique T_{AO}^* ($0 < T_{AO}^* < \infty$) which satisfies (22), and the resulting cost rate is

$$C_{AO}(T_{AO}^*) = c_0 \int_{T_{AO}^*}^\infty F(t)\theta e^{-\theta(t-T_{AO}^*)}dt$$

$$= \frac{c_N + \int_0^{T_{AO}^*} F(t)dt}{T_{AO}^*}, \tag{25}$$

which agrees with (4) when $T = T_{AO}^*$.

Table 2   Optimal T^*_{AO} when $1/\theta = 10.0$.

c_N/c_0	$\alpha = 1.0$ $1/\lambda$			$\alpha = 1.5$ $1/\lambda$			$\alpha = 2.0$ $1/\lambda$		
	100	150	200	100	150	200	100	150	200
2	97.9	147.7	197.7	21.5	28.3	34.5	10.6	12.7	14.5
5	102.6	152.5	202.4	25.2	31.9	38.1	13.9	16.0	17.8
10	110.0	160.0	210.1	30.5	37.3	43.5	18.9	21.0	22.7
20	123.6	174.2	224.6	40.3	47.1	53.4	28.9	30.9	32.6
30	136.1	187.4	238.2	49.9	56.6	62.8	38.9	40.9	42.5
40	147.9	199.9	251.3	59.6	66.2	72.2	48.9	50.9	52.5
50	159.1	211.9	263.8	69.5	75.9	81.7	58.9	60.9	62.5

Furthermore, comparing (24) with (6),

$$\int_0^T F(t)\mathrm{d}t - \theta T \int_T^\infty F(t)e^{-\theta(t-T)}\mathrm{d}t - \int_0^T [F(T) - F(t)]\mathrm{d}t$$

$$= T \int_T^\infty e^{-\theta(t-T)}\mathrm{d}F(t) > 0,$$

which follows that $T^*_{AO} < T^*_A$ given in (6). Thus, from (25), $C_{AO}(T^*_{AO}) > C_A(T^*_A)$, *i.e.*, the optimal policy with time T^*_A is better than the replacement overtime policy.

5.2   *Numerical Examples*

We give numerical examples when the failure time has an Weibull distribution $F(t) = 1 - \exp(-\lambda t^\alpha)$ and the completion of a job cycles has an exponential distribution $G(t) = 1 - \exp(-\theta t)$. Table 2 presents optimal T^*_{AO} which satisfies (24) when $1/\theta = 10.0$.

We can see that T^*_A increases with c_N/c_0 and $1/\lambda$. Further, we can see that T^*_A decreases with α. This indicate that we should replace the unit early to avoid failure when α is small.

6   Replacement First with Minimal Repair

Suppose that the unit is replaced at Nth job cycle or at time T, whichever occurs first. When the unit has failed, minimal repair is done, i.e., the unit after each minimal repair has the same failure rate as before failure. Some failures may occurs to replacement. In this model, c_0 is the loss cost of minimal repair. In later sections, we assume the system has a failure time distribution $F(t) = 1 - e^{-H(t)}$, where $H(t) \equiv \int_0^t h(u)\mathrm{d}u$ is the cumulative hazard function. We assume the failure rate $h(t)$ monotonically increases with t from $h(0)$ to $h(\infty)$.

Replacing $\int_0^T F(t)\mathrm{d}t$ and $F(T)$ with $H(T)$ and $h(T)$ formally, the expected cost rate is, from (3),

$$C_{PF}(T,N) = \frac{c_N + (c_T - c_N)[1 - G^{(N)}(T)] + c_0 \int_0^T h(t)[1 - G^{(N)}(t)]\mathrm{d}t}{\int_0^T [1 - G^{(N)}(t)]\mathrm{d}t}.$$
(26)

In particular, when the unit is replaced only at time T, the expected cost rate is

$$C_P(T) = \lim_{N \to \infty} C_{PF}(T,N) = \frac{c_T + c_0 H(T)}{T},$$
(27)

which agrees with (4.16) of [Nakagawa (2005), p. 102].

When the unit is replaced only at Nth job cycle, the expected cost rate is

$$C_P(N) \equiv \lim_{T \to \infty} C_{PF}(T,N) = \frac{c_N + c_0 \int_0^\infty h(t)[1 - G^{(N)}(t)]\mathrm{d}t}{N/\theta}.$$
(28)

6.1 Optimal Policies

We derive optimal policies which minimize the expected cost rates.

(1) Optimal T_P^*

We find optimal T_P^* to minimize $C_P(T)$. Differentiating $C_P(T)$ with respect to T and setting it equal to zero,

$$\int_0^T [h(T) - h(t)]\mathrm{d}t = \frac{c_N}{c_0},$$
(29)

and the resulting cost rate is

$$C_P(T_P^*) = c_0 h(T_P^*).$$
(30)

If $\int_0^\infty t\mathrm{d}h(t) > c_N/c_0$, then a finite T_P^* $(0 < T_P^* < \infty)$ exists.

(2) Optimal N_P^*

We find optimal N_P^* to minimize $C_P(N)$. Forming the inequality $C_P(N+1) - C_P(N) \geq 0$,

$$N \int_0^\infty h(t)[G^{(N)}(t) - G^{(N+1)}(t)]\mathrm{d}t - \int_0^\infty h(t)[1 - G^{(N)}(t)]\mathrm{d}t \geq \frac{c_N}{c_0}.$$
(31)

In particular, when $G(t) = 1 - e^{-\theta t}$,

$$\frac{1}{\theta} \sum_{j=0}^{N-1} \int_0^\infty [G^{(j+1)}(t) - G^{(N+1)}(t)] dh(t) \geq \frac{c_N}{c_0} \tag{32}$$

whose left-hand side increases strictly with N to $\int_0^\infty t dh(t)$. Thus, if $\int_0^\infty t dh(t) > c_N/c_0$, then there exists a finite and unique minimum N_P^* which satisfies (32).

(3) Optimal T_{PF}^* and N_{PF}^*

We find optimal T_{PF}^* and N_{PF}^* when $c_T = c_N$ and $h(\infty) = \infty$. Differentiating $C_{PF}(T, N)$ in (24) with respect to T and setting it equal to zero,

$$\int_0^T [h(T) - h(t)][1 - G^{(N)}(t)] dt = \frac{c_N}{c_0}, \tag{33}$$

whose left-hand side increases strictly with T to ∞. Thus, there exists a finite and unique T_{PF}^* $(0 < T_{PF}^* < \infty)$ with satisfies (33), and the resulting cost rate is

$$C_{PF}(T_{PF}^*) = C_0 h(T_{PF}^*). \tag{34}$$

In addition, because the left-hand side of (33) increases strictly with N to that of (29), T_{PF}^* decreases strictly with N to T_P^* in (29).

Next, forming the inequality $C_{PF}(T, N+1) - C_{PF}(T, N) \geq 0$,

$$\frac{\int_0^T h(t)[G^{(N)}(t) - G^{(N+1)}(t)] dt}{\int_0^T [G^{(N)}(t) - G^{(N+1)}(t)] dt} \int_0^T [1 - G^{(N)}(t)] dt$$

$$- \int_0^T h(t)[1 - G^{(N)}(t)] dt \geq \frac{c_N}{c_0}. \tag{35}$$

Substituting (33) for (35),

$$\frac{\int_0^T h(t)[G^{(N)}(t) - G^{(N+1)}(t)] dt}{\int_0^T [G^{(N)}(t) - G^{(N+1)}(t)] dt} \geq h(T),$$

which does not hold for any T, and $N_{PF}^* = \infty$. Thus, the optimal policy to minimize $C_{PF}(T, N)$ is $T_{PF}^* = T_P^*$ and $N_{PF}^* = \infty$.

6.2 Numerical Examples

We give numerical examples when the failure time has an Weibull distribution $F(t) = 1 - \exp(-\lambda t^\alpha)$ and the completion of a job cycles has an

Table 3   Optimal (T_P^*, N_P^*) when $1/\theta = 10.0$.

c_N/c_0	$\alpha = 1.5$			$\alpha = 2.0$		
	$1/\lambda$			$1/\lambda$		
	100	150	200	100	150	200
2	(54.3, 4)	(71.1, 5)	(86.2, 6)	(14.1, 2)	(17.3, 2)	(20.0, 2)
5	(100.0, 7)	(131.0, 8)	(158.7, 10)	(22.4, 2)	(27.4, 2)	(31.6, 3)
10	(158.7, 10)	(208.0, 12)	(252.0, 15)	(31.6, 3)	(38.7, 3)	(44.7, 4)
20	(252.0, 15)	(330.2, 19)	(400.0, 22)	(44.7, 4)	(54.8, 4)	(63.2, 5)
30	(330.2, 19)	(432.7, 24)	(524.2, 29)	(54.8, 4)	(67.1, 5)	(77.5, 6)
40	(400.0, 22)	(524.2, 29)	(635.0, 34)	(63.2, 5)	(77.5, 6)	(89.4, 7)
50	(464.2, 26)	(608.2, 33)	(736.8, 39)	(70.7, 6)	(86.6, 7)	(100.0, 8)

exponential distribution $G(t) = 1 - \exp(-\theta t)$. Table 3 presents optimal T_P^* which satisfies (29) and and N_P^* which satisfies (32) when $1/\theta = 10.0$.

We can see that T_P^* and N_P^* increases with c_N/c_0 and $1/\lambda$. It can be seen that T_P^* and N_P^* decreases with α. Futher, we can see that T_P^* and N_P^* are greater than T_A^* and N_A^* in Table 1 for the same parameters. This indicate that loss of minimal repair model is, for the same parameters, smaller than one of no repair model with loss cost per unit of time.

7   Replacement Last with Minimal Repair

Suppose that the unit is replaced at Nth job cycle or at time T, whichever occurs last. When the unit has fails, minimal repair is done, and c_0 is the loss cost of minimal repair.

Replacing $F(t)$ with $h(t)$ in (16), the expected cost rate is

$$C_{PL}(T,N) = \frac{c_T + (c_N - c_T)[1 - G^{(N)}(T)] + c_0\{H(t) + \int_T^\infty h(t)[1 - G^{(N)}(t)]dt\}}{T + \int_T^\infty [1 - G^{(N)}(t)]dt}. \qquad (36)$$

7.1   *Optimal Policies*

We discuss about optimal T_{PL}^* and N_{PL}^* to minimize $C_{PL}(T)$. Differentiating $C_{PL}(T,N)$ with respect to T and setting it equal to zero,

$$\int_0^T [h(T) - h(t)]dt - \int_T^\infty [h(t) - h(T)][1 - G^{(N)}(t)]dt = \frac{c_N}{c_0}, \qquad (37)$$

whose left-hand side increases strictly with T to ∞. Thus, there exists a finite and unique T_{PF}^* $(0 < T_{PF}^* < \infty)$ which satisfies (37), and the resulting

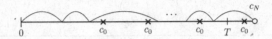

Fig. 1   Processes of overtime maintenance with minimal repair

cost rate is

$$C_{PL}(T_{PL}^*) = c_0 h(T_{PL}^*). \tag{38}$$

Next, forming $C_{PL}(T, N+1) - C_{PL}(T, N) \geq 0$,

$$\frac{\int_T^\infty h(t)[G^{(N)}(t) - G^{(N+1)}(t)]dt}{\int_T^\infty [G^{(N)}(t) - G^{(N+1)}(t)]dt} \left\{ T + \int_T^\infty [1 - G^{(N)}(t)]dt \right\}$$

$$- H(T) - \int_T^\infty h(t)[1 - G^{(N)}(t)]dt \geq \frac{c_N}{c_0}. \tag{39}$$

Substituting (37) for (39),

$$\frac{\int_T^\infty h(t)[G^{(N)}(t) - G^{(N+1)}(t)]dt}{\int_T^\infty [G^{(N)}(t) - G^{(N+1)}(t)]dt} \geq h(T),$$

which always hold for any N, and $N_{PL}^* = 0$. Thus, the optimal policy to minimize $C_{PL}(T, N)$ is $T_{PL}^* = T_P^*$ and $N_{PL}^* = 0$.

8   Replacement Overtime with Minimal Repair

Suppose that the unit is replaced at the first completion of job cycles over time T ($0 \leq T < \infty$). When the unit has failed, minimal repair is done, and c_0 is the loss cost of minimal repair.

The expected cost rate is, from (21),

$$C_{PO}(T) = \frac{c_N + c_0 \sum_{j=0}^\infty \int_0^T \left[\int_T^\infty H(u)dG(u-t) \right] dG^{(j)}(t)}{T + \sum_{j=0}^\infty \int_0^T \left[\int_T^\infty \overline{G}(u-t)du \right] dG^{(j)}(t)}. \tag{40}$$

8.1 *Optimal Policies*

We find optimal T_{PO}^* to minimize $C_{PO}(T)$. Differentiating $C_{PO}(T)$ with respect to T and setting it equal to zero,

$$\theta \int_0^\infty [H(T-t) - H(t)] dG(t) \left\{ T + \sum_{j=0}^\infty \int_0^T \left[\int_T^\infty \overline{G}(u-t) du \right] dG^{(j)}(t) \right\}$$

$$- \sum_{j=0}^\infty \int_0^T \left[\int_T^\infty H(u) dG(u-t) \right] dG^{(j)}(t) = \frac{c_N}{c_0}, \tag{41}$$

whose left-hand side increases strictly with T to ∞. Thus, there exists a finite and unique T_{PO}^* ($0 < T_{PO}^* < \infty$) which satisfies (41), and the resulting cost rate is

$$C_{PO}(T_{PO}^*) = c_0 \theta \int_0^\infty [H(T_{PO}^* + t) - H(T_{PO}^*)] dG(t). \tag{42}$$

In addition, when $G(t) = 1 - e^{-\theta t}$, (40) is

$$C_{PO}(T) = \frac{c_N + c_0[H(T) + \int_T^\infty h(t) e^{-\theta(t-T)} dt]}{T + 1/\theta}, \tag{43}$$

and (41) is

$$\theta T \int_T^\infty h(t) e^{-\theta(t-T)} dt - H(T) = \frac{c_N}{c_0}, \tag{44}$$

whose left-hand side increases strictly with T to ∞. Thus, there exists a finite and unique T_{PO}^* ($0 < T_{PO}^* < \infty$) which satisfies (42), and the resulting cost rate is

$$C_{PO}(T_{PO}^*) = c_0 \int_{T_{PO}^*}^\infty h(t) \theta e^{-\theta(t - T_{PO}^*)} dt$$

$$= \frac{c_N + c_0 H(T_{PO}^*)}{T_{PO}^*}, \tag{45}$$

which agrees with (27) when $T = T_{PO}^*$.

Furthermore, comparing (44) with (29),

$$\theta T \int_T^\infty h(t) e^{-\theta(t-T)} dt - H(T) - \int_0^T [h(T) - h(t)] dt$$

$$= T \int_T^\infty e^{-\theta(t-T)} dh(t) > 0, \tag{46}$$

which follows that $T_{PO}^* < T_P^*$ given in (29). Thus, from (42), $C_{PO}(T_{PO}^*) > C_P(T_P^*)$, *i.e.*, the optimal policy with time T_P^* is better than the replacement overtime policy.

Table 4   Optimal T^*_{PO} when $1/\theta = 10.0$.

c_N/c_0	$\alpha = 1.5$ $1/\lambda$			$\alpha = 2.0$ $1/\lambda$		
	100	150	200	100	150	200
2	45.6	62.1	77.0	7.3	10.0	12.4
5	90.7	121.6	149.3	14.5	19.2	23.2
10	149.3	198.5	242.5	23.2	30.0	35.8
20	242.5	320.8	390.7	35.8	45.7	54.0
30	320.8	423.4	515.2	45.7	57.8	68.1
40	390.7	515.2	626.4	54.0	68.1	80.0
50	455.0	599.5	728.7	61.4	77.2	90.5

8.2   *Numerical Examples*

We give numerical examples when the failure time has a Weibull distribution $F(t) = 1 - \exp(-\lambda t^\alpha)$ ($\alpha > 1$) and the completion of a job cycles has an exponential distribution $G(t) = 1 - e^{-\theta t}$. Table 4 presents optimal T^*_{PO} which satisfies (44) when $1/\theta = 10.0$.

It can be seen that T^*_{PO} decreases with α. This indicates that we should replace the unit early to avoid the failure when α (> 1) is large. T^*_{PO} increases with c_N/c_0. This indicates that we should replace the unit early to avoid the replacement cost when c_N/c_0 is large.

9   Conclusions

We treated some extended replacement policies: replacement first, replacement last, overtime model, and minimal repair models for above each models. For each models, we obtained, expected cost rate and discussed the optimal policies. We gave numerical examples for some models.

We have seen that optimal replacment time and number for minimal repair models are for the same parameters, larger than that of no repair model with loss cost per unit of time. It have been seen that it is not necessary to replace the unit early when the loss cost per unit of time is much smaller than the preventive replacement costs. We discussed optimal T^*_{AF} and N^*_{AF} which minimize the expected cost $C_{AF}(T, N)$ in age replacement first. And we discussed similarly for age replacment last, replacement last with minimal repair, and replacement last with minimal repair. Futher, we can see that we should replace the unit early to avoid the loss cost per unit of time when the mean time to failure is small.

These formulations and results would be applied to other real systems such as management of equipment in factory by suitable modifications.

References

Barlow, R.E. and Proschan, F. (1965). *Mathematical Theory of Reliability* (Wiley, New York).

Osaki, S. (1992). *Applied Stochastic System Modeling* (Springer Verlag, Berlin).

Osaki, S. (ed) (2002). *Stochastic Models in Reliability and Maintenance* (Springer, Berlin).

Pham, H. (ed) (2003). *Handbook of Reliability Engineering* (Springer, London).

Nakagawa, T. (2005). *Maintenance Theory of Reliability* (Springer, London).

Nakagawa, T. (2008). *Advanced Reliability Models and Maintenance Policies* (Springer, London).

Chen, M., Nakamura, S. and Nakagawa, T. (2010). Replacement and preventive maintenance models with random working times. *IEICE Transactions on Fundamentals*. E93-A, **2**, pp. 500–507.

Nakagawa, T. (2014). *Random Maintenance Policies* (Springer, London).

Nakagawa, T., Zhao, X., and Yun, W. (2011). Optimal age replacement and inspection policies with random failure and replacement times. *International Journal of Reliability, Quality and Safety Engineering*, **18**, pp. 405–416.

Zhao, X. and Nakagawa, T. (2013). Optimal periodic and random inspection with first, last, and overtime policies. *International Journal of Systems Science*. DOI: 10.1080/00207721.2013.827263.

Zhao, X., Qian, C. and Nakagawa, T. (2014). Optimal age and periodic replacement with overtime policies. *International Journal of Reliability, Quality and Safety Engineering*. **21**, 1450016.

Nakagawa, T. and Zhao, X. (2015). *Maintenance Overtime Policies in Reliability Theory*. (Spring-Verlag, London).

Chapter 19

Optimal Checkpoint Times for Redundant Nodes and Errors

Kenichiro Naruse[1] and Sayori Maeji[2]

[1] *Nagoya Sangyo University,*

[2] *Institute of Consumer Sciences and Human Life,*
Kinjo Gakuin University

1 Introduction

Most computer systems in offices and industries execute successively tasks, each of which has random processing times. In such systems, some errors often occur due to noises, human errors, hardware faults and software faults. To detect and mask errors, some useful fault tolerant computing techniques have been adopted [Lee and Anderson (1990); Siewiorek and Swarz (1982)]. Several studies of deciding optimal checkpoint frequencies have been made: The performance and reliability of redundant modular systems were evaluated [Pradhan and Vaidya (1992); Nakagawa (2008)], and the performance of checkpoint schemes with task duplication was evaluated [Ziv and Bruck (1997, 1998)]. The optimal instruction-retry period that minimizes the probability of the dynamic failure by a triple modular controller was derived [Kim and Shin (1996)]. The evaluation models with finite checkpoints and bounded rollback were discussed [Ohara *et al.* (2006)]. Furthermore, checkpointing scheme for a set of multiple tasks in real-time systems were investigated [Zhang and Chakrabarty (2004)].

In recent years, Big data processing is indispensable to various research for researchers, for example, risk management for finance, genomic analysis, estimation of seismic risks, and so on. When we achieve the results from the big data, we need to use high speed processing computer system, because it has many processing volume. However, a CPU clock speed is limited by some physical limits. One of technique to solve the above problem is to apply multi CPU node model. Multi CPU node model gathers a lot of CPUs and behaves as one virtual high speed processing unit. Naturally, the reliability of the multi CPU node is lower than one CPU model. We applies the checkpoint scheme for multi CPU node system to prevent from the lower system reliability. The checkpoint schemes have various methods [Ling *et al.* (2001); Pradhan and Vaidya (1994); Vaidya (1995)].

The checkpoint system in this chapter applies two types of checkpoint schemes. And, the checkpoint operates on the system which executes successively each task with random working times [Naruse *et al.* (2006); Nakagawa *et al.* (2009); Chen *et al.* (2010); Naruse and Nakagawa (2013)]: Checking times are placed at the end of the Nth ($N = 1, 2, \cdots$) task. When a failure occurs in the system, the system executes the recovery operation until the latest checking time and repeats such processes until the next checking time. We introduce checking costs and a loss cost from failure to the latest checking time, and obtain the total expected cost between checking times, using an inspection policy.

If some errors would occur in the system, the processed data might be lost. To prevent from data loss, we suppose the following checkpoint schemes such as Journal Checkpoint (JC) and Flush Checkpoint (FC) schemes (Figure 1) [ORACLE (2012)]: JC is placed at each end of tasks and FC is placed at the Nth ($N = 1, 2, \cdots$) end of tasks. JC stores command and result of a task to HDD, and FC updates the HDD database according to JC data. Suppose that task k has a processing time $Y_k (k = 1, 2, \cdots)$ with an identical distribution $G(t) \equiv \Pr\{Y_k \leq t\}$ and finite mean $\mu = \int_0^\infty [1 - G(t)] \, dt < \infty$.

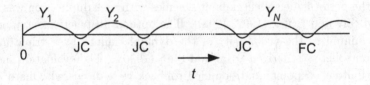

Fig. 1   Task execution.

Futhermore, we consider element of computer system in Sect 3, the computer system is made by a hardware and some software. Hardware has a bias degrade with a past time while software doesn't. Therefore, we consider independent failure rate system model.

2   RAICN and GRAICN System

A computer requires a high speed to process a SQL (Structured Query Language) command, to process big data, and so on. But, because a high speed computer is too expensive, we need to make high speed processing and high reliability computer with some inexpensive computers.

Most computer storage have recently used RAID (Redundant Arrays of Inexpensive Disk) architecture [Patterson *et al.* (1988)] as one of fault tolerant systems. RAID has 7 type of architectures: Most used RAID architectures are RAID 5 and RAID 6. RAID 5 needs three or more disks. For example, if we make RAID 5 storage with 4 disks, the storage system writes data to 3 disks, and calculates parity data and writes the parity data to one disk. When some errors occur at a disk, the system can work using the other disks, *i.e.*, the system reforms 2 data disks and 1 parity data disk. Therefore, the system can continue to work when one disk has failed.

2.1 *System Model*

This section applies an extended RAID architecture model which is a Redundant Arrays Inexpensive Computer Nodes (RAICN) model in Figure 2 and a Grouped Redundant Arrays Inexpensive Computer Nodes (GRAICN) model in Figure 3 for the multi database-nodes model which executes successively each task with random working times [Chen *et al.* (2010); Nakagawa *et al.* (2009); Naruse *et al.* (2006)].

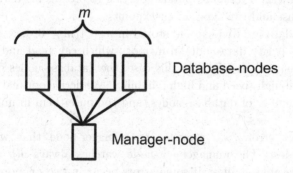

Fig. 2   RAICN system.

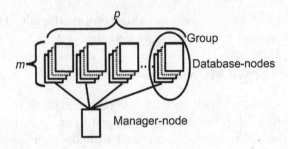

Fig. 3   GRAICN system.

We consider a RAICN system which is consisted of m database-nodes and one manager-node in a database system with RAID 5. The database-nodes process each task, and the manager-node watches the database-nodes. First of all, the database-nodes store database data from HDD to memory by dividing them into $m-1$ database-nodes, calculate parity bit from $m-1$ database-nodes, and store them on memory. Therefore, $m-1$ database-nodes can process each task with high speed. If some errors occur in a database-node, the system can continue the process by using remaining database-nodes data and parity-bit data. Therefore, the system forms an $(m-1)$-out-of-m system $(m \geq 3)$ [Nakagawa (2008)].

In addtion, we consider an extended model that is a GRAICN system which is consisted of p groups of m database-nodes and one manager-node in a database system with RAID 5 in Figure 3. It is for the multi database-nodes model with several computers applying to process big data with high speed response and two types of checkpoints.

The big data are divided and stored in $m-1(m = 3, 4, \cdots)$ database-nodes and 1 parity data-node on memory which can read and write over 100 times faster than HDD. In this case, the database-nodes can process big data with high speed and high reliability. We derive optimal checkpoint times and number of database-nodes, and compute them in numerical examples.

To detect errors, we provide the manager-node that watches the database-nodes. The management-node watches always $p(p = 1, 2, \ldots)$ (grouped) database-nodes. If some errors occur in two or more database-nodes, they are restarted by the management-node and transport a part of corresponding data from HDD to memory.

2.2 Performance Analysis

Let C_R be the overhead for JC time and Cs be the overhead for FC time($C_R < Cs$). Suppose that we have to execute the successive tasks with processing times $Y_k(k = 1, 2, \cdots)$ in Figure 1. Let W be the time for transferring all database data to each database-node and for calculating parity data, and R be its restart time. The mean execution times per one task are obtained, and optimal numbers N^* and m^* to minimize them are derived analytically. This is one of applied models with random maintenance times [Nakagawa (2008)] to checkpoint models. Such schemes would be useful when it is better to place checkpoints at the end of tasks than those at periodic times.

FC is placed at the end of task N ($N = 1, 2, \cdots$) and JC is placed only at the end of task $k(k = 1, 2, \cdots, N - 1)$ between FCs in Figure 1: When there is no error in the process of task k, the database-nodes execute task $k + 1$. When errors occur in task k, the manager-node restarts the database-nodes and restores the FC and JC data, and transfers them to database, irrespective of manager-node faults.

When the management-node does not detect any error until task N, the process of all tasks N is completed, and its state is stored. The database-node executes task $k + 1$. It is assumed that the database-node has a failure distribution $F(t)$ with finite mean $1/\lambda$. Let $\widetilde{L}_R(k, m, p)$ be the mean execution time from task k to the completion of task N. Then, we have the following renewal equations [Maeji *et al.* (2010)]:

$$\widetilde{L}_R(k, m, p) = \int_0^\infty \left\{ \overline{F}(t) \left[C_R + \frac{t}{p} + \widetilde{L}_R(k + 1, m, p) \right] \right.$$
$$\left. + F(t) \left[C_R + t + \widetilde{L}_R(1, m, p) + \frac{W}{m - 1} + R \right] \right\} dG(t)$$
$$(k = 1, 2, \cdots, N - 1), \qquad (1)$$

$$\widetilde{L}_R(N, m, p) = \int_0^\infty \left\{ \overline{F}(t) \left[C_R + \frac{t}{p} + Cs \right] \right.$$
$$\left. + F(t) \left[C_R + t + \widetilde{L}_R(1, m, p) + \frac{W}{m - 1} + R \right] \right\} dG(t), \qquad (2)$$

where $\overline{F}(t) \equiv 1 - F(t)$.

It is assumed that some errors occur at constant rate $\lambda(\lambda > 0)$, *i.e.*, the probability that one database-nodes have no error during $(0, t]$ is $e^{-\lambda t}$.

Then, the system with m nodes has a failure distribution

$$\overline{F}(t, m, p) = \left[me^{-(m-1)\lambda t} - (m-1)e^{-m\lambda t} \right]^p.$$ (3)

Solving (2) for $\widetilde{L_R}(1, m, p)$,

$$\widetilde{L_R}(1, m, p) \equiv \frac{\left(C_R + \frac{\mu}{p} + \frac{W}{m-1} + R \right) \left[1 - A(m)^{pN} \right]}{\left[1 - A(m)^p \right] A(m)^{pN}} + Cs,$$ (4)

where

$$A(m) \equiv mG^* \left[(m-1)\lambda \right] - (m-1)G^*(m\lambda),$$

and $G^*(s)$ is the Laplace-Stieltjes(LS) transform of $G(t)$, *i.e.*, $G^*(s) \equiv \int_0^\infty e^{-st} dG(t)$ for $s > 0$. Note that $\overline{F}(t, m, p)$ decreases strictly with m to 0 and $A(m)$ decreases strictly with m to 0. Therefore, the mean execution time per one task is

$$L_R(N, m, p) \equiv \frac{\widetilde{L_R}(1, m, p)}{N}$$

$$= \frac{\left(C_R + \frac{\mu}{p} + \frac{W}{m-1} + R \right) \left[1 - A(m)^{pN} \right]}{N \left[1 - A(m)^p \right] A(m)^{pN}} + \frac{Cs}{N}.$$ (5)

From the inequality $L_R(N + 1, m, p) - L_R(N, m, p) \geq 0$,

$$\frac{1}{A(m)^{p(N+1)}} \sum_{j=1}^{N} [1 - A(m)^{pj}] \geq \frac{Cs}{C_R + \frac{\mu}{p} + \frac{W}{m-1} + R},$$ (6)

whose left-hand side increases strictly with N from $[1 - A(m)^p]/A(m)^{2p}$ to ∞. Thus, there exists a finite and unique minimum $N^*(1 \leq N^* < \infty)$. which satisfies (6). We can derive an optimal number N^* analytically that minimizes $L_R(N, m, p)$ in (5).In general, it would be very diifficult to discuss optimal m^* and p^* analytically.

2.3   *Numerical Examples*

Table 1 presents optimal number N^* and the resulting execution time $L_R(N^*, m, p)/\mu$ in (5) for $\lambda\mu$ and N when $m = 4$, $C_R/\mu = 0.2$, $W/\mu = 5$, $R/\mu = 10$ and $G(t) = 1 - e^{-t/\mu}$. This indicates that N^* decreases with $\lambda\mu$, and its resulting execution time $L_R(N^*, m, p)/\mu$ decreases with $\lambda\mu$. Thus, the system don't needs to make a lot of frequency FC checkpoint (FC time > JC time) when low $\lambda\mu$, and when p increases with in same $\lambda\mu$, the execution time decrease not a lot in spite of increases nodes. This means that

p is a little effect when large $\lambda\mu$. But when low $\lambda\mu$, rate of execution time are smaller than large $\lambda\mu$.

The case of $N^* = 1$ means that we should provide no JC between FC. For example, when $\lambda\mu = 0.005$ and $p = 2$, we make 14 JC checkpoints between FC checkpoints. In this case, the job time is 12.477.

Table 1 Optimal number N^* and execution time $L_R(N^*, m, p)/\mu$ when $m = 4$, $Cs/\mu = 0.8$, $C_R/\mu = 0.2$, $W/\mu = 5$, $R/\mu = 10$ and $G(t) = 1 - e^{-t/\mu}$.

$\lambda\mu$	$p = 1$		$p = 2$		$p = 4$		$p = 8$	
	N^*	$\dfrac{L_R(N^*,m,p)}{\mu}$	N^*	$\dfrac{L_R(N^*,m,p)}{\mu}$	N^*	$\dfrac{L_R(N^*,m,p)}{\mu}$	N^*	$\dfrac{L_R(N^*,m,p)}{\mu}$
0.1	1	14.575	1	14.816	1	15.862	1	17.881
0.05	2	13.699	2	13.582	1	13.919	1	14.628
0.01	11	13.026	8	12.592	5	12.440	4	12.459
0.005	21	12.946	15	12.477	11	12.274	8	12.217
0.001	102	12.882	74	12.389	53	12.147	37	12.035
0.0005	204	12.868	147	12.378	105	12.132	75	12.013

From the inequality $L_R(N, m+1, p) - L_R(N, m, p) \geq 0$, we can compute numerically an optimal number m^* that minimizes $L_R(N, m, p)$ in (5) for $m \geq 3$.

Table 2 presents optimal number m^* and the resulting execution time $L_R(N, m^*, p)/\mu$ in (5) for $\lambda\mu$ and m when $N = 5$, $Cs/\mu = 0.8$, $C_R/\mu = 0.2$, $W/\mu = 5$, $R/\mu = 10$ and $G(t) = 1 - e^{-t/\mu}$. This indicates that m^* decreases with $\lambda\mu$ and the resulting execution time $L_R(N, m^*, p)/\mu$ increases with $\lambda\mu$. And, we attention the number of nodes, increasing nodes are not always good for this scheme in same $\lambda\mu$, the execution time decrease not a lot in spite of increases nodes,

Table 2 Optimal number m^* and execution time $L_R(N, m^*, p)/\mu$ when $N = 5$, $Cs/\mu = 0.8$, $C_R/\mu = 0.2$, $W/\mu = 5$, $R/\mu = 10$ and $G(t) = 1 - e^{-t/\mu}$.

$\lambda\mu$	$p = 1$		$p = 2$		$p = 4$		$p = 8$	
	m^*	$\dfrac{L_R(N,m^*,p)}{\mu}$	m^*	$\dfrac{L_R(N,m^*,p)}{\mu}$	m^*	$\dfrac{L_R(N,m^*,p)}{\mu}$	m^*	$\dfrac{L_R(N,m^*,p)}{\mu}$
0.1	3	15.594	3	16.737	3	19.894	3	27.132
0.05	4	13.910	4	14.229	3	15.005	3	16.751
0.01	11	12.183	9	11.906	7	11.948	6	12.218
0.005	16	11.874	13	11.509	10	11.437	8	11.544
0.001	45	11.535	36	11.079	29	10.887	23	10.835
0.0005	70	11.471	56	10.998	45	10.784	36	10.704

From the inequality $L_R(N, m, p+1) - L_R(N, m, p) \geq 0$,we can compute numerically an optimal number p^* that minimizes $L_R(N, m, p)$ in (5).

Table 3 presents optimal number p^* and the resulting execution time $L_R(N, m, p^*)/\mu$ in (5) for $\lambda\mu$ and p when $N = 5$, $Cs/\mu = 0.8$, $C_R/\mu = 0.2$, $W/\mu = 5$, $R/\mu = 10$ and $G(t) = 1 - e^{-t/\mu}$. The resulting execution time $L_R(N, m, p^*)$ decreases with m and increases $\lambda\mu$ except in case of $p^* = 1$.

Table 3   Optimal number p^* and execution time $L_R(N, m, p^*)/\mu$ when $N = 5$, $Cs/\mu = 0.8$, $C_R/\mu = 0.2$, $W/\mu = 5$, $R/\mu = 10$ and $G(t) = 1 - e^{-t/\mu}$.

$\lambda\mu$	$m = 4$		$m = 5$		$m = 6$	
	p^*	$\dfrac{L_R(N,m,p^*)}{\mu}$	p^*	$\dfrac{L_R(N,m,p^*)}{\mu}$	p^*	$\dfrac{L_R(N,m,p^*)}{\mu}$
0.1	1	16.022	1	17.139	1	18.697
0.05	1	13.910	1	13.959	1	14.249
0.01	5	12.430	4	12.118	3	11.974
0.005	10	12.231	8	11.868	6	11.672
0.001	49	12.068	38	11.662	32	11.423
0.0005	97	12.047	76	11.636	63	11.392

Finally, we find both optimal N^* and m^* that minimize $L_R(N, m, p)$ in (5) and (6). To compute optimal N^* and m^*, we substitute $m = 3$ into (6), and compute N_1^* , and compute m_2^* for $N = N_1^*$ from (5). If $m_i^* = m_{i+1}^*$ and $N_i^* = N_{i+1}^*$ then $m^* = m_i^*$ and $N^* = N_i^*$. This indicates optimal combination of the numbers of database-nodes and JC between FC.

Table 4 presents optimal number N^*, m^* and the execution time $L_R(N^*, m^*, p)/\mu$ when $Cs/\mu = 0.8$, $C_R/\mu = 0.2$, $W/\mu = 5$ and $R/\mu = 10$. This indicates that $L_R(N^*, m^*, p)/\mu$ decrease with decreasing $\lambda\mu$, and both N^* and m^* incearse with decreasing $\lambda\mu$.

Compared to Tables 1, 2 and 3 the execution times in Table 4 for $\lambda\mu$ are equal or smaller than those in every Tables 1, 2 and 3 in same $\lambda\mu$.

Since, we can compute number of required node by pm^* in Table 4, if $\lambda\mu = 0.005$, then the number of nodes are $16(p = 1, m^* = 16)$, $26(p = 2, m^* = 13)$, $44(p = 4, m^* = 11)$, $80(p = 8, m^* = 10)$ when the number of minimum execution time. Especially, when we compair the execution time in $p = 4(44 \text{ nodes})$ and $p = 8(88 \text{ nodes})$, though case $p = 4$ is faster than case $p = 8$ at the execution time, the number of nodes when case $p = 4$ is smaller than case $p = 8$. This means that we have to choose the suitable architecture and parameters, or we lose execution time what if we use a lot of nodes.

Table 4   Optimal number N^*, m^* and execution time $L_R(N^*,m^*,p)/\mu$ when $Cs/\mu = 0.8$, $C_R/\mu = 0.2$, $W/\mu = 5$, $R/\mu = 10$ and $G(t) = 1 - e^{-t/\mu}$.

$\lambda\mu$	$p = 1$			$p = 2$			$p = 4$			$p = 8$		
	N^*	m^*	$\frac{L_R(N^*,m^*,p)}{\mu}$	N^*	m^*	$\frac{L_R(N^*,m^*,p)}{\mu}$	N^*	m^*	$\frac{L_R(N^*,m^*,p)}{\mu}$	N^*	m^*	$\frac{L_R(N^*,m^*,p)}{\mu}$
0.1	1	5	14.561	1	4	14.816	1	3	15.613	1	3	16.947
0.05	2	6	13.500	1	5	13.545	1	4	13.919	1	4	14.628
0.01	4	11	12.168	3	10	11.862	3	8	11.862	3	6	12.074
0.005	5	16	11.874	5	13	11.509	4	11	11.422	3	10	11.500
0.001	12	34	11.496	10	29	11.051	8	25	10.868	7	21	10.826
0.0005	16	49	11.408	14	41	10.946	11	35	10.743	10	29	10.675

3   Hardware and Software Failures

This section applies a computer system with failures of hardware and/or software to the computer system which executes successively task with random working times [Naruse *et al.* (2006); Nakagawa *et al.* (2009); Chen *et al.* (2010); Naruse and Nakagawa (2013, 2015)]: Optimal checking times to minimize the expected cost per one task are derived analytically and numerically.

3.1   *System Model*

We consider a computer system which consists of hardware and software whose errors often occur independently. It is assumed that the hardware has a failure distribution $F_H(t)$ with finite mean $1/\lambda_H$. When hardware failures occur, we need to make some repair with mean time R_H. The software has a failure distribution $F_S(t)$ with finite mean $1/\lambda_S$. When software failures occur, we need to make the restart with mean time R_S with $R_S << R_H$.

We assume hardware has a bias degrade with a past time while software doesn't. because hardware is subject to wear, damage and so on. If some failures would occur in hardware or software, the data might be lost the data. To prevent from data loss, we apply checkpoint schemes in Sect. 1.

To detect failures, we provide a self-checking sensor for hardware and a self-checking program for software, irrespective of self-checking sensor and self-checking program failures. We assume C_T is the total time of a self-checking time for hardware and a self-checking program for software, and Cs is the overhead for their store.

Suppose that checkpoint is placed at each end of task k: When hardware and/or software checking cannot detect failures at the end of task k, the process of task k is correct and its state is stored. In this case, the process goes forward and executes task $k + 1$. However, when hardware and/or software checking detect failures, the process goes back and makes the retry of task k again.

3.2 *Performance Analysis*

The mean execution time of the process of task k between task N is given by a renewal equation:

$$
\widetilde{L}_T(k) = \int_0^\infty \Big\{ \overline{F}_H(t)\overline{F}_S(t) \Big[C_T + t + \widetilde{L}_T(k+1) \Big]
$$

$$
+ F_H(t)\overline{F}_S(t) \Big[C_T + t + R_H + \widetilde{L}_T(1) \Big]
$$

$$
+ \overline{F}_H(t)F_S(t) \Big[C_T + t + R_S + \widetilde{L}_T(1) \Big]
$$

$$
+ F_H(t)F_S(t) \Big[C_T + t + R_H + R_S + \widetilde{L}_T(1) \Big] \Big\} \, dG(t)
$$

$$
(k = 1, 2, \cdots, N - 1), \quad (7)
$$

$$
\widetilde{L}_T(N) = \int_0^\infty \Big\{ \overline{F}_H(t)\overline{F}_S(t) \left(C_T + t + C_S \right)
$$

$$
+ F_H(t)\overline{F}_S(t) \Big[C_T + t + R_H + \widetilde{L}_T(1) \Big]
$$

$$
+ \overline{F}_H(t)F_S(t) \Big[C_T + t + R_S + \widetilde{L}_T(1) \Big]
$$

$$
+ F_H(t)F_S(t) \Big[C_T + t + R_H + R_S + \widetilde{L}_T(1) \Big] \Big\} \, dG(t) \quad (8)
$$

where $\overline{F}_H(t) = 1 - F_H(t)$ and $\overline{F}_S(t) = 1 - F_S(t)$.

Solving (7) and (8) for $\widetilde{L}_T(1)$ which is the mean execution time between FCs,

$$
\widetilde{L}_T(1) = \frac{B\left(1 - A^N\right)}{(1 - A)\, A^N} + Cs \quad (N = 1, 2, \cdots), \quad (9)
$$

where

$$
A \equiv \int_0^\infty \overline{F}_H(t)\overline{F}_S(t) dG(t),
$$

$$
B \equiv C_T + \mu + R_H \int_0^\infty F_H(t) dG(t) + R_S \int_0^\infty F_S(t) dG(t). \quad (10)
$$

Therefore, the mean execution time per one task is

$$L_T(N) = \frac{B\left(1 - A^N\right)}{N\left(1 - A\right)A^N} + \frac{Cs}{N} \qquad (N = 1, 2, \cdots).\qquad (11)$$

We find optimal N^* which minimizes $L_T(N)$. From the inequality $L_T(N+1) - L_T(N) \geq 0$,

$$\frac{1}{A^N}\sum_{j=1}^{N}(1 - A^j) \geq \frac{Cs}{B},\qquad (12)$$

whose left-hand side is strictly increasing with N from $(1 - A)/A$ to ∞. Thus, there exists a finite and unique minimum $N^*(1 \leq N^* < \infty)$ which satisfies (11). If $(1 - A)/A \geq Cs/B$, then $N^* = 1$.

(1) Increasing Error Rate

When $F_H(t) = 1 - \mathrm{e}^{-(\lambda_H t)^m}$ $(m > 1)$ and $F_S(t) = 1 - \mathrm{e}^{-\lambda_S t}$, (10) is

$$A = \int_0^\infty \mathrm{e}^{-(\lambda_H t)^m}\mathrm{e}^{-\lambda_S t}dG\left(t\right),$$

$$B = C_T + \mu + R_H\left[1 - \int_0^\infty \mathrm{e}^{-(\lambda_H t)^m}dG\left(t\right)\right] + R_S\left[1 - \int_0^\infty \mathrm{e}^{-\lambda_S t}dG\left(t\right)\right].\qquad (13)$$

(2) Constant Error Rate

When $F_H(t) = 1 - \mathrm{e}^{-\lambda_H t}$ and $F_S(t) = 1 - \mathrm{e}^{-\lambda_S t}$, (10) is

$$A = G^*(\lambda_H + \lambda_S),$$
$$B = C_T + \mu + R_H\left[1 - G^*(\lambda_H)\right] + R_S\left[1 - G^*(\lambda_S)\right],\qquad (14)$$

where $G^*(s)$ is the Laplace-Stieltjes (LS) transform of $G(t)$, *i.e.*, $G^*(s) \equiv \int_0^\infty \mathrm{e}^{-st}dG\left(t\right)$ for $s > 0$. When $G(t) = 1 - \mathrm{e}^{-t/\mu}$, (14) is

$$A = \frac{1/\mu}{\lambda_H + \lambda_S + 1/\mu},$$

$$B = C_T + \mu + R_H\frac{\lambda_H}{\lambda_H + 1/\mu} + R_S\frac{\lambda_S}{\lambda_S + 1/\mu}.\qquad (15)$$

3.3 *Measure of Effectiveness*

We consider a measure of effectiveness in this section. We compare the execution time between the system and a conventional system whose checkpoint are made by FC in Fig.4 [Naruse *et al.* (2007)]. This is the same system when $N = 1$ in (11), and the mean execution time per one task is, from (11),

$$L_C \equiv \frac{B(1-A)}{(1-A)A} + Cs. \tag{16}$$

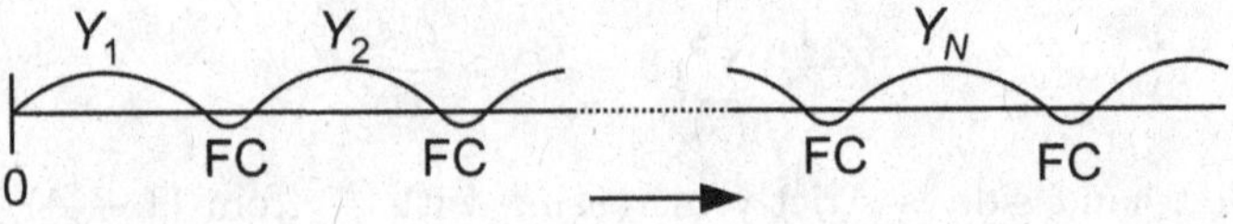

Fig. 4   Conventional system

It can be previously shown that if $(1-A)/A \geq CsB$, then a conventional system is better than the above one.

Tables 5, 6 and 7 present numerical examples of optimal N^* and the resulting execution time $\widetilde{L}_T(N^*)/\mu$ and L_C/μ in (11) for λ_H and λ_S/λ_H when $Cs/\mu = 0.8$, $C_T/\mu = 0.2$, $R_H/\mu = 10^5$, $R_S/\mu = 10^2$, $m = 1.25, 1.5, 1.0$, and $G(t) = 1 - e^{-t/\mu}$. These tables indicate that N^* decreases with λ_S/λ_H except when $N^* = 1$, and, N^* decreases with λ_H, and its resulting execution time $\widetilde{L}_T(N^*)/\mu$ decreases with decreasing λ_H. The case of $N^* = 1$ means that we should provide no JC between FC. For example, when $\lambda_H = 10^{-7}$, $\lambda_S/\lambda_H = 100$ and $m = 1.5$, we make 363 JC checkpoints between FC checkpoints. In this case, the job time is 1.206. Tables 6 and 7 indicate good performance. For example, when $\lambda_H = 10^{-7}$, $\lambda_S/\lambda_H = 100$ and $m = 1.5$, the mean time execution time is 1.205. This result means the above system has a good advantage in comparison with a conventional model. This model can reduce about 40% mean time execution time, compared with a conventional system. L_C/μ is lager than $\widetilde{L}_T(N^*)/\mu$ in all tables, therefore, two type of checkpoint scheme has an effectiveness for some checkpoint schemes. When λ_H decreases, N^* increases, because the system don't needs to make a lot of frequency FC checkpoint (FC time > JC time). And, according these table, when hardware error rate decreases, execution time do not so decreases. Therefore, the system needs to reduce the software error rate.

4   Conclusion

In Sec. 2, we have considered two types of checkpoints and database-nodes for the RAICN system and the GRAICN system, and have solved the prob-

Table 5 Optimal N^*, execution time $\widetilde{L}_T(N^*)/\mu$ and L_C/μ when $Cs/\mu = 0.8$, $C_T/\mu = 0.2$, $R_H/\mu = 10^5$, $R_S/\mu = 10^2$ and $m = 1.00$

λ_H	$\lambda_S/\lambda_H = 10$			$\lambda_S/\lambda_H = 100$			$\lambda_S/\lambda_H = 1000$		
	N^*	$\dfrac{\widetilde{L}_T(N^*)}{\mu}$	$\dfrac{L_C}{\mu}$	N^*	$\dfrac{\widetilde{L}_T(N^*)}{\mu}$	$\dfrac{L_C}{\mu}$	N^*	$\dfrac{\widetilde{L}_T(N^*)}{\mu}$	$\dfrac{L_C}{\mu}$
10^{-4}	11	11.446	12.111	4	12.700	13.112	1	23.121	23.121
10^{-5}	81	2.230	3.010	26	2.362	3.102	7	3.435	4.022
10^{-6}	334	1.306	2.101	110	1.325	2.110	33	1.448	2.201
10^{-7}	1096	1.212	2.010	361	1.215	2.011	114	1.234	2.020
10^{-8}	3480	1.201	2.001	1148	1.202	2.001	364	1.206	2.002
10^{-9}	11009	1.200	2.000	3633	1.201	2.000	1154	1.202	2.000

Table 6 Optimal N^*, execution time $\widetilde{L}_T(N^*)/\mu$ and L_C/μ when $Cs/\mu = 0.8$, $C_T/\mu = 0.2$, $R_H/\mu = 10^5$, $R_S/\mu = 10^2$ and $m = 1.25$

λ_H	$\lambda_S/\lambda_H = 10$			$\lambda_S/\lambda_H = 100$			$\lambda_S/\lambda_H = 1000$		
	N^*	$\dfrac{\widetilde{L}_T(N^*)}{\mu}$	$\dfrac{L_C}{\mu}$	N^*	$\dfrac{\widetilde{L}_T(N^*)}{\mu}$	$\dfrac{L_C}{\mu}$	N^*	$\dfrac{\widetilde{L}_T(N^*)}{\mu}$	$\dfrac{L_C}{\mu}$
10^{-4}	25	2.497	3.235	7	3.573	4.156	1	13.366	13.366
10^{-5}	111	1.288	2.074	34	1.411	2.165	8	2.458	3.076
10^{-6}	363	1.209	2.005	114	1.228	2.014	35	1.350	2.105
10^{-7}	1153	1.202	2.000	364	1.206	2.001	115	1.224	2.010
10^{-8}	3649	1.200	2.000	1154	1.202	2.000	365	1.205	2.001
10^{-9}	11543	1.200	2.000	3651	1.200	2.000	1154	1.201	2.000

lems of setting suitable checkpoints. We have derived optimal JC number between FC for the number of database-nodes, optimal database-nodes for the number of tasks for FC and optimal database-nodes and JC number between FC. It has been shown that the optimal mean execution time decreases when the rates $\mu/(1/\lambda)$ of the mean processing time with the mean error time decreases. We have considered one kind of system of processing big data with high speed and high reliability.

In Sec. 3, we have considered the checkpoint scheme with software and hardware failures, in which software failure has constant failure rate and hardware failure has increasing error rate. We have solved the optimization problems of setting suitable checkpoints, and derived optimal JC number between FC. Furthermore, we have compared the mean time execution time with that of a conventional model.

To get reduce failures in a computer system, we should use high-quality hardware parts, but they would be expensive. If this proposed scheme could be applied to some practical system, it could reduce greatly maintenance

Table 7 Optimal N^*, execution time $\tilde{L}_T(N^*)/\mu$ and L_C/μ when $Cs/\mu = 0.8$, $C_T/\mu = 0.2$, $R_H/\mu = 10^5$, $R_S/\mu = 10^2$ and $m = 1.50$

λ_H	$\lambda_S/\lambda_H = 10$			$\lambda_S/\lambda_H = 100$			$\lambda_S/\lambda_H = 1000$		
	N^*	$\frac{\tilde{L}_T(N^*)}{\mu}$	$\frac{L_C}{\mu}$	N^*	$\frac{\tilde{L}_T(N^*)}{\mu}$	$\frac{L_C}{\mu}$	N^*	$\frac{\tilde{L}_T(N^*)}{\mu}$	$\frac{L_C}{\mu}$
10^{-4}	33	1.482	2.234	8	2.530	3.146	1	12.266	12.266
10^{-5}	114	1.228	2.014	35	1.350	2.105	8	2.395	3.016
10^{-6}	365	1.206	2.001	115	1.224	2.010	35	1.347	2.101
10^{-7}	1154	1.201	2.000	365	1.205	2.001	115	1.224	2.010
10^{-8}	3651	1.200	2.000	1154	1.201	2.000	365	1.205	2.001
10^{-9}	11546	1.200	2.000	3651	1.200	2.000	1154	1.201	2.000

cost. We are sure that this proposed system could be applied to practically data backup system which uses software and hardware, and some embedding system and so on. This architecture would be applied to cloud systems and other database systems requested for high-reliability and high speed processing.

References

Chen, M., Nakamura, S., and Nakagawa, T. (2010). Replacement and preventive maintenance models with random working times, *IEICE TRANSACTIONS on Fundamentals of Electronics, Communications and Computer Sciences* 93-A, 2, pp. 500–507, 10.1587/transfun.E93.A.500, http://ci.nii.ac.jp/naid/10026863281/.

Kim, H. and Shin, K. G. (1996). Design and analysis of an optimal instruction-retry policy for tmr controller computers, *IEEE Transactions on Computers* 45, 11, pp. 1217–1225.

Lee, P. A. and Anderson, T. (1990). *Fault Tolerance Principles and Practice*, Dependable computing and fault-tolerant systems (Springer, Wien), ISBN 9783211820773.

Ling, Y., Mi, J., and Lin, X. (2001). A variational calculus approach to optimal checkpoint placement, *IEEE Transactions on computers* 50, 7, pp. 699–708.

Maeji, S., Naruse, K., and Nakagawa, T. (2010). Optimal checking models with random working times, in *Advanced Reliability and Modelling IV*, pp. 488–495.

Nakagawa, T. (2008). *Advanced Reliability Models and Maintenance Policies* (Springer, London).

Nakagawa, T., Naruse, K., , and Maeji, S. (2009). Random checkpoint models with N tandem tasks, *IEICE TRANSACTIONS on Fundamentals of Electronics, Communications and Computer Sciences* E92-A, pp. 1572–1577.

Naruse, K. and Nakagawa, T. (2013). Optimal checkpoint times for a majority database system, in *19th ISSAT International Conference on Reliability and Quality in Design*, pp. 333–337.

Naruse, K. and Nakagawa, T. (2015). Optimal checkpoint times for a computer system with hardware and software failures, in *Proceedings of The 2nd East Asia Workshop on Industrial Engineering*, pp. 159–163.

Naruse, K., Nakagawa, T., and Maeji, S. (2006). Optimal checkpoint intervals for error detection by multiple modular redundancies, in *Advanced Reliability and Modelling II*, pp. 293–300.

Naruse, K., Nakagawa, T., and Maeji, S. (2007). Random checkpoint models for a double modular system, in *13th ISSAT International Conference on Reliability and Quality in Design*, pp. 231–235.

Ohara, M., Suzuki, R., Arai, M., Fukumoto, S., and Iwasaki, K. (2006). Analytical model on hybrid state saving with a limited number of checkpoints and bound rollbacks(reliability, maintainability and safety analysis), *IEICE TRANSACTIONS on Fundamentals of Electronics, Communications and Computer Sciences* **89**, 9, pp. 2386–2395, http://ci.nii.ac.jp/naid/110007537954/.

ORACLE (2012). My sql :: Mysql cluster cge, http://www-jp.mysql.com/products/cluster/.

Patterson, D. A., Gibson, G., and Katz, R. H. (1988). A case for redundant arrays of inexpensive disks (raid), in *Proceedings of the 1988 ACM SIGMOD International Conference on Management of Data*, SIGMOD '88, ISBN 0-89791-268-3, pp. 109–116, 10.1145/50202.50214, http://doi.acm.org/10.1145/50202.50214.

Pradhan, D. and Vaidya, N. (1992). Roll-forward checkpointing scheme: Concurrent retry with non-dedicated spares, in *Proceedings of the IEEE Workshop on Fault-Tolerant Parallel and Distributed Systems*, pp. 166–174.

Pradhan, D. K. and Vaidya, N. H. (1994). Roll-forward checkpointing scheme: A novel fault-tolerant architecture, *IEEE Transactions on computers* **43**, 10, pp. 1163–1174.

Siewiorek, D. P. and Swarz, R. S. (1982). *The Theory and Practice of Reliable System Design* (Digital Press, Bedford, Massachusetts).

Vaidya, N. H. (1995). A case for two-level distributed recovery schemes, in *Proceedings ACM SIGMETRICS Conference Measurement and Modeling of Computer Systems*, pp. 64–73.

Zhang, Y. and Chakrabarty, K. (2004). Dynamic adaptation for fault tolerance and power management in embedded real-time systems, *ACM Transactions on Embedded Computing* **3**, 2, pp. 336–360.

Ziv, A. and Bruck, J. (1997). Performance optimization of checkpointing schemes with task duplication, *IEEE Transactions on Computers* **46**, pp. 1381–1386.

Ziv, A. and Bruck, J. (1998). Analysis of checkpointing schemes with task duplication, *IEEE Transactions on Computers* **47**, pp. 222–227.

Printed in the United States
By Bookmasters